THE RED CITY

THE RED CITY

*Limoges and the French
Nineteenth Century*

John M. Merriman

New York   Oxford
OXFORD UNIVERSITY PRESS
1985

Oxford University Press

Oxford London New York Toronto
Delhi Bombay Calcutta Madras Karachi
Kuala Lumpur Singapore Hong Kong Tokyo
Nairobi Dar es Salaam Cape Town
Melbourne Auckland

and associated companies in
Beirut Berlin Ibadan Mexico City Nicosia

Published by Oxford University Press, Inc.,
200 Madison Avenue, New York, New York 10016

Library of Congress Cataloging in Publication Data
Merriman, John M.
   The Red City: Limoges and the French Nineteenth
Century.
     Bibliography: p.
     Includes index.
     1. Limoges (France)—Industries—History—19th century.
2. Limoges (France)—Politics and government.
3. Labor and laboring classes—France—Limoges—History—19th century.
I. Title.
HC275.Z7L566   1985   307.7'64'094466   85-2938
ISBN 0-19-503590-9

Printing (last digit): 9 8 7 6 5 4 3 2 1
Printed in the United States of America

For Chuck Tilly

Acknowledgments

I owe much to many people. The director of the Archives Départementales de la Haute-Vienne, M. Jacques Decanter, and his staff have always been unfailingly helpful, particularly M. Jean-Marie Boubel. The Archives provided microfilm copies of the maps of Limoges that appear in this book. The personnel at the Limoges *mairie* graciously allowed me to examine the documents and censuses in the attic before they were classified and moved into the new Archives Municipales, under the direction of Mlle. Faye. I benefited from Alain Corbin's superb study of the Limousin in the nineteenth century and from reading Kathryn Amdur's recent dissertation on the labor movement in Limoges and St. Etienne from 1914 to 1922.* Jean-Claude Peyronnet, Michel Kiener, Pierre Vallin, and Louis Pérouas shared their knowledge of the Limousin and invited me to the annual meeting of the Historiens du Limousin, held in Solignac in 1980. Some of the material in this book, particularly in Chapters 1 and 2, first appeared in two essays.†

I am grateful to Yale University for a Morse Fellowship for the 1975–76 academic year; to the Whitney Griswold Fund and the Yale Center for International and Area Studies for summer research grants; and particularly to the John Simon Guggenheim Memorial Foundation for a Guggenheim Fellowship held during

---

* Alain Corbin, *Archaïsme et modernité en Limousin au XIXᵉ siècle, 1845–1885,* 2 vols. (Paris, 1975); Kathryn Amdur, "Unity and Schism in the French Labor Movement: Limoges and St. Etienne, 1914–22." Ph.D. dissertation, Stanford University, 1978.

† "Incident at the Statue of the Virgin Mary: Old and New in Nineteenth-Century Limoges," in Merriman, ed., *Consciousness and Class Experience in Nineteenth-Century Europe* (New York: Holmes and Meier, 1979); and "Restoration Town, Bourgeois City: Urban Politics in Industrializing Limoges," in Merriman, ed., *French Cities in the Nineteenth Century* (London: Hutchinson, 1982). This material is reprinted with the kind permission of these presses.

the 1979–80 academic year. Mary Whitney, Claire Shindler, Nancy Stone, and LaRue Brion each typed parts of the manuscript. The latter's skillful management of the Master's Office at Branford College facilitated my completion of the manuscript. At Oxford University Press in New York, the manuscript benefited considerably from the careful editorial attention of Henry Krawitz and from the design work of Jack Harrison. Nancy Lane is a superbly talented and patient editor with whom it has been a great delight to work.

Increasingly I have come to think of France's second city, Lyon, as its first. I have frequently enjoyed the hospitality of Yves Lequin, Maurice Garden, and their families, as well as of that transplanted Lyonnais, Roger Chartier. The T.G.V. has made these occasions even more frequent; the seminar at the Centre Pierre Léon at the Université de Lyon II has been as stimulating as the city's restaurants and *bouchons*. In Paris, Edward Rohrbach, my friend for many years, Joëlle Desparmet, and Monsieur and Madame Charles Bonis have welcomed me back each year. In Le Perreux-sur-Marne, Monsieur and Madame Daniel Taylor, Jean-Claude Petilon, and Dany and Diane Taylor have always made me feel at home. I have also appreciated the hospitality of Pierre Delaunay in Chambéry.

Many people made the research and writing of this book more enjoyable, including Alan Forrest, Steven Kaplan, Peter McPhee, Michelle Perrot, Elinor Accampo, Jeanne Innes, Richard Van Ham, Rory Browne, Roger Price, Natalie Davis, Cissie Fairchilds, Lenny Berlanstein, Robert R. Palmer, Judy Coffin, David Pinkney, Robert Herbert, Paul Hanson, Betsy Lambie, Keith Luria, David Bushnell, Mike Hanagan, Patricia Klaus, Robert Schwartz, Jack Censer, Joby Margadant, Robert Isherwood, William Parker, David and Toni Davis, Richard and Cindy Brodhead, and Louise Tilly. Mike Johnson watched over the Branford College Master's House, with its cartons of note cards and footnote fragments, and is always a source of good cheer; so, too, are Ivo and Manana Banac. Joan Scott, Gordon Wright, Jim McClain, and Edward Gargan offered helpful suggestions after reading a draft of the manuscript. Richard Cobb's work has influenced this book, particularly his essays, which evoke a "sense of place." Susanna Barrows and Michael Burns have heard about much of this over countless *comptoirs* and tables, ranging from Troisgros and La Cremaillère to Le Ralleye, place Stalingrad, in Paris; Au bout du monde, near Chambéry; La Bodega, A la galoche d'Aurillac, and the Tout va bien in Amboise (which we ended up calling the Ça va pas). Christopher Johnson and Ted Margadant, inspiring historians and *confrères,* carefully read the manuscript and offered useful suggestions. I value Peter Gay's collegiality and friendship, and am grateful to him for a thorough reading of the drafts of each chapter and his close attention to style, an art that he has mastered.

Carol Payne's own sense of history, impatient encouragement, and love for France have enriched this book, to say nothing of my life.

Charles Tilly has been mentor, *compagnon,* and friend for fifteen years. From

Hill Street in Ann Arbor to the Rue François Miron in Paris, from Amiens to Collioure and, yes, Limoges, he has shared his knowledge and understanding of economic, social, and political processes, and of modern France. His generosity, good humor, and spirit of the atelier have always matched his incredible energy, great ability to conceptualize historical problems, and exemplary research skills. This book is dedicated to him.

Contents

Introduction

Cities, towns, and bourgs spearheaded the transformation of nineteenth-century France. They reflected and accentuated the concentration of capital, the expansion of commerce, and large-scale industrialization. The continued growth of the centralized, bureaucratic state, such fundamental changes in social organization as the development of voluntary associations, the bourgeoisie's rise to political dominance, an emerging factory proletariat, and the political challenge of ordinary people for power were all most clearly associated with urban areas. Recurrent revolutions—1830, 1848–51, and 1870–71—were one of the most telling indicators of these changes. The contest for national power was waged more noticeably in Paris, from which regime after regime fled. The rapid population growth of Paris accompanied the capital's increasing domination of the nation. Louis Chevalier's classic restatement of the "uprooting hypothesis" claims that unchecked migration flooded Paris with a second race of people, the marginal "dangerous and laboring classes," who created a mood of criminality, if not outright revolution.[1] One would expect Paris to have been the center of rebellion and revolution, though not necessarily for the reasons Chevalier enumerates: Recent work has demonstrated that it was organized workers, not the disorganized, who rebelled.[2] But by the end of the century Paris had become more frequently a scene of nationalist demonstrations than left-wing insurgency. The social composition of the capital gradually changed as the rebuilding of Paris by Napoleon III and Baron Haussmann accentuated the emerging horizontal geography of class segregation in the Paris region; the "red belt" reflected the higher living costs in the center city as well as the location of more industry and workers on the periphery of the city.

Limoges, not Paris, was *la ville rouge* in nineteenth-century France. Of all other cities, only smaller Narbonne was also at the forefront of every wave of social and political conflict. The prominent place of Limoges in the radicalism of 1848 and the Second Republic was but one of the city's revolutionary awakenings; its tradition of militance stretched from 1830 to 1871, and despite the relatively dormant two decades that followed the Commune, it revived with the socialist municipality of the era of the belle époque (1895–1905), when a convergence of everyday life and political conflict seemed to occur. In that latter year, strikes and violent demonstrations—captured in a series of fascinating photographs—again catapulted Limoges into the headlines. These strikes anticipated the widespread strike activity elsewhere in France during the next two years. Once more Limoges was depicted as *la ville rouge*.

Why Limoges? The city grew rapidly, by French standards, during the century and became a center of industrial activity identified with its famous product, porcelain. But there were other burgeoning industrial towns and cities, urban centers whose changing forms of social organization and political activity encapsulated the dramatic process Agulhon has called "the descent of politics toward the masses."[3] Was there something specific about the experience of Limoges that provided continuity between the precocious working-class consciousness of 1848 and 1871 and the militancy of the fin de siècle that combined economic and political action, joining skilled and unskilled workers, men and women? A historian of the Paris Commune has called our attention to the importance of understanding the "complex sociocultural milieu" of the individual city,

> which can be defined by collective acquisitions that are at the same time technical (according to its dominant industries), historical, linguistic, or political—a particular mentality that is revealed at the deepest level of the lower classes and that also, in part, determines the capacity for action of its lower classes. In sum, the past thrusts itself into the present and becomes an important force in the creation of the popular community.[4]

Thus put, the individual city becomes something like the yeast that activates the dough provided by industrialization, the concentration of work, and the presence of an elite of skilled workers.

A number of successful recent studies have helped identify those themes that should help us place the nineteenth-century city in the context of the changes that helped shape the twentieth century: the impact of urbanization and large-scale industrialization on political life; the emergence of workers as contenders for power; the development of predominantly working-class neighborhoods, often on the periphery of cities; the relationship between city and country; the tensions between municipal governments and the centralized French state; and the interaction among urban form, planning, and political life. These studies—including those by Maurice Agulhon, Adeline Daumard, William Sewell, Jr., Joan W. Scott, Jeanne Gaillard, Ronald Aminzade, David Pinkney, Anthony Sutcliffe, Rolande Trempé, and Michael Hanagan—all have focused on specific themes and/or certain periods of time.[5] Yves Lequin's pioneering study of the workers of the Lyonnais (1848–1914) is the most complete account of the regional concomitants of large-scale industrialization and the experience of the proletariat during the last half of the century.[6]

Yet, surprisingly, we still have no study of a single city encompassing the period from the end of the Old Regime until our century, that great period of economic, social, and political transformation. There is, for example, nothing comparable to the study of eighteenth-century Caen by Jean-Claude Perrot, or that of Lyon during the same period by Maurice Garden.[7] Perhaps the emphasis on the economic, social, and political processes themselves has led us to de-emphasize the histories of individual nineteenth-century cities and to forget that no two are exactly alike. Early in the century the French humanistic geographers described the evolution of certain cities, concentrating on the functions of urban centers—administrative, commercial, industrial, military—but leaving out what arguably was the most important function of all for nineteenth-century cities: bringing ordinary people into political life.[8] The "new urban history" of the late 1960s and early 1970s emphasized quantitative analysis of social mobility but usually ignored political life.[9] Conventional labor history—and even some not so conventional works of significance—has relegated the individual city to little more than a stage, setting, or context.[10] Other historians, eager to pinpoint the "modernization" of rural France by examining the impact of cities on the countryside, have ignored the fact that the conflict between old and new also took place within cities.[11]

I thus set out to study political life in Limoges (1815–1914) through at least five regimes. After conducting research in the Archives Nationales, the Archives du Ministère de la Guerre, the Bibliothèque Nationale, the Archives Départementales de la Haute-Vienne, and the attic of the Limoges town hall, I needed an approach that would result in a book that avoided the diffuse nature of a French *thèse,* a format that would not be congenial for American publishers. Wanting to write an accessible book that might capture the essential dramas of a nineteenth-century city, I decided to follow several groups of people and neighborhoods throughout the century.[12]

I have therefore concentrated on the porcelain workers, the vanguard of the workers' movement, together with the butchers (and, to a lesser extent, the laundresses), juxtaposing the newer neighborhoods of the faubourgs with the traditional quarters of the ancient trades. I first became interested in the butchers in 1977. Their story represents, I think, the passing of much of traditional France during the century. The idea of using porcelain workers and butchers to illustrate how Limoges changed came to me when I learned of a brief confrontation, perhaps only seconds long, that occurred during the strikes of 1905, when a number of porcelain workers threatened the butchers' treasured statue of Notre-Dame-la-Pitié which still stands in the small square in front of the chapel of St. Aurélien

The chapel of St. Aurélien and the statue of Notre-Dame-la-Pitié

on the rue de la Boucherie. This was, as far as I can tell, the last such statue in the secularizing and socialist city. Two ways of looking at the world stood face to face.

My inclination in writing history has been to combine the approaches of two kinds of historians Emmanuel Le Roy Ladurie once called "parachutists" and "truffle-hunters." I have been influenced by the work of Charles Tilly and that of Richard Cobb, who, despite quite different approaches and conclusions, are not so unlikely a combination: Both appreciate the way a city works, shaping the routines of ordinary people.[13] I have tried to emphasize the dynamics of social change, as they would have been observed by a parachutist descending very, very slowly from the heavens over France, with the goal of unearthing the delicious truffles of the experience of real people (though, admittedly, those experiences themselves were not always so pleasing). In doing so, I have sought to weave both large-scale economic and social changes and ordinary people into an account that captured something of the texture of urban life.

In order to tell a long story of a large city, I have chosen to highlight three critical periods: (1) the end of the Restoration and the Revolution of 1830; (2) the last years of the Second Empire and the "terrible year" of 1870–71, with the Franco-Prussian War and the attempt to declare a Commune in Limoges; and (3) the socialist municipality during the belle époque (1895–1905). In each case I introduced Limoges in terms of a specific year: 1828, when an army officer visited the city for the purpose of accomplishing a *reconnaissance militaire,* that is, to prepare a plan for the defense of the city based upon a hypothetical attack; 1859, when a scientist from Poitiers visited Limoges at the height of the Second

Empire and was so impressed with its porcelain industry that he wrote an account of his impressions; and 1900, the turn of the century, when all France celebrated the universal exposition in Paris and all Limoges seemed to reflect upon the remarkable changes that had occurred. Each chapter of what might be called "thick description," in which I have tried to enmesh the significant changes shaping the city, neighborhoods, and workers, is followed by a description and analysis of the succeeding political events. While not excluding the Revolution of 1848, I have concentrated on three other events that represented great moments in Limoges's history and that of France: the Revolution of 1830; the Commune; and the socialist municipality of 1895–1905, ending with the strikes of 1905. Given this strategy, I have had to rely upon some rather "thin description" for the intervening periods (especially the 1840s and 1880s), depending upon the next *prise,* or *tranche* to keep the reader up to date. I have left aside the interesting glove-making town of St. Junien, thirty kilometers to the west on the Vienne River, whose radicalism was greatly influenced by Limoges.

Finally, I also emphasize the form and physical reality of the city, although I do not consider such related topics as the construction industry or patterns of building ownership. The growth of Limoges led to the creation of industrial faubourgs that remained inside the city limits instead of creating separately administered communes populated by workers outside the city. This meant that workers contended for political power within Limoges and not in a series of contiguous but separate communes like those found around Paris. Patterns of residence, street names, and iconography were all closely tied to the political evolution of Limoges. I have tried to integrate these, too, into a holistic study. I spent a considerable amount of time walking the streets of Limoges, convinced that "the stones of the city" are also historical artifacts from which the past leaps forward with the same effect as the names inscribed in the census of 1841, or in the rich police reports in the Archives Départementales.

My relationship with Limoges has been long and occasionally ambivalent. I first went to the city as a doctoral student. After working in the Archives Nationales, I finally took the train to confront both the Archives Départementales and Limoges. Limoges has always had something of a bad reputation in France, one virtually made official by the use of the verb *limoger,* meaning to dismiss, fire, or cashier. If someone has been *limogé*—sent to Limoges—it is thought to be a disgrace. Naturally I was apprehensive about conducting my research in such a spot. Disembarking at the Gare des Bénédictins, which immediately gave me a bad impression of the place, I crossed the Champ de Juillet and found a room for eleven francs a night at the Hôtel-Restaurant d'Isly. At that time I was playing basketball for a team in Paris and commuted by train on the weekends, an escape to which I greatly looked forward. To save money I took the 11:25 P.M. train back Sundays from the Gare d'Austerlitz (with the help of a *carte d'abonne-*

ment, which made the trip half price); upon arrival at 3:30 A.M., I spent the rest of the night sleeping in the second-class waiting room to save money. Occasionally the guard would come by to poke me and the smattering of *clochards* finding some shelter in what was then a very breezy room. At about 5 A.M. trains started coming in, with each arrival marked by recorded bells, and "Limoges, Limoges, changez ici pour Périgueux," or for "Guéret and Montluçon, via St. Sulpice Laurière." At about 8 A.M. I would sleepily take my bag to the hotel and then trundle up the avenue de la Libération to the Archives, just below the place Denis Dussoubs on the rue des Combes. The rest of the week I stayed in the hotel, eating dinner in one of several restaurants—all of which were full of businessmen, each with a copy of *Le Monde* or, more often, *France-Soir*—at a single table facing the television. My first encounter with Limoges was interesting but not much fun.

When I decided to write a book on nineteenth-century Limoges, friends told me that I must be a masochist, that such a state of mind might ultimately push me to a comparative study of Limoges and, say, Mulhouse, Agen, Angoulême, or some other similar place. I dreaded my return visits to Limoges. But a strange thing happened in 1978: I began to *like* Limoges despite its noted *froideur*. I stopped referring to the city as "horrible Limoges" or even "dreary Limoges." I looked forward to my return, although my visits were still very solitary. I think it was because I *knew* Limoges. And after Jean-Claude Peyronnet told me about the restaurant Marceau, I ate copiously and well. The year 1971 was the last time I slept in the railroad station. I finally settled upon the Hôtel de Paris, also on the Champ de Juillet, where from the window in room number twenty I could see the sun rise over the Gare des Bénédictins. As Cobb would say, it had all become familiar and reassuring once I had my routine down, and there is something to that. But there was more. I had begun to like Limoges at precisely the same time that the city seemed to rediscover and treasure its own past. Red signs went up under the standard Parisian blue and white street signs, proclaiming the street's former name; underneath the sign for the avenue de la Libération (which reminds locals not of Charles de Gaulle but of the heroic resistance in the region during World War II) appeared another sign announcing that the street had previously been called the avenue de la Révolution, that of 1830. The city rediscovered the shabby houses of the rue de la Boucherie and stripped off some of the pitiful facades that had covered the old beams. It has since become something of a tourist attraction. Several antique shops and restaurants opened onto the street. Aided by an active group of local historians and the Société archéologique et historique du Limousin, Limoges began to appreciate its past. One day I followed a demonstration organized by the C.G.T. on a route to the prefecture that demonstrators had taken in 1905. It was very exciting. The past came alive again.

Notes

1. Louis Chevalier, *Dangerous and Laboring Classes in Paris During the First Half of the Nineteenth Century* (New York, 1973).
2. George Rudé, *The Crowd in the French Revolution* (New York, 1959); Charles Tilly and Lynn Lees, "The People of June, 1848," in R. D. Price, ed., *Revolution and Reaction* (New York, 1975); Charles Tilly, "The Chaos of the Living City," in Tilly, ed., *An Urban World* (Boston, 1975).
3. Maurice Agulhon, *La République au village* (Paris, 1970).
4. Maurice Moissonnier, "Les Communes provinciales: Propositions pour une étude," *Mouvement Social* 79 (April-June 1972): 130.
5. Maurice Agulhon, *Une ville ouvrière au temps du socialisme utopique: Toulon, 1815–1851* (Paris, 1970).
6. Yves Lequin, *Les Ouvriers de la région lyonnais, 1848–1914,* 2 vols. (Lyon, n.d.).
7. Jean-Claude Perrot, *Genèse d'une ville moderne: Caen au XVIIIe siècle,* 2 vols. (Paris, 1975); Maurice Garden, *Lyon et les lyonnais au XVIIIe siècle* (Paris, 1973).
8. Among them one can cite: Philippe Arbos, *Etude de géographie urbaine: Clermont-Ferrand* (Clermont-Ferrand, 1930); and Jacques Levainville, *Rouen: Etude d'une agglomération urbaine* (Paris, 1913).
9. See, for example, some of the essays collected in Stephen Thernstrom and Richard Sennett, eds., *Nineteenth-Century Cities* (New Haven, Conn., 1969).
10. Kathryn Amdur, "Unity and Schism in the French Labor Movement: Limoges and St. Etienne, 1914–1922," diss., Stanford University, 1978; Joan W. Scott's *The Glassworkers of Carmaux* (Cambridge, Mass., 1974), is an example of the latter.
11. William Sewell, Jr., "La Classe ouvrière de Marseille sous la Seconde République: Structure sociale et comportement politique," *Mouvement Social* 76 (July 1971): 27–63; Rolande Trempé, *Les Mineurs de Carmaux,* 2 vols. (Paris, 1970); Jeanne Gaillard, *Paris, la ville, 1852–1870* (Paris, 1976); Adeline Daumard, *Les Bourgeois de Paris au XIXe siècle* (Paris, 1970); Scott, *The Glassworkers of Carmaux;* Michael P. Hanagan, *The Logic of Solidarity* (Urbana, Ill., 1979); Anthony Sutcliffe, *The Autumn of Central Paris* (London, 1974); David Pinkney, *Napoleon III and the Rebuilding of Paris* (Princeton, N.J., 1958); and Ronald Aminzade, *Class, Politics and Early Industrial Capitalism: A Study of Mid-Nineteenth-Century Toulouse* (Albany, N.Y., 1981).
12. Following the advice of Charles Tilly, "Peeping Through the Window of the Wealthy," *Journal of Urban History* 2 (1974): 135: "Begin with the structure of the community, locate your classes within it; make systematic comparisons of class and communities. Reason, in short, from the variables rather than from the constants."
13. Tilly, "The Chaos of the Living City"; idem, *The Vendée* (Cambridge, Mass., 1964); Richard Cobb, *Reactions to the French Revolution* (London, 1974); idem, *A Sense of Place* (London, 1975); idem, *Paris and Its Provinces* (London, 1974); idem, *Promenades* (London, 1980).

THE RED CITY

1

Life in a Restoration Town

In 1828 an army officer named Borel de Bretizel came to Limoges on the route de Paris from the north. He had been ordered to prepare a defense of the city in the event of an attack by any enemy of France. Like Arthur Young in 1787, he passed an ancient inn at a point called Maison Rouge, several kilometers above the town. Probably also like Young, the traveler found it an "execrable" place, with "a beggarly account of a larder" and, in any case, not far enough from Limoges to justify staying there. He continued on the road that the Limousin's most famous Intendant Turgot had made one of the sturdiest in France.[1] The route rose and then descended, bordered by chestnut groves, meadows, and ponds, through a ring of hills and into an amphitheater-like setting, with the spires of St. Michel-des-Lions and St. Pierre-de-Queyroix visible in the distance. The infertile soil of the Limousin temporarily seemed more promising as the estate of the wealthy noble Pierre Hippolyte Martin de la Bastide appeared off to the left. As he passed the customs barrier (*octroi*) at Les Lachères, small gardens lined the road. Beyond a large crucifix on the route de Paris, a few scattered houses, a former convent which served some sort of official function, a cavalry garrison, and two small porcelain factories represented the growth of a modest and even paved faubourg. The road ended at the circular place Dauphine; there a street led up a hill to the crowded cattle market at the place d'Aîne. To the left a less well-kept road sloped down to a muddy field which appeared *en pleine campagne*.[2]

Unlike Borel de Bretizel, most of Limoges's visitors had commercial, not military, business in the town in 1828. Many took a room at La Boule d'or, where the carriages stopped just above the place Dauphine (the junior officer's less elegant lodgings awaited him elsewhere), and after resting from the bumpy journey they followed one of two streets that led to the commercial quarters of the city. Their destination might well be the rue Manigne or the rue Banc Léger, the most prosperous in the maze of twisting and hilly streets of the center city. Wagons rattling through the town invariably found their paths encumbered, but the traffic suggested that in 1828, despite a year of some economic and political uncertainty, Limoges was an active and prosperous commercial center.

The officer's impressions of the southern approach to the city in 1828 were somewhat different, despite the similarities of the meadows, ponds, and chestnut groves on either side of the road. The first view of the city loomed more suddenly, after one passed through a hamlet of little more than ten or twelve buildings housing poor gardeners, weavers, and a few eager innkeepers and shopkeepers anticipating the arrival of weary travelers. As the road curved and ran down a rather steep slope, one beheld the old episcopal city, dominated by the Cathedral of St. Etienne on a hill, and, to the side, the bishop's palace, with manicured gardens sloping down toward the muddy banks of the Vienne River. At night *la bonne compagnie* could sometimes be seen chatting with the bishop and the prefect of Haute-Vienne.[3] An old abbey graced one bend of the river. When the route de Toulouse entered a small faubourg, the soldier might have noticed some tired textile workers stretching their limbs in front of their houses or bargaining with the merchant who brought them work. From the Pont St. Martial several mills and a small textile factory were visible. Hefty washerwomen, dressed in black and sporting white *coiffes,* knelt at the water's edge and hauled piles of laundry up the steep hill in the shadow of the cathedral, pausing to nod in the direction of small statues of saints occupying niches in the walls of some buildings. On both sides of the river boatmen steered logs downstream to a landing (*rameau*) which jutted out from both banks, where the timbers gathered until workers loaded them onto the dock of Naveix. A few fished, although, like modern-day fishermen on the Seine, they never seemed to catch anything. Any traveler who had business in the episcopal city—such as the priest in Balzac's *Le Curé du village*—walked along the river and up the hill.

Throughout most of Limoges's history such travelers would have been entering two separate and fiercely independent walled cities which were often bitter enemies and once fought a war. Limoges was originally Lemovicum, a Gallo-Roman settlement first mentioned in the early second century A.D., near the bridge over the Vienne River where two Roman roads met. A period of decline culminated in the sack of the city by the Visigoths in the sixth century, and the population may not have recovered its earlier size until the early nineteenth century. Those who escaped formed a second settlement at a slightly higher elevation above the river. The new settlement became known as Civitas (Cité) and the bishop of Limoges enjoyed the rights of a sovereign. Sometime in the seventh century another town grew up around the tomb of Saint Martial, who, according to legend, had been martyred after converting some twenty thousand inhabitants of Limousin and Aquitaine to Christianity. This new settlement, known as the "Château" after the residence of its vicomte, included the abbey of St. Martial, three churches, several chapels, and a small hospice.[4]

Unlike the ecclesiastical Cité, the Château developed rapidly as a center of local commerce and artisanal industry. Its burghers jealously guarded their right of self-government against the encroachments of the vicomte and the abbot, electing twelve of their own consuls. They preferred to think of the Cité as nothing more than their faubourg. The Château had numerous public *places* which served as markets; the Cité had but two open *places,* both adjacent to the cathedral. The Cité, which encompassed four churches, four convents, and a monastery, grew much more slowly than its rival. In 1371, during the Hundred Years' War, the Prince of Wales destroyed the Cité and massacred three thousand of its inhabitants; the Château survived and prospered for having supported the English.

Renowned for its enamels and silverwork during the Renaissance and favored by its location, Limoges developed into a major commercial center. At the town's three largest annual fairs Bordeaux wines were traded for iron and textiles from the north; spices and arms from the northeast were exchanged for oil and soap from the Midi; and eau-de-vie, salt, and spices from the west were bartered for hats made in the east. Commercial expansion pushed Limoges beyond the confines of its walled cities. In the seventeenth century several enterprising merchants defied municipal ordinances and set up businesses at major crossroads. A significant concentration of population developed between the two "cities," and a small settlement survived near the ancient Pont St. Martial, where the first *limougeauds* had gathered many centuries earlier. But most of the life of Limoges went on within the walls of the two cities, whose houses ringed their respective hills. During this time Limoges was known as *la ville rouge* because of the red tiles of its roofs, the first sign that one is at least approaching the Midi.

Some seventeenth- and eighteenth-century visitors stressed the Limousin's poverty and the unhealthy mien of its capital and inhabitants. One visitor found the streets "quite narrow, with high houses and leaning roofs, which render this town extremely dark and very dirty." He estimated the population of Limoges at the end of the seventeenth century at approximately twenty-six hundred households (*feux*) or about fourteen thousand people.[5] A series of eighteenth-century administrators improved the town in some respects. The intendants Aîne, Tourny, and Orsay constructed exterior boulevards and gardens which ultimately bore their names. Turgot constructed the boulevards of Montmailler, Pyramide, Collège, Promenade, and Ste. Catherine, which ringed the Château. He ordered the cemetery moved outside the city limits and improved the water system in a town noted for its fountains, imposed restrictions on the disposal of waste and garbage, and regulated the keeping of animals in the city. In response to a report on Limoges by Turgot, a royal decree in 1775 noted some diminution in illness and epidemics thanks to the demolition of several walls, which now permitted "a freer passage of air and sunshine." The king authorized further work in Limoges, "where the population and industries are progressing," in the hope that the city "will become more and more salubrious and at the same time more commodious if one can give its streets greater width and suitable direction." Turgot also organized a relatively large police force of thirty-seven and divided Limoges into six quarters, each under the authority of a bourgeois. Turgot used royal subsidies, taxes, loans, and contributions from subjects to widen and improve some streets. When the Château and Cité were officially joined in 1791, after the latter once proclaimed its independence at the time of the Revolution, Limoges had become a somewhat healthier town to inhabit than when it had drawn complaints from the royal official one hundred years earlier.[6]

Yet in 1828 Limoges remained a town with many vestiges of the Middle Ages. The Revolution and Empire brought war, social conflict, some violence, and virtually no urban progress. Limoges was still crowded, dark, and dirty. Its streets presented steep inclines that impeded traffic. Wagons that successfully negotiated the treacherous Pont St. Martial still confronted a formidable hill before reaching the central city. Almost all streets were quite narrow; the steep rue du Clocher, in the heart of the commercial quarter, was in some places no more than five meters wide; visitors to the rue de la Boucherie held their breath as they picked their way among the animal carcasses on a street that was no more than four to seven meters wide.

The *Annales de la Haute-Vienne,* the town's newspaper, admitted that "Limoges offers an image of disorder, an absence of all rules, policing, and planning." Our military observer noted, "If one can find anything more disgusting than the houses of the countryside, it is the houses of Limoges itself," which were fabricated from wood and flimsy plaster, cob-covered with a dirty pebble dash, and capped by the gray tile by then typical of the Limousin.[7] They seemed to tilt forward as if to meet above the street. Occasionally one collapsed because of erosion caused by underground water. Some of the houses recently commissioned for wealthier clients on the wider boulevards were more solidly constructed. Most houses lacked the barest sanitary facilities. Sewage still ran down small ditches cut into the middle of streets. Limoges's churches sometimes gave off a deathly stench because corpses were left unattended; in 1825 the prefect complained that the smell in St. Michel was so bad that the services could no longer be followed. Day laborers dumped their refuse randomly in other neighborhoods on the way to work. Their journeys could indeed be hazardous; one official complained in 1810 that "at any moment one can see water and garbage being thrown from the windows. . . ."[8] The Abbessaille quarter, where laundresses and *flotteurs de bois* spoke a particularly difficult patois, offered a particularly appalling scene. In the center of the commercial city the butchers' quarter gave off a disgusting and overwhelming smell. And in the *entre-deux-villes* section a filthy stream into which tanners carelessly tossed animal parts gave off a similar stench.

LIMOGES IN 1785

A. La Cité   B. Le Château   C. place Dauphine   D. Cathedral of St. Etienne

These ancient, crowded quarters were particularly susceptible to fire: The city had suffered six major conflagrations during the eighteenth century, the last in 1790, when the Manigne quarter burned to the ground.

Several factors aggravated overcrowding within the city. Limoges's physical expansion during the eighteenth century had been constrained by royal decrees and by the survival of the town walls. The limited space between the two original cities had been quickly filled in. Church property occupied one fifth of the space of the Château, and the cathedral, bishop's palace and gardens dominated the Cité.

Limoges's population growth during the first half of the nineteenth century, the fourth greatest rate of increase in France, compounded the serious overcrowding within the city limits, stimulating the growth of faubourgs and extending the physical limits of the city. The newer houses in the faubourgs stretching out from the place Dauphine and the place des Carmes were of a more "rural" type, with sloping roofs (a house for sale on the route d'Aixe in 1828 included a barn, a meadow, cultivatable land, and a garden).[9] Spurred on by commercial and industrial growth, Limoges's population increased by one third in the first decades of the nineteenth century, reaching over 27,000 in 1831. By 1828 all but about 3,000 inhabitants lived in the nucleated settlement of the city, including the faubourgs. Net migration accounted for this population increase, as Limoges usually had an excess of deaths over births. Only during the three years beginning in 1820 were more people born in Limoges than died there. Between 1820 and 1831 the excess of deaths was 811, while the town's population increased by at least 2,078.[10]

The central city had reached its maximum density during the 1820s. Only the parish of St. Michel continued to grow because of the expansion of Limoges to the north. Excluding two sections whose populations swelled because of the presence of charitable institutions and a prison, the most densely settled quarters were those that had developed between the two old cities: the faubourg Boucherie (so-called because it has served as a crossing point, or *bouche*) and the area around the Hôtel de Ville.[11]

There was little about Limoges to counteract these unfavorable impressions. Its inhabitants seem to have suffered from feelings of inferiority that visitors found quite justified. Even at its best, Limoges was the kind of city Stendhal claimed was "peuplés avec les âmes du sous-préfecture."[12] Despite the city fathers' attempt to convince the king that Limoges was "a second Rome," the town had neither a public monument nor any imposing statue, aside from numerous minor religious artifacts and cumbersome stone crosses that blocked key intersections. Only one old private residence seemed noteworthy: The Minister of Justice Martignac recalled some pleasant memories of the maison Nivet, where Balzac once stayed; in a somewhat generous understatement, the great novelist termed it "less grand and imposing than the Louvre and the Palais-Bourbon."[13] Limoges applied to the king for the designation of *bonne ville* in 1821 and 1825, a title that could be affixed proudly to the town crest. The petitioners reminded Louis XVIII that the "miraculous progress" of commerce and industry in Limoges had increased revenues by 20 percent in the past ten years. However, each time Limoges was politely but firmly informed that the country already had a sufficient number of towns of this rank. As several of these towns were smaller, the municipal council believed Limoges had become "a humiliating exception."[14] Its academy had been eliminated in 1814 after a short and undistinguished existence; for a time it seemed that the royal court would be transferred elsewhere, which would have dealt an economic blow and resulted in a considerable loss of prestige. Limoges seemed to be a forgotten town. A local booster despaired that the town's elite merely imported the modes and styles of Paris, and the effect was "similar to those light wines whose quality is diminished when they are transported." Even the dead seemed to suffer from having lived in Limoges, transported to the new cemetery in an awful wagon that resembled a dump cart more than a hearse.[15]

Yet the city fathers bristled at the idea that Limoges was a *ville perdue;* they took pride that "religious tradition [was] conserved with care" in "Holy Limoges," whose people were known for their Christian charity. There were many signs of religiosity in Limoges in 1828. A large mission cross stood before the Church of St.-Michel-des-Lions; the revivalist missions of the Congregationalists were eagerly followed by the majority of the population. The gates of the city had once been placed under the protection of the Virgin Mary and saints, whose statues had been erected when the walls were torn down in the eighteenth century. Street corner niches sheltered about two hundred statues of Mary (such as at a corner of the maison Nivet) and a variety of locally popular saints. The manner in which the saints were housed and even clothed indicated the wealth of the particular quarter. Each quarter celebrated the feast days of its patron saints. Notre-Dame-du-Pont, near the port of Naveix on the Vienne, was the object of a particularly lively cult. On the last Sunday of September the procession of the washerwomen (*buandières*) was led by a tiny king and queen, children whose parents had purchased their "titles" at an auction. Once or twice a year the poor went from door to door asking for "God's share" of specially baked cakes. On their day the laundresses returned to their riverside quarter with wine poured into their bottles by their clients. And before the small chapel of St. Aurélien, in the butchers' quarter, stood the statue of Notre-Dame-la-Pitié, which had survived war, fire, and revolution.[16]

In 1789 Limoges boasted one cathedral, thirteen parish churches, two seminaries, and twenty-three abbeys and convents. One tenth of the town's twenty-four thousand inhabitants were religious personnel. Several churches, abbeys, and nine chapels did not survive the revolutionary period. The religious orders were dispersed by the revolution, and the male orders never returned.[17] The Church of St. Martial, originally part of the abbey of the same name and the home of several confraternities, was destroyed. The Convent of Providence became an army barracks, and that of the Cordeliers served as the warehouse of the entrepreneur Pouyat. The ancient abbey of the Bénédictins served nicely as the regional prison. Clerics must have cringed when the purchaser of another convent divided up the space among a masonic lodge, a café, and a public bath!

Yet religious faith seemed to be restored along with the monarchy. Despite the loss of its stained-glass windows and the heads of most of its statues, Limoges's unfinished and rather graceless cathedral was often full, although the wealthy were no longer able to secure their burial in its gloomy reaches. The *Annales de la Haute-Vienne* advertised brochures describing "six months of the lives of the Saints of the Diocese of Limoges and all of the Limousin!" and listed all of the ecclesiastics who had died during the year. Most associational life in the town was religiously inspired. Nowhere outside of the Midi did the religious confraternities have such a public role, where one could witness

> these long lines of poorly aligned men, processional crosses covered with banderoles made from the richest cloth, lanterns placed on the ends of sticks, this fantastic procession, an almost barbaric sight, this garb recalling the classic costume of magicians emerging from the shadows in China.[18]

J. J. Juge, a chronicler of his changing town, emphasized that both "the great and the humble manifested an incredible zeal for their confraternities," meeting every Sunday. That of St. Martial was one of the most important; it had been credited with saving the relics of St. Martial from the Revolution. Reconstituted in 1806, membership was then limited to seventy-two men "of an honest life and without reproach." The most exclusive confraternity was that of the Pèlerins, whose members had undertaken a pilgrimage to St. Jacques de Compostelle in Galicia or to Rome. But the most visible confraternities were the seven associations of penitents.[19]

Limoges's penitents emerged in the religious fervor of the seventeenth century. The black penitents were founded by Bernard Bardon de Brun, a charitable *limougeaud* educated in Paris, who was known as the "lawyer of the poor." He subsequently established the blue penitents, and they were followed by the white (1611), gray (1611), *feuille-morte* (initiated by eight priests in 1615), and, later, the purple or red penitents (1661). As in much of France, the Limoges penitents stressed penance, devotion, and charitable works. However, they served an important social function as well; in the eighteenth century their fierce independence sometimes put them at loggerheads with the clergy. Each represented a distinct social group and distinguished itself from the others by the color of its belt, its own chapel, patron saint, feast days, and processions. The white penitents met on the first and third Sunday of each month, on any feast day associated with the Virgin Mary, and on selected other occasions to read the vespers of the Holy Virgin, psalms of penance, and the litanies of the saints. Their statutes required the frequent examination of conscience, the forgiveness of their enemies (usually other groups of penitents), works of spiritual and corporal *miséricorde,* assistance at the funerals of their confreres, the study of the works of religion and the commandments, and visits to the sick, the poor, and prisoners. The *feuille-morte* penitents prayed morning and night and were forbidden to play cards or visit taverns. If temptation got the best of them, they were to present themselves to their rector or prior and hold a cross while flagellating themselves. Just how many actually knocked on their prior's door can never be known.

The purple penitents undertook a special act of charity. Founded in 1661 when the black penitents refused to accompany one of their colleagues to his execution, the purple penitents accompanied the condemned man to the scaffold, passed the hat for his family, and offered prayers for his soul. They fell into official disgrace after what was probably their most charitable act, namely, helping a condemned man escape execution in 1743. But soon they were back in force each time the scaffold was erected on the place d'Aîne.[20]

Religious processions brought the penitents and other confraternities together, at least temporarily, to march, usually barefoot, through the narrow streets from church to church. A child dressed in a sheepskin as St. John the Baptist led the white penitents; the purple penitents trotted out an entire troupe of apostles in the middle of their procession. In the eighteenth century most males of any means were members of a confraternity—an estimated twenty-five hundred in 1750.[21]

The penitents survived the Revolution and the loss of several of their chapels, retaining many of the virtues and abuses that had characterized their life under the ancien régime. They fought to retain their traditional independence vis-à-vis the clergy and the municipality. Their pious and charitable function declined; they sought to outdo each other in their recruitment of members, processions, and prosperity. The Imperial Prefect Texier-Olivier reproached those members who left their homes and work to assist in religious ceremonies, burials, and processions, and then followed those good deeds with less ascetic trips to the cabarets of the city. He drew up some regulations intended to put the penitents under the watchful eye of the parish clergy.[22]

By 1828 the penitents probably had declined in number from the estimated 4,000 in 1804: The blue penitents had 140 to 150 members, the gray about 200, and the elite black penitents about 80. Their processions remained lively, although Bishop Prosper de Tournefort banned their boisterous dramas and ordered his clergy to lock them out of the churches if they became disorderly. But the town's other leading subjects were penitents. Though weakened in number, function, and perhaps even commitment, and occasionally mocked by a new generation who found them anachronistic, they still attested to the role of organized religion in the society, politics, and culture of Limoges.[23]

The religion of Limoges and the Limousin seemed a far cry from the dogmas and rituals approved by the bishop. As in rural Haute-Vienne, the clergy often complained that religious practices bordered on superstition, if not idolatry. The cult of the saints and the "magic fountains" (including one on the outskirts of Limoges) was quite alive.[24] Ordinary people in Limoges were more attached to the routines of organized religion—baptism, marriage, major festivals, and burial— than to dogma. The revivalist religious missions of 1827 and 1828 were "closely followed by the faithful, rich and poor." If Bishop Prosper de Tournefort railed against the excesses of the confraternity and claimed that their behavior would not be tolerated in any other city, he was privately grateful that the appeal of traditional religion in Limoges was still strong.

In 1828 the religious calendar dictated virtually all public events of significance. The septennial Ostensions, which had begun in 1519, lasted fifty days in the spring, from Quasimodo Sunday until Trinity Sunday. After the Paternoster at the final mass, a crowd of poor women came forward, as in the Old Regime, hoping for a cure for their sick children. The final processions included several thousand clergy, penitents, and other confraternity members, as well as children dressed as the Virgin Mary, apostles, martyrs, and saints. In September the confraternities marched in procession, together with the clergy, to the site of a former chapel on the plain of Montjovis, northwest of Limoges, the site of a miracle that occurred in 994.[25]

Other public ceremonies and celebrations were also inextricably linked to the Church. Te Deums and masses marked the birthdays of the king and his patron saint. A solemn funeral mass mourned the anniversary of the execution of Louis XVI on January 21. In 1821 the birth of the *enfant du miracle* following the assassination of his father, the Duc de Berri, was commemorated by masses of thanks, the illumination of the city, artillery salvos (which always ensured a large crowd), gymnastic displays, fireworks, a horse race, a free theater performance, and various balls. A banquet was offered to 250 "fathers of families, chosen among the most deserving and honest artisans." They humbly manifested submission and dependence while their superiors fulfilled the Christian duty of charity.[26]

One street, more than any other, guarded the traditions of the old Limoges. The rue de la Boucherie, the butchers' quarter, was one of the few neighborhoods still defined by a specific trade, although a corporative work structure and vestiges of a medieval town could be found elsewhere. A Bordeaux resident later recalled his visit to Limoges:

> I suddenly found myself in a street forming a horseshoe, humid, and closed tightly by relatively tall houses, which tried to hide their decay with a rather offensive whitewash. There I found only the exhalations of sweat and blood, a chaos of buildings, of muffled animal groans, and the hoarse moos of cattle; in the somber interior of the shops, nothing but ropes, hooks, and the dank smell of dead flesh . . . This was the rue de la Boucherie.[27]

The junior army officer, ordered to prepare an imaginary defense of the city, had also wandered into the rue de la Boucherie. Here is how he described its inhabitants:

[They] formed a type of corporation . . . and have nothing in common with the rest of the city; their clothes, their habits, the saints who protect them, their church, their language, indeed, everything is unique to them. They delight in the most excessive filth. Under no circumstances will they change their clothes . . . showing up at every gathering and public festival as though they were going off to the most disgusting tasks of their profession . . . even those people not ordinarily repelled stay far away.[28]

Small wonder that the butchers had been left alone to organize their own national guard unit.

The butcher's community on the rue de la Boucherie was based on ties of trade, neighborhood, family, and religion, having remained virtually unchanged for centuries. It was first mentioned as a *corporation* in 1322 but was probably constituted in the eleventh or twelfth century; the butchers traced their confraternity back to 930 to 931. A document from 1234 noted two métiers, wholesale and retail. Four elected *bayles,* or syndics, who arbitrated disputes among butchers, were put under the surveillance of the consuls of the Château. An act of 1533 or 1535 confirmed their monopoly on meat slaughtered in the city. Three centuries later that monopoly, although legally ended by the Revolution, remained virtually intact. Unlike any other trade or occupation, the butchers paid their customs, or *octroi,* taxes on goods brought into the city and their tax for slaughtering animals by subscription, or *abonnement,* dividing the tax among master butchers of the corporation according to the volume of their business. Waging war on the itinerant sellers of meat, they protected their privileges.[29]

Only butchers, their families, and domestics lived on the rue de la Boucherie and the several tiny adjoining streets. There were six clans of butchers, as there had been at the end of the seventeenth century: Plainemaison (which dated as far back as 1344), Cibot (1362), Parot (1535), Pouret (1536), Malinvaud (1561), and Juge (1575). In 1828 there were fifty-eight heads of household, almost all of whom owned their own houses. Virtually all marriages were arranged within these families. Those children who did not marry remained in the household; single adults of both sexes were common.[30]

The Revolution only nominally ended the tradition of primogeniture on the rue de la Boucherie. Younger sons remained in the household, working for their elder brothers; when one married the daughter of another butcher (marriages within the ten branches of the Cibot were particularly common), they set up their household in the home of their father or eldest brother. Widows or daughters without brothers could inherit the family business, but as the butchers had many children, a male offspring was invariably available to assume the patriarchal role of his father. The absolute paternal authority passed from father to son was often a weighty charge indeed because of the butchers' legendary large families. One Cibot had twenty-three children and another sent sixteen into the crowded street; there were fourteen Malinvaud offspring in one family and fifteen in another. No one ever bothered to count cousins because almost everyone was related. The patriarch arranged each daughter's dowry and marriage and taught his sons the trade. The sons left the Congregationalists' school—if they went at all—at the age of twelve or thirteen, accompanying their fathers and brothers to the markets of the region. They also helped slaughter animals on the adjoining streets or at the back of the shop. The daughters worked at home under the direction of their mothers, who were responsible for the maintenance of these large households.[31]

In the nineteenth century as in the sixteenth, butchers went by traditional nicknames, which were necessary to differentiate the various Martials, Léonards, and Jeans; otherwise there would be a good number of butchers named Martial Malinvaud, Léonard Cibot, or Jean Parot in the community of five hundred people. The nicknames had their origins in personal habits, characteristics, or experiences, and, like the family business, were inherited. Martial Pouret *dit* l'Abbé was pious; François Cibot *dit* le Pape was also pious and perhaps bossy; Parot-Chérant was known for his high prices; Parot-Nez-Plat had a flat nose; Eloi Cibot père *dit* Boiteux was lame, and his son inherited the name but presumably not the limp; Malinvaud-Mantoue had once been in the army and fought at the battle of that name in 1797; Cibot *dit* Maisonneuve had built a new house, or else one of his immediate predecessors had; Plainemaison *dit* Louis XVIII had once cried out "Long Live Louis the Eighteenth!" (which would have been fine except that it was at the height of the First Empire)—his son proudly carried the name long after the king had died. For others we can simply guess at their origins: Jean Pouret *dit* le Dragon; Barthélemy Pouret *dit* Jambon; Barthélemy Cibot *aîné dit* Sans-quartier, and so on. When the butchers signed agreements with the town concerning the taxes they would pay, they often signed only their nicknames: Moissieux (the sufficient), Parpaillaud (from *volage,* fickle, flighty, or inconstant), Missard (*qui flâne*), Petit Monsieur, and so on.[32]

The only outsiders on the street (and often the only residents not born in Limoges) were the butchers' domestics. In the tradition of the corporation, they ate their meals with the family and were allowed to participate in the religious processions and festivals. They remained in the quarter until they married (never into the butchers' families), in exchange for their room, board, and a very small wage. A few worked as apprentices in the trade, but without any rights of inheritance or familial recognition in the neighborhood.[33]

Each night the patriarchs gathered at a corner to discuss—or, rather, to fix—prices, do business, and prepare for the next day's thirty-to-forty-kilometer foray to the markets of the region, such as that in Eymoutiers. Their dogs terrorized the adjoining streets, "an imposing battalion, like their masters, when united."[34]

The butchers were fervently religious. Among the "hacked and hanging pieces of meat, the glistening livers and salted hams, and the blue heads of dead cattle . . . punctuated with large pools of blood, were niches sheltering pretty statues of saints or rich madonnas with azure coats starred with gold, before which burned religious lamps."[35] Many of the houses had enclosed statues on the outside walls that were visible from the street. The life of the community centered, as it had for centuries, on the small chapel of St. Aurélien. St. Martial, the patron saint of Limoges, had been sent to the region by Saint Peter to convert the Gauls. Martyred, he was succeeded by St. Aurélien as bishop. Sometime early in their history as a corporation, the butchers chose Aurélien to be their patron saint. A chapel was constructed in either 1453 or 1475 (probably built where another had stood) on the rue Torto, or Torte, a twisting street on which the butchers had settled. The relics of St. Aurélien were lodged in this modest chapel, which had several beautiful *vitraux*. The upkeep of the chapel of St. Aurélien was the duty and originally the raison d'être of the confraternity of St. Aurélien. The confraternity could not be distinguished from the corporation in terms of its members and leadership. The members treasured the statue of Notre-Dame-la-Pitié, which stood in the small *place* before the chapel, about twenty feet from the door.

The butchers paid dearly to preserve the chapel during the Revolution. Two of the wealthiest butchers, Barthélemy Cibot and Maurice Malinvaud, purchased it as a *bien national* for thirty-five hundred francs on the eleventh of Germinal in the year III. Secretly they did so on behalf of the entire corporation of butchers, who also held on to the sacristy and a small adjoining building for another thousand francs. "Woe to those who would be bold enough to violate the sanctuary that sheltered the venerated relics of St. Aurélien" served warning to the Jacobin club of Limoges, which included only one butcher, *le citoyen* Audoin Malinvaud *dit* le Petit, who, the radicals assumed, gathered information for the butchers' corporation. In 1793 a mob killed the priest Chabrol not far from the rue de la Boucherie, but the chapel, its windows, the statue, the relics, and the corporation and confraternity of the butchers survived Limoges's Jacobins. While the statues of the cathedral were beheaded, the butchers heard mass in the dark in their chapel. Only during the Restoration did the chapel again become the legal property of the confraternity of butchers; the fifty-eight masters signed a notarized agreement to that effect in 1827, pledging to pay fifty centimes a month for its upkeep. Each male child's name continued to be inscribed in the register of the confraternity and two francs a year was paid in his name until he was old enough to pay the *cotisation* himself.[36]

Public processions were an integral part of the butchers' community life. They celebrated the feast day of St. Martial with the other confraternities of the city, marking their own *fête du boeuf engraissé* on February 24. Other feast days particularly dear to the confraternity of butchers were St. Joseph (March 19), St.

Anne (July 26), and, above all, St. Aurélien (on May 10 or the first Sunday after that date), when they finally changed their clothes, appearing in the saint's colors of white and green. They played a central part in the above-mentioned Ostensions, during which the remains of St. Martial and other saints were paraded about town in a procession involving a total of 292 relics in 92 reliquaries and 8 grand *châsses*. The confraternity of butchers auctioned off to one of their own the right to carry the most precious relics, an honor that would cost as much as 100 francs. The butchers also escorted the bishop of Limoges, fired off their muskets during the final procession (in one case forcing the court to suspend testimony because of the noise), and entertained the clergy at a series of banquets. The butchers' wives maintained their own confraternity, Notre-Dame-des-Sept-Douleurs, and celebrated the feast day on the third Sunday of September, known locally as Notre-Dame-des-Petits-Ventres, by preparing steaming plates of tripe.[37]

The years of the Revolution had only further solidified the butchers' devotion to the monarchy and the royal family. The devoted clans still claimed a centuries-old right to escort princes of the blood into Limoges, a tradition that stretched back to the visit of Henry IV. Legend also has it that they once saved the life of this monarch, to whose memory they were particularly attached.

When the Duc d'Angoulême arrived in 1814 and again in 1815, the butchers greeted him at the town's outskirts in their finest processional garb. The first of these royal encounters proved somewhat embarrassing, as the butchers cried out "A bas lou rats!" ("Down with the tax collectors!"). The duke misunderstood their patois as "A bas les rois!" ("Down with kings!"), but the momentary crisis passed after some hurried explanations. In 1828 the Duchesse de Berry, the mother of the *enfant du miracle,* the Comte de Chambord, visited Limoges. The butchers rode out to meet her and were thus described:

> Mounted on their ponies, the butchers are identified by their blue outfits with yellow sleeves, the immense plume that crowns their shako, and especially the noisy acclamations with which they fill the air while brandishing swords which seem to have been borrowed from some panoply of the Middle Ages.[38]

The butchers, invited to the reception for the duchess, stood with the bishop of Limoges and the prefect, as well as the mayor, Monsieur Martin de la Bastide. The duchess agreed to visit the rue de la Boucherie, a decision she might later have regretted, the piety and loyalty of its inhabitants notwithstanding.[39]

Yet the relations between the corporation of butchers and Limoges's civil authorities were not always ideal, despite the almost mystical fervor with which the butchers embraced the political and religious ideals of the Restoration. For one thing, there were countless complaints—quite justified—about the appalling filth of the street. The butchers' stalls made the street virtually impassable. The unpaved rue de la Boucherie had only a ditch running down the center for drainage. The narrow streets, such as the rue Huchette and the rue Vigne-de-Fer, that radiated from the rue de la Boucherie offered minimal space for killing animals. An ancient decree had proclaimed that slaughtering was to be done on the street so that buyers could see—undoubtedly more than they ever wanted—that they were getting fresh meat.[40]

Even more vexing for the butchers' neighbors in nearby quarters—especially for anyone walking in the direction in which the wind was blowing—was the utter, inescapable, putrid stench given out by the rue de la Boucherie. Particularly noxious were the older houses, toward the upper end of the street, where there was no division between the store area of the ground floor and the area where the butchers prepared and stored meat, animal parts, and skins. The upper reaches of the houses had space for the hanging of meat—often right over the street. The police only occasionally prosecuted a butcher for allowing chickens to run wild through the streets or for failing to sweep the front of his house at night.

The municipal council first considered the construction of a slaughterhouse in 1825. Three years later they were still debating. The noble Martin de la Bastide limited himself to infrequent friendly reminders that tossing dead cows into the Vienne River was not in the best interests of the city. Police investigated complaints that butchers occasionally sold meat at false weights or unloaded spoiled meat on the public, but they took no serious steps. The only municipal decree had been issued in 1825, when the butchers, who had complained that they could not use the famous fountain of Aigoulène for their purposes, were told that during particularly hot weather they were to slaughter only when and where authorized.

The butchers were faithful and prosperous political allies of the Bourbons if the need arose. Thirty-four were included on the 1834 list of those eligible to vote by virtue of taxes paid. Their considerable wealth included plots of grazing land in the city's hinterland. Four butchers, led by Cibot *aîné dit* Sans-quartier, paid even more taxes than Dumont St. Priest, a young lawyer who went on to become the procureur général in Limoges.[43] The butchers' declared fortunes represented, as everybody knew, but a part of their wealth, which was hoarded or used to purchase expensive chalices and religious trappings for their festivals and not invested in large chunks of the countryside and secondary residences.

Imposing change on the rue de la Boucherie had never been easy. When the king sent an agent in the seventeenth century to check up on the butchers, the former was "mistreated" and sent on his way. In April 1814 they categorically refused to pay their taxes and recaptured prisoners seized by the tax officials and police. During the Restoration the corporation signed an agreement with the municipal administration. Their *abonnement,* set at fifty-eight thousand francs in 1816, rose to over sixty-five thousand francs in 1825; whereas the butchers complained that they were paying too much, particularly when meat consumption in the city fell, most *limougeauds,* particularly the police, believed that the butchers were amassing vast fortunes at the public's expense. The butchers insisted that any rise in the *abonnement* would be reflected in the higher price of meat. They bitterly protested the *octroi* regulations, such as the hours the gates were closed. They opposed even minimal supervision of their corporation by the town authorities; the mayor had the right, dating back to an unknown time, to select the syndics of the corporation from a list of candidates elected by the master butchers.[44]

The Viraclaud, another old quarter, was largely identified with an equally ageless trade associated with the flesh, namely, prostitution. Hard times, leaving the poor without resources, increased the number of *femmes publiques*. Prostitution in Limoges was tolerated during the Restoration, although in principle it was limited to thirty local women. Should the number fall below thirty (which it never did), the available spot was to be filled by whichever outside "applicant" demonstrated the "least offensive morals." In 1828 twenty-three houses of prostitution were in operation. Some were rooming houses that also accepted full-time lodgers with other occupations. Nine of these "received all girls who wanted to be prostitutes." Forty-five women, despite the legal limit, worked the fourteen "official" houses. These houses were found primarily in Viraclaud, near the rue des Combes, particularly the rue Froment. Some were also cabarets, where "drinkers sing and pass the night away." Soldiers were regular customers, including one who, in January 1828, tried to fight his way into a house with sword drawn.[45]

The policing of prostitution had but two goals in Limoges: to limit the number of prostitutes by sending away women who were not from the city and to prevent public scandal. Such scandals included prostitutes propositioning openly in the streets, attempting to lure minors into their lairs, or loud carousing into the night. In 1816 a *fille en service* was allowed to enter the municipal jail, where "elle avait fort connaissance avec un condamné à six ans de réclusion." In this case only marriage could lessen the "scandal"; the prosecutor allowed them to marry before the prisoner was returned to a more chaste confinement.[46] One prostitute was ordered out of town because of her "conduite peu réservée," and when she returned without a passport, she was returned by the gendarmerie to her home in Benevent, in the Creuse.[47] Complaints about Limoges's prostitutes were frequent. "Nothing stops them," went one report, "because they know all of the tricks necessary to reach their goal." In April 1827 the residents of the rue Froment bemoaned the "scenes of disorder" that troubled their rest night and day. They particularly cited one Verthou, called "Red Nose," who employed six prostitutes in what her angry neighbors called "her den of thieves." The prefect, Baron Coster, adopting a more rigorous policy than his predecessor, ordered some prostitutes returned to their villages and incarcerated those suffering from venereal disease in the *dépôt de mendicité*. He received a letter of thanks from one Madame Gossely for having rid Limoges of so many "public women from outside of the city." She had more on her mind than the defense of public virtue; in particular, she was referring to the scandalous Souvaroux sisters from Guéret, who were wreaking havoc in many households, including her own.[48]

Who were the prostitutes of Limoges? In November 1824 forty-three *femmes publiques* were known to be working in the city. Of these twenty originally hailed from Limoges. The others all came from rural Haute-Vienne, the Creuse, the Corrèze, and one from the Dordogne. Those born outside Limoges were somewhat younger, averaging about twenty-five as compared to nearly thirty for the *limougeaudes*. Most did not bother to list any other occupation, but four claimed to be seamstresses, three day laborers, two spinners, and one each a tailor, merchant, braider, and ink maker. Those born outside of Limoges had spent an average of 8.4 years in the city. They had come in their late teens or early twenties, perhaps after becoming pregnant in their communes. Marie Tricaud, twenty-six in 1824, was born in the small textile town of Felletin, in the Creuse. She arrived in Limoges in 1814, claiming some skill as a seamstress. She had spent most of the time since then in a *maison de tolérance* on the rue Froment. An "outsider," she was ordered to leave the town and was handed a passport with a fixed itinerary to lead her back to the Creuse. But Marie did not leave, or else she soon returned, as did most of the others. Françoise Lafond, twenty-one in 1824, had arrived from the Charente in 1821 without any trade. Like many of her fellow prostitutes, she gave no permanent address, continuing to live in the *dépôt de mendicité* because she had venereal disease. Louise Ester, the oldest registered prostitute at forty-six, had apparently reached the end of the line. She had come to Limoges from Meymac, in the Corrèze, in 1808. Since that time her name had turned up in a police register for having "led a youth to debauchery." Now she lived on the rue du Cheval Blanc with what was diagnosed as an incurable case of venereal disease. The doctors refused to see her anymore. Arrested during the cold night of December 18, 1828, for being on the street after 10 p.m., she had nowhere else to go. Here we lose any trace of her, but we must assume that she did not have much time left. Marie Versavaud, called Claris, had arrived in Limoges from Chalus in 1814 at the age of sixteen. She now lived on the rue des Trépassés and was "sometimes given to madness."

In 1824 the recently arrived and ambitious Prefect Baron Coster ordered most of the "outsiders" to be returned to their own communes. One self-proclaimed day laborer from Negrondes, in the Dordogne, was told to sell her belongings by the end of the month; another was given a reprieve when the banns of her marriage were suddenly posted. Most of those who were not incarcerated returned home, or possibly never left. Several remained under legal surveillance, undoubtedly because they had committed crimes. Others escaped the census because they were *sans domicile fixe,* worked only part time, or stayed in the city only briefly. Prostitution remained rather effectively limited to several streets. The Restoration government tolerated and, to some extent, even indirectly protected the local talent against outside competition. The municipal government was much more concerned with control of the spread of disease than with prostitution per se, and took steps to force the "public women" to be inspected twice monthly by a doctor at the *dépôt de mendicité.* For example, in September 1818 the *femme* Adélaïde refused to see the doctor, claiming no obligation because she saw her own clients at home. The prefect threatened to put her, together with sixty other women, in the *dépôt de mendicité* if she refused to cooperate.[49]

The police saw prostitution, then, as part of the evil in the world, interfering only when public order or decency seemed gravely menaced. During the first years of the reign of Charles X the number of prostitutes increased along with the growth of the urban population and the small garrison. Local authorities returned to a limited policy of containment, perhaps because the economic crisis and political events came to occupy more of their time.

Work left little time, opportunity, or need for the development of literacy. The Haute-Vienne trailed virtually every department throughout most of the century in the percentage of literacy. Even to the departmental General Council it seemed that "Haute-Vienne lags behind civilization, and the rapid movement that has advanced it in other regions is hardly felt there beyond the walls of the town." A military observer's less generous explanation was that "the intellectual facilities of the Limousins are hardly precocious." Prefect de Castéja had found his charges "little adapted to the culture of reading" in 1819. Indeed, 123 of the department's 200 communes had no schoolteacher during the Restoration. Only slightly more than half of the men (an estimated 55 percent in 1825–26 as compared to about 31 percent in the year VI) and only a little more than a quarter (about 27 percent in the year VI) of the women were literate.[50]

Illiteracy and the use of patois were specific characteristics of *le peuple,* half of whom had migrated from Limoges's backward hinterland. The royal *collège* enrolled about 325 students, of whom 125 were boarders. A small seminary disappeared in the late 1820s. Boys in Limoges could attend any of three schools, two of which were run by the Sisters of St. Vincent de Paul. In addition, Limoges boasted about thirty or forty private school teachers or tutors and a number of charitable institutions for young girls and orphans. But most children of workers entered the work force at a young age and could not attend school. Exceptions included the sons of the *artistes en porcelaine,* including turners and moulders, whose skills in reading and writing further distanced them from the mass of the working population.[51]

The 1820s were years of fairly stable prices and gradually rising wages. In 1819 the prefect claimed that "abundance is everywhere; the worker lives without effort, and three days of work are largely sufficient for the necessary expenses of the week." The average worker in the city earned somewhat more than 1.70 francs per day. One local historian has classified the workers according to, on the one hand, those who were "happy" (*heureux*), earning between 2.50 and 8 francs a day (the latter figure attained only by a few *artistes en porcelaine*), or average workers who took home between 1.75 and 2.50 francs; and, on the other, the "unhappy" laborers, who earned less than the daily average wage. The latter included day laborers, dyers, workers in the kaolin mills, and women in any industry. Children brought home only a fraction of the wages of an adult male worker, but this additional income often contributed to the survival of the household.[52]

Approximately 60 percent of a worker's family budget was set aside for the purchase of food, and the majority of that for bread alone. This was rarely bread of the first quality, usually rye bread. Rents were relatively low, accounting for somewhere between 7 and 12 percent of the budget; another 10 to 12 percent was spent on heat and light. Approximately 7 percent paid for clothes, of which most workers had two sets (winter and summer), made from the coarse cloths produced in the city. Rye bread was a staple, with buckwheat prepared as pancakes (*galettes*) cooked in grease or served with milk and chestnuts. The workers' diet included potatoes, lard soups, and cabbage and turnips soaked with rye bread (*bréjaude*). Meat seldom appeared on the workers' tables, although the raising of animals was such an important regional industry that the level of meat consumption may have been higher than in other relatively poor regions. *Porc gras salé,* for example, was common, but chicken and local fish were less so. Water remained the principal drink, although some of the justly inexpensive local wines produced in Aixe, Verneuil, and Isle (which turned to vinegar after a short time) were consumed. Beer and cider remained luxuries.[53]

Just what we know about prices and wages, which rose slightly, would suggest that the worker and his family could have survived rather easily in Limoges during the Restoration. However, wage rates, when they can be determined, are not a reliable indicator of the standard of living because of the perpetual problems—for the historian as well as for the worker—of unemployment and underemployment. The porcelain industry, which had the widest scale of wages and paid its skilled workers well, is a good case in point; the industry had its own *morte saison,* when inventory was taken, and was subject to relatively sudden plunges in demand. The level of wages reflects only payment during the time the worker was employed. Furthermore, most skilled workers in the industry had to pay for their tools and materials, as well as supply the wages of those who assisted them in their task. The turners, molders, and decorators were paid by the piece, but had the cost of the *fente*—damages to products or breakage that had occurred during the process of production, particularly during baking—subtracted from their wages. This tradition reduced their real wages and was bitterly resisted and, later, contested.[54]

Furthermore, Limoges's industries and, consequently, its workers were particularly vulnerable to years of crisis. The margin of economic survival remained narrow in the first half of the century. Personal disaster (such as an accident or an untimely pregnancy) could push a person or an entire family across the line between "getting by" and misery.[55] A harvest failure, which invariably brought a commercial and industrial crisis in its wake, could have ruinous consequences. Skilled turners and molders, and even decorators, were vulnerable because a decline in demand left them without work.

However, most workers benefited from fairly stable prices during the Restoration. For example, the price of beef was about 80 centimes per kilo from 1820 through 1837; the price of potatoes, a staple, rose sharply only during the first years of the Restoration and again in 1824, falling back to normal levels in following years. But the threat of agricultural crisis still loomed. Two major crises of the Restoration dramatically drove up the prices of bread, the staple of the poor: one in 1816–17 (and, to a lesser extent, 1818) and another in 1828–29, the effects of which were still being felt in 1830. These crises arrived slightly later and remained longer than in some regions. The price of wheat, 18.25 francs per hectoliter in 1815, rose to 30.50 during the terrible year 1816, before falling back to between 14 and 17 francs from 1821 to 1827. Thus, first-quality bread rose from 33 centimes a kilo in 1815 to 70 centimes briefly in 1817; the price fell to between 27 and 32 centimes between 1821 and early 1828, when prices again rose sharply, although never again to the 1816–17 level.[56]

An economic slump affected the bulk of the city's population. Workers with virtually no income to spend left shopkeepers with overstocked shelves and artisans without customers. Large numbers of the poor became dependent upon private and public charity; a flood of impoverished *campagnards* arrived. The municipal council voted sums for public works projects and sometimes sent people to other regions to buy grain. The bishop and the prefect discussed how the needs of the worthy poor could be met, if at all. Priests drew up lists of the "deserving" poor who were known to be religious and might qualify for some charity from the ladies of the city. The death rate rose, as did the number of abandoned children taken in by the kindly but overburdened Sisters of St. Alexis. During hard times some workers returned to the countryside to look for work and live with relatives. How different were their trips to the environs from the excursions of the elite to their country estates!

We can catch only glimpses of the culture of poverty in Limoges. *Le peuple limousin* were considered "gapers," loving impromptu performers, clowns, storytellers, puppets, and charlatans, all of whom were "always surrounded by a numerous and absolutely attentive crowd." Workers, like the peasants of the region, enjoyed cards and drink—the latter sometimes to excess—although in general both were known for their reserve and "resignation." They could be extremely sentimental, as one prefect attested: "It is not difficult to bring these good people to tears. Upon hearing of a tragic event or listening to a touching ballad or song, even the largest gathering will suddenly burst into tears. Woe to those who conserve dry eyes—it will be said that they are heartless."[57] *Le peuple* enjoyed the religious festivals of their city, region, and of their corporation or trade. They enjoyed the annual markets and fairs that brought the smallish, long-haired, fierce-looking Limousin peasants, as well as merchants from other regions, to town.

Public order was easily maintained in Limoges. Occasionally the police interrupted a charivari: for example, a noisy crowd of three hundred who serenaded a woman who had just been married for the third time—in this case the new groom stormed out of the house and snatched away one of the offending musical instruments; or another involving young men from "les meilleures maisons de Limoges" following a theater performance in 1820.[58] Only one major incident involving a crowd had posed a threat to public order in the Restoration, when *les gens du peuple* made their only collective appearance during the Restoration.

In 1816 the price of grain rose sharply following a poor harvest. The price of rye reached twenty francs per hectoliter—twice the price it commanded in nearby St. Junien. Costly white bread reached forty-four centimes a kilo, leaping to seventy centimes the following year. The price of potatoes, a staple of the poor, almost doubled. While the municipal administration and the prefect commissioned merchants from the city to go to Orléans to buy grain for the Limoges market, rumors of hoarding spread.[59]

On June 18, 1816, several wagons filled with grain—purchased at a price the poor could not afford—left Limoges for Montauban. Some distance beyond the Pont St. Martial, they were stopped by a mob of between three and four hundred people, mostly women. The police intervened and escorted the merchant, who lived in Limoges, to the hamlet of St. Lazare. But there another crowd intercepted his wagons at the cotton-spinning factory of Monsieur Constantin. This time they hurled rocks and damaged the wagon with a pitchfork. One of the women who was arrested explained simply that "the driver was taking the grain out of the department." When news of the arrest of several women spread, a huge crowd gathered in protest at the prefecture; another woman was arrested for loudly making a "seditious statement." The prefect posted a warning against hoarding; the police monitored the bakers' stock, which helped get more grain on the market, and the National Guard patrolled the streets night and day. The price of grain fell briefly, only to climb to record heights during the next year. But by 1828 these events had been long since forgotten. Officials and the town's leading citizens assumed that "the people are incapable of reflecting wisely," but aside from the fear that they could "be put up to something," they were not seen as a threat to public order in Limoges.[60]

Police duties therefore focused on assisting the *octroi* employees; watching the swarms of vagrants who descended upon the city in bad times or who arrived alone or in pairs in normal years; noting the arrival of travelers, particularly *colporteurs,* passing through the city; tracking army deserters; and breaking up drunken brawls between soldiers and civilians, or between rival *compagnons*. The police commissioners checked the registers of Limoges's hotels and numerous inns, removed cadavers, and kept an eye on the city's cafés. Their duties also included overseeing "workers' *livrets* and arresting prostitutes," the two being perceived as needing similar moral supervision. The Ministry of the Interior provided funds for undercover agents *au niveau de peuple* and occasionally in the prison, where security was notoriously lax and escapes not infrequent. But among the people there were no political plots to sniff out or political opposition to fathom.[61]

Nor was crime a great problem. Murders were exceptional events which dominated conversations for weeks, particularly when they were savage and gory. In December 1827 a peasant named Jean Doirat, who lived near Bellac, in the commune of St. Symphorien, hacked to death his wife, oldest daughter, and a neighbor with an ax, wounding several other people before he dove into a pond and drowned himself as the fire he had set consumed ten houses in his village. In 1828 there were only two reported murders in the entire department; one was sufficiently brutal to occupy the public's attention for weeks: A peasant woman beat a neighbor to death after he had chased her animals from his property. And early in December 1829 the body of an elderly priest was found some distance from Limoges on the road to Angoulême; he had defended himself bravely against four attackers, shooting one of them before he expired. Even though the killers were captured, many *limougeauds* remained terrified of the wooded area outside the city, even when another murder in the vicinity turned out to be a crime of passion involving infidelity and jealousy. Murders were rare events, almost as unusual as escaped circus bears killing children, which occurred once in the vicinity of St. Yrieix. Suicides were more common and were discussed in hushed tones: a domestic taking poison after discovering that she was pregnant; or the suicide of Laval *dit* Poiron, a noted local scoundrel in Limoges who claimed to have been one of the assassins of the Princesse de Lamballe during the Revolution, dealt in stolen merchandise, lived in sin, and sold the *boulettes de poudre fulminante* to the young anticlerical bourgeois who disrupted the missions in the spring of 1828.

Thefts were considerably more common than murders, yet they were rare enough to receive much attention. Those apprehended for such crimes sometimes found themselves exposed and ridiculed at a public square. In 1824, for example, only three were reported in the entire month of September in the department of Haute-Vienne, and only four were recorded the previous April. Three attempted robberies in Limoges in April 1826 created a panic and even caused some people to lock their doors. But in December of that year only one theft in the city was reported. One had to be wary of pickpockets and confidence men at the annual fair of the Innocents (and even more so in May during the fair of St. Loup), particularly of *colporteurs,* who were suspect. The major theft in December 1828 turned out to be embarrassing for the police: Someone stole 160 francs from the police station during the night. More common were thefts from stores or shops by men "who appeared to me to be Auvergnat."[62]

Most of the *procès-verbaux* of the police were citations of those who violated basic municipal regulations: shopkeepers, particularly bakers, who cheated on weight and quality; residents who let their animals run in the street, failed to sweep the frontage of their buildings each day, blocked traffic by leaving their wagons unattended, or dumped garbage in the street; wagon drivers who sped across the narrow bridges, occasionally killing helpless pedestrians; or shopkeepers who ostentatiously worked on Sunday. A part of the small fines resulting from such contraventions—usually one franc—went to the poor. Vagrants and prostitutes—at least those who failed to pass the obligatory medical inspection—were incarcerated at the *dépôt de mendicité*. Prisoners convicted of major crimes joined those convicts from four other departments at the *maison centrale*.[63] But executions were rare. The *esprit publique* section of the daily police report had very little to say. At the end of 1822 the police commissioner reported that not one event of interest had occurred in Limoges.

A seventeenth-century tourist once claimed that the people of Limoges were far more concerned with their commerce than with the care of their houses or even their bodies. Prefect de Castéja, arriving in the spring of 1819, thus characterized his administrative charges: "The inhabitants of this department are distinguished by the shrewdness of their judgment, their calculating and practical minds, and a great aptitude for commercial operations."[64] At least one lifetime resident found this taste for speculation offensive: While justly proud of the "brilliant reputation" of his city's commercial bourgeoisie, he worried that relative newcomers were tarnishing Limoges's once sterling reputation with their "wild speculations" and seemingly endless quest for new luxuries.[65] In 1816 a "friend of the king" had written an anonymous denunciation of Limoges's deputy mayors; he complained that not only were they *sans connaissances,* but they were so preoccupied with their businesses that they neglected the affairs of Limoges. One of them, the textile merchant Muret de Bord, was recognized for "infamous public conduct," perhaps inspired by his father, who, the secret detractor alleged, had enjoyed 190 mistresses. Some of Limoges's commercial leaders urged stricter codes and regulations to discourage unscrupulous commercial practices, but most prided themselves on the "thrift, patience, energy, and good faith" of the group of families and friends who dominated the commerce of the city.[66]

Limoges's geographic position had favored its development as a thriving commercial center for the exchange of goods from the North, East, and Midi, enriching the branches of the Pouyat and Pétiniaud families, among others, who owned considerable property in the communes surrounding the city. Increasing *octroi* receipts reflected prosperity, jumping from 186,000 francs in 1812 to 220,000 francs per year during the period 1819–24, and rising to 252,000 francs in 1827. In 1818 ten merchants and two commercial transport entrepreneurs were among the leading *censitaires* of the city. Among municipal voters in 1834, sixty-eight whole-sale merchants represented by far the second most common occupational category, behind *propriétaires*. Twenty-eight paid more than 300 francs, nineteen paid between 200 and 300, and twenty-one paid between 100 and 200. Their houses on the rues Manigne and Haute-Vienne were among the most elegant in Limoges.[67]

But if Limoges lived by commerce, much of it was retail. In 1819 the prefect estimated that at least two thousand of the approximately twenty-five hundred buildings in Limoges housed boutiques, stores, or small workshops on the ground floor. Limoges's merchants sold a wide variety of products, ranging from staples and rugged, locally produced clothing for the poor to colonial products by way of Bordeaux, luxury *articles de Paris,* and even "fresh" oysters available each day (though one may doubt how fresh they could have been after the long, jolting, and dusty journey from the coast). The shops on the rues Haut and Bas Lansecot greeted peasants arriving to buy the products of the urban market. "There, nothing is spared to seduce them, to tempt the variety of villagers, and bring about the extremely painful separation of the peasant and his money."[68]

Yet in 1819 the prefect de Castéja had been struck by a marked shift in the economy of Limoges. It was not just salon conversations that convinced him that some of the capital which had been used to finance wholesale commerce was now going into the manufacture of Limoges's two most noteworthy products, textiles and porcelain. One could see ever-increasing quantities of wood being hauled up from the Vienne River to fuel the porcelain kilns. The settlements across the river were alive with domestic textile production; several small factories along the Vienne were busier than they had ever been. Country people were coming to Limoges in ever greater numbers in the hope of finding better-paying jobs. Furthermore, Limoges's manufacturers began to send their own representatives to other towns and markets. Thus, the number of wealthy commercial transport entrepreneurs declined from seventeen in 1817 to seven at the time of the Revolution of 1830. Wholesale commerce (particularly of woolens) seemed to be losing out to competitors in the North and Midi. The fall onslaught of Auvergnats "selling whatever they can in warmer areas" was thus resented. But, at the same time, the preeminence of the porcelain manufacturers Alluaud, Baignol, and Tharaud, all of whom had begun as skilled turners in the industry, came to match their wealth. In 1828 no manufacturers of porcelain, flannels, paper, and wax were among those eligible for election to the Chamber of Deputies. Limoges was becoming a manufacturing town.[69]

The production of textiles was the largest industry in the city in 1828, although Limoges could not successfully compete with the Nord and other departments. The production of textiles favored by Limoges's location on the Vienne and the availability of labor, which included the prisoners of the central prison, had expanded since Turgot first brought spinning wheels from the Nord; over one thousand laborers spun or wove coarse cloth flannel and druggets. Yet a visitor would have had little immediate sense of the size of the textile industry because the putting-out system still dominated production. Textile workers could be found in most quarters of the city, but particularly in the faubourg St. Martial and the streets near the Vienne. Limoges merchants sold cotton and wool clothes and blankets at the fairs of Bordeaux, Clermont, and Beaucaire. They returned with merchandise to sell in Limoges or to send up North. The production of cotton had declined rapidly in the face of stiff competition from the textile departments of the North, but the wool industry was thriving. In the late 1820s a few manufacturers tried their hand at finer types of production, including calicoes and cashmeres.[70]

Before 1825 thirteen manufacturers of flannels had been located near the Pont St. Martial, but during that year several moved into the commercial quarter of Manigne; nine hydraulic spinning machines were located in factories along the river, and at least two hundred looms were at work. The mechanization of spinning in about twenty small shops increased domestic employment possibilities for weavers in the faubourg des Casseaux, along the rue des Petites Maisons, and in the settlements of St. Lazare and Bellevue on the other side of the Vienne. Forty looms spun cotton near Pont St. Martial, and another 150 workers spun cotton and linen, this despite the decline of these industries. The health of these workers suffered because of the excessive humidity and cramped working conditions associated with their tasks, which for some lasted sixteen and seventeen hours a day. The more prosperous manufacturers of druggets and flannels employed their own dyers, although a few of the latter worked independently in the vicinity of the polluted stream that ran through the tanners' quarter.

The decline that gradually pervaded the textile industry did not threaten Limoges's second product, porcelain. For although it was still the major employer in the city, the textile industry remained largely dependent upon a regional and local market, with little hope of competing nationally.[71] The porcelain industry had greater hopes. Limoges porcelain owed its origin to the accidental discovery in 1765 of kaolin, a fine white clay, by a doctor's wife, who found the substance near St. Yrieix, thirty kilometers southwest of Limoges. Encouraged by Turgot, the first porcelain factory was established in Limoges six years later and survived as a branch of the royal manufacture at Sèvres until 1791. The production of fine porcelain revived during Thermidor, and in 1797 Baignol, a former skilled turner from the royal manufacture, moved his own small operation from St. Yrieix to what had earlier been the convent of the Petits Augustins in Limoges. One of his former co-workers, François Alluaud, originally an engineer, who had taken charge of the royal manufacture in 1790, began a small factory on the rue des Anglais which was staffed by skilled artisans brought from Paris. But Alluaud died in 1799 before he could realize his dream of building a large factory suitable for new production techniques. His son, François, returned to Limoges in 1801 from the army and took over his father's business. Soon he and Baignol accounted for three quarters of the total porcelain produced in Limoges. They relied upon skilled decorators, turners, and molders from other cities, as well as workers trained by the school of industrial design that the local Société d'agriculture et des arts established in 1804. They were paternal overseers of their workers, alongside whom they frequently labored. The fete of the *patron* became that of his workers, and when Baignol died, they fought with the penitents to which he had belonged for the right to carry him to his grave. The constant wars and deflated market conditions, however, severely limited the expansion of Limoges's newest industry.[72]

The Restoration first brought hope to the industry and then prosperity. Limoges was favored by its proximity to Bonneval, which was relatively near the kaolin quarries in St. Yrieix and Coussac. The woods of the Limousin produced fuel for the porcelain kilns; the Vienne River provided the means to transport the logs to the port of Naveix in Limoges. The wood was lifted from two *rameaux,* or barriers, which reached from each side of the river, by the *flotteurs de bois* and other day laborers and was hauled to the factories. The Vienne also provided power for the mills that ground the kaolin into a paste, from which the pieces of porcelain were shaped. A number of skilled decorators, turners, and molders lived in Limoges, and from among these artisans emerged several able entrepreneurs who were familiar with every stage of production. Furthermore, the Limousin offered a surplus of unskilled labor willing to abandon the infertile countryside for possible jobs in the city. In Limoges both the skilled and unskilled worked for wages lower than those in Paris. Several manufacturers left Paris for the provinces, settling in Vierzon, the Nièvre, the Indre, as well as the Limousin. By 1819 four factories produced porcelain in Limoges, which increased to seven three years later and nine in 1824. Alluaud purchased land in the sparsely populated faubourg des Casseaux, near the Vienne, above the port of Naveix. He constructed the first building in the city planned as a factory. The municipal council granted Alluaud a year's exemption from the costly *octroi* tax on wood, an advantage that was apparently not resented or opposed by other entrepreneurs, although several later applied and were refused this same privilege. Tharaud, another artisan-turned-manufacturer, was among this number; he had established his factory in the open faubourgs north of the city, on the road to Paris.[73]

The manufacture of porcelain required a relatively large outlay of capital for raw materials, transportation, and labor. As a result, the movement of the porcelain industry to lower production costs in the provinces was accompanied by some dispersion from Limoges into its hinterland. Factories were established in Magnac Bourg (1819), Coussac Bonneval (1819), the abbey town of Solignac (1824), St. Brice (1825), and up the Vienne River in St. Léonard (1825). Such factories were nearer the kaolin quarries and benefited from the lower wages paid outside of

Limoges. Increased production and slightly lower production costs reduced the price consumers paid for porcelain, thereby stimulating demand. At the same time, the German, Spanish, and Italian markets began to open up to French porcelain. Thus, despite the rise in the price of wood and a slump associated with the economic crisis of 1826–27, the region's porcelain industry prospered.[74]

In 1828 between eight and nine hundred porcelain workers toiled in Limoges.[75] Generally the level of required worker skill increased at every stage in the production process. Unskilled, poorly paid rural workers extracted kaolin from the quarries and transported it to small *moulins à pâte,* several of which were owned by Alluaud and Baignol, where it was dried in the sun, purged of visible impurities, ground up by a water mill until a smooth texture was obtained, and then passed through a silk screen. It was then shaped into balls and delivered in wagons to the factories. There workers beat and kneaded the pastelike substance to remove air bubbles. Then turners shaped the cakelike *pâte* on a pottery wheel with a knife. The molders removed further impurities and shaped each piece, often with the assistance of a mold. The pieces were now baked in enormous wood-heated ovens, which were stoked by the *hommes du four* and then dipped into enamel (feldspar and powdered quartz diluted with water). The final baking took between thirty and forty-five hours at a greatly increased temperature. The *enfourneurs* were responsible for this process and thus worked exceptionally long hours in great heat. The porcelain was baked in clay vessels, prepared by workers called *engazetiers,* in order to protect the product from ashes or cinders from the wood fire.

Next the *useurs de grains* checked the porcelain for impurities; burnishers and polishers finished the process that resulted in the plain, white porcelain, the most popular variety at the time. The final stage of production for some of the porcelain, however, occurred in small, separate decoration workshops in Limoges or Paris, where the *artistes en porcelaine* added the painted designs and final decorative touches to the product for which the city became known. By far the most highly paid workers, they usually labored at home. Earning between five and eight francs a day, they were quite mobile geographically, as their skills were much in demand in Sèvres, Vierzon, and Paris. Most had arrived from these other cities at some point during the Restoration. Dignified, literate, prosperous, and relatively independent, they were as close to an "aristocracy of labor" as existed in Limoges. Only the other artisans in the industry, the turners and molders, approached their skill. Once the decorators had finished their tasks, the porcelain was briefly reheated in *moufles,* or smaller ovens, and then declared ready for shipment.[76]

The conditions of work in the industry were already notorious. Chemical fumes and dust filled the workshops. Porcelain workers could be readily identified by their "pale complexion, and a sad, suffering countenance." The small children and apprentices were initiated early into an unhealthy world of dust, fumes, suffocating heat, and workdays approaching fourteen hours.[77] Porcelain workers were particularly susceptible to tuberculosis and other lung diseases.

Porcelain was a high-risk, high-profit venture for manufacturers. Alluaud corresponded with his counterparts in Sèvres and other cities and had won a silver medal at an exposition in Paris in 1819. But cruel bankruptcies in 1823 and 1826 closed two operations. The porcelain *fabricants* petitioned municipal and national authorities, asking for permanent exemption from the *octroi* tax. They faced the possibility that their skilled workers would leave, just as they had been lured to Limoges. Political crisis spelled danger; uncertainty and indecision could bring ruin if demand for porcelain was significantly reduced. Alluaud (who wrote several articles on the floating of wood down the Vienne and on the extraction of kaolin) and the other *patrons* closely studied every step of the production process. His was one of two factories in Limoges that employed more than one hundred workers. The workers, skilled and unskilled, accepted a 20 percent wage reduction in 1826. But Alluaud and his colleagues maintained their optimism. Fourteen ovens were in operation in Limoges in 1828.[78] Porcelain seemed to be shaping the future of the city, indeed, the entire region.

Limoges's other industries were considerably less significant. The region's major economic mainstay, the raising and selling of livestock, generated the tanning industry. Seven tanneries, most of which bordered a stream that ran through the entre-deux-villes section, obtained their dyes from the abundant chestnut trees outside the city. Shoes, galoshes, and *souliers de pacotile* were also produced for a regional market. Eight small paper manufactures employed a total of less than one hundred workers along the Vienne. There was some bookbinding and printing, a manufacture of weights and measures (seventy-five workers), an iron forge with twenty-five workers, and several brasseries that catered to the taste for beer which Napoleon's soldiers had brought back from Germany. Limoges's growing population also supported the typical range of artisans who supplied the local market, such as coppersmiths, tinsmiths, metalworkers, cabinetmakers, pin makers, and a few remaining silver and enamel workers with little but centuries of proud tradition to support them. These artisans maintained their traditional corporate structure; journeymen and apprentices still spoke of "my bourgeois" when referring to the master.[79] No inhabitants discussing work in the city of Limoges would have failed to mention the two most traditional groups supplying food to the population, namely, the bakers, whose organizational heritage went back for centuries, and the corporation of butchers, who were isolated from the city, on the rue de la Boucherie, by mutual consent.

In order to characterize urban politics in a Restoration city, we must first briefly sketch its power structure. As in all French cities, Limoges's elite included only a relatively small proportion of the population. Class structure here seemed relatively uncomplicated. The most striking aspect of class relations in this Restoration town was not the differences within the "middle classes," but their shared self-perception and role, which opposed and distanced them from the mass of the working population and, at least partially, from the remnants of the traditional *noblesse* in the Limousin. Economically, socially, and culturally the middle classes shared much in common in Restoration Limoges. Contemporaries claimed that the scions of commerce, law, magistrature, and industry were drawn from essentially the same milieu in the small world of Limoges. First, we can roughly identify the number of *limougeauds* who were, and would have proudly considered themselves, "bourgeois," as opposed to being of the *peuple* or members of the *noblesse*. We are here considering far less than one fifth of the population.[80]

Limoges's population of slightly more than 27,000 in 1831 included about 6,700 households (with an average family size of a little less than four) and 6,585 males between the ages of twenty and sixty. More than two thirds of the some 6,000 male heads of household were workers, from journeymen artisans down to casual laborers. The number of armed and uniformed guardsmen provides a good estimate of the Limoges bourgeoisie, including master artisans. In 1822 the guard had included 1,530 out of a population of 19,650. In 1831 the National Guard rolls listed 1,774 males, of whom 1,519 possessed a uniform and 1,341 owned suitable rifles. The guard had grown very little over the nine-year period, confirming that the increase in the city's population resulted from the arrival of unskilled labor in the city, workers not admitted to the elite guard. The list of municipal voters (*censitaires*) from July 1834 suggests an even more accurate figure. That year 1,083 taxpayers contributed the minimum sum and another 147 qualified by virtue of some other status (retired officials or officers, for example). The total of 1,230 represents every level of Adeline Daumard's pyramid structure of the bourgeoisie in Paris, from François Alluaud, the city's second leading taxpayer (assessed at 1,625 francs), to Jean-Baptiste Descampes, master hatmaker (who paid 6,106 francs).[81] Based on figures provided by the National Guard rolls and the list of municipal voters in 1834, just over 20 percent of the population were bourgeois.

A much smaller group dominated the economy and politics of Limoges. In 1816 the National Guard included about 500 "elite" members after having excluded an unspecified—but certainly quite small—group because of their "bad political opinions." The guest list for one of the official celebrations of the Restoration at the prefecture included 400 guests, a number fairly close to the 443 electors who paid at least 200 francs in taxes or otherwise qualified to be electors in 1831, the first year of the July Monarchy. However, the franchise requirements of the Restoration in 1828 were much narrower and included only those *près au pouvoir*. There were but 36 eligible voters who paid more than 1,000 francs in taxes (and 53 two years later).[82] These included 13 officials, 12 wholesale merchants, 7 property owners, 3 lawyers, 1 banker and 1 pharmacist. The term "officials" is misleading, since these gentlemen were hardly harassed functionaries of modest means. Pierre

Etienne Montréal Allouveau was *conseiller à la cour royale,* but his 1,184 francs in taxes (paid in four communes) and his position came from his status as one of the department's leading property owners. To dismiss Jean-Baptiste Maurensanne de Puyimbert simply as a "member of the departmental General Council" would be to ignore the fact that his position stemmed from his vast land holdings. Likewise, Martial J. B. Julliac, the deputy mayor, could have been considered an "official," but he had been appointed because of his influence as a leading property owner; although he owned a spacious apartment on the boulevard de la Promenade, he also possessed considerable land outside the city. Jean-Baptiste Lamy de la Chapelle, the *conseiller à la cour royale,* belonged to one of the very oldest noble families in the Limousin and owned land in five communes. The *éligibles,* then, included the wealthiest citizens in Limoges—the very purpose of the restricted franchise—and excluded a large number of prominent *limougeauds* whose fortunes were based on the city's developing commerce and industry.[83]

As Table 1 illustrates, we can expand this group to include the 145 adult males who would have been eligible to vote but not to run for public office in 1828 (listed as municipal electors in 1834) and those who were eligible to vote after the Revolution of 1830:

TABLE 1

	1828 "censitaires"	postrevolution "censitaires"
property owners	27	72
commerce and industry	97	248
liberal professions	13	63
officials	8	60
	145	443

The Revolution of 1830, by enfranchising many more citizens, increased the number of voters in each category. Commerce and industry (wholesale merchants were by far the largest group here) already dominated statistically in 1828. This group of approximately five hundred men, paying what they considered a large sum in taxes, demanded to be heard in the political arena, as they were in the businesses of the city. The vast majority were excluded from politics by the electoral laws of the Restoration. The arbitrariness and complexity of taxation and personal proclivities for diversified investments keep us from making more of the division between property owners and those whose precise occupational denomination clearly suggests that their wealth came from commercial and industrial interests. The *patente* represented a relatively small proportion of taxes for the wealthy.[84] But evidence suggesting a split among the men of commerce and industry, and the region's nobles, the prefect, and the bishop, emerges from different sources. The handful of eligible voters—principally rural property holders and "gentlemen"—and the prefect and other officials seemed more concerned with staging a gracious reception for the Duchesse de Berry in 1828 than with looking after the larger interests of the city. The number of middle-class *limougeauds* eligible to participate in political life was considerably smaller than the number of subjects of means who thought that they *ought* to be able to participate and believed that a coalition of the nobles and the Church, which seemed to determine government policy, was preventing this from happening.

To some extent there was a social geography in Restoration Limoges. The locus of industry, as noted earlier, was near the Vienne River, but it had also expanded toward the periphery of the city to the north. Textile workers lived near the far bank of the Vienne River; for example, on the rue St. Affre, near the cathedral, and especially the faubourg St. Martial. Porcelain workers settled near their workshops, particularly to the north of the city. But workers' quarters were not characteristic of Limoges in 1828, aside from a concentration of laborers and *flotteurs de bois* in the Naveix and Abbessaille quarters near the river, and the developing faubourgs to the north. On the boulevard de la Cité some poor laborers lived among relatively wealthy rentiers and property owners. Artisans could be found everywhere, from the boulevard de la Promenade, the residence of Martial J. B. Bourdeau-Julliac, a wealthy landholder, and Jacques Delor, a wholesale merchant, to the commercial streets of the rue du Consulat and rue du Clocher. Wealthy and poor houses could be found side by side, "the former built of granite and the latter of wood."[85]

Yet some neighborhoods and streets remained exclusive. The *éligibles* preferred to live in the old Château area or along the relatively spacious boulevards that had been built over the site of the old walls. At the Porte Tourny, *le beau monde* strolled about the tree-lined allée des Bénédictins, which no longer led to the old abbey of the Bénédictins, now a prison.[86]

The most powerful men in Limoges were to be found on several streets in the old Château area. The rue Banc-Léger included Pierre Tharaud, a wealthy wholesale textile merchant; Joseph François Noualhier, another merchant from one of the most eminent ancien régime families; the banker J. B. Tarneaud, who loaned money for some of the enterprises of his neighbors; Lamy de la Chapelle, *conseiller à la cour royale* and heir to the fortunes of an old noble family. The rue Montant-Manigne housed François Maurice Noualhier-Masbatin, a wholesale merchant; Joseph Pétiniaud, *propriétaire,* and the printer Roméo-Pierre Chapoulaud. Some of the city's wealthiest wholesale merchants occupied the nearby rue Haute-Vienne: Lamy and Théophile Ranson, the father of a future mayor of the city; J. J. Thévenin, a shoe merchant, and Péconnet, the *juge d'instruction,* whose six-year-old son, Othon, also later served as mayor. Among those who made their home on the rue Andeix-Manigne were: François Pouyat, a kaolin merchant, whose son, a deputy mayor and commercial transport entrepreneur, lived on the

place Tourny; Georges Pétiniaud-Dubos, heir to a commercial fortune; and François Joseph Buisson, a wholesale cloth merchant. The adjacent rue Manigne was
chosen for the homes of prominent wholesale merchants, as well as the manufacturer of flannels, Raymond Laporte, and another member of the prominent Pétiniaud family, Pierre Pétiniaud-Champagnac, one of whose relatives had bailed the city
out financially during the Revolution. Limoges's few public places were particularly desirable places to live. Like the place Tourny, the place Royale had developed a reputation for elegance; it housed, among others, François Alluaud, Jacques
Pénicaud, a shipping contractor, and the *propriétaire* Henri Dechabacque. Thirty
of the hundred leading taxpayers resided on these above-mentioned streets or on
the place de la Liberté. Thus, although there was not a rigid geography of class
segregation, there were streets traditionally occupied by Limoges's most prominent residents. They roughly corresponded to the area of the old Château, identified with Limoges's commerce as the Cité was with the Church. Beyond the
boulevards bordering the old Château stretched Limoges's developing porcelain
industry; at the end of the faubourgs—already described as stretching "un grand
quart de lieu" from the center in 1821—and across the Vienne to the south lived
day laborers, sharecroppers, and gardeners, who had one foot in the rural world,
the impoverished countryside of the Limousin, which was broken only by the
comfortable secondary residences of the urban elite.[87]

The culture of the elite has left a good number of traces. The pleasuring of *la
bonne compagnie,* more easily documented, excluded their social inferiors. Salons
flourished through the year except during the summer and fall vacations. Invitations to the prefecture were particularly prized. Horse racing was also a social
event in the region, which prided itself on the quality of its animal husbandry.
Martin de la Bastide raised horses on his estate north of the city, using his official function to assure the upkeep of the hippodrome. His horses raced those
owned by such other members of the Limousin's old *noblesse* as de Roulhac,
Barbou, de Royère, and de Venteaux. Large sums of money changed hands and
honor was won or lost on these races. The biggest sporting event of 1828 was a
heavily staked challenge race in which Martin de la Bastide's finest bested "le
Brillant," an English horse owned by M. le Chevalier Ferdinand de la Place.[88]

Music played a considerable social role in public and private events in Restoration Limoges. Martin de la Bastide's daughter warbled, accompanied by the
piano, at official receptions. The Société philharmonique and the literary circle
sponsored concerts, such as one in 1826 for the benefit of the Greeks, whose rebellion against the Turks fired the romantic imagination of Europe. The theater
in Limoges struggled with a small municipal subsidy after its authorization was
approved in 1824, but it managed to survive despite the fact that it was housed
in a small building with poor acoustics, as Limoges had no real *salle de spectacle.*
It presented traveling troupes of actors, including the regional troupe and several
from Paris. Classical taste in Limoges dominated in the theater as well as in

music and literature. *Les Annales de la Haute-Vienne* reviewed the productions and proclaimed the standards to be met: "Have a good troupe, give good performances in delicate taste . . . reject these absurd melodramas and the public will come; in Limoges, as elsewhere, we love the comedies of manners, beautiful operas, good verses, good music!" Popular singers and troupes of actors were encouraged to return. The prefect also contributed funds (for example, by financing free performances on holidays), viewing it as "a useful, healthy, and moral diversion for the urban population when controlled." He noted that the theater was a good place to monitor the activities of the city's incorrigible *oisifs*.[89]

Yet the theater fell upon hard times. When a popular troupe returned to the city in 1827, the *Annales* claimed that the mere arrival of one Mademoiselle Georges, a favorite actress of the time, had saved the theater from extinction. "The public came in droves" to see and hear her play a number of roles, including that of Joan of Arc. But the director, M. Jausaurand, a former actor, was frequently absent. Furthermore, the audiences were often boisterous and frequently unruly; the *Annales* reminded the harried performers that provincial actors "sometimes forget that on the stage they belong to the public, which has the right to whistle and to criticize them . . . the public buys them." Occasional disputes between the elegant young army officers and their bourgeois rivals contributed to the uneasy ambience. The increased popularity of dancing deflected interest in the theater and concerts "And what dance!" exclaimed Juge. "Not that studied according to the rules of the art but a tumultuous and fatiguing dance." But none of these diversions could compete with the arrival of a circus or any other extraordinary presentation imported from the outside, for these memorable events had popular appeal as well.[90]

Old Limoges, as almost any town in traditional society, had little associational life aside from the Church. An agricultural society, created in 1759, experimented with exotic plants; after languishing during the revolutionary era, it had revived as the Société d'agriculture, des sciences et des arts in 1801. The Cercle littéraire, dating from 1762, shared its members. They sometimes invited women to their literary soirees, which prompted Juge to note that, in contrast to the English, "French gallantry never allows the members to leave the ladies by themselves." In 1826 they held a ball to celebrate the blessing of the standard given the National Guard by Charles X on the occasion of his coronation at Reims. The literary circle remained one of the preeminent social centers of Limoges, numbering among its members "the most highly recommended merchants and bourgeois of the city," who paid an annual fee that financed the purchase of books and journals. Little is known about a second circle that may have limited its reading to liberal newspapers. In any case, those interested in more serious reading could peruse any of the municipal library's eleven thousand volumes, most of which were left over from the old Jesuit library. Two *cabinets de lecture* brought together "connoisseurs of novels and political pamphlets," suggesting the probable role of these gatherings in the evolving political life of the city.[91]

A philharmonic society was active and offered concerts, the proceeds of which benefited the poor during the harsh winters that followed the harvest failures of 1817 and 1827. In 1828 a masonic lodge, whose members included many of the younger and more liberal bourgeois, worried the prefect and offended the bishop. The development of associations offered a means of political education, organization and, ultimately, opposition. But one should not overestimate their political role at the expense of their social function. Juge associated increased visible sociability with the evolution of his town: "Numerous glittering gatherings are, in the eyes of outsiders, the true measure of our progress."[92]

Limoges's other associations were nominally charitable, based upon the conspicuous patronage of the poor. An old Limousin adage went, "When a beggar finds himself among others, he tells them, 'Go to Limoges; there you will lack nothing!' "[93] The Bureau de bienfaisance, founded in 1793 and now sponsored by the prefect and the bishop, provided resources for fifteen sisters of St. Vincent de Paul, distributed food, and cared for the sick, carefully removing the "unworthy" poor from its lists. A Société de charité maternelle gave layettes to poor mothers of sufficient virtue; the Dames de la Charité lodged orphans and provided some technical training to girls. The Maison de bons secours of the Sisters of St. Alexis, originally intended for beggars, opened its doors to epileptics, the destitute elderly, the mentally retarded, idiots, and, above all, more than fifteen hundred foundlings from the entire region.[94]

J. J. Juge's little book, *Changements survenus à Limoges depuis cinquante ans,* published in 1808 and brought up to date in 1817, contended that commercial wealth had precipitated a moral decline in his city "because of the increasing taste for luxury" which accompanied the attempt to ape the styles and habits of Paris. "Luxury," he argued, "is followed in its steps by the quest for pleasure, and pleasure leads to laziness." Every bourgeois now seemed to aspire to the wealth of the most prominent *marchands en gros* or the noble de la Bastide family. The new houses built along the exterior boulevards sparkled with fancy furnishings and table settings. Juge called for a return to the simple virtues of old Limoges.[95]

He had been particularly struck by the recent growth of café life and social drinking in Limoges. Before this wave of depravity associated with the city's commercial and industrial growth, *jeu de paume* had been the only acceptable form of public amusement for *la bonne compagnie.* There were several billiard tables where "libertarians and cheats" gathered; any scion of a prominent family discovered in such places risked a severe parental reprimand. But the expansion of commerce crowded the cafés every day, particularly during major markets and fairs.[96] In 1822 the Prefect de Castéja voiced a similar fear:

> The air of the cafés is not pure; idleness, the passion for gambling, and the taste for strong drink characterize such places. Frequenting these establishments reflect or can

produce problems in business; political aberrations, and errors in judgment may follow; they are caused by such related phenomena as newspapers that encourage licentiousness. Such disorders cause these kinds of men to lose control of their passions.[97]

In 1817 fifty-eight cafés and cabarets dotted Limoges. A report compiled in 1822 listed twelve cafés (seven of which subscribed to papers) according to clientele and politics: Four were frequented by "the lower classes" and therefore subscribed to no newspapers (one of them, the café de la Comédie, offered card games); at the Café des Colonnes, the scene of several disputes that led to duels, *jeunes gens de famille* with varied political opinions gathered. Another catered to "young people of the middle classes" with "bad political opinions." The Café de la Monnaie, it was claimed, remained a "gathering place for Jacobins." Preferring the Parisian opposition papers none of these latter cafés subscribed to the quasiofficial newspaper of the prefecture, *Les Annales de la Haute-Vienne*.[98] Undoubtedly there were more in 1828, for by 1837 there were ninety cafés and cabarets, in addition to sixty-five inns. Many promoted gambling, a passion that had spread during the Restoration. Fortunes were won and lost at the gaming tables during the fair of St. Loup. Early in the Restoration a prefect refused the request of a number of bankers to open a game in a café even when they offered to donate money to the *hospice*. Such a gambling den, the prefect insisted, would be the ruin of those *pères de familles* too weak to resist temptation.[99] One did not have to know the Rastignacs of Paris to see that drink, a lack of skill, poor odds, or bad luck could spell financial catastrophe. In the spring of 1828 the suicide of a young man in a small neighboring town focused public attention on the problem. The *Annales* associated the taste for gambling with the march of urbanity and chastised its readers:

> Knowing how to play cards and being resigned to losing money when one is unskilled in such practices have become indispensable for the man of society. They have become the obligatory passport for any parvenu.[100]

A young bourgeois without the gaming fever seemed to his peers ill equipped for conversation in the salons or cafés, unable to "faire briller d'urbanité."[101]

Hotels and inns, too, had their particular clienteles. Royalist *propriétaires* stayed only at the Hôtel du Lion d'Or, on the boulevard Montmailler, toward the north. The political opinions of the owners were, as was to be expected, "good." Travelers arriving from the north took rooms at the liberal Hôtel de la Boule d'Or, on the boulevard de la Poste aux Chevaux. Poorer salesmen tended to stay at the less expensive Hotel de la Pyramide, located in the center of town on the rue Haute-Vienne. The Bonne Foi, Gorsas (boulevard du Collège) and Hôtel de l'Aigle d'Argent (place de la Mairie) had a mixed clientele.[102]

Two more elite amusements were characteristic of life in Restoration Limoges, both largely unavailable to ordinary people. Before the Revolution a critic complained that people rarely took baths in Limoges.[103] Old habits were not easily broken. The *Annales* ran a series of articles on the importance of bathing and tending properly to the sick during an influenza epidemic.[104] People who could afford baths had apparently not installed proper facilities; this could partially be explained by the fact that their houses, built in the eighteenth century, relied upon the same inadequate means of providing water as those of the poor; few but the young would have bathed in the Vienne under the gaze of the laundresses and river workers, to say nothing of the bishop, whose garden overlooked the river. By 1828 three public baths operated in Limoges, one on the banks of the Vienne. The most elegant was the fancy Chinese baths on the fashionable rue Banc-Léger, where de la Bastide had his apartment. Monsieur Reix boasted "a complete thermal establishment," including minerals, steam, and other healing baths—even food. The *Annales* announced as "news" that "at any hour that you present yourself to one of these establishments, you will be received politely and served promptly and properly." The prices equaled or went far beyond the daily wages of most Limoges workers: 1.25 per bath (or five baths for 5 francs), with a shower at 2.50; *bains de bottes à la gilles* at 2.50; and the luxurious Russian bath at 4 francs. M. Reix became one of the wealthiest men in Limoges and was eligible to run for public office by 1829.[105]

Finally, the ultimate recreation and mark of wealth was, as today, the freedom to leave the city for a secondary residence. The prosperous invested in land, and for the vast majority of eligible voters the *patente* represented a relatively small portion of their taxes. Forty-three country houses lay in the immediate vicinity of the city, occupying the most fertile lands in the department. They included: Virolles, owned by François Alluaud, who also owned land in Aixe and Cognac; Fontjaudran, the property of the Restoration politician Martignac; Parpaillat, belonging to the Pouyat family; Beaublanc, owned by Pierre Disnematin Desalles (who paid taxes on land in six communes); and the holdings of the Ardant family, just outside the city and still clearly marked on the map of the city drawn up in 1838. Other pleasant spots nestled around the city that were designed for "rustic excursions and other purposes of pleasure" included the amorous woods typical of many French nineteenth-century cities, where young lovers and sometimes even prostitutes retreated from the prying eyes of city dwellers. Summer and fall vacations were spent in the countryside by those who could afford the luxury. Others traveled; some of the wealthy had been to Paris and other major cities for business and for pleasure. The *Annales* carried advertisements for luxury establishments in La Rochelle, reached by way of Angoulême and Saintes. Money had its prerogatives; the wealthy could afford to leave Limoges.[106]

That commerce and industry were transforming Limoges made the fact that they seemed overtaxed and underrepresented even more galling. The businessmen of the place Haute-Vienne and the rue du Clocher had breathed life into Limoges, not the clergy of the Cité or de la Bastide and his own château and hippo-drome.[107] Yet commerce and industry at least had one organization representing its interests. In 1804 an imperial decree recognized the "usefulness" of a Chambre des manufactures et du commerce. But this body left no written record and few traces until 1822, when the prefect summoned the commercial and industrial elite, including Alluaud, to elect a new Chambre consisting of six members. Thereafter the group could annually replace two of its members, at first chosen by lot and then by seniority. But the two "departing" members were invariably reelected without a dissenting vote.[108]

The Municipal Council reflected the limited nature of political life in Restoration Limoges. Rarely meeting more than once a month, its function was limited to establishing and administering the budget. But another, probably more important reason for its seeming harmony and the absence of disruptive political issues was its composition. The council, whose members were appointed, was overwhelmingly comprised of like-minded social equals, including such scions of several noble families as de Villelume, Roulhac, Pétiniaud des Mont, Noualhier, and, of course, Mayor de la Bastide.[109]

The council's discussions in 1828 included the question of enlarging the municipal cemetery of Louyat, located to the north of the city; the possible location of a proposed slaughterhouse; the use of two available scholarships to the local *collège;* preparations for the visit of the Duchesse de Berri in Limoges; the finances of the hospice; and *octroi.* A decided casualness characterized the activities of the council; several members missed one meeting when they claimed that they had not been notified and did not hear the voice of the mayor's valet, who came to alert them. Martin de la Bastide, mayor since 1821, was rumored to be ill and, in any case, spent as much time on his estate as possible, cared for by his staff of twenty-eight, while the aged deputy mayor, Pouyat, penned his correspondence.[110]

Yet beneath the calm of Municipal Council meetings and the daily reports of the police, some voices of dissatisfaction could be heard. But how far down the pyramid of wealth were they? The workers were outside the city's political life. They were not involved in the only disturbance in Limoges in 1828 to break the ordinary tranquility of provincial life and have political repercussions. The event surrounded the arrival of the controversial mission, which consisted of traditionalist revivals of fire and brimstone orchestrated by the conservative congregations. The curé of the church of St. Pierre, unpopular among the youthful bourgeois, brought the mission to Limoges. Young men who "belong, for the most part, to commerce" tossed containers of sulfuric acid and another "substance of an intolerable stench" into two churches. Almost a month later, after one young bourgeois had been sentenced by the court for his participation in the disruption of the missions, religious ceremonies were interrupted by shouts of: "Down with the Jesuits! Hang the *calotins!"* and "Down with the *choristes!"* (referring to those who attended the missions). A scuffle broke out when the protesters—perhaps as many as four or five hundred—attempted to rescue several of their number arrested by the police. Both the prefect and the bishop noted that the workers of the city were outraged by this behavior and had followed the missions with fervor and interest, later chanting: "Long Live the Missionaries!" Mounted troops kept order the following days; groups of workers, as well as the butchers, had to be restrained from taking revenge on the middle-class "calicots."[111] No reference to the mission incidents appeared in the summaries of the Municipal Council meeting, which were supposed to be above petty politics.

Neither the municipal council nor the police had to be concerned about strikes or attempted "coalitions" of workers in Restoration Limoges. There were no mutual aid organizations in 1828—skilled porcelain workers established the first a year later—and the traditional compagnonnages have left few traces. Verbal work agreements and artisanal traditions of apprenticeship and mutual responsibility persisted. Workers carried livrets, and when disputes arose, the word of the master was always accepted. Employers sometimes complained about the undisciplined nature of the workers of Limoges, but they were referring to the mass of the laboring population and not to skilled workers. Alluaud's factory on the faubourg Casseaux was held up to industrialists as a model establishment because it was "ingeniously" designed to prevent "any false moves" by the workers. The central prison seemed even more ideal because the workers were literally prisoners; the Maison Centrale offered "an inexhaustible nursery of submissive and disciplined weavers." The inauguration ceremony for the Conseil des Prud'hommes, established in 1825, hinted at difficulties in the relations between employers and workers. A proclamation, undoubtedly written by Alluaud, cited "the prodigious growth of industry and the important and continuous relations which have been established between the classes of citizens, which did not previously exist at all in this ancient city." The goal of the Conseil des Prud'hommes was more than just arbitration in the numerous disputes over cracked porcelain or broken contracts between journeymen and masters. The Conseil was charged with a moralizing function:

> We therefore had to take the steps necessary to guide these various laborers from birth—childlike by virtue of their perceived self-interest, sustained by vanity and nourished by obstinacy . . . we needed an institution that could combine the paternal relations of a family gathering with legal authority to prevent, through the special expertise of the Council in matters of legal dispute, mistakes of bad faith, and to silence the [workers'] exaggerated demands arising from their wrongly perceived interests.[112]

During its first year the Conseil, which included the porcelain manufacturers Baignol and Tharaud, successfully arbitrated all but four of the cases it considered, with these latter going before the Tribunal de Commerce.

"The misery here is great," the prefect of Haute-Vienne had written of his department in March 1817, "but the inhabitants bear it with a resignation that indicates a proper spirit and a profound submission."[113] The municipal police and the gendarmerie easily maintained public order without recourse to the small reserve garrison. Limoges's wealthy citizens voiced an occasional fear about the "eight hundred scoundrels, in open revolt against the laws of society," in the regional prison, guarded by only ten men.[114] The guard had been reorganized in 1816 and apparently performed regular duty at the prison and in selected other posts during the following year, when the economic crisis and rampaging rumors of Bonapartist conspiracy and insurrection seemed to warrant preparedness. By 1817 the prefect had removed those few guardsmen of Bonapartist sentiments from the rolls. But officers were hard-pressed to find "two or three willing to take a minute off from their businesses" to perform night duty. When posts were formed, the guardsmen usually left for home long before dawn. In 1822 the guard's disciplinary council handed out over one hundred sentences consisting of twenty-four hours in jail for those failing to show up when convoked for duty. However, these penalties could hardly be meted out to the notables, and it was difficult to convoke even the disciplinary council. Those penalized were "amnestied" at the time of the coronation of Charles X, but the guard's record failed to improve. The prefect asked the Minister of the Interior to suspend the "purely illusory" service, and the Municipal Council voted only half of the usual annual allotment for drums and trumpets. After 1826 the almanacs stopped listing the officers of the guard, and the Municipal Council cut the budget from three thousand to six hundred francs. However, it was always assumed that in case of an invasion, a massive prison uprising, a jacquerie, or the arrival of bands of incendiaries, the guard could be relatively quickly and easily constituted as a reliable backup force for the gendarmerie and the army.[115]

Yet political dissension was already festering among the Limoges middle class, which was excluded from political life by the electoral franchise of the Restoration. Young bourgeois, like their precursors during the Revolution, no longer unquestioningly accepted the traditional institutional and political role of the Church. They complained about the lack of urban progress in a city recently even denied the title of a *bonne ville*. If J. J. Juge had earlier complained that bourgeois parvenus had imported an insidious, impious taste for luxury, some of Limoges's new elite complained that the eyes of Pierre Martin de la Bastide and the others entrusted with municipal authority were trained on the countryside and the cathedral and not on their city, which visitors found lacking in the most basic urban amenities. The butchers' quarter symbolized the lack of urban progress in Limoges. Merchants and *fabricants* demanded an atmosphere conducive to prosperity and commercial success. It was not surprising, therefore, that some of them, particularly the younger ones, joined the faction of opposition in 1827— and a few even earlier. This challenge called into question the political system of the Restoration, which seemed to lag behind the economic and social changes occurring in one of France's most rapidly growing towns.

Army officer Borel de Bretizel, a visitor in 1828, would have been surprised at the bitter political divisions visible in Limoges had he returned two years later. He would have been shocked to learn that Limoges would earn a reputation as a politically turbulent city during the remainder of the century, and that future officers would be much more concerned with plans of defense against working-class insurrections than any external threat to Limoges.

2

The Bourgeois Revolution of 1830 and the Workers

In 1833 several events occurred in Limoges that would have been inconceivable in 1828. A crowd of protesters, largely republicans, drawn from the lower middle class and especially the workers, greeted a newly appointed prefect with insults and rocks, necessitating the intervention of the police. Several months later skilled porcelain workers, angered by cuts in their wages, went out on strike, supported by money from their new mutual aid association. And, finally, a crowd stormed a church, demanding that a priest bury a friend of theirs who had taken his own life. Within three years of the Revolution of 1830, the recently installed officials of the July Monarchy worried about the spread of republican and even socialist ideas in Limoges. The years surrounding the Revolution of 1830 are worth examining in detail. The political life of Limoges would never be the same again. Such changes resulted from the economic and social transformation of the city.

Before 1827 there were few signs of organized opposition to the government of the king. The bourgeoisie of Limoges resented the arrogance of the Church and the weak regional nobility but accepted the Restoration as long as the Charter of 1815 kept old privileges at bay. Limoges had been a Jacobin town during the Revolution; the Jacobin club exerted considerable influence, particularly after the moderate club of the Amis de la Paix had been dissolved in 1790; the principles of the Terror of 1793–94 were later accepted, with nobles and other suspects imprisoned with the strong support of the population. But the period was not particularly bloody, save for the murder of the priest Chabrol in July 1792, one day after *la Patrie* had been declared *en danger*. The *haute bourgeoisie* sought a restricted electorate, while the *moyenne bourgeoisie* sought political participation. The imperial prefect Texier-Olivier later asserted that "the same hands that overturned the alters soon put them back up again." However, he may have underestimated the impact of the Revolution when he claimed that "the revolutionary crises and agitation that troubled the peace in many other cities would not have been felt here if they had not been fomented by several enthusiasts and seemingly sanctioned by the example of several neighboring departments."[1] With the exception of a handful of men who made their fortune while serving the emperor, few remembered Bonaparte fondly. Limoges had welcomed Napoleon back during the Hundred Days with little more than "sympathetic admiration" for his various exploits. Most businessmen had breathed a sigh of relief when the Napoleonic adventure finally ended, bringing peace and prosperity.[2]

Yet a gendarmerie report at the end of 1817 noted a "marked tendency for the liberal principles professed in the Chambers." Several liberal pamphlets surfaced and a few seditious cries echoed in 1818; wild rumors of the return of Napoleon, with huge Turkish armies or by other miraculous means, reached the town. One petition "asking for the maintenance of the Charter" circulated briefly in Limoges. In 1822 a list of cafés and hotels compiled by Baron Coster, the prefect, identified a handful of liberals who could be found in the Café de la Monnaie ("a gathering of Jacobins"), while noting that another café catered to "young people of the middle classes [with] bad political opinions." Two literary circles subscribed to "liberal" Parisian newspapers, and readers could find an occasional opposition brochure or pamphlet on the tables there. But the few local families of "pronounced royalists" (Ultras) voiced no concern about any move to the left of Limoges's voters until 1827.[3]

As the elections of that year approached, however, Baron Coster confronted the possibility that his friends, the "true royalists," would not be returned to the Chamber of Deputies. Some of the old commercial families were still loyal to the Bourbons, "but without being particularly disposed to make any sacrifices." Other bourgeois were constitutional monarchists, particularly those families new to the city, whom Juge had accused of importing a taste for speculation and luxury.[4] The government found little or no support among those men recently enfranchised in Limoges. The Villèle ministry also lost the allegiance of many voters representing commerce and industry, hit hard by the economic crisis of 1826–27, which began with a harvest failure. Liberals, who were active and organized in Paris and the provinces, efficiently capitalized on the business community's belief that their interests were being ignored by the government, while some prefects indignantly complained of the "ingratitude" of the men of business.

Pierre Alpinien Bourdeau, a member of the Corps législatif during the Empire, led the liberal opposition in Limoges. Bourdeau and his friends convinced many eligible voters to register; their number increased by 250 percent between August 15 and September 30, 1827—by far the largest percentage in all of France. Bourdeau helped his cause by locating and reprinting a confidential circular from the prefect to his subordinates instructing them to influence the outcome of the election. The Aide-toi society and probably also the Société des amis de la liberté de la presse also worked for the liberal cause.[5]

Baron Coster's career, which he knew might depend on engineering a government victory over the constitutional faction, was thus threatened by what he disdainfully called "a mob of small property owners and merchants" now eligible to vote. Others who were previously eligible to vote only in the district *collèges* could now join the elite departmental *collège,* which included the wealthiest landowners of the countryside, who had always been so unwavering in support of the king's government. There Coster faced "an alliance of liberals of all shades," many of whom would be voting for the first time out of a desire to exact some degree of revenge against those "gentlemen" loyal to the government who had treated them with no small measure of contempt. Coster could count on the support of nineteen magistrates and functionaries in the departmental *collège* who knew that a vote cast for the opposition would bring a sudden and inglorious end to their careers. But the votes of forty-one merchants and ninety-two other "plebeians living from commerce" could not be assured.[6]

In Limoges several opposition candidates included: Pétiniaud-Champagnac, a wealthy merchant with few visible talents and little support aside from his many relatives in the region; Desalles Beauregard, a wholesale merchant who had served as a National Guard officer during the Hundred Days; François Guillaume Dumont St. Priest, a forty-one-year-old lawyer of some means, "full of finesse and ambition," a liberal despite (or perhaps because of) his marriage to the daughter of the procureur général; François Pouyat, a porcelain manufacturer, loyal to the throne but never forgiven by the rural gentlemen for having served as mayor during the Hundred Days; and François Alluaud, a porcelain manufacturer, judge at the Tribunal of Commerce and member of the Municipal Council, who had married a woman above his station who was known for her social graces.[7] Of Alluaud Coster wrote that "his manners are gentle; having risen from a very low class—his father had originally worked as an engineer for the Department of Bridges and Highways—M. Alluaud regretted the return of the old nobility and appears to dread the influence of the court and the clergy."[8]

Alluaud's dread of the clergy may be traced to his childhood. Born on the commercial rue du Clocher in 1778, Alluaud later recalled that the priest who had assumed responsibility for his education when he was nine had greatly favored the sons of the nobility, while "the pitiless cruelties of our teachers were reserved for the children of the bourgeoisie." During the Revolution Alluaud's enterprising father, a Jacobin and the department's district director (1792–93), had obtained a scholarship for his bright son in Paris. There the "study of the Declaration of the Rights of Man and of the meaning of 'men are born free and equal in rights'" replaced the Ten Commandments and the catechism as the young Alluaud's topics for study and reflection. During the Hundred Days the imperial prefect noted Alluaud's loyalty. Although he was without political ambition and preferred to spend his time improving the production of porcelain, Alluaud now (1827) seemed a natural leader to represent men disenchanted with the lack of attention the government gave business.[9]

Against these candidates Coster could only propose the incumbent, Jacques Mousnier Buisson, who, secure in his position as a magistrate and president of the departmental General Council, could prominently display his award of the Order of St. Louis for years of loyal but uninspired service. The two wealthiest men in the region would faithfully represent government and rural interests as they had in the departmental *collège:* de Montbron, who fled his feudal château during the revolution; and de la Bastide, mayor and commander of the Limoges National Guard, another émigré. De la Bastide had inspired the *prévôtale* court established during the White Terror in the first year of the Restoration. Coster described him as "full of fire at the moment of danger; but in ordinary times he becomes entirely consumed by his passion for fine horses." He refused to campaign actively, ignoring the warnings of his friends that the businessmen now wanted a deputy of their own.[10]

Prefect Coster worked frantically, pressuring, imploring, and threatening the thirty-six eligible functionaries with dismissal should they vote for liberal candidates. But the liberals were also organized, sending electoral circulars to voters throughout the department. A dinner in Limoges in honor of Bourdeau attracted so many people that the theater performance had to be canceled for the evening. Liberals discussed two petitions that opposed a newly ordained change in the postal service between Lyon and Bordeaux that would bypass Limoges. Coming a month before the election, the move seemed to prove that the government ignored the interests of local business, particularly those of the porcelain industry.[11]

Pierre Bourdeau was easily elected in the Limoges district on the first ballot, as was a liberal manufacturer, Terraux, in the district of St. Junien. But in the departmental *collège,* which met a few days later, the more restricted suffrage pulled the official candidates through. On the first ballot de Montbron failed to win a majority, as de la Bastide's friends refused to abandon their reticent idol. But de Montbron defeated Desalles Beauregard on the second ballot, joining the old standby Mousnier Buisson as deputy of the departmental electoral *collège.*

Successful candidates usually offered a short victory statement before the electoral *collège* disbanded to the obligatory chorus of "Long Live the King!" Mousnier Buisson's brief speech contrasted with his 1825 address to the General Council at the accession of Charles X, when he had reminded his listeners that the throne of France was the natural protector of landed property (perhaps alluding to the national debate over the possibility of the return of *biens nationaux* to their original owners). Now, in 1827, he emphasized that commerce and industry should stand at the side of agriculture, the first source of France's wealth. His speech betrayed the tension between landed and acquired wealth in Limoges. Even if some old landed families had commercial interests and businessmen often bought land with their profits or made money from rural holdings, sharp differences in the political views of the two groups developed in Limoges during the late 1820s. At issue was the place of commerce and industry in politics.[12]

Two nights of brief disturbances followed the election in the departmental *collège;* disappointed young merchants and clerks, disguised for the most part, "offered" a charivari to the ministry's newly elected deputies at the home of Mousnier Buisson and the hotel lodging de Montbron. Some of the youthful bourgeois carried makeshift musical instruments out of the Café Renommé while shouting, "Down with the Jesuits! Down with the Ministry!" They returned another night, only to be dispersed by the police. Scandalized, Coster wrote that "the time has come to imprint on this new generation a wise sense of direction." He quickly pointed out that *le peuple* took absolutely no part in the event; the guilty were "young men whose social position should have rendered them more circumspect." For Coster had little patience with the political pretentions of business, "which, adopting the opinions of liberalism and peddling its lies, continues its own speculations and enterprises"; despite constant complaining, Limoges's businessmen "build and enhance the luxuriousness of their houses."[13]

In 1828 a special election took place after Mousnier Buisson resigned in a huff, angered by liberal attacks in the Chamber of Deputies following his narrow victory the previous year. Coster convinced him to change his mind and oppose Dumont St. Priest, a lawyer. Mousnier Buisson's campaign, orchestrated by the prefect, received an unexpected boost from the brief visit of the Duchesse de Berry in the fall, which brought vacationers back from the countryside. Dumont St. Priest campaigned in defense of the charter. Without systematically opposing the ministry, he reasoned, one must carefully examine its acts. He promised to appeal to the king to examine the situation of industry and commerce, now suffering from a business slump. However, the landed interests in the departmental *collège* proved too strong and Dumont St. Priest lost again, this time by the narrow margin of eighty-seven to eighty-two.[14]

The elections of 1827 and 1828 reveal the evolution of urban politics in Limoges: in the verbal protests of the young bourgeoisie, accompanied by the "rough music" of one of Europe's popular rituals borrowed from *le peuple;* in the perceptive assessments of a prefect who had come to understand his changing town; and in the cautious speeches of a successful deputy and his challenger. The liberal opposition emerged from these elections with two of the department's four deputies, some organizational experience, and a commitment to oppose the politics of the ministry on several issues. They proposed the election of the municipal council (now appointed by the king and meeting only with the written permission of the prefect), opposed the unpopular tax on drink (the bane of the town's wine merchants as well as the poor), and complained about the conditions of the royal roads on which their merchandise traveled. Among those talking seriously of tax resistance were the deputy Bourdeau and François Alluaud's son, who successfully petitioned to become a voter by virtue of the increased tax he was paying on his profitable businesses. Not all those who joined the liberal camp were merchants and manufacturers; nor were all staunch supporters of the government critical of business interests. But Baron Coster nonetheless summed up the prevailing division in Limoges when he assessed the city's commercial and manufacturing interests: "Liberal doctrines are widely held in this class, which inevitably dreams of an equality in conditions and honors."[15]

The next two winters did little to improve morale in Limoges. The winter of 1828 brought a fever that carried off a number of children from the city's most prosperous families, those, the prefect believed, whose relatively sheltered lives gave them the least physical resistance to illness. While Parisian journalists exaggerated the gravity of the health situation in Limoges, grief and fear of an epidemic precluded the usual winter social activities of the elite.

The following winter the poor contemplated starvation. Bread prices soared and, among "murmured complaints" from *le peuple,* Baron Coster suspended the licenses of several bakers who had deliberately kept their stocks low, thereby driving up prices and leaving the city with an alarming deficit as the temperature plunged in December. Ordinary people bore their misery well; the only two thefts that month were committed by "well-dressed" men. Coster believed that the police, aided by undercover agents for whom he requested additional funds, could predict and prevent any trouble from ordinary people. As for the bourgeoisie, he planned to "distract them from politics by occupying them" with various municipal projects they desired, including the construction of a slaughterhouse. Free gymnastic exhibitions and fireworks on the feast day of the king also offered "a fortunate diversion from the maneuvers of the Paris newspapers." But liberal catcalls interrupted a play authored by a fervent Bourbon supporter. A duel pitted a young man who had insulted the king against an offended army officer. Local commerce suffered; a letter from Limoges printed in the Parisian newspaper *Le Constitutionnel* blamed the political uncertainty on the controversial appointment of the intransigent Polignac ministry. Many bourgeois openly worried about the future of their children.[16]

Coster knew that Limoges's only newspaper, *Les Annales de la Haute-Vienne,* spoke for the prefecture in this battle; the director was an employee of the prefecture. This "administrative, political, literary, commercial, and agricultural journal" survived because of its prefectorial subsidy, administrative pressure on the department's mayors to subscribe, and its status as the only available outlet for the traditional *annonces et avis divers.* The *Annales* preferred to avoid political issues, for such discussions implied "a division of spirits"; before the 1827 election it had "regretted having to speak of the ministry and of an opposition—we would prefer to see only one political opinion in France, as there is only a single sentiment of love and recognition for the king and for the Bourbons." But Coster and the *Annales* faced growing political opposition and the paper now found itself "having to speak the language of the time in order to be heard."[17] If Limoges had a "language of the time," it was that of commerce; and that was not a language that the *Annales* spoke well. After the opposition had selected its candidates for the 1827 election, the journal's editor observed that "by its choice, the opposition announced that it wanted to give its heart to commerce."

The appearance of a liberal newspaper had been rumored during the fall of 1829. On February 15, 1830, the editors and directors of *Le Contribuable* published their prospectus. Most were young, "not yet masters of their own fortunes," but, as one *Annales* subscriber admitted, "with a number of good and even brilliant qualities." The editor, Aimé Mallevergne, who had won a first prize for rhetoric in school six years earlier, put the initial 250-franc "caution" money on deposit; the managing director, Abria, a clerk for a local merchant, had earned another first prize at the seminary in 1826. Several of their friends were in the magistrature, including Peyramont, later an Orleanist deputy. The managing director was Dumas, a retired army officer and former Jacobin who had been cited in 1816 as an "enemy of the government."[18]

The prospectus of *Le Contribuable* reflected the emergence of the self-conscious and organized voice of commerce and industry. *Le Contribuable,* journal "of all citizens paying taxes," was to be the voice of business in Limoges:

> A town of thirty thousand people, rich and commercial, with relations extending to every point in France, has clamored for a newspaper that would be the faithful echo of its wishes . . . Limoges owes all of its importance to its commerce and its industry. Let us thus consecrate a great part of our columns to these two great causes of its prosperity. Commerce and industry live on confidence and liberty. How could they not be suffering in a region where confidence cannot exist because liberty has been under attack?

The constant mood of political uncertainty and outright hostility surrounding the acts of the ministry had taken its toll on business. "Commerce suffers because of it, public credit is affected, money remains sterile in the justly hesitant hands of capitalists, and industry awaits with anxiety outlets for its products."

What had the ministry done to restore business confidence?

> Insolently and disdainfully they insult all of commerce through paid hacks; and, to neutralize the influence that the *patentés* [those who pay the business tax], as they scornfully call those of fortune and wisdom, they now threaten to reduce their influence . . . Commerce scorns these insults and laughs at these threats.

Affirming itself, above all, "always faithful to the principles of the Charter," *Le Contribuable* offered a prophetic warning:

> Commerce knows well that [for the government] to try to replace the legally constituted regime with a regime of ordinances would be the height of folly. If ever the ministry embarked on this foolhardy course of action, we would be the first to counsel resistance to any acts that could endanger what France encompasses with its love and reverence.[19]

The *Annales,* drawn into a weekly polemic with its rival, railed against these "poor, misled children of the century of light" who now "associate themselves with offensive and revolutionary writers." Coster instructed the *Annales* to stop doing business with its printer because the latter had taken its rival as a client, and ordered the prosecution of Aimé Mallevergne for accusing the government of having "betrayed its oath." The prefect even worried that improvements in the department's mail service might serve to expand the readership of the liberal paper.[20] Undaunted, *Le Contribuable* began to publish twice weekly in June, attacking the Polignac ministry and voicing unqualified support for the Charter of 1815 and the public liberties it guaranteed, demanding the inclusion of more voters on the electoral lists.

Three issues formed the basis of the liberal critique of the Restoration. First, as suggested above, was the place of commerce and industry in local and national politics. The number of businessmen paying taxes had increased in the late 1820s; so had the number of taxpayers eligible to run for the Chamber of Deputies by virtue of being assessed a minimum of one thousand francs annually. In 1816 there had been but twenty, including five merchants, four property owners, one manufacturer, one transport entrepreneur, two lawyers, two magistrates, and five others. Between 1828 and 1830 the number of *éligibles* increased substantially, from thirty-six to fifty-three. Of the eighteen new men who could run for the Chamber of Deputies, no fewer than six were merchants, four were industrialists, and the others included two wholesale merchants and a transport entrepreneur. These *éligibles* and voters worried Coster:

This region, essentially commercial, furnishes a great number of modest voters by virtue of the tax on business, over whom the administrative authorities have little influence; the great landed interests are weakly or not at all represented here.[21]

Le Contribuable accused the "enemies of commerce and industry" of trying to reduce the influence of "merchants and manufacturers, incorrigible men stubborn enough to love the Charter . . . [who have] the good faith to believe that it offers the protection necessary to their business and to the happiness and prosperity of France." And yet business in Limoges was overtaxed and underrepresented in the Chamber of Deputies. The *patente* was, with a few exceptions, insufficient in itself to earn the right to vote; by raising the tax on business, the ministry had increased its revenue without significantly increasing the number of voters. *Le Contribuable* proclaimed the right of taxpayers "to occupy ourselves with the business of government." The group that Coster referred to as "a mob of petty merchants and shopkeepers" now openly discussed the possibility of tax resistance. Some signed the statutes for an "Association Limousin," which, like the national Association Breton, would coordinate such efforts. The Chambre consultative des arts et manufactures demanded a location more suitable than the courthouse for its business meetings, protesting when Coster tried to force them into an old convent hall.[22]

The Church provided the second focus for the liberal critique, particularly the controversial bishop, Prosper de Tournefort, the most powerful of Coster's political allies. The bishop, who had briefly been imprisoned during the Empire in 1811, now lived in a palace described by Arthur Young in 1787 as "large and handsome . . . the garden of which was the finest object to be seen in Limoges, for it commands a landscape hardly to be equalled for beauty."[23] The bishop remained a staunch traditionalist who complained about the "profane representations" during Limoges's religious processions, as he did about nude bathing in the Vienne. Upon his arrival in Limoges he asserted that bishops had always "signaled the dangers that threatened the alliance of altar and throne." Like Coster, he had little use for the parvenu bourgeois, frequently remiss in fulfilling his religious duties. He refused to accept the idea that anyone could publicly discuss or question the acts of the king's government. Believing that "corruption has never been as universal and as deep," he advised the Minister of Ecclesiastic Affairs in February 1830 that "France needs to be conquered morally, as it was physically . . . she must be invested, as by the allies, with all that is required to reform minds, beginning with the young." He urged the ministry to withdraw the freedom of the press, the antithesis, he believed, of a properly controlled state.[24]

Le Contribuable assailed the Church, asserting that the "liberty" achieved during the French Revolution, the beginning of an emancipation movement that had shaken all of society, was now threatened by arbitrary actions, notably by the infamous sacrilege law of 1825. Rumors that the king would reestablish the *dime* tax had contributed to the mood of fear and mistrust of the Church. Shortly before the 1827 elections, a sizable crowd turned out in Limoges to attend the funeral of an actor denied a church burial because the bishop found his humor offensive. Prosper de Tournefort neither forgot nor forgave the incidents during the missions in 1828. *Le Contribuable* attacked the bishop, his budget, the seemingly exorbitant salaries of these "gladiators in cassocks," and demanded lay instruction.[25]

Even the Church's charitable work during the harsh winter of 1829–30 brought complaints. The temperature plunged to record lows in December, following a summer drought. The price of bread rose to levels even higher than those during the winter of 1827–28, and the rural poor swarmed to the city seeking food and shelter. The Municipal Council funded charity workshops, but soon it was too cold to work. Many wretched, homeless beggars huddled in the doorways of churches, facing death from exposure. The Municipal Council allocated money for a municipal soup kitchen which would provide heat, bread, an "economical soup," and religious instruction for the poor between the hours of 8 A.M. and 4 P.M. What happened to the homeless poor at night is not clear.[26]

Prosper de Tournefort opposed this modest act of charity, first because the soup kitchen was to be located in the chapel of the royal *collège,* where only a temporary barrier would separate the shelter from the holy sanctuary. Worse, the sexes would be mixed. But Baron Coster's frequent promise that the poor would kneel on the cold stone floor to say their prayers before eating caused the bishop to relent, and he donated fifty pots of soup. The literary circle held a ball for the benefit of the poor and the "dames of society" sponsored an auction, selling, among other discarded items, a "charming armchair" owned by the bishop. The maternal society ventured out into the cold to bring sustenance to 177 poor mothers of suitable moral character. Traditional forms of charity helped the poor survive the winter, but the episode of the soup kitchen once again put the Church in an unfavorable light. The cold subsided, but not the biting criticism of "the priestly party."[27]

Limoges's liberals also wanted to guide the affairs of their own growing town. This was the third issue of contention. But, as we have seen, Mayor de la Bastide seemed uninterested in municipal affairs and rarely came to town.[28] Some people complained about the long-neglected urban environment, particularly the rue de la Boucherie. The departmental General Council had allocated money for the construction of a slaughterhouse just southwest of the city, on the plain of Beaupeyrat. The project was frequently discussed at Municipal Council meetings, but no action followed. De la Bastide did not oppose the project, but he admired the religious devotion of the butchers and may have been protecting their interests. The baron seemed to turn a deaf ear to complaints of the "fetid and poisonous odors" carried by the wind from the street, and from the tanneries in the old Cité, both far from his country estate. He ignored the "pitiful state" of the rapidly deteriorating eighteenth-century boulevards while improving the route de Paris—which, incidentally, led to his estate.

But there was much else that needed to be done in Limoges, which, in addition to a slaughterhouse, lacked a *halle aux grains* and a *salle de spectacle* or any place for large numbers of people to gather, aside from church services. Furthermore, the fairground, located at the place d'Aîne, near the commercial quarters of the town, was far too small to accommodate Limoges's expanding commerce. On market day the streets leading to this field were completely blocked by cattle, pigs, and sheep, as well as by hordes of townspeople and peasants. On several occasions the Municipal Council had discussed the possibility of significantly enlarging the existing market ground by expanding it to include the old cemetery of the gray penitents. But in 1826 the Municipal Council decided to pursue a new ploy by which the *champ de foire* would be moved to a new locale, the terre de Poilevé, which would be purchased from its owners. This humid and muddy land, which had earlier been considered as military terrain for the cavalry, lay far from the commercial quarters of the town, down the steep hill well below the place Dauphine. The claim of the municipal administration that a new quarter would spring up around the new fairground did little to assuage the fears of the merchants, some of whom complained that they would be ruined. The move made even less sense given the fact that the most significant urban project of the Restoration in Limoges had been work on a new street that led from the central commercial quarter to the place Dauphine. A petition signed by 110 men in 1825 had made a strong case against the proposed move, the men insisting that their interests should be taken into consideration. They received not a single response from the mayor over a period of two years, not even after publishing their case in *Raisons de décider dans le choix d'un nouveau champ de foire pour Limoges* in 1829. Martin de la Bastide enjoyed the prestige of his office and the salons but never really felt at home listening to the complaints of the sons of commerce, even if many shared his passion for land and horses. Three leading bourgeois liberals associated with *Le Contribuable*—Abria and Descoutures, as well as the younger Alluaud—even offered to donate land to expand the present *champ de foire*. Still they heard nothing. Baron Coster thus received little help from his mayor in his ploy to "distract" the bourgeoisie from politics with long-awaited urban projects. "A secret power" seemed to paralyze the administration.[29]

The spring of 1830 carried national and political debates beyond the stage where mere distractions were enough. The defiant vote against the king's address by 221 deputies in the Chamber and the preparation for the election of June further polarized local political opinion. *Le Contribuable* urged all businessmen who had earned the right to vote to cast their ballot against "the enemies of liberty and commerce!"

> For a long time, when we shopkeepers, lawyers, and peasants have wanted to occupy ourselves with what they call politics, the men of *La Gazette* [an intransigent royalist newspaper] and generally all those who want absolutism sent us rudely back to our business.[30]

The issues at stake also seemed clear to the *Annales:* "To vote for the 221 deputies is to vote for pure democracy, that is, anarchy." Noting the increase in the number of voters in Limoges since the election of 1827, the voice of the prefecture again arrogantly challenged those electors risen from commerce and industry:

> To any man of good faith it is evident that landed proprietors, for whom the electoral right is granted through tax assessment, desire that the powers of the authorities be strong in order that evil be prevented and good conserved. Men who risk their fortune in commercial speculations or in perilous enterprises should be very pleased to see the extension of liberties, as they are ready to run several more risks. Their electoral right is flexible, and for that reason their vote is less reasoned.[31]

The bishop promised to do his part to defeat the liberals—as he had in 1827—by counseling the wealthy faithful to vote for the candidates of the government. *Le Contribuable* took advantage of the opportunity afforded by its trial on a press offense to counter the administration's propaganda efforts with its own. Its editors predicted that "all of the dinners at the prefecture, all of the dinners at the bishop's palace, all of the circulars of the administration, and all of the instructions of the congregations will not deprive us of one single vote." A liberal electoral committee, led by François Alluaud's son, prepared for the victory of commerce and industry.[32]

On June 23, 1830, the liberals triumphed: Both Dumont St. Priest, the liberal lawyer, and Bourdeau-Lajudie were elected in the departmental *collège*. One of the voters had included a man in his seventies who, ignoring the orders of his doctor, traveled miles to Limoges, where he was greeted with applause, to vote against the Polignac ministry. All four of the department's deputies were now liberal; the perfunctory cries of "Long Live the King!" were surpassed by the defiance of "Long Live the Charter!" *Le Contribuable* celebrated its victory:

> An immense revolution has occurred in our culture. The periodic press taught us to defend ourselves . . . each day public liberties make new conquests; each day the Charter sees the number of its defenders increase. The generation that is growing up is taking root and replacing the one in decline.[33]

Neither a public execution in Limoges nor the news that Alger had fallen to French troops distracted public opinion from the political crisis. On July 26 *Le Contribuable,* referring to rumors that a coup d'état was imminent, warned against any attempt by the ministry to attach the right to vote, freedom of the press, or to attempt to dissolve the Chamber of Deputies or lower the *patente* so as to eliminate the most "troublesome" voters: "So it will be by coups d'état that the ministry thinks of conserving its power. Well, let it make such an unfortunate attempt, and it will see! We are resigned to undergo any test!"[34]

That very day, in a veritable coup d'état, five ordinances appeared in Paris, dissolving the Chamber, restricting the number of voters by increasing franchise qualifications, and curbing freedom of the press. On that hot Monday Parisian artisans took matters into their own hands. Some of them had been locked out by their employers, who were eager to see them on the streets protesting the government action. The raising of the revolutionary tricolor on one of Notre Dame's towers symbolized the alliance of the top hat and the smock against the Bourbon king, the old nobility, and the Church. The appointment of Maréchal Marmont, the betrayer of Napoleon, as military commander roused their fury. Charles X, woefully unprepared to defend Paris and his throne, abdicated, fleeing Saint-Cloud with his court. Embraced by the republican hero Lafayette, Louis Philippe, the Duc d'Orléans, became Citizen King, promising that his monarchy would extend the definition of "capacity" and have a larger electoral franchise.

Limoges first learned of the ordinances on the twenty-eighth of July. Thereafter liberals gathered to await the arrival of the mail coaches for what news might be gleaned from the official proclamations and rumors from the capital.

The manager of *Le Contribuable* threatened its printer with a lawsuit if he did not honor his contract to publish the paper. Several porcelain manufacturers seemed on the verge of dismissing many of their workers to "make them unhappy and ready to protest."[35]

Prefectoral proclamations called for calm, counteracting a rumor that a sentry at the château of de la Bastide had been found with his throat slit. On the twenty-ninth the National Guard, dormant since 1826, took arms, proclaiming itself ready to march to Paris in defense of the Charter of 1815. *Le Moniteur* later reported that some three thousand workers gathered in their *quartiers* to yell "Long Live Liberty!" The Municipal Council met on the thirtieth, with nineteen members present—without de la Bastide—and voted four thousand additional francs for the beleaguered Bureau de Bienfaisance. Finally, on the first of August Baron Coster received word of the abdication of Charles X. He turned over his departmental administrative functions to Alluaud, naming him mayor. The passing of the municipal reins from de la Bastide to Alluaud symbolized the end of the Restoration in Limoges. De la Bastide could now remain permanently on his estate, which lay, together with his interests, outside the city.

Alluaud immediately banned all public gatherings and established a 10 P.M. curfew. The nominal commander of the Guard, a favorite of the bishop, resigned and was replaced by Dumas, who promised to fulfill the "wonderful mission" of keeping the peace and protecting property. Public order was briefly challenged on August 2, when the inmates in the regional prison refused to work. Limoges's small garrison joined the Guard in restoring order, which they accomplished by killing one prisoner and wounding six others.[36]

A mood of celebration and genuine optimism prevailed. Patriotic ladies sewed and distributed tricolor *cocardes* and many inhabitants spontaneously illuminated their houses. The National Guard triumphantly hoisted the tricolor on August 3; in subsequent days it organized a patriotic banquet and a festival in honor of those wounded during the "three glorious days" in Paris. *Le Contribuable* boasted that its city "offered the most imposing of all sights, that of a great population, strong and generous, [ready to] take up arms in anger" and rush to the aid of the Paris insurgents.[37]

If few disputed the notion that "Limoges had risen as one man," the implications of the revolution led to vigorous disputes within several weeks. The successful coalition that had opposed the last Bourbon ministry soon began to crack as the policies of the new regime in Paris were gradually revealed. The allies of the spring began to part company in the fall. The municipality wrote to urge the other towns in the department to join them in an address supporting the constitutional and hereditary monarchy of the Duc d'Orléans and a "truly liberal Charter" that would "guarantee our rights and liberties forever." However, the extent of those rights and liberties inevitably began to be debated. How far was the revolution to be carried?[38]

Contemporaries agreed that the revolution changed political life in France. First, 1830 was very much a bourgeois revolution, despite the fact that land continued to be the basis of wealth during the July Monarchy. The conventional interpretation of that revolution had been refined and nuanced, but seems essentially correct. Most of those now given the vote in Limoges were industrial or merchant capitalists, even if it was extremely rare that the business tax alone gave them the right to vote. In Table 2 the first numerical column of eligible voters in 1834 in Limoges lists those who would have qualified to vote according to the laws of the Restoration (i.e., they would have had to pay at least three hundred francs in taxes). The second column lists those voters enfranchised by the revolution and subsequently added to the register by virtue of contributing between two and three hundred francs in taxes. Half of the new voters eligible to vote in Limoges were wholesale merchants.

The year 1830 saw an increase not only in the political participation and power of the bourgeoisie but in their self-awareness as a group, conscious of being men of "capacity," as defined by their income, business activity, and contribution to the reputation of their city. During the Restoration all men of commerce were usually lumped together in the list of voters as *négociants*. Now they were listed with greater precision, as *marchand en gros, marchand de fer en gros, marchand de kaolin,* and so on. Jean-Baptiste Reix was now listed as an *entrepreneur des bains publics,* the sixteenth leading taxpayer in Limoges. In 1831 these men elected the merchant Philibert Chamiot-Avanturier as deputy from Limoges's district. Grateful for the assistance the government gave industry and commerce

TABLE 2

Eligible Voters	300 francs or more	200–299
property owners	56	16
wholesale merchants/industrialists	68	35
retail merchants	84	55
liberal professions	36	17
functionaries of the king	18	6
functionaries/mayors	6	2
military	4	2
dignitaries	3	0
honorific voters	1	0
clergy	0	0
others	26	6
Total	302	139

Source: Madame J. Léger, "Etude des listes électorales du département de la Haute-Vienne sous la monarchie de Juillet (1830–48)."

after the revolution, they became the bulwark for the Orleanist regime and were already dubbed the *juste milieu*.[39]

Second, the revolution curtailed much of the political influence of the Church in France and in Limoges. Controversial Bishop Prosper de Tournefort no longer had the ear of the prefect and was less able to influence local politics; his relations with the chief secular authority in the department were often strained. His successor in 1844 was careful to please local authorities. It was no coincidence that the popularity of the local religious confraternities began to wane after the Revolution of 1830, and that several local religious festivals declined. In the interest of safety, the Municipal Council banned the traditional ceremonial fires of St. Jean on June 23 and on the last day of the Ostensions. The *fête des vendanges,* traditionally held on the site of the old Montjovis chapel, disappeared. Other traditions that soon ended included the burning of mannequins suspended from lanterns, wearing masks during the carnival, and the baking of special cakes for the king's feast day (which itself had suddenly changed).[40]

Third, the revolution accelerated municipal political life. Henceforth, "men of capacity" would elect their own municipal representatives. The July victors in Limoges insisted that "the council seats should in no way be perpetuated in the same families and among the same people . . . the leading inhabitants of the town should be called upon, in turn, to serve and to pay the tribute of their enlightenment and their devotion to their fellow citizens in the discussion of common interests.[41] Thereafter seats on the Municipal Council were politically contested. In the 1832 municipal elections the liberal paper *Le Contribuable* supported a list containing twenty-seven candidates, thirteen of whom were *industriels*. Business acumen and success were subsequently viewed as important qualifications for the council ("affaires commerciales très étendues," or "prudence remarquable, commerce considérable"). In May 1832 the paper called for the council to account regularly for the use of funds at its disposal and applauded the preliminary measures taken to lower the tax on liquor as a first step toward the elimination of "the odious system of taxes on the poor." In the municipal election the "party of movement," as it came to be known, lost out to the Orleanist "middle party" or *juste milieu,* which it accused of "profiting from the influence that comes with wealth." But *Le Contribuable* could rightly claim that the left opposition had already had "a pronounced impact" on municipal politics, "due less to its numbers than to its consensus, and especially its liaison with the lower classes, from which it draws strength and indeed its life."[42]

The Municipal Council, now elected and no longer needing the permission of the prefect to meet, could turn its attention to the city. "We should agree that for thirty years Limoges had not been on the path of progress from the perspective of cleanliness," *Le Contribuable* claimed, challenging those who doubted its assertion to walk its streets.[43] "Towns should not fear to undertake loans in order to execute major public works projects," the liberal paper claimed in March 1832, a sentiment that anticipated the Second Empire.[44] Alluaud's administration emphasized public works in part because the charity workshops provided a labor supply that demanded work but primarily out of conviction. And the Municipal Council began to meet more than three times as frequently as it had before the revolution. In 1826 there had been eleven sessions of the council, seven in 1827, eight in 1828, and ten in 1829. During the first seven months of 1830—until the revolution—the council came together eighteen times. The council met fourteen times in the last five months of 1830, and between thirty and thirty-four times in each of the next four years. It initiated a series of urban projects that had been awaited in vain during the Restoration, indeed, since the time of Turgot.[45]

The wishes of the majority of the population were answered when the new administration expedited the construction of a slaughterhouse. The municipality purchased land at Beaupeyrat, south of the city, in January 1831. Construction began near the Vienne, funded by a loan of 140,000 francs from local businessmen and a gift of 50,000 francs from the new government, which was eager to please its urban constituents. It remained to get the butchers into the slaughterhouse. They were already unhappy about the right of the mayor to choose (from a list they provided) the syndics with whom the municipality would negotiate. The corporation had been arbitrarily divided into three groups, determined by the kind of meat each butcher was licensed to sell. The mayor had usually picked the wealthiest butchers, who sold every kind of meat. In 1832 the corporation collectively protested the new slaughterhouse in a pamphlet entitled "Observations des bouchers de la ville de Limoges." Their little pamphlet claimed that the new slaughterhouse would raise the price of meat for the consumer by increasing their own costs. After presenting a careful but somewhat suspect analysis, they sarcastically noted that the people of Limoges probably believed that such calculations were beyond their mental capacities. They protested many of the proposed conditions under which they would work—the number of scalding tubs (*échaudoirs*), plans for the upkeep of the building, and the hours the slaughterhouse would be open—and contested the municipality's insistence that they be collectively responsible for any damages done to the slaughterhouse by them or their dogs. Furthermore, they complained that itinerant meat sellers and other people brought animals into the city without paying any tax (this was a frequent complaint against the butchers themselves).

Their written protests exhausted, and facing the determination of the new municipal admininistration, the butchers gathered in their tiny chapel and decided not to slaughter any animals as a form of active protest. They refused to sign the annual agreement with the city and withheld their collective tax payment (*abonnement*), thereby jeopardizing the repayment of the municipal debt. Finally, after twelve meatless days, the butchers capitulated and sullenly returned to their lucrative trade. The annual negotiations with the city over the amount of the *abonnement* were thereafter always difficult, with the butchers annually forcing the municipality to prepare for a return to the old system of counting each and every animal brought through the *octroi* before an agreement could be reached. Though the slaughterhouse marked a victory for the new municipal administration, the task of cleaning up the street remained.[46]

Other projects followed. The bourgeoisie believed that their municipal revolution augured well for the future, and the leading citizens loaned the municipality money. The plan to move the fairground away from the place d'Aîne and closer to the commercial quarters was scrapped, and work was begun to expand its size. The site of the *champ de foire* was soon fixed above the place d'Aîne and the place d'Orsay and was enlarged to include an old cemetery. The terre de Poilevé became the Champ de Juillet, a place for promenades by local residents and drilling exercises for the bourgeois National Guard. A residential quarter soon developed there, expanding Limoges toward the east. The construction of a number of streets was begun and others were aligned. A third bridge, to be called the Pont de la Révolution, was discussed but its construction never begun during the Restoration; it eventually became the major route across the Vienne in the nineteenth century. Limoges soon had a *salle de spectacle* like other cities. In several years Alluaud and his immediate successors contributed more to the physical improvement and development of their city than the entire period of the Restoration, Empire, and the Revolution.[47]

The Revolution of 1830 also gave the local Chambre consultative an unprecedented importance. Alluaud, its president, led discussions of the economic and political crisis and allocated the funds provided by the new regime in Paris to local industries. Blaming the legislation of the Restoration and the attitudes of the nobility toward commerce and industry for the relative backwardness of Limoges's development, the members of the Chambre consultative demanded lower taxes and sound commercial legislation—with respect to bankruptcy, for example—to protect honest and hard-working entrepreneurs against unscrupulous speculators. Improved credit arrangements would allow more responsible men to enter business, discouraging "men who flock to engage in what really becomes a game of chance." The monarchy could only end the crisis of confidence through economic reforms and wise financial policies.[48]

And they demanded order. Alluaud and the Chambre consultative recognized that continual popular disturbances were disastrous to France's limited credit facilities. Some bankers had panicked during the political crisis that led to the revolution, withdrawing their money from circulation. Early uncertainty about the policies of the new regime and popular disturbances during the succeeding months compounded the lack of credit. Hotheaded liberals seemed to have forgotten the virtues of patience and encouraged, or at least tolerated, popular disorders. The Orleanists would not.[49] The "principles of the July Revolution" were liberty and public order.

The reconstitution and revitalization of the National Guard, that fundamental bourgeois institution, had followed naturally from the municipal revolution that occurred in Limoges in 1830. In October funds were allocated for a guardhouse at the town hall. In 1831 the Guard drilled regularly on the new Champ de Juillet, which had been terraced by workers temporarily employed by the city; the bourgeois corps seemed "remarkable for its handsome dress, precise maneuvers, and zeal for service." Colonel Dumas reminded the corps of its duty in 1831: "Let each of us, quitting our bourgeois attire, leave behind cares of the day and say: I am a soldier today. . . ." The first anniversary of the revolution was marked by the public marriage of a young National Guard officer to an "honest girl nobly provided with a dowry by the Guard."[50]

In principle, the National Guard was to enroll all males between the ages of twenty and sixty—over sixty-five hundred males in Limoges. In reality, only the bourgeoisie, including master artisans, joined the National Guard of Limoges. The Guard registers in 1831 listed over seventeen hundred members (about 35 percent of the eligible age group), but only slightly more than thirteen hundred of these men owned a uniform, somewhat less were armed, and fewer than one thousand were fully outfitted—just about the number of eligible municipal voters in 1834. Colonel Dumas organized the Guard into two battalions of four companies each and three "elite" companies, of *cavalerie, voltigeurs,* and *grenadiers.* But throughout the July Monarchy the Guard was never organized by quarters, which was recommended by the relevant law of 1831. *Le Contribuable,* having already broken with the Orleanists, called for such a reorganization in April 1831; a plan proposed in 1834 would have created a number of neighborhood companies but would have maintained the elite companies and the right of officers to serve in any unit in which they had been elected. The organization of the Guard by quarters never took place; if the Guard had never been opened up to every male citizen, a prefect surmised, "companies of aristocrats and companies of proletarians would have been created," the latter by the rapid expansion of the industrial faubourgs. The National Guard of Limoges, then, remained "irregularly" constituted, overseen by a *conseil de recensement* that had the right to refuse anyone admission. On that council served Alluaud, Desalles Beauregard, Pétiniaud Dubos, Dumont St. Priest, Peyramont, Talabot, and the other leaders of the *juste milieu* in Limoges.[51]

The National Guard stood ready to enforce order during the July Monarchy, despite a lapse into apathy following the resignation of Colonel Dumas late in 1831. Though they were on alert at the time of the October riots in Paris in 1831 and in Lyon in November 1831, relatively few answered the call during a violent protest against the arrival of a new prefect in Limoges in 1833. An official blamed "the deplorable indifference of a population preoccupied with business and speculation to an institution whose utility it cannot appreciate in the current state of calm in which we live." The bourgeoisie at first stampeded to fill the prestigious rank of officer, but the nightly guard posts were filled only with extreme difficulty. The Limoges bourgeoisie would put aside its business attire and don the uniform of the Guard only when its interests were threatened.[52]

The *juste milieu* demanded order and stood ready to defend its interests by donning the uniform of the National Guard after the Revolution of 1830 because its victory soon was challenged. The threat to public order at first emerged in Limoges not from the supporters of the Bourbons but from ordinary people. Soon thereafter those young left liberals, dissatisfied with a conservative interpretation of the revolution, mounted an organized opposition to the politics of the Orleanists. Out of this movement there gradually emerged republicans and then socialists in Limoges, not only among the young bourgeois radicals but within the working class as well. The Revolution of 1830 thus moved into its second stage.

While Limoges's elite had begun to debate the accomplishments of the revolution that had just occurred, the poor worried about the necessities of life. Many workshops had closed their doors as the revolution brought the struggling economy to a standstill. On August 9 the municipal council allocated funds for charity workshops and sent several merchants to Rochefort to purchase grain for the Limoges market. Daily incidents occurred at the *octroi* as peasants and townspeople, as elsewhere in France, refused to pay up; the liquor tax could not be collected during the entire month of August. Rumors of "plots" to destroy the tax registers alarmed tax officials. Workers went to the town hall to ask for official intervention to combat hoarding and prevent any further rise in the price of bread. Stories of mysterious "gatherings" in the woods around the city followed ill-considered statements by some employers that wages would have to be lowered.[53]

At the end of August municipal authorities announced an increase in the price of bread, as they had during the previous winter, when the bakers had been blamed—with some justification—for the bread shortage. On the morning of the thirty-first angry workers began to assemble but were dispersed by the police; they reassembled at the place Tourny in the afternoon. About two thousand marched to the gardens of the town hall, where they believed that a number of the unscrupulous bakers had taken refuge. Many in the crowd had armed themselves with sticks and pitchforks; a few had pillaged pistols from a gunsmith's store. Finding no bakers in the gardens, they attacked two nearby bakeries, whose owners, Gérald and Misset, barely escaped before their grain and bread were distributed among the crowd, furniture was smashed, and tools destroyed. The crowd then turned its fury on a third baker, one Samie, whose store on the rue des Petites Maisons, between the cathedral and the town hall, turned out to be well stocked, thus confirming their suspicions. These desperate acts lasted about an hour and a half, long enough for the National Guard to assemble and make thirteen arrests. However, the recent transfer of power limited the effectiveness of the repression: A prosecutor had been dismissed that morning, and local magistrates, "hardly used to dealing with riots" in Limoges, released most of those arrested. Troops, gendarmes, and Guardsmen patrolled the streets and the night passed without further trouble; they dispersed small groups of workers the next morning, amid rumors of an attack upon the prison to release the inmates.[54]

Dumont St. Priest, now procureur général, ordered an investigation, at first blaming political agitators—legitimists—because he believed the workers "sensible, honest, peaceful, professing the respect religion accords persons and property." He heard that notes had been sent to the rioters telling them where to assemble, but he doubted that "rich and influential men" would initiate such disorder; he suspected one Catherinaud, an illiterate porcelain worker who, to hide his identity, was believed to have instructed a comrade to spell out carefully the place and time the riot was to begin. Yet the only evidence for any conspiracy was a letter with mysterious "Masonic" figures and words in argot, as well as "Down with the National Guard!" hastily scrawled by an unpracticed hand. None of the 150 witnesses provided any credible testimony pointing toward Carlist or republican troublemakers and secret payoffs.[55]

Who rioted? Of the sixteen suspects interrogated whose records survive (twelve men and four women, nine of whom were born in Limoges), we can identify two weavers, six day laborers, one pottery worker, two bootblacks, one apprentice carrier, one wheelwright, and the wives of a carter, a porcelain worker, and another day laborer. Most could not sign their names and all had "no resource other than their labor." The weaver Duraney claimed to have been working when someone he did not know brought a letter "urging the workers to go to the champ de foire." Finding nothing there, he heard someone saying that "everyone should go to the town hall, where they are considering the bread tax." On the way he found himself caught up in the mob at one of the bakeries. There he struck one baker's basket with a stick. Then J. B. Lafleur convinced him to go out and drink a bottle with him—a fact which explains to the historian as well as the contemporary prosecutor why this fifteen-year-old boy happened to be called "Carnival."

Other explanations seemed somewhat less likely. One Raymond insisted that he was being helplessly pushed along by the surging crowd when some of the grain thrown from a bakery landed on him. Jacques, who believed that he had been born in Limoges, had heard that the mayor would distribute bread to the poor. So he took a huge hunk of bread when someone offered it to him, "but I received it without any bad intentions." While walking away, a "bourgeois told me to put it back, and I turned it over to him without any resistance." He told the judge that "before this unfortunate event, no one could reproach me for anything, and the ladies in the hospice, who have known me for a long time, can attest to my good conduct." Anne Auriat took a little bread with a clear conscience, having gone to the town hall "because of the rumor that people were going there to lower the price" of bread. Léger Gauthier, a bootblack on the place Royale, who gave his age as sixteen or seventeen, told a similar story. Jean Brissaud, a fifteen-year-old pottery worker, admitted taking four candles and some rye bread because "inexperience and youth put me in this sad position." A woman admitted haranguing the crowd at the place Tourny, "telling them that some people want to make the poor die and that the bakers were rascals." Having seven children, she did not want the price of bread raised. Police arrested Françoise Gery as she was carrying a sixty-pound bag of grain to her home on the place des Carmes; when it became too heavy, she offered a small amount of the grain to a passerby in exchange for his assistance.[56]

We may assume, with the commander of the gendarmerie, that the rioters were "women and workers of the lowest class of people." Indeed, several groups of skilled workers indignantly wrote Dumont St. Priest, denying their participation. One letter sought to counter "the most injurious rumors circulating about the *artistes en porcelaine*" expressing irritation that those with skills were sometimes confused with common day laborers. The fact that all twenty-five could sign their names clearly distinguished them from the mass of the working population. Those employed by Tharaud on the place Tourny, where the disturbances started, also insisted that they had not been involved in the "tumultuous meetings held by day laborers from all sorts of trades." Another letter from porcelain workers—these less literate, with only nine out of thirty-six being able to sign their names—assured the public prosecutor that "the workers of the factory of Latrille and Company" remained in their workshops; the letter insisted that "a single word from our director made us return to our tasks." They asked only some assurance from the mayor in the face of rising bread prices, with another miserable winter only months away. Similar attestations were volunteered by the laborers of Naveix and a number of textile workers.[57]

By underlining the plight of workers, the economic crisis therefore helped raise the "social question" in France, dividing the allies who had ousted the Bourbons.[58] Over the next few months the economic crisis led to two major bankruptcies in the city. In its session of October 25, the Chambre consultative expressed the "anxiety of our fellow citizens, justly alarmed at the thought that so large a number of people might participate in disturbances fearing a lack of work during the winter."[59]

Alluaud convoked the wealthiest businessmen of Limoges to finance a loan of over sixty thousand francs with which to purchase grain, which was sought first in Châteauroux, then in Orléans, and was finally obtained in Rochefort; a subsequent government loan during the winter helped finance workshops for some five hundred unemployed workers.[60]

Popular ferment, however, continued. One month later another crowd stormed the tax offices at the *octroi* and attempted to burn the registers. A petition sponsored by a wholesale liquor merchant named François Villegoureix, who owed five hundred francs in taxes, demanded the abolition of indirect taxes. Dumont St. Priest, who had earlier refused to believe that bourgeois could incite a grain riot, now expressed amazement that "rich and influential men now desire an anarchist uprising from which they would have the most to lose." One of the architects of the revolution in Limoges, he now called for absolute order. The leading magistrate in the Haute-Vienne already regretted some of "the changes in ideas and hopes spawned by the glorious July Revolution." Alluaud's two elderly deputy mayors, Georges Pouyat and Bourdeau-Juillac (seventy-five and seventy-seven years of age, respectively), resigned to allow more vigorous men to aid the mayor in keeping order. Juge St. Martin and Philabert Avanturier proudly represented the "bourgeois electoral corps"; they supported Casimir Perier's interpretation of the revolution.[61]

Troops and the National Guard could, Procureur Dumont St. Priest reasoned, put down further disturbances from *le peuple*. The "advanced" young liberals of *Le Contribuable* posed a more difficult challenge since they attacked the "men of order" who carried on the business of government as if a revolution had not even taken place. They first complained that a complete purge of old Bourbon supporters had not occurred: "The same men who a short time ago, adorned with white sashes, prostrated themselves before Monsieur de la Bastide now, wearing tricolor sashes, crowd around M. Alluaud."[62] Those who had eagerly awaited invitations to the prefecture from Baron Coster now anticipated the call of the new Orleanist prefect, Baron de Theis. *Le Contribuable* urged the appointment to the Municipal Council of men of commerce not tainted by having served the Bourbons. The departmental General Council, the Arrondissement Council, and even the Comité de bienfaisance still seemed to be composed of men "who had always marched for the other side" before the July Revolution.[63]

By early October the new prefect complained that the dissatisfied liberals were secretly meeting, discussing their "doctrine" openly.[64] The break between the two factions that had opposed the last ministries of the Restoration became irreparable later that month. *Le Contribuable* chided the new depositories of political power for failing to enact reforms beyond increasing the narrow electoral franchise. Did not the government comprehend that France was entering a new era? Content, for the moment, to attack the new administration, the paper defiantly warned that "we will, if necessary, be republicans tomorrow." The newspaper printed the statutes of the Limousin branch of the Aide-toi society, which circulated in the cafés and even some workshops of the city.[65]

Dumont St. Priest now symbolized the *juste milieu* of Limoges, which, having won its political rights, sought to pull up the drawbridge behind it in the name of order. The procureur général thereafter came under attack from *Le Contribuable* when he accepted the Légion d'honneur:

Would it be for having bravely hidden himself in Orléans until the danger had passed, after having left our walls behind in July [as deputy], with the enthusiastic acclamations of the entire population . . . for having made such a great sacrifice for the country by accepting a position worth fifteen thousand francs a year . . . for having constantly voted in the Chamber for measures restricting or preventing our liberties and our rights?[66]

The ambitious magistrate had married the daughter of a noble who had betrayed the Bourbons and had served as imperial procureur général. Having himself achieved the same position, the man elected as a liberal in the 1830 election had now decided not to run for the Chamber, his enemies claimed, because the judiciary position offered lucrative financial advantages and would allow him to wield his political influence in Limoges. Dumont St. Priest seemed to be "one of those cold and egotistical men who saw the July Revolution as nothing more than a mine to be exploited for the purposes of unlimited ambition." Frequent disturbances outside his house on the boulevard du Collège—including an unruly charivari—only stiffened his stance as a "man of order."[67] *Le Contribuable* inquired:

Why do we no longer feel the bonds of sympathy that united us when the great tremor of July 1830 shook the earth? What became of this magnificent future that was opening for the nation, that we could only contemplate with tears of joy in our eyes? What became, above all, of the devotion that molded so many generous souls into one?[68]

On what issues did those who had assumed political power in Limoges as Orleanists and their leftist critics—future republicans—disagree concerning the consequences of the Revolution of 1830? The Church, although its diminished influence was assumed, remained one source of political division. The July Revolution intensified anticlerical ferment among the left; the Masons soon revived. The cross that stood before the Church of St. Pierre was pulled down in December as a relic of "fanaticism." *Le Contribuable* campaigned against the mission cross in front of the Church of St. Michel-des-Lions, a reminder of the influence of the Congregationalists in France. For twenty years the Municipal Council "had been devoted to every form of despotism and to all of the Congregationalists." Now, with only four resignations since the revolution, the "representatives of the Congregationalists" still seemed to have a majority on the council."[69] The "new" administration appeared to woo the clergy. Dumont St. Priest made peace with Bishop Prosper.

Yet the bishop seemed to thrive on controversy. The events of the revolution had only briefly served to divert popular attention from his insistence that every commune in his diocese purchase two new, very expensive church missals (at a cost of seventy francs), which was beyond the means of most communes, particularly since the armament of the National Guard and the expense incurred by official ceremonies after the revolution had seriously depleted the already modest resources. Even the office of the Minister of the Interior noted that "this forced distribution of the new missals appears to be a [financial] speculation." In September the bishop banned the old missals, but the new Orleanist Minister of Public Instruction ruled that communes could not be forced to buy the expensive ones. Other complaints against the Church followed. A local man complained that a priest had heard his wife's deathbed confession only upon receiving a sum of money. Prosper denied a church burial to a former municipal employee who had earned his disfavor. Louis Philippe's name was only added to the mass prayers sung in the cathedral on February 20, 1831, as a crowd menacingly gathered outside. The mood of anticlericalism reached such a fever pitch following talk of "secret meetings" at the bishop's palace that a rumor began circulating that a mob intended to slit the throats of the seminarians. Prosper rushed to the seminary to warn that "revolutionary impiety" would soon close all churches. He then ordered the seminarians to flee Limoges for Guéret, where he would join them unless Alluaud guaranteed his safety. He finally agreed to remove the controversial mission cross before St. Michel. Popular resentment against the bishop and his clergy even surpassed that of the government, which already seemed to "favor the priests and the partisans of the old government."[70] In September 1831, when rumors circulated that Carlist arms were hidden in the bishop's elegant palace, crowds chanted "Down with the Carlists!" and "Down with the *juste milieu!*"[71]

The disenchanted liberals assailed the new regime for ignoring the plight of the workers. "The July Revolution was begun and carried out by the popular classes," asserted *Le Contribuable*. "This is a fact that no one can deny." The artisans of Paris had fought largely without recompense; nothing had been done to alleviate the tax burden that weighed them down. At the same time, *"le parti moyen,* or of the *juste milieu,* if you insist, although acting with little cohesion, has profited from the influence that wealth makes possible." Now they blocked "the full development of the consequences of the July Revolution," which included improving conditions for the poor. The liberals discussed the "social question," proclaiming that "le peuple est tout." Who could blame the poor of Paris for expressing their irritation and for now asking that "we pay some more attention to them"? How could it be surprising that "they want social institutions for their benefit in compensation for the burdens and sacrifices they have suffered"?[72]

Both the spokesmen for the new regime and their liberal critics understood that continued popular disturbances were accentuating the economic crisis. But they both drew very different lessons. While Dumont St. Priest thundered for order, his former allies accused the ministry of contributing to the crisis of confidence through heavy-handed policies of repression—the same attack previously levied against the last government of the Restoration. Instead of encouraging positive action to develop commerce and industry while aiding the workers, the government prevented its citizens from exercising the liberty won in July 1830. "From where do revolutions come," asked *Le Contribuable*, "if not from social malaise?"[73]

What could be done for Limoges and its workers? The new administration could also encourage the development of associations. *Le Contribuable* welcomed the establishment of a *banquet de secours* and published a series of articles explaining its financial operations; its relatively low interest rate (5 instead of 6 percent) had saved several businesses and permitted the operation of the charity workshops, which remained open through the spring of 1831. The editors urged its readers to form *sociétés anonymes*, "today the only means that one can apply successfully to undertakings of great public utility." The freedom to form associations seemed to them to be one of the conquests of the "three glorious days" of July 1830. In addition to facilitating the growth of the economy and thus bringing prosperity to the bourgeoisie and workers alike, associations could provide the means by which citizens could defend themselves against any attempts to curtail the free expression of their liberties. The Aide-toi Society had been instrumental in mobilizing opposition to the Bourbons before the revolution and its revival seemed consistent with the rights of citizens. Yet the new government claimed that the members of the Aide-toi society were "malcontents, conspirators, or anarchists who want to levy taxes, regiment everybody, and bring us back to the politics of 1793."[74] The 1834 law concerning associations was the result of such thinking.

There had been little talk of republicanism before or immediately after the Revolution of 1830. Alluaud, in an address forwarded to the Chamber of Deputies from "the people of Limoges" on August 6, stated that "a few people talk of a republic, but the general opinion does not at all adhere to this idea." By October the editors of *Le Contribuable* warned that if the reforms suggested by the revolution and implied in the meaning of "liberty" and "sovereignty of the people" were not enacted, they would become republicans. During 1831 and 1832 republicanism won a strong nucleus of supporters in the city, among them a nineteen-year-old lawyer named Théodore Bac, who, despite his youth, had already earned a considerable reputation as a brilliant orator. Some two hundred men met at the Café de L'Europe in March 1831 to discuss the statutes of the Aide-toi society.[75]

The arrival, in 1832, of several Polish refugees passing through the city encouraged other republican gatherings. Two merchants were arrested at the theater for shouting "Down with Kings!" One of them had sung the "Marseillaise," had yelled "La République nous appelle," and, worse, was alleged to have said, "D'ailleurs, j'emmerde le Roi citoyen comme les autres!" The identification of several republican *"jeunes têtes"* in the National Guard convinced the prefect that the republican spirit in Limoges was gradually "assuming the character of a political party." By November 1832 the informal gatherings of republicans in cafés or at Théodore Bac's house on the rue Gaignolle had become full-fledged "opposition banquets." The following year the prefect routinely began to count the number of "democrats" among the voters. Republicanism had become a significant opposition political force by the end of 1832.[76]

In the spring of 1831 the first of several Saint-Simonian "missions"—offering a marked contrast with the missions of the Church in 1828—arrived in Limoges in the person of the earnest but bizarre Moïse Retouret of Paris, who addressed about a hundred people on two occasions. Police reported a "third Saint-Simonian production" on April 25 and another in July. By the fall utopian socialist influence among *"les classes aisées"* was worthy of attack by Dumont St. Priest in his speech opening the session of the Royal Court.[77] Young Bac, Retouret's friend from their school days in Paris, defended the Saint-Simonians, who

> agreed with you [the Orleanists] that property is the basis of all society . . . the amount of which is to be determined by ability and compensation for work, and want the amelioration of the condition of everyone, the abolition of all of the privileges and idleness, and the reign of work. These are their doctrines.[78]

This distinction between producers and the idle was critical in Saint-Simonian theory, as established by Saint-Simon's rather untimely parable (given the assassination of the Duc de Berri) of 1820: Society could afford to lose kings and queens, nobles and bishops, but it could ill afford to lose men of science and business, artisans and farmers. We find Saint-Simonian influence in *Le Contribuable:* The highly paid functionaries of the July Monarchy were compared to the idle nobles and high clergy of the ancien régime and the Restoration. Exorbitant salaries for largely ceremonial tasks remained—the first president of the Royal Court was paid fifteen thousand francs a year but had not been seen in Limoges for thirteen months. The Orleanists had maintained a high salary and budget for the bishop. In their own self-interest the *juste milieu* had left untouched the most fundamental economic problems, particularly that of taxation. It was not unreasonable to tax the sources of progress—the producers—defined in the broadest sense as those who labored productively. Indirect taxes should be eliminated, or at least greatly reduced; nonproducers—nobles, clergy, large property owners, *rentiers*—should bear the weight of the *fisc.* The existing tax structure merely served to "consolidate the regime of riots" by weighing so heavily on the poor that they rebelled—as they had in Limoges after the revolution—thereby further disrupting business. The economic crisis had only gradually begun to recede in 1831, but not before two large commercial houses, those of Pétiniaud-Juriol and Lamy de la Chapelle, had declared bankruptcy.[79]

Other Saint-Simonians came to Limoges in 1833. In February two disciples arrived "in costume" before traveling to St. Léonard, and in May the tanner Rives and Ganichon, a marble polisher, arrived. A letter from Rives to Dr. Guépin, an ardent Saint-Simonian living in Nantes (and, like many of these young utopian socialists, a militant during the Second Republic), mentioned "numerous warm friends," republicans, discovered during their twelve-day stay in Limoges. Each day they held Saint-Simonian "productions," "ceremonies," and "rituals," attracting up to three hundred people, at least once dressing up a café waiter in some sort of inspiring costume. Besides these tantalizing glimpses, we have little information as to what occurred during these meetings. There Bac delivered impassioned discourses against the *juste milieu,* which, he claimed, "believes us impotent" but has "more enemies than it realizes . . . we are the authors of our revolution . . . we have emancipated the French, who are scornfully called *les hommes du peuple.*" The Saint-Simonians distributed five hundred copies of a brochure written by the president of the Society of the Rights of Man in Paris, solidifying the link between utopian socialism and republicanism in the early 1830s.[80] The Saint-Simonians did not return, but their influence remained and affected the development of republicanism and the early evolution of socialism in Limoges.

A demonstration and a strike in 1833 proved how quickly Limoges had changed since the Revolution of 1830. Jean Scipion Mourgnes, the newly appointed prefect of Haute-Vienne, did not sympathize with the Poles. His anticipated arrival in Limoges therefore angered the left; about sixty people streamed out of a café and gathered in protest across the square in front of the prefecture. The next night a crowd of three hundred poured into the place St. Martial after learning that the new prefect's coach would soon arrive from St. Junien, where he had already been greeted with shouts of "Down with the *mouchard* of the *juste milieu!*" Police dispersed the unruly crowd, which, apparently egged on by another eight or nine hundred sympathetic onlookers, reassembled at the place Royale. They ran to greet the carriage with rocks and stones as it descended the rue Turgot. Gendarmes escorted the new prefect and his terrified aunt and niece to their lodgings; troops with fixed bayonets scattered the protesters after the legally required three warnings and arrested several people.

The disturbances continued the next day when the Haute-Vienne's chief administrator went to the cathedral to attend a mass for those killed during the July Revolution. There he also heard a chorus of shouts of "Down with the Prefect! Down with the Tyrant of the Poles!" For the second time in two days the National Guard responded to the call in limited numbers; most of these men were government employees who dared not be absent. Officers, alarmed by the decline in discipline in the Guard since the resignation of Colonel Pierre Dumas as commander the previous year, called a full review the following day to restore morale and counter the republicans with a show of force.[81]

The trial records from this seemingly minor protest reveal the event's true significance: Workers had now joined the radical bourgeoisie in Limoges in their republican protest. Those prosecuted included: a commercial clerk whose father, embarrassingly enough, served on the Municipal Council; a sabot maker; a miller; an apprentice baker; two porcelain workers; and Bac, who proudly declared to the court that he was both a Saint-Simonian and a republican. The participation of the miller and apprentice baker is striking, differentiating this event from the earlier popular disturbances that were directed against millers and bakers. The trial, as other such legal proceedings during the July Monarchy, played into the hands of the republicans by permitting them to publicize their own case against the government. Bac admitted joining the charivari at the prefecture the previous night, "affirming in principle that this mode of expressing an opinion belongs to the people." Moïse Retouret took advantage of the opportunity to speak on his comrades' behalf and launched into a discourse on Saint-Simonian theory. Two convictions and one duel resulted from the trial, which enhanced the popularity of the republicans.[82]

Limoges's first recorded strike followed several months later. The *artistes en porcelaine,* or decorators, had formed the first mutual aid society in the city in 1829. Turners and molders formed similar organizations during the first year after the revolution. We can only guess at their impact, but the timing of such an association fits the national pattern and again underscores the significance of the Revolution of 1830 on workers. Although strikes were illegal, the meager funds at the disposal of mutual aid societies could provide covert assistance to strikers.

The porcelain manufacturers had been struck hard by the economic crisis that accompanied the Revolution of 1830. As the industry slowly began to recover in 1832, reaching the level of production of 1829 only in 1833, they cut by about 20 percent the wages paid their turners and molders. In December 1831, shortly after the Lyon insurrection, an anonymous letter to two porcelain workers allegedly tried to "excite them to demand a raise in salary" to the previous level. On September 12, 1833, after two of their comrades were fired, two hundred turners and molders struck five of Limoges's eight manufacturers. Letters seized by the police indicated that the Limoges workers were exchanging information about the piece rates paid in Paris and Vierzon. The manufacturers announced that they would train the workers necessary to maintain continued production. The strikers demanded the return to the rates paid at the time of the July Revolution. Some left to find work in the porcelain workshops of other towns. A few turners and molders returned to work when offered a 5 to 10 percent raise—which was still below the wages paid in 1830—but the others held out for four weeks. On October 10 the workers again collectively demanded a return to the piece rate of 1830. Tharaud agreed to their proposal and the other manufacturers followed suit by October 22. In early November only one factory remained closed, and the strike was soon settled. Shortly thereafter groups of tailors and some café waiters gathered to demand higher wages, and a number of the former briefly stayed away from work. Was the example of the skilled porcelain workers consciously followed?[83]

François Alluaud had already resigned as mayor in August 1833, announcing that he would not seek election to the Chamber of Deputies. He wanted to devote all his time to his business; furthermore, his brother and a nephew had recently died—probably during the cholera outbreak the previous year—and his aged mother had urged him to withdraw from public life. But there was another reason for his decision. Alluaud had been disappointed and frustrated by the behavior of a growing number of his fellow citizens. He complained of the embarrassing reception given the new prefect with "large groups that had gathered at the place de la Préfecture running through the town [shouting] 'Long live the Republic!' [and singing] songs that recalled the most disastrous periods of our revolution, accompanied by dances not the less odious!" He had personally pleaded with the rebellious young bourgeois republicans and with the workers, cautioning them against "disorders whose implications your inexperience will prevent [you] from seeing in advance . . . I entreat you as a father, as a friend . . ." A few days later he resigned. Several months thereafter the prefect publicly applauded his "firm resolve [in the] struggle with the striking workers."[84]

In some important ways Limoges had changed in the five years that had passed between 1828—when François Alluaud's son, Victor, had had to petition the Bourbon administration, still seemingly in the hands of the nobles, and the clergy to obtain the right to vote—and 1833, when his father resigned as mayor. Some physical differences in the city evidenced deeper and more meaningful changes. The Sunday strolls of the bourgeoisie were now likely to take place on the Champ de Juillet, which included a *jardin de plaisance,* an elegant place to dance, and a drill ground for the National Guard. The crosses in front of the churches of St. Michel and St. Pierre had been removed—under the threat of being torn down by angry crowds. The place Dauphine had become the place de la Liberté. The first stone of the Pont de la Revolution was laid on July 27, 1832, the anniversary of the "three glorious days." The butchers had been forced into occupying a new slaughterhouse, and a decree on March 3, 1832, reaffirmed regulations for keeping the streets clean. These projects stemmed from the outcome of the revolution, which brought a self-conscious bourgeoisie to political power. The transition from the noble Baron de la Bastide, an anachronism in an industrializing town, to Alluaud symbolized for *limougeauds* the evolution of their own town. The ascribed honor of being designated *une bonne ville,* denied Limoges on the several occasions the town had applied, disappeared with the revolution. The optimistic mood of 1830 suggested that the city could make its own way.[85]

The Revolution of 1830 reflected and accelerated a contest for political power waged throughout France. In Limoges the revolution was bloodless, but it was nonetheless a revolution, carried out by commercial and industrial interests unhappy with the politics of the Restoration. They found in Orleanism a political credo that could satisfy the desire for an atmosphere conducive to economic achievement and a stable social order; both seemed inseparable. Even after the acrimonious split between the conservative and liberal factions of the prerevolutionary coalition, both sides agreed that the revolution had been a victory for the bourgeoisie, particularly for business. *Le Contribuable,* while heaping invective on the opportunistic *juste milieu,* continued to publish articles informing its readers how banks operated and extolling what business could do for Limoges. The Saint-Simonians trumpeted the possibilities of commercial and industrial expansion and envisioned a republic of producers. *Le Nouveau Contribuable*—its official name as of November 1831—had neatly summarized the rapid maturation of French political life during those dramatic years following the Revolution of 1830:

> Is not the eldest son of the July Revolution actually the youngest son of the bastard aristocracy of Louis XVIII? . . . henceforth government must receive its sanction from the people; let it gain strength through the electoral urn, let it also become a national institution . . . and let it democratize its pedigrees and its bases.[86]

By 1833 Dumont St. Priest asserted that a republican party now existed in Limoges. Of 366 eligible voters who were expected to exercise their franchise (out of a total of 455 eligible voters), at least 184 would support the government on all issues and another 60 or more formed the dynastic or moderate opposition. Another 32 were Legitimists (20 of these were considered intransigent). But there were also about 90 "democrats" or republicans—at least 40 of whom were "pronounced" in their political opinions—who elected several National Guard officers. And although Philabert Chamiot-Avanturier, a thirty-seven-year-old merchant and deputy mayor, was easily elected to the Chamber of Deputies, his election was greeted with a charivari and shouts of "Down with the *juste milieu!*"— which were now quite familiar echoes in Limoges. A strong republican tradition in the city was born.[87]

Officials before 1830 had often noted that "the people take no part in the political debate." Now, in the words of *Le Nouveau Contribuable,* it seemed that "each day the people become more enlightened as to their real interests."[88] There is no indication that at this time the workers of Limoges thought of themselves as "the working class." It was the radical bourgeoisie that began to call them just that. Workers in Limoges certainly had a loosely defined sense that the new administration owed something to them as *le peuple,* the laboring poor in the broadest sense. Craft solidarities remained strong and only the most skilled, prosperous, and organized workers struck the porcelain industry in 1833. Several porcelain workers were among those arrested during the protests against the new prefect because they were more literate and politically conscious. They joined this demonstration as allies of the radical bourgeoisie and were not yet conscious of themselves as a class; it will be recalled to what lengths the skilled porcelain workers went to distinguish themselves from the mass of unskilled workers in denying rumors that they had participated in the pillages of the bakers' shops at the end of August 1830. Since Orleanism quickly demonstrated that it had little to offer the workers, the latter gradually turned to republicanism. Class consciousness was not far away.

Workers also began to manifest the vigorous anticlericalism of the bourgeois radicals, whereas in 1828 some of them had rushed to defend the clerical missions. In October 1833, a member of the National Guard killed himself, leaving his pregnant wife a widow. A priest refused to bury the poor man, which enraged the latter's friends. The next day a large crowd transported the body to the church and, finding it locked, placed it on a table outside. Police reports paid particular attention to the fact that some workers from the faubourg Montmailler were among those shouting insults at the curé and demanding that the church be opened. The priest finally complied upon receiving instructions from the town hall—before 1830 he would have consulted the bishop. The crowd poured into the church, the poor man was buried, and the incident was quickly forgotten.[89]

A political disturbance in which workers joined the radical bourgeoisie in protest. A strike. The refusal of a priest to bury a man and an outraged crowd forcing the church to open its doors. Small events in the history of nineteenth-century France, but telling moments in the political evolution of an industrializing city.

On April 27, 1848, Limoges's workers, led by the *porcelainiers,* disarmed the bourgeois National Guard and took control of the city, albeit briefly.[90] The *affaire de Limoges,* as it came to be known, witnessed the dramatic appearance of workers as organized contenders for political power, just fifteen years after Dumont St. Priest had expressed his amazement at the workers' newfound interest in politics. Limoges had become an industrial city of some thirty-eight thousand people, with workers concentrated in the burgeoning industrial faubourgs. These workers predominated in the Société populaire, Limoges's radical club. If Alluaud and most bourgeois had at first been surprised and then irritated by the early signs of organized insubordination and political awareness among the workers in 1833, by 1848 they were truly afraid. The procureur général wrote the Minister of Justice three days later, "Limoges is still in the hands of the workers; their posts occupy . . . even the courthouse from where I am writing you. Terror continues to reign in the town."[91]

Like the Revolution of 1830, that of 1848 was anything but a simple reaction to events in the capital. The political mobilization of 1848 emerged as the result of an alliance forged during the July Monarchy between bourgeois republicans and the working class, an alliance whose outline could be seen by 1833. Industrialization in Limoges generated the seeds of republicanism and socialism. The issues in the spring of 1848—the freedom of assembly and association, as well as the "right to work," unified both skilled and unskilled workers. Workers demonstrated a generalized sense of class consciousness based upon the dignity of work, identifying capitalists as individuals whose interests were opposed to their own. Evidence of the workers' *prise de conscience* during the July Monarchy in Limoges is sketchy—and the social historian must proceed with caution—but the city's second strike, which occurred in 1837, revealed skilled workers grasping for a sense of class that extended to unskilled workers as well. The attraction of workers to the republican party may have helped break down barriers between skilled and unskilled workers, at least on the political front. A heated controversy in 1847 involving the National Guard helped sharpen perceived class lines and conflict.

Hurt by competition from the German states and the Berry, in 1837 the porcelain manufacturers lowered the piece rate for their skilled workers that had been established after the previous strike. This move, combined with some layoffs, led about forty workers—mostly turners and *modeleurs* employed by Romanet—to gather, despite miserable weather, at a racetrack north of Limoges. On April 15 about five hundred workers in five factories stayed home, and a sixth was struck soon thereafter. The workers sent representatives to the other porcelain factories in the Limousin and in the Berry to learn about rates paid there and to ask for financial assistance. They carefully drafted a letter to the prefect, offering assurances that their actions were not politically inspired.[92]

After a seventh manufacturer closed his doors on April 26, some one thousand additional mostly unskilled workers were left jobless. Strikers received contributions from those sympathetic to their cause and spent the meager savings of their mutual aid society, although such use of funds was illegal. Charity and some municipal assistance aided those put out of work by the strike. Some workers held out through the summer, but many gave up, leaving to find work elsewhere. Finally, their resources exhausted, some workers capitulated and returned to their workshops. On August 12 most of the others returned, accepting a one-third reduction in their wage rage.[93]

Although the strike failed, it produced one interesting document, a pamphlet entitled "Précis sur la situation véritable des ouvriers et artistes en porcelaine, sans travail, de la ville de Limoges, pour servir à faire apprécier à leur juste valeur des dires de certains ennemis des ouvriers." The strikers asserted that they were *ouvriers* and not an aristocracy of labor, as claimed by those who were against their cause. These "enemies" appear to have been unskilled workers, as well as the manufacturers, who exploited the rivalry between skilled and unskilled workers. The strikers insisted that their real wages were much lower than they outwardly appeared: They had to pay the cost of raw materials, tools, light, and helpers out of the daily sum of five francs. They earned two and a half francs a day, which they insisted was not enough to maintain a family. Layoffs, inventory periods, and increasing food costs further cut into their standard of living, as evidenced by the fact that not a single worker could afford to make a deposit in the recently established savings bank. In order to earn a few francs, they had to toil most of the day, as did their less skilled co-workers. They reminded their employers that "a man is not a machine destined only to eat and to produce; the human dignity of self must also be satisfied, and noble faculties must not be left to perish." Beyond the daily requirements of bread and lodging, "one must find something for the future, for sickness and old age, to guide and support the youth of our children." They struck because a worker's salary "must satisfy all of these things in order that the worker may truly *live.*" Their employers, "blinded by their speculations" and therefore encouraging overproduction, did not comprehend this.[94]

The strike affirmed the dignity of work, but it also revealed the limits of working-class strike action. Differences in skill, organization, literacy, and the standard of living distinguished these skilled porcelain workers both from others in their industry and from workers in other industries. It is unlikely that the strikers had the support of these unskilled laid-off workers. Only one of the five mutual aid societies supporting porcelain workers included relatively unskilled workers (*mouleuses* and *garnisseuses*). Associations like the Société philanthropique des artistes en porcelaine (founded in 1843) offered members little more than minimal financial assistance during periods of illness or bereavement, both of which were beyond the means of most workers during the first half of the century. They joined workers of the same trade or similar occupations.[95] In 1847 some workers seemed to share the utopian socialism of Pierre Leroux, who visited the city that year and whose presence in his brother's printing shop in Boussac, in the Creuse, offered something of a center of diffusion for the former's socialist "religion of humanity."[96]

The events of the spring of 1848 nonetheless demonstrated at least a generalized sense of the dignity of work and class consciousness and a decided awareness that the aims of the bourgeoisie as a class were hostile to the interests of the workers. Specifically, the National Guard appeared as the arm of bourgeois reaction. In 1847 the apathy of the middle class toward active participation in that institution ended amid evidence of solid support among workers for the republicans and rumors of "communist" meetings of socialists in the woods around Limoges. Despite chronic apathy, demonstrated by relatively small turnouts to elect officers and difficulty in finding men to fulfill the patrolling and posting duties of the Guard, most bourgeois would have vigorously resisted its dissolution. Members had paid one hundred francs for a uniform and the Guard embodied municipal pride and readiness in the event of a threat.

This threat now came from the faubourgs. Because of the preponderance of workers in some quarters, the Guard was never reorganized according to neighborhoods, as had been strongly urged by the relevant law of 1831, because "companies of proletarians" would have been created. Although companies (excluding the elite artillery and the grenadiers) maintained the names of quarters (Cité, quartier des Arènes, Consulat), officers and ordinary guardsmen could reside in any district.[97] The Guard came alive. Officers first petitioned that all members be required by law to own the expensive uniform of the Guard and, several months later, insisted that the names of all guardsmen without the uniform be stricken from the National Guard's rolls. The petition became a political issue, giving republicans considerable momentum and increasing their support among workers, who had been gratuitously compared to the convicts in the regional prison as potential threats to order and property.[98]

Workers had found a political ideology: Republicanism, stressing the dignity of all men, could easily be combined with a primitive socialism that looked to the state to ensure them the "right to work" and permitted workers to form socialist associations. Workers followed such radical republican leaders as Théodore Bac and Marcel Dussoubs Gaston. The republican movement found strength in the *petite bourgeoisie* of the city. Republicans had gained several seats on the Municipal Council despite the limited franchise, at least partially because of a tactical alliance with the legitimists, who hated the smug men of the *juste milieu* as much as the republicans. A reform banquet held on July 24, 1840, in honor of opposition leader Michel de Bourges gave the police a chance to assess the strength of republicanism in Limoges. Among the 100 people who attended, "no bourgeois or commercial notable, no functionary or employee of the public administration" could be seen. Only 20 of the 280 banqueters drawn from the entire region were eligible to vote in the legislative elections by virtue of their wealth. The bourgeoisie listened to toasts in honor of electoral reform and property, issues that interested fifteen lawyers, many merchants and clerks of moderate wealth, and twenty master artisans, as well as one David, *artiste en porcelaine,* who was later compromised in the *affaire de Limoges.* But the police were quick to point out that although the admission fee was reduced from 5 francs to 1.50 for workers (which was still a day's wages for many), "the working population showed no sign of interest, nor emotion." The vast majority of the bourgeois populace spent the afternoon promenading, as was their custom, on the Champ de Juillet and the place de la Liberté, symbols of their Revolution of 1830.[99]

The Revolution of 1848 encountered no such indifference. It raised two crucial issues that the workers had adopted as their own, creating a second revolution that followed that of February: the role of workers in national political life and the "social question." Within a few days of the fall of the July Monarchy, the Société populaire, most of whose members were workers, began to meet, pressing for the election of strong republicans. Skilled and unskilled workers joined forces, looking to the state to guarantee them the "right to work" and the freedom of association and assembly. Such rights would protect them from the power of capitalists. Influenced by the utopian socialists, they imagined a republic of producers. The Société populaire established a commission to study the "organization of work," which the Luxembourg Commission was discussing the same

LIMOGES IN 1838

A. Champ de Juillet   C. Cathedral of St. Etienne   E. place de la Liberté
B. *champ de foire*   D. Prefecture   F. rue de la Boucherie

issues in Paris. Delegates, led by Bulot, another *artiste en porcelaine,* "of the workers" joined the provisional municipal administration to entreat the government to provide assistance. At the same time a popular press, freed from Orleanist censorship, worked to educate the laboring poor concerning their rights and duties as citizens. The "democratic and social Republic" seemed to be taking shape.[100]

The upcoming legislative elections, the threat of reaction, the dire economic crisis, and the bitter issue of active working-class participation in the National Guard as armed equals intensified class tensions. A moderate club began to meet. Conservative candidates for the National Assembly presented themselves in the department, seemingly sure of the rural vote. Disappointed with the results of the election and fearing a rumored attack by the bourgeois National Guard (into which they had yet to be integrated), members of the Société populaire stormed through the city, forcibly disarming the bourgeois Guard and propelling a new, more radical provisional administration (which included a number of workers) into power. Troops sent by the provisional government in Paris put an end to this situation. Limoges was spared the bloodshed that simultaneously occurred under similar circumstances in Rouen and Elbeuf. The *affaire de Limoges* anticipated the June Days by almost two months.[101]

Limoges's workers were directly responsible for the city's reputation as *la ville rouge;* this holds true even if one places the emergence of the left in Limoges at the beginning of the July Monarchy. The elections of May 1849 brought all Montagnards to the National Assembly from the department.[102] A by-election in 1850 confirmed the emergence of a leftist consensus in the department. The repression took a tremendous toll on the *démoc-soc* leadership and movement, weakening the strength but not the commitment of much of the leftist organization in Limoges. Workers continued to be politically involved, gradually assuming a greater role in the Montagnard movement in the last two years of the Republic. Several attempts by porcelain workers to begin producers' cooperatives demonstrated the influence of utopian socialist ideology, particularly of Fourier and Cabet (with cooperative schools and gardens planned). The government soon turned against all workers' associations because they raised the prospect of working-class control over production. The range of skills within the industry also contributed to the difficulties of these organizations, although one of them survived well into the Empire.[103] The National Guard, which had been dissolved after the *affaire de Limoges,* was replaced by an officially approved but illegally constituted corps of bourgeois "Volunteers" that nervously patrolled the city during the Republic. Louis Napoleon organized the coup d'état without any assistance from the Guard; units considered unreliable had long since been dissolved and disarmed. The National Guard was dead. The Volunteers applauded the coup. Republican socialists attempted to spark resistance in the rural hinterland. The march of the peasants of the village of Linards and several other nearby communes was short-lived. Protest in Limoges was limited to the exhibition of "seditious" red symbols and a large number of abstentions and negative votes during the plebiscite.[104] The Second Republic was over, but the political mobilization of 1848 could not be undone. The bourgeoisie had retained the political domination achieved in 1830. What they had not bargained for in 1830 had become a threatening reality in 1848 and a haunting specter by 1851: the consciousness and political awakening of the workers of their city.

3

Urban Growth and Industrial Concentration: Old and New Neighborhoods in Second Empire Limoges

In September 1859 A. de Louguemar, a scientist and writer from Poiters, attended a national scientific congress in Limoges. Rail service to Limoges from the north had been initiated three years earlier, and so Monsieur de Louguemar arrived by train. As would anyone traveling between two towns not on the main trunk lines to and from the capital, he complained, albeit philosophically, about the length of the journey; although Limoges and Poitiers are only 120 kilometers apart, the trip lasted an entire chilly night and took him, at added expense, through Tours, Orléans, and Châteauroux. Ten days of meetings in Limoges left little free time, but de Louguemar managed to see some of the city, recording his impressions for a newspaper in Poitiers. He was intrigued by much of what he saw.

De Louguemar, recoiling from the "hideous and repulsive spectacle of the rue de la Boucherie," marveled at the development of what he called a second city, industrial Limoges, rising along the Vienne River and in the faubourgs to the north. Along the valley of the Vienne, where "the landscape becomes a panorama and leaves nothing to be desired . . . [we] were strangely surprised to see the darkness of the valley suddenly illuminated by gigantic torches whose vacillating flames seemed to emerge from the bowels of the earth. The high chimneys of the factories and workshops gave further evidence of the incessant activity, tireless even during the night, of this laborious population, to whom rest seems almost unknown."[1]

The scientific congress of 1859 offered Limoges its first opportunity to welcome a considerable number of distinguished visitors from all parts of France. The city now thought of itself as an appropriate choice for a gathering of men of science. François Alluaud, now an octogenarian, served as honorary president of the congress. He carefully described the techniques of production he had introduced. De Louguemar was among those paying homage to his factory near the river, finding it "an entire world to manage, but the tasks are so well organized that each person employed in its numerous workshops performs all of the phases of production without mishap and without noise." Then de Louguemar joined the group of scientists visiting the new factory of David Haviland, whose name eventually became synonymous with the industry itself. He thought that the Haviland porcelain had additional charm, principally because of its colorful decoration and gold trim. If de Louguemar admired Alluaud's factory, he was awed by that of Haviland, which was far larger and even more efficient.

In 1855 David Haviland, who had come to Limoges in 1842 in search of porcelain to import to the United States, had constructed his factory on the newly laid avenue du Crucifix, which ran from the place Tourny until it intersected with the route de Paris, near where an ancient crucifix had announced the approach to Limoges. Haviland fulfilled his dream of combining the operations of production and decoration. The factory, built to contain two giant kilns and twenty smaller ovens, employed almost one thousand workers by the mid-1860s and became the largest single producer of porcelain in France. Designed by the architect Regnault, it was so imposing that the guidebook *Limoges et le Limousin* listed the Haviland factory as one of the major monuments in the region. Its single compound, closed to the public, included four large workshops for decoration and another four for molding, sculpture, and for the preparation of colors. A warehouse sixty meters long and twelve meters wide included the company offices on the ground floor, a workshop for polishing and dusting, another for burnishing on the second floor, and a packing and shipping office.[2]

Most people who viewed the imposing new structure first noticed the clock over the main door, which distinguished this factory from that of Alluaud or any other in the city. One local guidebook described this "handsome Wagner clock" that regulated the arrivals and departures of the Haviland workers. The main door of such factories became, as described by Michelle Perrot, the nerve center of surveillance of workers.[3] The Alluaud manufacture, it will be recalled, had been "ingeniously calculated to prevent any false moves" by its workers. The Haviland factory had a central vantage point "from which every movement in the factory [could] be observed." The other manufacturers followed Haviland's lead in this and other aspects of production.

The porcelain industry had conquered a major share of the national market. Yet the prosperity of that industry and the city was tied to American demand; by the end of the 1850s about half of the porcelain produced in Limoges went to the United States. Some inroads had been made into England (particularly after the liberalization of tariffs established by the Cobden-Chevalier Treaty of 1860), as well as Spain, Prussia, Italy, Mexico, and even Egypt. The growth of these markets only somewhat reduced the devastating impact of the Civil War on trade with the United States. Several large commercial houses joined Haviland as successful exporters of porcelain, aided by the recognition that accompanied their

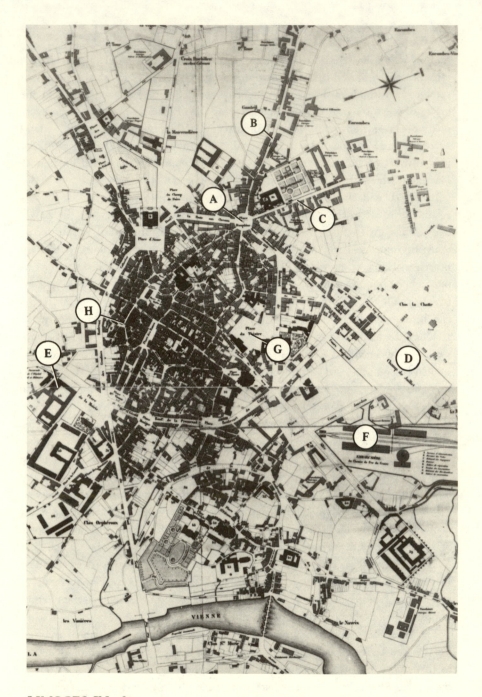

LIMOGES IN 1851

A. place Dauphine (formerly place
   de la Liberté)

B. faubourg Montmailler

C. route de Paris

D. Champ de Juillet

E. Town Hall

F. Railroad Station Construction (proposed)

G. place du Théâtre (formerly place
   Royale)

H. rue de la Boucherie

participation in expositions in Paris and London. According to Corbin, two types of men predominated among the manufacturers: the few descendants of old, wealthy manufacturing or commercial families dating from the end of the previous century; and those who, like Alluaud, were former skilled workers. David Haviland was an exception in that he belonged to neither group. Yet in the future there would be more wealthy outsiders like him.[4]

Technological advances in casting and imprinting helped enlarge the scale of production as Limoges manufacturers adjusted their product to satisfy consumer demand for more decorative pieces. De Louguemar observed and described a new technique by which porcelain could be decorated with decals uniformly turned out by a lithographic press. This procedure was still in its infancy in the late 1860s; although only semiskilled labor was required and more and more women were brought into the industry, the skilled decorators survived because of the demand for painted porcelain. Here again Haviland enhanced the industry's success by inspiring imitation. Before Haviland arrived in the Limousin, the shortage of skilled *artistes en porcelaine* had forced manufacturers to ship their porcelain to Paris for decoration. Only Alluaud owned both a factory for production and a workshop for decoration, and these operated independently. During the Second Empire the porcelain manufacturers began to encourage the training of the local skilled decorators to replace those trained in Paris or Sèvres who had left the region or who had died. Municipally subsidized courses in molding and casting, drawing, and mathematics were begun in the mid-1860s.[5]

But the most important reason for the progress and prosperity of the industry during the Second Empire was the gradual replacement of wood with coal as fuel for the kilns. The arrival of the railway in 1856, which opened up new markets (for example, in England via Bordeaux), reduced the cost of raw materials; this dramatic advance could not have come at a better time, as the cost of wood increased by 40 percent from 1856 to 1862. In 1861 coal fueled sixteen of the forty porcelain ovens in Limoges. Factories beyond the city limits closed their doors; the advantage of the railroad outweighed the slightly lower labor costs in towns like Magnac Bourg and Pierre Buffière.[6]

Thus, despite the economic crises of the late 1830s and the late 1840s, the number of factories, workers, and batches (*fournées*) of porcelain produced had increased dramatically, as Table 3 on the following page demonstrates. The average number of porcelain workers had also increased, reaching 117, a figure far surpassed by Alluaud (who had employed 100 workers in the largest factory in 1828) and Haviland. The separate decoration workshops were considerably smaller, averaging 12.6 workers each, a figure that probably included some home workers; their average number had decreased greatly as the largest factories had begun to do their own decoration. At the same time, the number of women employed in the industry increased dramatically.[7]

The rapid expansion of the porcelain industry dwarfed the textile industry;

TABLE 3

	1828	1837	1861
factories	7	11	27
workers in production	8–900	1, 200 (200 women and children)	3,166 (2,237 men, 688 women, 281 children)
decoration workshops	?	12	65
workers in decoration	?	250–300	819 (552 men, 265 women, 2 children)
journées	?	535	1,664

Sources: Camille Grellier, *L'Industrie de la porcelaine en Limousin* (Paris, 1908), pp. 242–61; and Alain Corbin, *Archaïsme et modernité en Limousin au XIXᵉ siècle, 1845–1880* (Paris, 1975), vol. 1, p. 45.

thirty years earlier the latter had been the largest in the city. Despite the damaging impact of the Cobden-Chevalier Treaty, about 950 workers were employed in sixteen workshops and perhaps another 1,000 worked at home in the early 1860s. Yet the industry was largely restricted to supplying the modest needs of the region, in addition to some sales in Brittany, Anjou, and the Bordelais.[8] The shoe industry, however, had developed steadily, with about forty establishments employing some 1,250 workers and about the same number of manufacturers of sabots paying another 250 workers. Several hundred other workers were employed in the related tanning and leather-dressing industries (while the production of gloves continued to thrive down the Vienne River at St. Junien); the manufacture of weights and measures, hats, and printing employed several hundred workers each, and nearly 2,000 were occupied in the booming building industry, at least during the early years of the Empire.[9]

Swollen by industrial concentration, the population of Limoges increased rapidly during the July Monarchy, and particularly in the Second Empire (see Table 4). In 1864 about 57 percent of the population derived their income primarily from industrial or artisanal work, an increase of 12 percent since 1851.[10] Limoges expanded so rapidly, by French urban standards, that some streets were still without names and many houses lacked numbers, as the Municipal Council noted when it urged the adoption of the blue and white street signs of Paris.

Large-scale industrialization pushed the city to the north and northwest, along the faubourg Montmailler and the route de Paris, as can already be seen from the map of the city drawn in 1851. The place d'Aîne had become more active, giving way to the rue Mauvendière and other increasingly busy streets. The porcelain industry now shaped Limoges. Some factories remained on or near the Vienne: those of Alluaud on the faubourg des Casseaux; Collot, Trotté and Company, on the river; and Tharaud on the place Tourny. But by 1864 most porcelain factories were located on the northern edge of the town; seven on the route

TABLE 4 The Rising Population
of Limoges, 1821–66

Year	Population
1821	21,757
1831	27,070
1841	29,870
1846	38,119
1851	41,630
1856	46,564
1861	51,053
1866	53,022

Source: *Almanach Limousin,* 1862,
1867, 1873.

de Paris and two each on the faubourg Montmailler and its new extension, the faubourg Montjovis. These locations offered the advantage of open space, easy access to the route de Paris and, above all, proximity to the railroad station after 1856. The industrial railroad depot of Montjovis was later constructed on that faubourg.[11]

The shift of the locus of industry to the edge of the city intensified the settlement of workers, particularly porcelain workers, in the faubourgs. In 1848 porcelain workers comprised 23.5 percent of the males; day laborers, most of whom worked in the same industry, accounted for another 20.8 percent on the faubourg Montmailler and the route de Paris. For the faubourg Montmailler, a longer and more developed road at the time, the percentages were 31.1 and 16.8 percent. Thirty-four percent of the 610 adult males identified by the unofficial and incomplete census, taken during the spring of 1848, of males working in the porcelain industry lived on one of these two streets, 12 percent on the route de Paris, and 22 percent on the faubourg Montmailler. Furthermore, many other porcelain workers inhabited streets leading to these two principal arteries, such as the rue Prépapaud. The nearby avenue du Crucifix and new cross streets such as the rue Aigueperse shared this same geographic concentration.[12] By 1864 the proporiton of the total number of porcelain workers listed as heads of households and residing on these two major routes had declined as other streets and quarters developed, but the two faubourgs continued to be most closely identified with the industry. In 1876, 188 of the 190 houses on the route de Paris and 65 of the 80 houses on the faubourg Montmailler included at least one porcelain worker who was a head of household; the route d'Aixe, faubourg d'Arènes, route de Bordeaux and the rue d'Angoulême, all streets leading away from the city, also had many porcelain workers, men, women, and children, living on them. The house at 113 route de Paris was owned by a cabinetmaker whose wife owned a grocery store on the ground floor. The heads of households living there included the following:

a *retoucheuse;* a turner whose wife also was a *retoucheuse;* a *couleur en moules* whose son had the same job; a shoemaker whose son was a porcelain painter; a turner; a widowed day laborer who lived with his three sisters (one of whom was a seamstress and another a burnisher); a widow supported by her son; a *moufletier;* and another porcelain worker. These examples could be multiplied on this street and extended to the other faubourgs. The life of the faubourgs and their predominantly working-class families was inextricably linked with industrial work.[13]

Migration still accounted for virtually all population growth, although in the 1860s births finally began to outnumber deaths in Limoges. More than 80 percent of the migrants came from the Haute-Vienne, particularly the southern part. Almost all of the remainder came from the adjacent departments of the Charente, Creuse, and Corrèze.[14] Most migrants thus shared the culture and patois of the region (the dividing line between French and the patois influenced by old Provençal ran north of Limoges). The faubourgs had a higher percentage of inhabitants born outside the city, as was to be expected; for example, in 1848 about 60 percent of the male porcelain workers living on the route de Paris and the faubourg Montmailler had not been born in Limoges, while the proportion was 46 percent for all males residing on the streets. In the center city more workers had been born in Limoges; for example, thirteen day laborers on the desperately poor rue Rajat, below the cathedral, had been born in Limoges.[15]

During the middle decades of the century the range of migration for porcelain workers became narrower, since skilled workers and decorators could be trained in Limoges. Yet even in 1848 some skilled workers were relatively recent arrivals from other porcelain centers in France (Paris, Nevers, Villedieu in the Indre, and Vierzon). A few were well traveled. In 1848 one turner living on the rue Raffiloux, in the center of the city, was a Belgian brought to France as a child. He grew up and then worked in Vierzon, where his father died, and then moved on to find work first in Paris and then in Limoges. After leaving the Limousin for a time, he returned, perhaps in pursuit of the woman he finally married in Limoges, which became his home.[16]

Not surprisingly, workers of the same town sharing similar work tended to live together. Ten men lived at 22 route de Paris, near several porcelain factories (seven of whom were married, with a combined total of fifteen children). The oldest, a forty-seven-year-old *useur de grains* aptly named Thomas Fourneau, was married and had two children who, like himself, had been born in the city. A skilled turner and a worker identified as a "miller"—almost certainly a worker in the mills that processed kaolin—were also born in Limoges. The only resident not involved in the industry was a shoemaker from St. Yrieix who may have followed a relative, who was a porcelain worker, to the city. The others were born either in nearby Solignac—coming to Limoges when they were, respectively, thirty-seven years of age in 1843, seventeen in 1844, and 23 in 1842—or Villedieu, in the Indre. Twenty-five workers at number 14 jammed into what one would hope was a large building, since it also housed nineteen wives and thirty-six children; a wood merchant with eight children also lived there. The residents included porcelain workers from St. Amand, Villedieu, and Paris. The building at number 24 included two brothers from Solignac, both porcelain workers, who had come to Limoges in 1843, and another from the same town, who arrived in 1840, and presumably found his two friends a place to live in the faubourg.[17]

By the 1860s the notion of a "faubourg" was usually associated with the working class. The *gens du faubourg* were workers, often newcomers to the city. For many bourgeois, faubourgs seemed menacing and forbidding; perhaps they associated them with the traditional uncertainties of the immediate countryside, particularly the wood, where robbers, brigands, and prostitutes were said to lurk. Earlier one of Louis Philippe's ministers had revealed this mistrust when he warned the Citizen King at the beginning of his reign, "Sire, your police prefects are allowing the capital to be blocked by a hundred factories; this will be the cord that one day will strangle us." The bourgeois of Limoges in the heady days of 1848 may have had this in mind. Six of those arrested for participation in the *affaire de Limoges* and many of the members of the radical Société populaire resided on the faubourg Montmailler.[18]

Alain Corbin has stressed the division between the old town and the new quarters, the latter possessing "a more anonymous physiognomy. The population of the old town was attached to the traditions and structures of another time; the recently implanted working-class population was much preoccupied with re-creating the conditions of rustic life on the periphery" of the city.[19] At the far end of the faubourgs, where the houses still lacked identifying numbers, day laborers and weavers mingled with gardeners, sharecroppers, truck farmers, and tenant farmers. Workers in the faubourgs enjoyed easier access to open space than their comrades in the central city. As the faubourg Montmailler and the route de Paris spread outward, the space between them increased. This open area permitted the maintenance of small gardens, particularly by migrants from the countryside, who, it was commonly believed, were more likely to own houses. One of the authors of a local guidebook contrasted the relatively fresh air of the suburbs with the stifling density of the old town, which subjected even the inhabitants of the relatively elegant houses on the boulevards or on the Champ de Juillet quarter to some discomfort.[20] The inhabitants of the old city viewed the faubourgs as a clear indication of the transformation of their city.

The fair of St. Loup at the end of May brought merchants and tradesmen, as well as peasants, from other regions to Limoges. This, the largest fair in the Limousin, seemed to have changed little over the centuries, which reassured those citizens already lamenting the transformation of their traditional city. The narrow streets of the city, the few public places of any size, and the boulevards that traced the shape of the old walls of the original two "cities" were packed with people and animals. The loud stomping of dancing sabots emanated from the place d'Aîne, under the watchful eyes of *le grand* Tistout, the reowned caller from nearby Panazol, who refused to allow the polka to be played because he highly disapproved of what he scornfully called "Parisian dances." Livestock encumbered the adjacent *champ de foire,* where pigs competed for space with scrap iron merchants and an assortment of charlatans.[21]

Standing on his calèche in front of the Palais de Justice, a man hawked a magic "African balm." Despite "the disdain of all of the doctors in their black suits who glance at me in passing," he was willing to consecrate "the immense knowledge I acquired during my studies and my long trips . . . this incontestable talent . . . to the poor and to the workers, because I am their friend . . . Buy, buy my elixir!" Entire villages arrived together to witness the thousand and one marvels visible at the place Royale, where cafés were full of animated customers, shouting, laughing, arguing, making deals, talking politics, and doubting at least some of what they had seen. For fifty centimes a sorcerer would let you see "a beloved object" in his mirror. Waffle sellers pushed their way through crowds lined up to see "exotic" wrestlers, the human cannon, and *le grand esquelette du Nord,* who had fought white bears in the snow of Sénégal and lived to tell the story in Limoges. The famous Marseillais grappled with a Sardinian strong man; gawkers could discover that the woman with eight fingers on her left hand and no right toes was nonetheless gracious and pretty; they could gape at a huge tattooed black man or be awed by the skills of a fellow who claimed to be the number one juggler of His Majesty, the emperor of Japan. Wild animals that could be viewed from a safe distance included skinny lions, two enraged hyenas, a bear who seemed to have an awful cold, and a couple of vigorous monkeys, "too vigorous, perhaps, frolicking in a manner to prevent a mother from taking her daughter into the large booth." More genteel public animal behavior could be found at the circus of Monsieur Aurillon, where a small but determined pony named Coco had been taught to play dead, leap to her feet, and jump through a hoop.[22]

Despite the annual reassurance of St. Loup, those who lived in the 1860s were convinced that they were witnessing the passing of many traditional sights and sounds of their city. The *Almanach Limousin,* acutely aware of these changes, attributed them to the growth of Limoges and its industries, the decline of the role of the Church in the life of the city, and the coming of the railroad.

The first train reached Limoges on June 30, 1856, when the city's station was inaugurated by a minor government official (another snub, since the emperor had been expected). The small, square, squat building reminded one wag of a coach stuck in the mud, confronting travelers and those awaiting passengers with an awkwardly steep entrance. Four trains a day arrived from Paris and as many departed for the "city of light." De Louguemar, the Poiters scientist whose trip to Limoges had assumed some of the dimensions of an epic journey, could have attested to some of the problems of early rail travel. The trip to the capital could take up to twelve hours in the winter. *Le Courrier de Limoges* regularly reported tardy arrivals, frequent mishaps, and derailments. The *Almanach Limousin* related weak jokes about travel to and from the capital. The train schedule during the Second Empire must have been a nightmare to interpret for travelers, almost all of whom were necessarily inexperienced with respect to such things. Because of longitudinal differences, each town was minutes ahead or behind other French cities in time. Thus, anyone traveling north had to be aware that Limoges was four minutes behind Paris (centuries, Parisians would insist), whereas Brest was twenty-seven minutes behind the capital and forty-nine behind that of Strasbourg.[23]

The train's influence could not be overlooked. The arrival of coal by rail transformed the porcelain industry. Some of the ambulatory trades began to disappear, but the Auvergnat umbrella sellers, peddlers from St. Gaudens, and chimney sweeps from St. Flour ("A ramouna lo cha, haut à bas!") still appeared regularly. Bordeaux wine merchants, advertising the delivery of cases of wine to the Limoges station, cut into some of the brisk trade of local wholesale merchants. The aged Spanish match seller now began his daily trek through Limoges at the railroad station, where he picked up his product. Mail to Paris, which took twelve days in 1760, now took but one night. Advertisements for rented villas in Arcachon began to appear in the local paper. A company based in Paris offered help for students wanting to pass the *bac* exam; a doctor Clertan promised wonders to those who purchased his "ether pearls," which could easily be delivered by rail. The train even helped speed up the changeover of roofs of the city, as slate from Angers gradually replaced curved tile. Train travel could expand the horizons of even the most urbane *limougeauds*. *Trains de plaisir* left to discover the roman bridge of Ahun, in the Creuse, or to visit Paris, which most of those locals who complained about the capital had undoubtedly never seen.[24] A few years earlier there were only between 45 and 50 travelers reaching Limoges each day; now the Hôtel Boule d'Or expanded to 80 rooms and 120 beds. Périgueux seemed as close to Limoges as St. Léonard or Pierre Buffière. Yet train travel was beyond the means of the laboring poor, costing almost 25 francs for third-class travel to and from the capital (45 francs in first class and 34 in second). Not everyone was happy about this new relative proximity to the capital. The *Almanach* complained that now, more than ever, "we are subject to the despotism of the fashionable." Stores such as the Maison de la belle jardinière tried to outdo each other with large, gaudy, enticing signs, announcing the latest novelty from Paris. Echoing the bitter complaints of J. J. Juge over forty years earlier, the royalist printer and author Henri Ducourtieux complained of the further erosion "of the solid virtues that characterized our fathers." The result was, he claimed, that children were now pampered like "exotic plants," while the "most noble aspirations of our nature are constantly under attack from the material preoccupations that absorb us without truce or mercy."[25]

In November 1858 the cafés of the place Royale and the place Dauphine seemed empty. "The billiards were still, the playing cards and dominos were sadly arranged on the shelves of the counters." Café owners could blame no prefectoral decree or natural disaster. The first café concert had opened its doors in Limoges, an event that to some people loomed almost as large as the arrival of the first train two years earlier. So many people thronged to the place Fitz-James to salute the mediocre entertainers that the beaming entrepreneur moved his tables and chairs outside. The *Almanach Limousin* poked fun at the "incense burned at the feet of these demigoddesses." All of Limoges, including the gamins who loitered about the public places, sang the frivolous song of the café concert:

> *Folichons et folichonnettes,*
> *Sautons et folichonnons,*
> *Gué, gué, gué, violons et musettes,*
> *En avant les folichons.*

Inspired by this success, another entrepreneur began an even larger rival establishment at the Champ de Juillet in a building that had served as a ballroom and banquet hall for the elite of the July Monarchy and, more recently, had housed a horticulture exhibition. But within several years the initial appeal of the cafés concerts had waned. Both entrepreneurs were ruined, left with little more than the memory of the crowds of the first weeks. Not only had the performances been found wanting aesthetically, but the cafés concerts had become notorious lairs for prostitutes. Once again Limoges seemed to have aped the modes and fashions of the capital with limited success; the less elegant cafés easily recaptured their clients.[26]

Of Limoges's annual religious festivals only Mardi Gras remained relatively unaltered, although its religious significance had been greatly watered down, if not washed away, by the great quantity of drink consumed. Most workshops and factories closed on the first day of Lent following this "forty-eight hours of madness," not for reasons of piety but to provide a necessary day of recovery. Before 1830 mannequins were hung from lampposts during Carnival and then ceremoniously burned or drowned, but this traditional means of reinforcing popular values had disappeared. Likewise the charivari had vanished during the July Monarchy, after having been briefly adopted as a form of political protest by the republicans. The village festivals (*frairies*) of the immediate vicinity had also changed: The festival of spring on Passion Sunday in March in the hamlet of St. Lazare, once the "festival of the cuckolds," now only served as an occasion for *limougeauds* to breathe the fresh air of the nearby countryside, while "paying tribute" to the young males of the commune. Its religious significance was forgotten. Only a few of the corporate festivals in Limoges's traditional trades continued to be celebrated, in addition to those of the washerwomen and the butchers. The procession of the gardeners on the outskirts in honor of St. Fiacre brought them into town, although they no longer brought baskets of their finest fruit and vegetables to the clergy.[27]

The confraternities of penitents were moribund by 1864. The bourgeoisie gradually lost interest in these colorful vestiges of old Limoges. Louis Guibert, sad chronicler of this decline, blamed "the recent revolutions and the flood of ideas that then took hold in the bourgeoisie and the working class. . . ." Unlike other cities in France, no return to poetic and artistic Romanticism aided their revival. The black penitents, though still retaining the allegiance of the wealthiest bourgeois families of Limoges, had only forty members. Despite the efforts of the Ardant family, the banker Firmin Tarneaud, and Armand Noualhier, former deputy and mayor of the city, only eighteen penitents remained in 1869, and but nine were left five years later. They prayed together for the last time in 1871, the last sign of life of the penitents in the nineteenth century.[28]

The white penitents, with only twenty members in 1848, revived after the coup d'état through the efforts of the banker Faucher. But of seventy-six nominal members in the early years of the Empire, only twenty paid their fees. When their beleaguered treasurer passed away, only five or six showed up to bury him. The survivors had to enroll a number of workers as associate members on the occasion of the funeral, and these poor surrogates carried the treasurer to his grave. The purple penitents, including Alluaud and Guibert, had previously accompanied a condemned man to the scaffold in 1854. They had recruited the last postulant in April 1848, a small ceremony lost in the revolutionary violence of that month. In 1863 there were only three members, hardly enough for a meeting, to say nothing of a procession. The register of blue penitents ended in May 1851, and records of their income and expenses ceased ten years later; the gray penitents last appeared in 1868 for a funeral. The *feuille-morte* penitents outlasted the others because most of their members were butchers; they held exercises until 1865 and probably afterward.[29]

The penitents last marched together during the Ostensions of 1862. Mothers brought their sick children to the alter on Quasimodo Sunday during the final mass said by the archbishop of Toulouse, hoping for a cure. But as the archbishop looked over the assembled faithful, he saw only a smattering of penitents and fewer members of the confraternities. Only those of St. Aurélien and St. Martial remained active.[30] Even by then some of the processional crosses, robes, books, and trappings of the penitents occupied a place in the municipal museum. Some of their former members were still alive to see those mementos of the old city, some of which were subsequently exhibited for the curious on the Champs-Elysées in Paris.[31]

The bells of the Angelus were still heard in the early morning hours; during the Restoration these bells had summoned virtually the entire town to prayer. Now they served only to remind the workers to hurry to their workshops. When he died, no one replaced the old ragpicker who had recited the Angelus on the streets as he went about his work. The editors of the *Almanach Limousin,* fondly recalling the days when religion was honored, now admitted that

> the porcelain ovens have little by little replaced the fallen steeples. Is not the flame that shoots up, roaring from their tormented bowels, the striking image of the feverish but fertile activity that began with the great movement of '89?[32]

Changing attitudes toward death also reflected the increased secularization, apparently inseparable from the emergence of an industrial town. Gone was the inscription of the Chapel of Death at the corner of the ancient cemetery of St. Pierre-de-Queyroix: "Passant par où tu passes, j'ai passé, tu passeras, comme toi vivant j'ai été, comme moi mort tu seras." Church bells were no longer slowly rung to commemorate the dead. The sacristan no longer carried sad news to every quarter: "Messieurs, qui êtes de la confrérie des Agonisants, priez pour l'âme de . . . qui est à l'agonie de la mort." The Louyat cemetery was far from the city and death and mourning was a more private affair, in which the role of organized religion had been considerably reduced. Several monks brought to Limoges during the July Monarchy to work in the cemetery appeared incredibly out of place, a remnant of another age in their traditional garb.[33]

The Church did retain some of its influence in Limoges through teaching and charitable activities. Nine congregations of sisters resided in the city, including those who worked at the prison, the hospital, or operated schools for poor children. Various lay religious organizations drawn from the upper classes supplemented their efforts for the poor, providing food and teaching the catechism, while urging those "living in sin" to legitimize their union through the sacrament of marriage.[34] But contemporary observers and subsequent historians have agreed that the practice of organized religion had declined in the Limousin. De-Christianization, common in the Massif central and other regions during the century, has been measured in terms of the increase in time between the birth of a child and baptism, as well as in the decline in the number of religious vocations. It is confirmed by an analysis of episcopal proclamations and other contemporary opinion. Most migrants to Limoges were already de-Christianized, presuming they had ever been truly "Christianized," given the well-established superstition of the rural Limousin. Among contributing factors were what Corbin called "the rigidity of mental structures" in the backward region, the relatively low quality and aged character of the clergy (particularly when compared to the previous century), the revived influence of the Masons, and the experience of the revolutions of 1830 and 1848, which reflected a decline in religious adherence among a considerable proportion of the bourgeosie and among even more of the lower classes. The workers of the faubourgs lacked the bases of religious tradition and collective memory—reinforced by the ceremonies, celebrations, processions, or voluntary associations—of the nearby central city. The northern faubourgs did not even have a parish; those who went to church had to walk to St. Michel. The city's approximately two hundred religious statues were virtually all in the old town. The chapel of Montjovis, once far in the countryside, had long since disappeared, buried beneath the expanding faubourg of the same name.[35]

If the Second Empire and the Church were at peace, the assault on the role of organized religion in public life continued in a more private sphere. A minor event in 1862 was prophetic. On the night of October 14 someone cut off the right hand of the statue of St. Martial, which adorned the fountain of Aigoulène. Traditionally it had been worse to curse St. Martial than Jesus Christ in Limoges. When the mutilation of the statue was discovered, the butchers demanded that if the culprit were caught, he should have his right hand cut off, which reflected the justice of the Middle Ages. The rebuilt statue was soon sporting a new hand.[36]

If the Poitiers scientist de Louguemar had been impressed with what he saw in Limoges, most visitors were not. A Parisian journalist named Assolant who visited a small exposition in 1860 was given a tour of the city. When asked his opinion of what he had seen, he haughtily replied, "Limoges is a sewer!" The wound was widened when the same cruel description appeared in a newspaper in the capital.[37] Then train made the city more accessible, and thus more vulnerable, to the condescending scrutiny of outsiders. Two years later a small illustrated guide to the city of Limoges went on sale for fifteen centimes in the new railroad station. M. Napoléon Chaix's *Guide-Indicateur illustré* flattered *limougeauds* by proclaiming that Limoges was "an important town that one must visit with care." But his brochure was not worth even its modest price because of numerous errors that suggested that the author had never actually taken the time to come to Limoges. Among other sites, Chaix urged tourists to visit the Church of St. Martin [*sic*] and the promenade de Fourny [*sic*]; to look for the Church of St. Martial, and particularly its clock of *haute antiquité* (both had disappeared during the French Revolution); and to browse in Limoges's three libraries (there was but one).[38] Napoléon Chaix's commercial effort did not enhance Limoges's reputation despite its burgeoning industry. Urban progress had not kept pace with the rapid march of economic and social change. The traditional quarters of Limoges seemed to have hardly changed at all.

"What strikes a visitor to Limoges," admitted the *Almanach Limousin,*

is no longer the ridiculous statue posed in the middle of the Aigoulène fountain . . . or the view of our unfinished cathedral, which can leave one only partially satisfied . . . or the Hôtel de Ville offering the singular anomaly of a bourgeois house crowned by a bell tower . . . [It is] arriving in the butchers' quarter, proceeding through it slowly, stopping in astonishment before the butchers' stalls, and encountering characters of a countenance that one has never encountered before, and that one will find in no other place.[39]

Limoges's leading citizens may have tried to steer visitors toward the scenic Vienne and the bishop's fine gardens, or to the Haviland factory. One man who came upon the butchers' quarters never forgot the experience:

> The rue Torte (as it was called centuries before because of its shape) is, without any contradiction, the most disgusting street in France . . . twisting, dirty, fetid, stinking, bones and smoking animal guts, scraps of flesh . . . the houses of the street are black; crossed on the facade by pieces of wood placed diagonally to form an "X," unequal in height, smoky inside, red with blood from the stalls and from the axes. Only if Hercules reappeared could the place be cleaned up . . . Nonetheless, it is in these unhealthy hovels . . . that the butcher of Limoges, rich and avaricious, is born, marries, raises his children, falls ill, and dies.[40]

The religious lamps of the rue de la Boucherie still burned with religious fervor. In 1862 the ancient corporation took its long-accustomed place at the head of the processions of the Ostensions, its members dressed as princes, carrying their beautiful processional crosses, flags, and reliquaries. Those who insulted Limoges's favorite saints or the butchers themselves ran grave risks.

The butchers defended their traditional right to escort "princes of blood" into the city. Although they insisted that the Bourbons were France's legitimate monarchs, in 1845 they proclaimed their right to accompany the Duc de Nemours, Louis Philippe's son, royalty being royalty. To do so they had to outrace the less sturdy sons of commerce to the outskirts of Limoges, returning with the Duc de Nemours in tow. In 1858, when the Bonapartist Prince Jérôme arrived for Limoges's first exposition, the butchers debated as to whether such a prince could really be considered royalty, but they turned up (uninvited) at a reception for him.[41]

The butchers were familiar sights in the markets of the region. A contemporary offered the following portrait of one of their number:

> Look at him there, in the middle of the market, with his rough appearance and swollen veins, his neglected beard, his hair long and tangled, his chest large and bare. Watch him brusquely clasp the calloused hand of one of our peasants and discuss, in a loud voice, the sale of a cow or calf . . . Listen to his voice, rude and rasping, speaking a heavy patois which, nonetheless, is not without some charm.[42]

Indeed, the butchers were hard to miss, wearing full-length coats over harlequin clothes, short pants of blue velvet or a dull, greasy green, hats blackened by smoke and the years, gray wool stockings, old shirts, and well-worn sabots. Their notoriously bad-tempered wives sometimes accompanied them; one seemed—at least in the eyes of a hostile observer—to "share all of the dirtiness of her husband . . . her *coiffe* is dirty, her clothes of gray serge, a dirty apron of cloth . . . the butchers' wives habitually do their laundry in the muddy stream that runs through the street and also carries away the garbage." Their sons assisted their father with the gruesome tasks of the slaughterhouse. The butcher's son was described as "the miniature of his father. He does not go to school, cannot read or write, is at heart an idler," practicing his future trade by "cutting off the tails of dogs [and] mutilating cats . . ." To outsiders the butchers exhibited distinct physical characteristics, undoubtedly reinforced, over the decades, by intermarriage within the five families. Most seemed to have small heads, glaucous eyes, prominent cheekbones ("as with all irascible people," proclaimed the *Almanach Limousin*), Roman noses ("indicating, at the same time, both virile energy and guile"), chestnut-colored hair, and rather large mouths. Their complexions reflected an "intensity of coloring" that made them appear somewhat distinguished, due, it was though:, to "une nourriture où domine le régime animal."[43]

An incident in August 1855 at the Laurière cattle market, thirty kilometers north of Limoges, demonstrated the continued cohesiveness of the corporation. One butcher offered an extremely low price for some cattle and the others followed suit, offering no more than the original derisory offer. A policeman took two of the butchers aside to discuss the consequences of such "horrible conduct," but he, in turn, was "mistreated" by them. The butchers then boycotted the Laurière market until the desperate mayor of that unhappy bourg knelt to entreat the patriarchs of the butcher clans.[44]

Only very minimal changes had occurred on the rue de la Boucherie by 1864, which still emitted a stench detectable at a distance of one kilometer. Although the butchers had resisted the advent of public latrines, at least raw sewage no longer ran down the center of the street, which was now regularly washed by the water from the nearby fountain of Aigoulène. Gaslight had replaced street lanterns in 1844. The butchers' dogs "no longer waged war against the calves of slow-moving passersby," their fearful reputation having ebbed slightly since that night in 1838 when war almost broke out between the butchers and the soldiers of the garrison after the former unleashed their dogs on a night guard.[45] But butchers' stalls still obstructed circulation. Plans for aligning the street had been drawn up after the Revolution of 1830, but they were never carried out, although the adjacent rue Vigne-de-fer was widened. The butchers did not seem to fear fire on their crowded street, perhaps because they attributed their good fortune at the time of the catastrophic blaze of 1790 to the fact that they had hauled out the relics of St. Martial.

Delivering the mail to the rue de la Boucherie remained difficult for anyone who did not know the quarter and its occupants very well. In 1864 only five Limoges butchers were not blood relations of the five families, and these may have been related by marriage: Chastenet on the rue des Combes; Bayout on the avenue du Cité; Lamontre on the rue Haut Cité; Glangeaud *dit* le Diableau; and the widow Monastier on the faubourg Montmailler. Twenty-three were Cibots, fifteen Malinvauds, thirteen Pourets, twelve Parots, three Plainemaisons (led by their patriarch, Plainemaison *dit* Louis XVIII), and two Juges. One did not need a census list to verify what the nose quickly discovered: Sixty of the sixty-four heads of household on the street were butchers. These households occupied fifty-five houses, an exceptionally low figure for any nineteenth-century street in France; on the average, there were more than three households per building in Limoges. Only one barber, a joiner, and two grocers were outsiders. Eight families of butchers also lived on nearby streets, such as the rue Bas Lansecot and the place de la Mothe. Each butcher from the families had been born in Limoges's most famous neighborhood.[46]

The Viraclaud quarter, particularly the rue Froment, had only reinforced its reputation as the center of prostitution in Limoges; one angry neighbor alleged that "there is not a single hour, day or night, when there are not orgies and brawls; what goes on there horrifies the human species and generates very bad principles in our youth." The introduction of gas lighting made vice even more visible. Many of the twenty-two *maisons de tolérance* (eight more than in 1828) were found in the quarter, sixteen on the rue Viraclaud alone. Prostitution increased with the growth in population of the city, which now included as many as fifteen thousand people inscribed on the rolls of the Comité de bienfaisance during the Second Empire. Statistics compiled for 1879 may approximate the situation in 1864, although they undoubtedly err on the side of caution: There were seventy-four registered prostitutes in the brothels, with another eighty-nine women authorized to entertain clients at home. The number of unauthorized prostitutes was believed to be about two hundred. There was action elsewhere, too, at the notorious Chemin de Beaubreuil, the "amorous" woods near the estate of Martin de la Bastide, and even at a windmill in the adjacent commune of Condat, where "passersby and children behold the most scandalous things." Prostitutes solicited revelers at dances, tempted workers at the new railroad station, bargained with soldiers from the garrison, one third of whom were treated for venereal disease in 1858. "Clandestine" prostitution troubled the municipal and departmental administrations but compromised public order less than the round-the-clock activity in the Viraclaud quarter, where nightly commotion, drunken fights, and public indiscretions bore witness to the persistence of ills in a neighborhood seemingly unaffected by a century of progress.[47]

In the Abbessaille quarter, located on the hill beneath the cathedral, one found a cluster of run-down houses seemingly propped up against the hill above the river only by habit, a motley mix of ramshackle constructions sharing an uncommon degree of filth. Those who gaped at the *cabanes* of the Naveix fishermen at the bottom of the hill were greeted with stares as cold as the Vienne. The Navetau was "King of the Vienne," passing along to his son the skills of negotiating the shallow but treacherous river in flatbottomed boats while controlling the floating wood with lances. These *flotteurs de bois* mostly lived between the thirteenth-century bridges of St. Martial and St. Etienne. The wood merchants dominated their corporation. The *ponticauds* stood at the bottom of this modest hierarchy because they did not work in the water.

Some of the women in this old quarter were the same washerwomen encountered earlier, hauling laundry slowly up the hill from the river by balancing formidable stacks on their powerful red arms and atop their heads. Their traditional costumes consisted of a unique white *coiffe,* large earrings that made them look like gypsies, and a black jumper with two huge pockets. Like the men of the river, they passed on the secrets of their trade to their offspring. They had retained their patois, speaking proper French as little as possible, as well as their religious fervor, festivals, and statues.

This quarter had evidenced some signs of change—more than the rue de la Boucherie or Viraclaud. The quay being constructed along the Vienne had reached the first houses of the Abbessaille. A new steam-cleaning establishment at Trou-du-Loup, at the edge of the city, had taken away some of the laundresses' business. Considerably less wood arrived at the port of Naveix; the substitution of coal for wood as fuel for the porcelain industry threatened the livelihood of the *flotteurs de bois.* The *flotteur* could now be found—arms firmly crossed, smoking his ever-present pipe—with in his *chantier* located on the other side of the river, too proud to seek temporary work as a common day laborer.[48]

The Parisian journalist's rude assertion that Limoges was a sewer incited a vigorous debate. Most people believed that the city had reached an important turning point in its long history. As delighted and intrigued as many civic leaders were with the impact of large-scale industrialization on Limoges, "where the increased scale of everything occurs with a speed that is truly prodigious," they were also deeply concerned with the lack of urban progress. The expansion of the city had done little to alleviate the overcrowding in the central city, whose densely populated, chaotic, and dirty quarters "continued to leave visitors with a sad impression." The discouragement was such that the *Almanach Limousin* asked rhetorically if it might not be wiser to abandon the old town and move all of Limoges in the direction of the faubourgs to the plateau above the city. The memory of an outbreak of cholera in 1854 added to the sense of urgency.[49]

The Second Empire was the era of the rebuilding of Paris and significant public works projects in other cities, notably Lyon and Marseille.[50] Those who visited Paris felt further shame at the squalid quarters of Verdurier, Rasja, Masgoulet, Viraclaud and, above all, the rue de la Boucherie. With the Second Empire urban planning passed from the utopian critics of the nineteenth-century city, such as Fourier and Cabet, to the centralized and authoritarian French state. For better or worse, the result reflected what Pierre Lavedan has called the impulse of *l'urbanisme démolisseur.*[51] Since Limoges was not intimately associated with the national grandeur and prestige of France, the government took little active interest in improving the city. The Municipal Council enjoyed increased government funding, but most of the impetus came from the emerging middle class's sense of pride and independence *from* central authority, continuing the municipal revolution of 1830.

The municipal government of the July Monarchy had not been inactive. The rue Aigueperse now ran east from the route de Paris, and the rue de l'Amphithéâtre linked the *champ de foire* to the place des Carmes; the rue Verdurier cut through the dilapidated quarter of the same name, which finally received some sunlight when several houses on the boulevard des Pyrénées were torn down. The city replaced the battered pavement of other streets and added sidewalks to a number of major thoroughfares. The sections of wall adjoining the old port Tourny were removed, thereby expediting traffic. At the same time, the *salle de spectacle,* which reflected little improvement over its shabby predecessor, was completed in 1840. Gas lighting, introduced in the 1840s, illuminated many streets; 359 lampposts, placed approximately 80 to 100 meters apart, replaced the dim street lamps that had survived since the old lanterns of the ancien régime disappeared in 1776.

Without a master plan for an urban transformation of Limoges, and lacking resources for such an undertaking, the Second Empire public works projects in Limoges proceeded in a hit-or-miss fashion. But by the early 1860s enough progress was apparent that the *Almanach* devoted several articles to these changes and published summaries of the relevant Municipal Council deliberations for readers seeking to confirm the *Almanach's* contention, expressed in 1862, that "recently our town has changed its appearance with kaleidoscopic speed."[52] By the mid-1860s Napoléon Chaix's insulting and inaccurate guide to Limoges was no longer the only one available, for it was replaced with the serious and reliable *Limoges et le Limousin: Guide pour l'étranger.* This small book, published by the Ardant family, proudly associated Limoges's urban revival with the expansion of local commerce and industry. Observing that "questions of public works increasingly impassion city dwellers," the guide sought to reassure potential visitors to Limoges, who might have read the most unfavorable commentaries published after the 1858 exposition:

> Fifty years ago Limoges did not have a single healthy quarter. Its narrow, winding, poorly designed [*mal orientées*], badly paved streets, flanked by tall wooden houses of fragile appearance, only rarely saw several rays of sunlight . . . Happily our efforts, battling against these old customs, have considerably improved these foul alleyways [*ruelles*].[53]

The first decade of the Empire witnessed more paving, the construction of a sewer, the building of a covered market (the marché Dupuytren on the place de la Mothe), and the opening of the boulevard Fleurus (1854–56), which connected the place Tourny to the place Boucherie and the avenue du Crucifix. The new quarters near the railroad station were spared the pell-mell crowding characteristic of even the wealthier bourgeois quarters in the center. The boulevard Fleurus, for example, now "offer[ed] all the comfort required today in the home [*le home*] of the most modest bourgeois." New houses on the boulevard Ste. Catherine stood out like veritable chalets in Limoges.[54]

In 1861 Othon Péconnet, who succeeded the ineffectual Joseph Noualhier, unveiled a more systematic series of projects. During the next few years some streets—including the faubourg d'Arènes and the nearby rue de la Mauvendière, to the northwest—were widened by eliminating a number of houses that impeded traffic. Pedestrians could now plan their itineraries with an increasing number of sidewalks in mind. The rue Ste. Valerie was joined to the rue Turgot, permitting direct access from the *champ de foire* and the place d'Aîne to the Champ de Juillet. Both the squares adjacent to the cathedral and the place St. Pierre were further widened, while the place Royale was increased in size when an awkwardly located house (the "maison des suisses") was demolished. At the same time, quays along the Vienne were completed, the rue Viraclaud was widened, and the rue Turgot was lengthened. New water closets for men and women at the 1860 carnival caused as much discussion as the human cannon.[55]

Tragically, the largest undertaking of the Empire followed in the wake of a catastrophic fire in 1864, by far the most serious of the more than 600 fires since 1793 (and 4,000 chimney fires). A series of strikes had ended that August. The police commissioner hoped that his city would henceforth be spared such "unfortunate preoccupations" and would joyously celebrate the feast day of the emperor on August 15. In a region where it can rain 125 days a year, the summer drought of that year was surprising, reaching such proportions that a novena was held in the butchers' chapel to implore God to bring rain. He sent fire instead. Virtually the entire population watched a fireworks display at the Champ de Juillet as—miraculously, it seemed—a few drops of rain fell on the crowd. In the Arènes quarter, one of the most densely settled in the city, the wife of a hatmaker, hurrying to the festival, carelessly put out the light in their apartment at 7 rue des Arènes. The bit of candle she tossed behind her began to smolder. The fire quickly spread, since the firefighters and volunteers were hampered by insufficient water. Calls for assistance went out by telegraph to Châteauroux and Périgueux.[56]

The fire raged through the night. The butchers carried out some of their precious relics in the hope that they would be spared. No one was killed, principally because the neighborhood was empty when the fire started. A total of 109 houses in the Arènes quarter, bounded by the boulevard Ste. Catherine and the place d'Aîne, were completely destroyed. Many families were not insured and, in any case, insurance companies did not have the capital reserves to meet the claims of those who were. About 2,000 people were ruined. A national campaign to provide assistance for the dispossessed brought in over 650,000 francs, and the quarter was rebuilt within a few years. Three parallel streets now led to the place d'Aîne, improving communication and also contributing to the growth of the faubourgs by forcing some families to abandon the quarter. Thereafter all houses built in central Limoges had to have stone facades.

The 1864 fire demonstrated that much more needed to be done to make Limoges a cleaner and safer city. There remained virtually no direct route through the center of the city; a trip from the place Dauphine to the Hôtel de Ville subjected one to a veritable labyrinth of winding streets. The quarters of Viraclaud, Verdurier, Abbessaille, and that of the rue de la Boucherie remained insalubrious eyesores. Despite the many ponds and streams in the vicinity, the water supply was woefully inadequate.[57] Recurring cases of diphtheria, typhus, cholera, and various less pernicious diseases were believed to be the result of high humidity levels in the relatively low-lying and cramped quarters. Limoges's municipal revival also engendered what seemed to be a modest intellectual renaissance in a city hardly known for the life of the mind, this despite its sixteen printers and eighteen bookshops. The level of education remained pitifully low. The literacy rate had not improved since the Restoration: about 55 percent for men in 1825–26 and 56 percent early in the Second Empire, with the rate for women about 7 percent lower. Of 1,500 workers inscribed on the list of *livrets* in 1856–57, only 520, or 34.6 percent could read. Three quarters of all weavers were illiterate. Enrollment in Limoges's primary schools had risen very slowly. In the early 1860s about 1,200 children attended four primary schools operated by the Brothers of Christian Doctrine, and there were another 306 lay students. Limoges's population was swollen by largely uneducated migrants from the department.[58]

The number of students in secondary schools also lagged far behind the national average. In 1864 there were 409 students in the imperial *lycée,* most of them coming from middle-class families. A number of special courses prepared other young men for careers in commerce, although a few went on to law or medicine. A small *collège* offered some chance for advancement for students of modest means. In addition, there were ten private *écoles libres* with over 500 students. Truly exceptional students went on to the universities at Poitiers or Bordeaux; only once in a while did a student promise make it into the Ecole Saint-Cyr or to one of the *grandes écoles* in Paris. The cultural impoverishment of Limoges, noted by academic inspectors, journalists, and the *Almanach Limousin,* embarrassed the local citizenry. Aimé Mallevergne, who had won first prize in his school days before leading the opposition to the Restoration prior to the Revolution of 1830, presided over an association of alumni from the *lycée* that sought to encourage local education. There was much work to be done.[59]

Limoges seemed an unlikely place for two literary papers to begin, and few people were surprised when *L'Essor* and *Le Figaro Neveu* both failed after a couple of issues. But they represented a start. The *Almanach Limousin* began to summarize and even review local cultural events, as well as the few books published by local savants. It voiced concern over the unfailing mediocrity of the theater, which had never prospered—even after the *salle de spectacle,* which could seat twelve hundred patrons, was constructed in 1840. After the Revolution of 1848, the workers filled the theater in a wave of exhilaration evident that spring; the local troupe petitioned the government for funds so that the theater might "moralize" the workers. But by the end of the republic some of those performances the workers might have flocked to see, such as "Charlotte Corday," "Le Pacte de famine," and "Louis XVI," had been censored because of their political implications. Now, in 1864, the local theater seemed "in full decline." Only opera and comic opera retained a modicum of interest. The high cost of staging performances and the lack of sophistication of the general public (of course) were blamed for mediocre productions. One went to the dark and humid theater only "to kill time, if at all."[60]

Nor was Limoges identified with brilliant music—indeed, one musician complained that he later faced discrimination merely for being from Limoges. The Société philharmonique had developed into little more than a large salon, a "mutual admiration society," in the opinion of the lordly *Almanach Limousin*. Yet here there was progress. Three choral societies attested to the popularity of music, if not necessarily its quality; the Union chorale and the Enfants de Limoges were the local favorites in the competition held in July 1864 in Limoges. Large and enthusiastic crowds—forty thousand according to one estimate—attended the competition and expressed their delight with "shouts, wild dances, a veritable *furia.*"[61]

The first significant steps to enhance Limoges's reputation as a center of industry stemmed from the activities of local businessmen, particularly industrialists, serving in the Chamber of Commerce. François Alluaud presided over the Société d'agriculture, sciences et arts de Limoges, founded in 1844, which published an annual bulletin and sponsored the scientific congress of 1859. The society encouraged the first regional exposition of local products in 1858, when Prince Jérôme visited Alluaud's factory, an event that led Audiganne, the observer of industry and work in France, to assert that the manufacturing elite of Limoges were improving the image of their city. Such élan could only help the center region. He noted that the efforts of Prefect de Coëtlogon, the financial concurrence of the Municipal Council, the assistance of the Chamber of Commerce, and the work of a planning committee had overcome serious doubts about the chances for success of the 1858 exposition. A small medical and pharmaceutical association attested to the growing interest in science in the city. The Société des amis des arts, founded the same year as the scientific congress, sponsored an exhibition in 1862, aided by prefectorial and municipal subventions. Among the canvases exhibited was Corot's early *La Bohémienne*, painted in the 1850s. The *Almanach Limousin* applauded the efforts of industrial Limoges "to escape the dry and cold spirit of Commerce." Some sixty thousand francs' worth of paintings were sold, including seventy-nine canvases to local citizens; these joined some of the Aubusson tapestries now seen on the walls of the fancier houses along the boulevards. The local elite had demonstrated that "beyond the talent of earning money, they have the capability to spend it well." The association claimed that in Paris, where, of course, it mattered, the Limoges effort was considered the very best in the provinces.[62]

Amid such a revival, some citizens lamented the fact that their city did not have a public monument, with the exception of religious statuary. They beamed as a statue of Marshal Jourdan was unveiled, on the site that bore his name, on September 30, 1860, adjacent to the old place Tourny. Their delight was tempered only by complaints that the emperor had not come, once again sending an obscure marshall; that the music for the ceremony had been poorly chosen and badly played; and that one of Jourdan's legs seemed considerably shorter than the other.[63]

Finally, after long years of planning by Adrien Dubouché, Limoges's ceramic museum opened its doors in 1864 with a derisory budget. Its debut was inauspicious, marred by murmurs that the displays were chaotically organized. Worse, there were allegations that the Sèvres porcelain was given top billing. But with gifts from successful manufacturers (Alluaud, Pouyat, Ardant, and Jouhannaud) the museum expanded its collection from eight hundred objects in 1866 to over four thousand six years later. Now the national porcelain museum, it was the most lasting and appropriate symbol of Limoges's revival during the Second Empire, reflecting its search for identity.[64]

4

"La Ville rouge": Republicanism, Socialism and the Commune

In February 1852, while the departmental Mixed Commissions were still meting out stiff punishments to *démoc-socs*, a number of business leaders gathered to consider ways of "moralizing" Limoges's workers. They discussed ways of "restoring, as much as possible, the confidence between employers and workers." They contributed 845 francs to begin a retirement fund for workers. They volunteered to serve as honorary presidents and members of mutual aid associations, which were to foster the workers' return to the virtues of patience, caution, and submission.[1]

Four years later, the central police commissioner sent the prefect names of working-class families with children born on March 16—Louis Napoleon's birthday—who had applied for the "honor of the godparentage of the emperor." Police investigated the moral and political antecedents of each family, finding that one shoemaker was immoral, lazy, and drank heavily, but his wife, happily, was honest and hardworking; another shoemaker sang in church—an excellent recommendation; a third, also a shoemaker, lived "in a state of near misery and merits our attention." The seven children selected did not fare well in life. Four of the babies died within little more than a year and a fifth died four years later. Two children survived until 1868, when each received fifty francs. One of the workers, a shoemaker, petitioned the government for help four times, at least twice receiving one hundred francs and another fifty francs for the child's first communion.[2]

Limoges's reputation as *la ville rouge*, which brought the businessmen together in 1852, lay behind the search for imperial godchildren from the ranks of the proletariat in 1856. Both were part of a campaign to "moralize" the workers of the "city in France where socialism has found," in the opinion of its prefect in 1850, "the deepest roots . . . nowhere else has it found more passionate disciples, nowhere else will the challenge of its organizations be welcomed with more enthusiasm by the workers and followed with more attention and devotion."[3] Manufacturers hoped that the "lessons" of 1848 had been learned by the workers. But the manufacturers had, by all accounts, virtually no influence on the workers. In Limoges *patrons* and workers lived in "a state of complete antagonism" in 1855. One found "none of the farsightedness or protection that give the worker roots, make him more moral, and spare him from the current of passions that engenders habits of disorder." The working class of Limoges betrayed its "bad spirit" by expressing

> opinions that reflect the hatred of those who give them their bread; this [situation] should also inspire manufacturers to employ the means which, in the manufacturing centers of the North and East, moralize the worker and thereby attach him to the industry that looks after his needs. The use of these means is unknown in the manufacturing centers of the Center of France. Thus the relations that exist between bosses and workers here are not such that they will change the attitude of the working class, which is held in check only by surveillance and by force.[4]

Yet if one looked only for reports of major disturbances, it would appear that the workers' militancy had perished with the Second Republic. During the first thirteen years of the Empire, there were but two incidents of workers meeting illegally and only three short strikes.[5] But despite the apparent calm, the procureur général still insisted as late as 1855 that workers were "imbued with the false ideas of socialism and the principle of equality . . . the doctrines of 1848 and the passions that they set ablaze are far from being extinguished."[6] The militance of Limoges's workers only seemed hindered, not eliminated, by the campaigns of "moralization," imperial promises, or police repression. Large-scale industrialization and the development of working-class consciousness lay beneath the transformation of political life that occurred in the nineteenth century. Manifestations of class consciousness are easier to find than the precise moment when some or all workers in any town, region, or nation began to think of themselves as a class apart, transcending preexisting trade or craft loyalties and solidarities or their absence. Class consciousness was a social and political reality embedded in both industrial work and daily life. Sometime between 1830 and 1871 some French workers—but not all—came to see themselves as a class.[7] This did not automatically generate collective action, joining workers of different trades or skilled and unskilled workers: Rivalries, tensions, and gaps in levels of skill and remuneration, as well as differences in geographic mobility remained. One must keep in mind that French history, like all national histories, is often as much characterized by discontinuities as by continuities. One must be cautious about assuming a linear evolution of the working class in which the French workers of 1848 were necessarily more class conscious than those of 1830, those of 1871 more than those of 1851, or the workers of 1895 more class conscious than those of the

Commune era. Such an evolution occurred in Limoges, but systematic comparisons across trades, cities, and time must be made before generalizations about class consciousness can be accepted without qualification.

Most historians would agree that a combination of several factors, in varying proportions, was crucial to the emergence of working-class consciousness during the middle decades of the nineteenth century in France. Artisans with an inherited tradition of skill and control over the process of production came to see themselves as exploited, sharing a common fate with other workers. Organizational and technological changes in the structure of work exposed them to "the logic of capitalism." The abolition of the guilds during the French Revolution brought a flood of newcomers into trades skilled artisans had once controlled. The clothing trade, for example, was radically altered when tailors were no longer protected and were forced to accept piecework at reduced rates from merchant capitalists. Such organizational changes were more important in France than technological changes that later abruptly reduced artisans to proletarians (the glassworkers of Carmaux provide a splendid example).[8] Small wonder that artisans dominated the revolutionary crowds in nineteenth-century France. Ultimately they passed on the perceptions of their situation to unskilled workers, as master artisans had passed on trade secrets to younger workers.[9]

Artisanal organization and class consciousness were inextricably linked. Trade organizations of artisans, particularly the *compagnonnage* and its successors, the mutual aid or friendly societies, prepared the way for associations that reached across trades, thus forming what Sewell has called "the confraternity of proletarians."[10] The link between these workers' associations and the social and political mobilization of workers in the Parisian spring of 1848 is clear.[11] The most important aspect of the Revolution of 1848 was the generalized sense of class consciousness that workers manifested irrespective of whether they looked to the state or to themselves to take the first steps toward emancipation from capitalism.

In Limoges skilled porcelain workers led the way. They were not, properly speaking, artisans, although the decorators called themselves *artistes* and had the same pride of craft and sense of dignity, if not the same status, that characterized some artisanal trades. Unlike Paris and other major French cities, Limoges offers the historian little continuity between the traditional confraternities of journeymen and the first organizations that joined workers of different trades. The *compagnonnage* was weak in Limoges, off the beaten path for most *compagnons*. The porcelain industry, it will be remembered, began in Limoges only late in the eighteenth century, developing after the revolutionary and imperial wars. Large-scale industry in Limoges, then, manifested some of the features of the English model of large-scale industrialization: relatively high numbers of workers per employer; significant division of labor; and considerable technological changes that reduced the status and control of the most skilled workers. But it was skilled workers, not artisans, who were at the forefront of the workers' movement in Limoges.

Class-conscious workers assume, indeed live, a sense of separateness or "otherness."[12] Gradually the bourgeoisie came to be seen as a class with other, antagonistic interests, as the disciples of Saint-Simon in the early 1830s extended their mentor's definition of nonproducers to include the bourgeoisie along with the clergy, nobles, and other idlers. However, as in the era of the sansculottes of the French Revolution, the term "bourgeois," like that of the older term "aristocrat," sometimes referred less to a specifically defined social class than to a certain kind of political behavior that seemed to oppose the interests of ordinary people. Workers benefited from the democratic patronage of the radical faction of the bourgeoisie, but they increasingly looked to go their own way, as they had in the last two years of the Second Republic.[13]

Class consciousness both shaped and depended on the development of an ideology that transformed class solidarity into a way of looking at political power and the state. The development of republicanism, utopian socialism, and republican socialism as ideologies, largely the contribution of radical bourgeois, justified and accelerated the political action of ordinary people in mid-century France.[14]

The changing spatial organization and separation of work and residence contributed to the emergence of working-class communities. Class segregation, the commonality of work experience, and the cohesion of the family (particularly as more and more women were brought into factory and industrial production) helped generate consciousness and militancy.[15] We have already noted the concentration of industry and workers' residence on the periphery of the city, specifically in the faubourgs. Here the café, too, played a significant role in the shaping of working-class community. By 1864 there were over six hundred establishments licensed to sell liquor in Limoges, one for every eighty-six people. In 1828 one could find three cabarets and three *auberges* on the faubourg Montmailler and two auberges on the route de Paris; in 1864 the two faubourgs offered twenty-five and twenty-eight drinking establishments, respectively. Such cafés served as the "just judiciary," or parliament, of the people. When the government began rounding up republicans and socialists after the attempted assassination of the emperor in 1858, the *cabaretier* Dérignac was among the first to go. When a flood of requests from country people to open cafés in Limoges arrived at the prefecture, the prefect promised to view such requests "with severity" and lamented the social, physical, and political "demoralization" that seemed to be a direct consequence of the proliferation of such drinking establishments, which catered to workers and benefited from the increased distribution and cheaper cost of liquor made possible by the train.[16]

The commercial and industrial bourgeoisie of Limoges admired but did not love the emperor. Fearing the lower classes and remembering the *affaire de*

Limoges and the whispered menaces of 1851, they looked to Louis Napoleon to guarantee order and economic prosperity. It was thus easy for those who had proclaimed themselves loyal to the Orleanists to support the Empire. There was considerable continuity between the supporters of the Orleanist monarchy and the "party" of Louis Napoleon Bonaparte.[17] When the procureur général said of the Limoges middle classes in 1858 that "they are only moderately attached to the form and attractions of a government that they do not dominate, but they serve and support it out of egoism and calculation," he might have been speaking about Dumont St. Priest and the *juste milieu* of the July Monarchy.[18] Some bourgeois, among them several in the magistrature, still favored an Orleanist revival, for a hereditary monarchy seemed to be the greatest guarantee of order. There were, of course, men who fervently supported the Empire out of conviction, such as Joseph Noualhier, whose father had loyally served Napoleon I. Louis Napoleon Bonaparte named the son mayor and the government made sure that he was elected to the Corps législatif. The Empire could prove that local businessmen had something to gain by supporting the regime. The emperor certainly won favor when the train first arrived in 1856. Putting the nightmare of the Second Republic behind them, Limoges's commercial and industrial elite went back to making money. They were not active in their support for the Bonapartists or Orleanists. But even when the Cobden-Chevalier Treaty of 1860 angered some businessmen, they did not join the republican opposition.[19]

Delighted to be protected, by virtue of imperial power, from the workers, many businessmen were willing to sacrifice the National Guard, one of the municipal liberties achieved in 1830. Henceforth they depended on the army of the centralized state. The army realized that the bourgeois Guard could be trusted, but it was always thought to be less effective than the army. The Guard was not even mentioned in the contingency plans drawn up in the early 1850s in case of a working-class insurrection. The small guardhouse at the town hall was pulled down, marking the end of the Limoges National Guard.[20]

In addition to some intransigent Orleanists, what other possible political opposition confronted Bonapartists in this industrializing city? Legitimism was not an important force in Limoges, despite the long years of service of such old rural noble families as de Montbrun and de Léobardy to the Bourbon cause, the printing dynasties of Limoges, the wealthy clan of Lamy de la Chapelle, and a few members of the clergy. One found none of the popular royalism that characterized such cities as Toulouse or Nîmes, where skilled artisans and unskilled day laborers were economically dependent upon the patronage of the urban nobility. Legitimists could hardly expect to develop a following in a city whose laboring class was anticlerical and whose bourgeois elite had helped unseat the Bourbons in 1830, particularly after the Empire made peace with the Church. The prefect could only name one legitimist in 1853 who could be viewed as "dangerous," and he was without influence.[21]

The absence of republican leadership and the heavy weight of repression limited republican opposition activity to individual acts of defiance, such as a placard
left at the entrance to the Palais de Justice in December 1852, denouncing "Messieurs les Exploiteurs de décembre . . . Mort aux aristocrates! Vive la République
démocratique et sociale!" Bac, who returned to Limoges for a trial, seemed aston-
ished by the indifference he encountered in his city in the second year of the
Empire, this despite the fact that the trial attracted a larger crowd than usual to
the courtroom, especially women, who "wept a great deal upon hearing the
lamentations that this monsieur knows so well how to deliver."[22] A police spy
named Henry Benoît reported that the republican socialists were constantly afraid,
"seeing only the police everywhere." Opposition to the Empire could only be
manifested through abstentions during the "elections" that followed the coup
d'état, when several thousand workers stayed away from the polls.[23] Signs of
political protest were seen during the subsistence crisis of 1853–54, the last of the
traditional agricultural crises in France; this was yet another indication that a
fundamental transformation had occurred during the middle decades of the nineteenth century. Increased productivity, vast improvements in distribution largely
but not exclusively related to the coming of the railroad, and the military victory
of the laissez-faire economics of food supply eliminated the cycle of the dreaded
chereté des grains and the grain riots that pitted urban and rural consumers
against producers, transporters, marketers, and police. At the same time, commercial and industrial enterprises were less vulnerable to the sudden withdrawal
of credit and waning demand, at least partially because of the political stabiliza-
tion and active government economic intervention during the Second Empire.[24]

The poor blamed the hoarders and the municipal officials, who failed to control
them, for the obvious dearth of grain at the market and high prices for several
consecutive days. Limoges had, at the time, no central grain market, and so its
commerce was, according to one official, "hidden." Several millers controlled the
supply of grain; the largest mill, in nearby Aixe, was owned by a group of
wealthy shareholders, including some municipal councilmen, all of whom had
been elected as government candidates. The profitable operation was not illegal,
but the poor blamed these leading citizens for artificially creating a rise in the
price of bread. A police commissioner remarked that the shareholders would have
been happy to pull out of the operation if they were not making so much money.
When the price of poultry also rose, people talked of an arrangement between
rural suppliers and the cranky *revendeuses,* who hawked fewer birds at higher
prices. The number of poor in Limoges was swollen by a flood of beggars arriving from the countryside with certificates of indigence obtained from mayors who
were happy to see them leave. Several placards left during the night on public
buildings attacked "the regime of hoarders" and "our mayor and his friends the
hoarders," and threatened "death to all these thieves!" One with words spelled
out with more enthusiasm than accuracy read "A bas Napollesont, Mor au

mouchar, vive la République démocratique, plus de jésuite!", and another "O sainte République, quand reviendra tu pour tes enfants et tu chassera les tyrans, vive la guillotine, vive Barbès!" In January 1854, two police agents arrested a mason for singing "Plan, plan, rataplan, vivent les rouges, à bas les blancs."[25]

But there were no more grain riots in Limoges. Crowds of beggars (including one ninety-three-year-old man hauled in by the police) and gamins still hung around certain public places—despite a prefectorial decree in 1859 forbidding mendicity—and proved that they were still adept at their only trade, namely, getting by. But the begging poor, who found no other refuge than the entrances to churches, posed no threat to public order. The police and the bourgeoisie remained preoccupied with the organized working class.[26]

As a police spy, Henry Benoît spent much time in the workers' cafés. His task was to identify *démoc-socs* and assess what was left of the movement. His report of September 16, 1853, stressed the influence of utopian socialism in Limoges: "Toute la famille des travailleurs est socialiste."[27] Dérignac, forced to reside in Pau after the coup, had returned to his café on the rue du Canard. In Benoît's estimation, he "belong[ed], by virtue of his modest position, to the family of proletarians," although he had received a modest education. Wanting to improve himself, Dérignac had read philosophy, thereby acquiring a "scientific argot" that allowed him, it seemed, "to flatter and caress the workers" who came to his café. In 1853 Benoît heard Dérignac complain that his friends were no longer stopping by for fear of getting into trouble. There were other such cafés: the Brasserie de Jacob on the avenue du Champ de Juillet, whose owner had been influenced by Pierre Leroux; the Café Paul Thomas on the rue Fitz James, which was filled with porcelain workers on Sunday and Monday; the Café National on the boulevard Ste. Catherine; plus several establishments on the avenue du Pont Neuf and in the industrial faubourgs. There were workers in virtually every trade who seemed "dangerous." Skilled porcelain workers were still the most militant. The spy observed that "the porcelain worker is a special man," who thinks he is "invaluable." The decorators complained that they embellished beautiful plates for the rich but were paid only modestly. Several of the twenty workers Benoît mentioned lived on the faubourg Montmailler, including one who claimed to be a follower of Proudhon.

Shoemakers and sabot makers were second on his list of "dangerous" trades; he named fifteen, including one who founded a trade association and another a "communist" momentarily jailed in Guéret. Benoît added such trades as tailors, joiners, locksmiths, and watchmakers, including a disciple of Cabet ("born in the tradition of the strike"). One cabinetmaker, a certain Vallière, also had followed Cabet; Benoît pointed out indignantly that these Icarians, who were supposedly nonviolent, were actually revolutionaries. The vast majority of the over one hundred people he identified were workers.

A more systematic report of those involved in *démagogie,* as it was called in

1854, noted that porcelain workers were again the leading activists among the 125 people listed, with 10 porcelain painters and another 14 porcelain workers. Shoemakers and cabinetmakers were also noteworthy. Among the bourgeoisie, clerks and lawyers were well represented.[28] Subsequent reports in 1856 and 1858 (the latter following Orsini's attempt on the emperor's life) brought forth essentially the same assessment of those imprisoned or sent into exile in 1852, whether or not they had returned to Limoges.[29]

The alliance of bourgeois republicans and workers created what Corbin has called the "permanence" of political opposition to the Empire.[30] The 1857 election marked the reemergence of organized republican opposition in France: A relatively unknown republican candidate named Bastide won 49.6 percent of the vote in Limoges, compared to 31.8 percent for the official candidate Noualhier, who was elected by the department as a whole. On the second day of the election the workers cast their ballots "in order and silence, as a well-disciplined army," for the republican. "Wherever there was a factory, a workshop, or men working in great numbers in the same place," it seemed that "the spirit of the vote was bad."[31]

When Limoges's industries languished, complaints could be heard. The political reforms unveiled by the emperor "did not appear to have moved the lower classes"; they seemed indifferent to the successes of the imperial army in Italy in 1859. The following year workers helped elect several republicans to the Municipal Council, although in general the former seemed to take little interest in municipal affairs. They would, the government thought, "obey their instincts and their rancor against their employers, the rich, the bourgeoisie" in any election. Most voted for Bac in his unsuccessful campaign waged against Péconnet to win a seat on the departmental General Council. After republican gains in Paris, the region's chief magistrate warned "of the intimate union of proletarians marching together to the ballot box . . . one must ask if this revolutionary contagion will stop there."[32] Even with an upturn in the porcelain industry in 1863, due primarily to successes in the Italian and British markets that compensated for the Civil War in America, the political dispositions of workers appeared to turn even more against the Empire. Relative prosperity engendered a bolder stance toward the *patronat,* particularly among porcelain workers.[33]

Early in the 1860s nine of Limoges's twenty mutual aid societies were under the patronage of the government and received municipal subsidies. Although only one of these associations—the shoemakers of St. Crispin—resembled the religious associations of the Midi, elite patronage continued to leave its mark on these organizations in Limoges. They still had honorary presidents and honorary members—among them Alluaud, Pouyat, and Noualhier—who contributed money and came to the meetings. When honorary member Texier Lachassagne died in 1869, shoemakers and weavers were among those attending his funeral.[34] They met only under the watchful eye of the administration, with the police often present to ensure that only "acceptable topics" were discussed. In 1863 Mayor Péconnet distributed medals to some of the one thousand workers in mutual aid organizations; the medals bore the image of Napoleon III, "whose paternal solicitude," the workers were told, "is ever watchful of the true interests of the laboring classes."[35]

Mutual aid societies could offer artisans and skilled workers more than just minimal protection against the uncertainties of employment and the pauper's grave. They provided organizational experience and an opportunity for exchanging information and discussing common problems. They also served as *sociétés de résistance* by providing funds to support illegal strikes, as they had done in 1833 and 1837. But mutual aid societies could really only defend the interests of those workers no longer supervised by honorary presidents and elite members.

Many workers still had faith in other associations with more ambitious goals, such as the elimination of the *patronat,* thus guaranteeing for themselves, it was hoped, the "right to work" by controlling production. The Revolution of 1848 had brought a proliferation of not only mutual aid societies but also numerous fledgling producers' and consumers' cooperatives. Bernard Moss has rightly pointed out that the defense of artisanal trades and the cooperative movement were two aspects of the "socialism of skilled workers."[36] The Société philanthropique des artistes en porcelaine had been founded in 1843 as a mutual aid society. In May 1848, the two hundred members of the association drew up statutes to transform their organization into a producers' cooperative (see Chapter Two). Convinced of the "power of association," they had looked to the state to provide the capital with which to begin. Their hopes and plans had reflected the influence of utopian socialists; they planned to withdraw to the nearby commune of Solignac to begin their operation, where they would establish a bakery and a butchershop, start a garden, and hire a schoolteacher. But the tone of their project was decidedly moderate, their deference to capitalists and the state markedly evident. Their project involved only workers of their trade and revealed their sense of distance from other workers in the industry, as well as their own dignity.[37] Several attempts to begin cooperatives during the Second Empire seemed more radical, involving a variety of occupations within the industry. These sustained the dream of production without capitalists, although the tensions among workers possessing different skills contributed to the failure of these varied experiments. The hope, engendered by the Revolution of 1848, still lingered that the "right to work" included the assumption that the state would provide capital to skilled workers and permit them to escape the exploitation of the wage system through the organization of cooperatives. Several cooperationists corresponded with workers in London, in particular with Alfred Talandier, an exiled *démoc-soc.* But the cooperative era seemed at an end. Cooperative associations had moved workers conceptually closer to the goal of organization across trades, but no practical steps had been taken. If anything, the movement had revealed the persistence of rivalries and tensions among workers of different levels of skill. Despite the socialist opinions of Richroch and other cooperationists, the movement failed to generate militancy.[38] Strike action did.

In May 1864, the Empire legalized strikes in France, a major step in the liberalization that characterized that regime's second, and last, decade. Skilled porcelain workers immediately struck and workers of virtually every other major industry followed suit. Even though the prefect accused the socialists of "facilitating" the strikes of 1864, strikes "in which they could not have had any material interest," they seemed to have done little more than generate an awareness of the problems workers had encountered in raising sufficient capital in order to sidestep the industrial capitalist.[39] The strikes of 1864 drew national attention; the prefect asserted that war had been declared between capital and labor in Limoges. What led him to this conclusion was the fact that for the first time workers seemed to cooperate across trades in strike action, although they still were deprived of the right to assemble and unions still remained illegal.

Shortly after the passage of the law legalizing strikes, carpenters and carriage makers voted in favor of tentative demands for salary increases and shorter workdays. But the movement really began among the porcelain molders and turners. These skilled workers, it will be recalled, combined their talents to give the *pâte* its form for baking. The turners gave the molded forms to the *englobeurs,* who first placed them in receptacles, called *gazettes,* and then put them in the oven. After the first baking, the person responsible for quality control tapped each unit. If the resulting sound was "full," the baking had been successful. But often the porcelain had cracked; the sound, like the porcelain, was less than perfect. Traditionally the manufacturer had deducted the cost of this failure from the workers' wages.

Turners and molders had often demanded that this practice be abolished, and fourteen workers had briefly struck one factory in April 1855. The manufacturers, who paid turners by the piece and *englobeurs* by the day, blamed the turners for these losses and claimed that if the crack, or *fente,* were eliminated, this would "excuse the *artistes en porcelaine* from responsibility for their work, [which] would be prejudicial to the interests of the manufacturers and the honor of all good workers." The turners claimed that the *englobeurs* were often to blame, and the procureur général agreed after investigating this issue. The turners and molders therefore threatened to walk out after learning that the *patrons* had met and agreed to hold firm and to blacklist any striker. On May 15 the workers drew up a manifesto outlining their case. They constructed a circular placard, around which their names were rather hesitantly traced from the center of the paper, calling the design the "sword of Damocles."[40]

Such an image did not reassure the manufacturers. They met on May 17 and named a commission of five, headed by Alluaud, who had led the resistance to strikes of 1833 and 1837. The commission met with a delegation of workers, consisting of one representative from each factory, which warned that workers would strike after the standard period of eight days if their demands were not met. In fact, workers had already left one factory as a result of their irritation with a foreman. Eight days later between 550 and 600 turners and molders stayed away, laying off about another 2,500 workers in 24 of Limoges's 28 porcelain factories.[41]

What happened next frightened the manufacturers and the government but encouraged workers. As if by prearranged signal, workers of virtually every major trade in Limoges began to present wage or other demands to their employers: Carriage makers and carpenters, *retoucheuses* and *brunisseuses* of porcelain, bakers, weavers, dyers, cabinetmakers, hewers and stonecutters, shoemakers, masons, earthworkers, scale makers, sabot makers, metalworkers, and even some of the washerwomen (sparking a brawl reminiscent of a scene in Zola's *L'Assommoir*). The number of those striking ranged from just a handful to five hundred weavers and fifteen hundred shoemakers. The shoemakers and the tailors quickly won a modest victory.[42]

The long strike of the porcelain workers dominated the public consciousness. Officials first suspected that republicans "occupying a higher rung on the social ladder" were behind the strikes. Bac had arrived in town on July 17, but the republican opposition profited from the strike, not the other way around. The workers acted on their own.[43] On June 2 the manufacturers announced that they would not readmit any workers to their factories until every worker had returned. Their financial resources rapidly dwindling—despite sixteen hundred francs in contributions from Paris, Vierzon, Bordeaux, and even London—the workers managed to hold out until July 2. The prefect thought that the workers had been taught a lesson they would not forget for a long time.[44] Yet the strikes of 1864 demonstrated that the co-option of mutual aid societies by the government and leading citizens had failed.

Workers were still forced by law to limit public gatherings to no more than twenty people, or, for larger groups, to slip away to the outskirts of the city in order to meet secretly. While the manufacturers met in the Palais de Justice, the workers gathered and trekked five kilometers from town to the fields, to the quartier des Roches, and beyond the Pont St. Martial. During the month of May they met almost daily within their trades, five hundred shoemakers in one case, two hundred carpenters dispersed by the police in another. Strike committees were formed; that of the porcelain workers wrote comrades within and outside France and printed tracts exposing their grievances.[45]

In addition to the legalization of strikes, the relative prosperity of some of the industries also helps explain the timing of the 1864 strike wave. The carriage makers, for example, chose the moment to strike when their employer had just signed a lucrative contract to repair the postal wagons. The action of the various trades was mutually reinforcing; the status of the negotiations in the porcelain industry clearly influenced the behavior of the shoemakers, although there is no evidence that workers of different trades met collectively. Furthermore, there

were hints of continued antagonism between the skilled and semiskilled or unskilled workers, who were laid off because of the porcelain strike and were forced
to go into the countryside in search of work; this was the case for the *hommes
du four,* who were let go early in June, and between the turners and *englobeurs.*

The strike forced the porcelain manufacturers to work together—something
that they did not always do. United, the Limoges industrialists could have outlasted their striking workers (although rumors circulated that the wealthier manufacturers were permitting the strike in order to force their weaker rivals out of
business). As Corbin notes, it was no coincidence that they formed the Union des
fabricants en porcelaine the following year.[46] The growing reputation of their industry and the relative absence of competition from other cities had thus far
saved them from having to form the kind of employer associations found elsewhere in France. They benefited from the tacit assistance of the local authorities,
particularly the prefect. While Mayor Péconnet attempted to reconcile the two
parties, Prefect Boby de la Chapelle blocked the use of mutual aid funds for the
strikers, threatened to dissolve their associations, and ordered the police to break
up several meetings of workers outside the city. He even offered to put the army
at the disposal of the industrialists.[47]

Despite small gains by the shoemakers and several other trades, the failure of
most of the strikes, notably that of the porcelain workers, weakened the workers'
organizations. Whereas the strike of 1837 had encouraged the porcelain workers
to enhance their ties with the republican opposition, the defeat of 1864 led to only
limited signs of republican political activity. The strike had not been marked by
any violence, but the Minister of War received several letters imploring him to
increase the size of the garrison. At one point a rumor circulated—in the wake
of the tragic fire of that August and an unusual number of small fires that followed—claiming that someone was trying to burn down the city.[48]

The unsuccessful strike bolstered the morale of the industrialists against the
republicans, who had voiced support for the workers. After Bac's death in May
1865, no strong republican leader emerged in Limoges in the last years of the decade. Further republican successes in the municipal elections of September 1865
attested to the growing strength of working-class opposition to the Empire. In
1867 the upper class began to worry about the impact the liberalization of the
laws governing the press and public assembly might have.[49] Supported by workers, Chamiot, a republican *commissaire* in the spring of 1848, Chiboys, another
old forty-eighter, and the notary Nassans were elected to district councils.

But without a local republican leader capable of winning departmental election
to the National Assembly, Limoges attracted two republicans of national reputation who wanted to capitalize on the liberalization of 1868: Jules Simon and
Georges Périn. Simon, one of the men most firmly identified with the revival of
the republican party, arrived in Limoges in October 1868 to lecture on the responsibilities and duties of *les pères de famille,* as well as to make contact with local

republicans. The workers first found him "too pale, too bourgeois," but when he returned in December several hundred porcelain workers turned out to greet him at the station, many with fists raised in the air in support. When he returned again in March 1869 to further his hopes, thousands greeted him. Even though the official candidate Noualhier emerged victorious—Simon was unknown outside Limoges—the electoral campaign enhanced the organization of local republicans.[50]

Périn arrived from Paris to begin a republican newspaper, *Le Libéral du Centre*. A lawyer from Arras, he was educated in Paris. He had never been to the Limousin before disembarking at the Gare des Bénédictins in 1868 at the age of thirty-one. *Le Libéral* published its prospectus on August 18: It called for the defense of local interests, freedom of the press, an end to unearned privilege, complete freedom of assembly, lay and public education, the abolition of permanent armies, and increased power for the Chamber of Deputies, which would assume the duties of the centralized state in deciding questions of war and peace.

Le Libéral appealed to the workers of the city, who were known to read opposition newspapers aloud in their workshops. It promised a forceful, if sometimes condescending, leadership of the working class, printing letters such as the following: "We are happy with you and your newspaper, which performs great services in our workshops . . . so nicely expressing the thoughts we have at the bottom of our hearts and which we have been forced to keep there . . . in you we have a guide who will lead us along the path of progress . . . you know that the working class is well-meaning and asks only to be able to do good things."[51] Périn's editorials attacked the Church, reporting tales of priestly misdeeds and misadventures whenever possible and applauding civil burials and other symbolic setbacks for the Church. *Le Libéral* also reflected the clear link between the republicans of 1848 and the radical revival in the late 1860s, publishing letters from Louis Blanc and Jules Michelet, printing a moving tribute to Denis Dussoubs, reminding readers of republican anniversaries, and offering obituaries of local militants. *Le Libéral* urged workers to send delegates to socialist congresses in Bâle and Genève, and to discuss the "social question." At the same time, the newspaper orchestrated a chorus of complaints against the imperial government, focusing on urban projects promised and now forgotten (such as an adequate water supply near the factories), criticizing the butchers' quarter ("qui s'huile et se graisse de jour en jour davantage du rez de chaussée à la mansarde"), and noting the continual refusal of the mayor to allow them to publish an account of council meetings. The Chamber of Commerce's pleas for a suitable place to meet went unheeded. Even the supporters of the Empire were irritated by the snub Limoges porcelain received in winning only one silver and one bronze medal, plus an honorable mention, in the 1867 exposition. They blamed Noualhier for failing to look after the interests of the city and welcomed any proposal favoring the decentralization of administrative power.[52] In many ways the challenge of these republican radicals against the imperial regime echoed that made forty years earlier before the Revolution of 1830. *Le Libéral* drew the wrath of the government, paying over four thousand francs in fines. It closed down in November 1868 and reappeared for six months in 1869, publishing its last issue on August 15, 1869.[53]

As the decade ended, manufacturers complained that the endemic and seemingly perpetual hostility between capital and labor had increased the undisciplined behavior of their workers. Denis Poulot, a Parisian employer of modest means, had noticed the same thing and published a remarkable description of this phenomenon entitled *Le sublime, ou le travailleur comme il est en 1870, et ce qu'il peut être,* colorfully categorizing the working population of the capital according to their proclivities (*les fils de Dieu, les sublimes,* and so on). Deference seemed dead, weakened by political agitation, drowned in drink.[54]

If workers would willingly vote for Jules Simon and thank Georges Périn for attacking the government, their leaders were of their own class, particularly two porcelain workers, Bergeron and Vallière, both of whom were hounded by the imperial police for their political views in the 1850s. Rumors abounded claiming the International's influence in Limoges. Workers discussed the possibility of forming *chambres syndicales* that would dispense with honorary members, represent the interests of workers, and set wage demands. Bergeron wanted to establish a *chambre fédérale* that would coordinate the demands of each *chambre syndicale,* overseeing the activities of each *chambre.* Strikes were said to be planned.[55]

Old François Alluaud passed away right after the 1864 strike, once again disappointed with the workers. He would have been even more angered had he lived to see the signs of organization and mobilization in the late 1860s. "It would be a great error to think that the socialist doctrines that agitate the public meetings at Le Redoute and Le Pré-aux-Clercs [in the capital] are limited only to the greatest centers of the population," wrote one magistrate. "The workers of our city suffer these same errors, and would also like to cross, in one step, the distance that separates them from the bourgeoisie."[56] Limoges, too, now heard "the frightening echo of these meetings, where the very basis of modern society and even the principle of government are discussed."[57] In the spring of 1870 the imperial state and the Limoges industrialists faced their greatest challenge, before diplomatic disasters led France to war and the debacle. This mobilization of the workers of Limoges culminated in *l'année terrible,* the last of the nineteenth-century revolutions, a synthesis of class consciousness, republicanism, and nascent socialism among the workers of the city.

The smoke rising above Paris at the end of May 1871 revealed the smoldering ruins of a devastated capital and the corpses of some twenty-five thousand Communards killed during *la semaine sanglante.* Few historians would deny the significance of the Commune for both the political left and the right in France: for the former, inspiration, a moment when the ordinary people of Paris were for a brief instant "masters of their own lives"; for the latter, a terrifying, haunting specter for the bourgeoisie. Most historians of the period have long assumed that the Paris Commune was "a unique event, born of an exceptional situation located in an exceptional city."[58] Only with the centenary of the Commune did students of the period turn their attention to the insurrections, riots, and other disturbances in provincial urban centers, the *communes de province*. These events reflected not just the timing of the Franco-Prussian War and the debacle, but crises in the economic, social, and political processes that had transformed France in the middle years of the century: industrial capitalism, state building, and urbanization. The porcelain workers were, to utilize an apt analogy, the yeast that worked the urban dough. The accentuated centralization of the Second Empire pitted municipalities such as Limoges, proud of her recent development, against the state. Marseille, Lyon, and St. Etienne led the opposition to the Empire in its declining years. The specific historical circumstances of the frightful year—the suddenness with which the Empire disappeared, the siege of Paris, and the absence of effective authority—left Limoges to its own devices. Its conflicts took on an added sense of urgency or crisis. On April 6, 1871, the workers of Limoges attempted to proclaim the Commune, just when militance was waning in other radical cities. Over half a century of industrial and urban development was drawing to a close.

During the first months of 1870, the Second Empire faced its sternest and ultimate challenge from the republican opposition and the workers. Limoges republicans profited from the law of June 18, 1868, permitting public meetings. In mid-January 1870 three consecutive days of "seditious demonstrations" occurred in Limoges; a young porcelain painter harangued the workers at public places. Instead of celebrating the generally favorable economic situation, the prefect's monthly report complained that if opposition *manifestations* had subsided, they "continue in the minds and attitudes of the working-class of Limoges," whose members are hostile to "their bosses, or state authority." Two porcelain workers organized a meeting, consisting of about three hundred workers, on January 23 in the Ponchet hall, rue du Consulat, the goal of which was to select a commission to form *chambres syndicales* of workers from each métier. One of them, Bergeron, was out to organize associations that would dispense with honorary presidents and honorary members drawn from among local notables. On the thirtieth and thirty-first porcelain workers elected twenty of their number to form a new *chambre syndicale*. Manufacturers and foremen of the large industrial establishments increasingly complained of the insubordination of their workers. "Demogogic journals" were now "found every day in the large workshops, read out loud there."[59]

Although the impetus for the thirty or so meetings in every major trade came from local militants, the arrival of two Parisian workers, Minet and Benoît, certainly helped spark the movement. In retrospect it seems clear that these two outsiders recruited Limoges workers to the International. A letter from the Société céramique in Paris was read to assembled porcelain workers seeking a 20 percent increase in wages. The hat was passed for the Le Creusot strikers at gatherings of leather dressers, sabot makers, locksmiths, mechanics, carriage makers, and scale makers. Like the porcelain workers, they began to establish *chambres syndicales*.[60] Was the International behind this movement?

It is difficult to assess the strength of the International. In the crackdown after the Commune, prosecutors claimed that thousands of workers in Limoges were members. Industrialists then streamed in to denounce the International, naively identifying all shop-floor insubordination with political conspiracy. We know that hundreds of workers—perhaps as many as seven or eight hundred—attended each of several public meetings and listened to the Parisian workers tell the assembly that *chambres syndicales* were springing up all over Europe: "We are only a little stream and this stream will become a torrent, and when the torrent will have swept everything away, we will be masters of the situation."[61] In September 1868 five delegates traveled to Bâle from Limoges to attend the fourth congress of the International and may have formally affiliated themselves with it. But thousands of workers in Limoges were not members of the International. Bergeron and Vallière, porcelain workers, and the shoemaker Dupré *dit* Duprat were, at the very least, familiar with the International, and so were many of their followers. They perceived the struggle of the working class against capitalists as an international struggle.

In mid-March the Limousin's first magistrate reported a strike by tapestry workers demanding a shorter workday. He blamed their leader, Bergeron, for the strike. Workers seemed more militant and more organized:

> This first evidence of the struggle that seems to have been growing for several months in Limoges is not in itself serious . . . but is significant because of the organization that brought it about. It is tied to a movement of emancipation that is occurring and spreading with remarkable unity within all of the workers' corporations.[62]

When the porcelain decorators submitted the statutes of their new association for approval, the prefect attempted to refuse authorization. The minister replied that unless the association had political objectives it would have to be tolerated because of the recent liberalization. The two stated goals of the *chambre* were to aid members without work and to "support and raise wages by all legal means that the union will have judged necessary and fair." The Empire seemed to have planted the seeds of its own demise by giving workers the right to strike in 1864.[63]

When members of fourteen different *chambres syndicales* gathered to consider forming a *chambre fédérale,* the Minister of the Interior asserted that such a grouping of different trades into a federation could represent a "gathering of forces that society has the right and the duty to be anxious about." The organization would be subject to criminal prosecution.[64] Yet the delegates of the *chambres syndicales* met on April 28 in the large hall at 3, rue Palvézy, not far from the cathedral.

The workers' mobilization continued into the summer. Some one hundred stonecutters and masons struck, backed by a pledge from other workers to contribute fifty centimes from their daily salary to the strike fund. On July 27 about three hundred porcelain workers voted to refuse the lower wage rates proposed by the manufacturer Guyot; only one worker voted against the proposition. On August 1 the carpenters elected new syndics, listening as the omnipresent Bergeron urged them to demand higher wages and to establish a newspaper. Local officials and employers feared a repetition of the strike wave of 1864.[65]

To many *limougeauds*—if not most—the Empire had seemed to have run its course before the plebescite of May 1870. Even many of its supporters had tired of the oppressive centralization at a time when provincial cities were boldly demanding increased municipal liberties. "The moment has come for collective action," proclaimed the *Almanach Limousin;* "centralization is losing its absorbing prestige as certain illnesses lose their intensity." When Louis Napoleon "crowned the edifice" by granting further reforms, he only succeeded in spurring the mobilization of his enemies. But even they could not have anticipated the speed with which the Empire collapsed.[66]

When war was declared, the Municipal Council of Limoges refused to join a patriotic address to the emperor; some isolated protests against the declaration of war were heard. Yet most people desired and expected a quick French victory. The procureur général reported that his charges believed it was better to fight the Prussians than each other. In Limoges the conflict of class seemed much more pressing than war with the Prussians. The workers elected to the Conseil de prud'hommes refused to take their oath of loyalty and talked about establishing a new paper with the provocative title *Revendication*. On July 29 the officials still seemed much more preoccupied with French workers than with Prussians.

> Every day the revolutionary spirit manifests itself in an unequivocal manner in the ranks of the working-class of this city; one sees civil burials multiply in number, attempted strikes follow one another, and evil newspapers gain more ground every day . . .[67]

Municipal elections in August demonstrated that even "a certain segment of the bourgeoisie" was willing to support the workers' "detestable sentiments"; they elected Bergeron, Dupré *dit* Duprat, as well as several other radicals. Two gun shops were pillaged on August 10, a poorly documented incident that may have been part of an attempt to storm the prefecture.[68]

The fall of the Empire, the proclamation of the Republic in Paris on September 4, and the struggle between the remnants of the French army and Prussian troops left Limoges republicans with two overriding concerns: to prepare the defense of the city and to fortify the nascent Republic against its internal enemies. But they faced the ravages of the economic crisis that inevitably accompanied the declaration of war and the bad news from the combat zones. The economic crisis and the political future of France would divide republicans and monarchists, capital and labor, and the conservative bourgeoisie and the working class.

Limoges gradually assumed the appearance of a military camp, the initial signs of which had been considerable activity in the red-light quarter of Viraclaud. Rumors of French losses in the North intensified anxiety in the Limousin's capital city; arrests of suspected Prussian "spies" included a traveling peddler of songs, a journalist from Orléans, a priest from the vicinity of Toulouse, and another from the Savoie. The National Defense Society of Limoges, established about a week before the proclamation of the Republic, raised money for the defense of the region and discussed building fortifications around the city. The National Guard was reconstituted and officers were elected; a *garde mobile* and two units of *francs-tireurs* were organized. The official departmental Comité de défense discussed plans to construct cartridge and cannon factories. One imaginative patriot submitted a plan for a local fleet of incendiary balloons that could drive the Prussians away.[69]

Left to its own meager resources, how was the municipality to cope with a devastated economy? Where would the money be found to feed the workers and maintain municipal workshops? On September 7 the Municipal Council agreed to advance funds to manufacturers who, despite vanishing credit, could keep their factories operating. The council voted to negotiate a sizable loan to be financed by a tax to be collected over the next thirteen years.

However, the reimbursable loan of 400,000 francs could not be raised. The council then convoked the thirty leading taxpayers to discuss ways of borrowing even more money to tide the city over during this crisis of seemingly indefinite length. On September 28 the council voted to make a loan of 1 million francs obligatory for the 471 leading taxpayers in Limoges, who would be paid back at 5 percent interest by the grateful city.[70] There was a precedent: The council recalled that the wealthy Beaupeyrat family had bailed out the city during the French Revolution and was repaid during the Restoration.[71] Limoges's credit seemed good.

But David Haviland, a member of the commission to arrange the loan, strongly objected, claiming that it should be voluntary and amount to no more than one and a quarter times the annual tax paid by each of the wealthy men. "Capital," Haviland said, "is something so elusive and so cosmopolitan" that any attempt to tax it would only serve to drive it away.[72] In fact, the provisional government vetoed the forced tax, leaving the municipality back where it was—unable to pay for the workshops, which were costing thousands of francs a week, or to subsidize the porcelain factories. On November 19 the beleaguered council finally approved a voluntary loan of 600,000 francs, to be repaid at 6 percent interest by the additional tax previously approved. The municipality, realizing that this sum was insufficient, initiated negotiations with a northern French banker for another loan. When that financier's shaky empire collapsed and he disappeared across the border into Belgium, such hopes vanished. Only about a fifth of the voluntary loan ever came in. The municipality thus found itself in almost the same position as its predecessor in the spring of 1848.[73]

The political club had characterized the revolutions of 1789 and 1848. Peter Amann writes that clubs characterized "societies in transition" before the establishment of mass political organizations.[74] With the fate of France uncertain, two such popular societies began to meet regularly in September, perhaps even before the Republic had been declared. Both pressured local authorities to republicanize and laicize the administration and magistrature, as well as the official defense committees. That the prefect continued to use the monarchist newspaper *La Discussion* to relay official dispatches and notices could not have reassured republicans.

Limoges's clubs shared a vigilant republicanism but differed in other ways. The Société pour la défense républicaine was the more moderate club. Many of its bourgeois republicans had been prominent *quarante-huitards*. Publishing a paper beginning in October, it was unrelenting in its attack on Bonapartist functionaries who had retained their posts as well as against the Church. Anticlericalism permeated its meetings. Legitimist municipal councilman Adolphe Bourdeau found only "the hatred of God" and "an arbitrary republic with a sense of fraternity that several times revealed its red skin" when he visited the club.[75] Its political program echoed that of 1848: universal male suffrage; a more equitable distribution of taxes; freedom of the press and of religion; free primary education; and the end of subventions for the Church.[76] This club demanded administrative decentralization and the extension of municipal liberties. The imperial regime's high-handed measures had not been popular in Limoges, nor had Bonapartist mayor Noualhier.[77]

Forty years earlier the bourgeoisie had found that Orleanism combined liberalism, social conservatism, and locally generated municipal development. Now the imperial debacle had shattered the prestige of centralization. The fact that provincial cities were now left to fend for themselves in organizing local defense underscored the feeling that Limoges would not only have to act independently in order to ensure the defense of the city but that this relative independence ought to characterize the relationship between the city and the central government. Regional liberties were no longer just code words for returning power to monarchist notables. Some bourgeois republicans, like their Girondin predecessors, began to break with the tradition of Jacobin republicanism.

The other club, the Société populaire, like the club of the same name in the spring of 1848, was numerically dominated by workers. Its leaders, too, were workers, like Elie Dubois, or petty bourgeois, like the jeweler Rebeyrolle. The

Société populaire grew out of the preliminary organization of the Chambre fédérale earlier that year. The proclamation of the Republic had carried the hopes of the workers even further. On September 11 an *orateur populaire,* a porcelain worker, addressed a large crowd gathered at the place Dauphine, just below the faubourgs, on "the past, the present, and the future." The police commissioner thought this particular orator to be a veteran of the *hangars* and music halls of Paris and its working-class clientele. At the same time, Limoges's mutual aid so-cieties met frequently to consider not only their desperate financial situation, in view of mounting unemployment, but also the political future of France. These workers turned out for meetings of the Société populaire in the same somber, humid hall on the rue Palvézy. Workers participated actively on electoral com-mittees before the municipal elections, and on September 26 one councilman de-manded, "in the name of his comrades," that the workers be armed.[78]

During the months of the siege of Paris, the two clubs agreed on the necessity of a united republican front against the Prussians, nobles, and the Church. *La Défense nationale* had noted the frequent meetings of the Société populaire with interest.[79] One man urged the bourgeoisie of the city—for whom the term "club" conjured up fearful, turbulent images—to come and see the workers exercising their rights as citizens by voting on issues by acclamation.[80]

Alfred Talandier became the spokesman for the Société pour la défense répub-licaine. He had returned to France from exile in England during the mid-1860s and was subsequently elected to the Chamber of Deputies from the Seine. Now he extolled the memory of the Second Republic through editorials and serialized histories in *La Défense républicaine,* and gave speeches at the society of the same name.[81] Despite his being attacked as a "communist" by the monarchists, Talandier had left his radical days behind. He helped move the Société pour la défense républicaine further away from the more radical Société populaire. The first issue of *La Défense républicaine* had sharply criticized the utopian socialists Cabet, Fourier, and Proudhon, all three still revered names among the workers. Talandier emphasized the importance of educating workers so that they might gradually assume a larger role in the political life of the nation, a theme to which he con-stantly returned. First the Republic had to be assured and the clericals and mon-archists vanquished; then meaningful reforms could be instituted. Sounding a bit like Haviland, he warned the workers not to frighten away capital, which alone could offer the means by which society could take care of "its physical and moral needs." Talandier believed that workers could sidestep capitalist exploitation by forming producers' cooperatives once they had accumulated sufficient capital. He thus opposed the attempt to make the loan obligatory, that is, forced upon the leading taxpayers of Limoges.[82]

This view put Talandier and the moderate club at loggerheads with the Société populaire. The leaders of the latter club, particularly Dubois, its president, and

Rebeyrolle, its secretary, accused the commercial and industrial bourgeois of betraying the city and the Republic by refusing to provide funds for the municipal workshops. The monarchist minority on the Municipal Council had opposed the forced loan. As early as September 22 police had reported the resentment of the workers against "the rich," who refused to help out.[83]

In mid-December both clubs marched together to the prefecture from the Champ de Juillet to mobilize support for the Republic and for continued resistance to the Prussians. When the Société populaire wanted to stage a second demonstration the following day, the more moderate club refused to join, fearing that such an act might provoke a severe reaction. The Société pour la défense républicaine declined to send delegates, together with those of the more radical club, to Bordeaux in order to demand that the provisional government authorize a Committee of Public Safety in Limoges, an idea incompatible with the decentralized bourgeois republicanism of the moderates. And while both clubs agreed that the National Guard should be armed, the latter club was wary of the workers. The prefect Massicault had warned the leading taxpayers that the Société populaire was conspiring against "capital." Many of their candidates seemed unacceptable to a number of bourgeois republicans. A stormy meeting of the Société populaire on December 17 demanded the addition of more radical members to the Bordeaux government and called for the election of radicals as National Guard officers.[84]

The municipal elections took place during one of the gloomiest Christmas seasons imaginable. Citizens mourned the son of a municipal councilman who had carried a copy of the statutes of the Société pour la défense républicaine to his death in battle against the Prussians. Complaints echoed that the contingency plans for the defense of Limoges were inadequate. The Municipal Council drew some of the blame, particularly as, embarrassingly enough, it had not been able to meet twice within the last month for lack of a quorum. The situation in the capital became increasingly desperate. Although not surrounded by Prussians, Limoges had its own problems.[85]

The strength of the two clubs and their combined commitment to some kind of republic ensured that the new Municipal Council was overwhelmingly republican in composition. The two societies had agreed on eighteen candidates, with the moderate club proposing fifteen moderates on their own list, and the Société populaire sixteen radicals on theirs. Elie Dubois, the watchmaker Rebeyrolle, the porcelain worker Aragon, the weaver Tharaud, and the gunsmith Nicot all were elected as candidates of the Société populaire. When the prefect officially convened the new council, he announced his satisfaction at seeing such "diverse elements" represented. The tone for future disagreements was immediately set when one councilman, a member of the more radical club, demanded that all police reports written before the proclamation of the Republic be turned over to the council for inspection. Such views clashed with those of the moderate republicans, represented by Talandier, Ransom (the mayor), Nassans (a notary who had served as mayor in September), and Adrien Debouché, whose commitment to the idea of a porcelain museum had helped spark the municipal revival of the 1860s.[86]

A strike at the Gibus porcelain factory by skilled workers compounded the problems of the new council in the first month of what everyone hoped would be a much better year. Gibus, who had been able to continue in operation, first put his workers on three-quarter time and then on half time. He also began enforcing regulations that prohibited the workers, who were paid on a piece rate, from entering and leaving the workshops, as they had wished, when they had nothing to do. The *chambre syndicale* of porcelain workers, having assumed the responsibility for setting wage demands, threatened to blacklist all workers who continued to work for Gibus. The strikers were willing to work fewer hours because of the economic situation and also because January was normally the period of inventory. But Gibus began withholding 3 percent of the workers' salaries—the *fente* that had initiated the strike of 1864—apparently going back on his word, given after the strike, when his workers had been the last to return to work. He explained that he wanted his employees "to be a little more careful with their work." The strikers appealed to the "tribunal of public opinion," as they put it, claiming that Gibus and his colleagues did not want "honest and intelligent workers" but simply *machines à travail*.[87]

Once again the workers' anger was focused on capitalists. Almost all had refused to lend the city money. Although the war had cut off major sources of their credit, most people assumed that they had considerable money available. A few had demanded what seemed to be exorbitant sums to keep their factories open. Some were suspected of being Orleanists. The manufacturers, on the other hand, were irritated by the constant demands and insubordination they faced from their workers. J. P. Virasse, president of the Tribunal of Commerce, later claimed that the workers "were all imbued with the idea that capital should disappear and that they should replace the bosses."[88]

The Municipal Council, supported by the workers, sympathized with the strikers. Two monarchist newspapers joined the conservative bourgeoisie of Limoges in condemning the "socialism" of the Municipal Council. On January 14 discussions between the municipality and the porcelain manufacturers ended because it was clear that the city could not afford to subsidize production.[89]

After days without any news from the capital, it was learned that heroic Paris had capitulated. The council addressed a letter to the government calling for a *guerre à outrance* unless the Prussians accepted the conditions of peace proposed by Jules Faure. The Société populaire once again called for the establishment of a Committee of Public Safety.

But the war was over, if not the shock and humiliation of defeat. The attention of republicans and socialists turned to fortifying the Republic. With the announcement that elections for the National Assembly would be held in February, the

Société populaire discussed how the antirepublican sentiments in some of rural Haute-Vienne might be overcome. The reaction of the countryside to the events of 1870–71 offers a striking contrast to the experience of the Second Republic. Neither the war—with its calls for ever more conscripts, beginning with the harvest of 1870—nor the unemployed workers of Limoges—occasional marauders in the hinterland—were popular in the countryside. Unemployed workers in Limoges muttered about the high prices charged by country people for their produce; police reports mentioned fights in the city marketplaces. Armed patrols outside Limoges had arrested several groups of urban pillagers in October. The rural Haute-Vienne turned a deaf ear to calls from its capital for a continuation of the war. It now elected a slate of Orleanist notables. Limoges, like Paris, seemed to be surrounded by enemies.[90]

The political attitudes of the men sent to the National Assembly from the Haute-Vienne in February 1871 had been formed by the Revolution of 1830 and reinforced by that of 1848. A liberal but socially conservative monarchy seemed to offer sufficient guarantees against the lower classes; such "order" would facilitate the expansion of commerce and industry, which set them apart from the legitimists. Mallevergne and de Peyramont, it will be recalled, had been two of the bright young bourgeois leaders of the liberal opposition to the Restoration. The year 1830 had been their time, their revolution. In his pre-electoral statement, Mallevergne reminded his department that "during the last years of the Restoration [he had] defended liberal ideas with talent and had had the honor to be convicted of a press offense." He had been rewarded by Louis Philippe with a position in the magistrature. De Peyramont, who held the position of *conseiller à la cour royale,* was proud that he never really transferred his allegiance to the Empire; he liked to tell people that when asked if he would stay on as procureur général, he had warned the prefect after the coup d'état, "Do not insist . . . If I should keep my position, I would be obliged to arrest you." The other prominent Orleanists elected were Carreyron, Benoît de Buis (the president of the Agricultural Society, whose pre-electoral statement claimed that he was continually surrounded by adoring peasants), and St. Marc Girardin, son of the Orleanist deputy.[91]

The next weeks brought not an end to the economic crisis, as some anticipated, but its intensification. Business activity remained paralyzed because of a lack of credit; successive extensions of due dates for previous loans piled up. The Chamber of Commerce tried to assist the flow of credit, but only the porcelain industry showed any signs of returning to normalcy. Even the few industries that had done well because of the war—for example, those producing military uniforms and equipment or turning out the almost endless newspapers and official *affiches*— now faced grave difficulties.[92]

The Société populaire demanded the retention of the municipal workshops, despite their weekly cost of thirty thousand francs, while empty coffers dictated their closure. The council meetings became so boisterous, in the presence of an almost frantic public, that a post of National Guardsmen had to keep order. Unable to raise money, on March 13 the Municipal Council threatened to resign; one member wryly suggested that a council of monarchists would have better luck turning up funds. But at the urging of the prefect and the Société populaire, the council agreed to stay on. On March 19 it took the difficult decision to close the workshops, while the radical clubs accused capitalists of trying to strangle the Republic by withholding funds. Talandier did not like monarchists, but he admitted that the workshops were too expensive to maintain, further distancing him from the Société populaire. In his editorial of March 19 he expressed the fear that the workers of the city might be tempted to rise up, following the slogan of the silkworkers of Lyon almost forty years earlier, "Vivre en travaillant, ou mourir en combattant!" They were, after all, demanding weapons as they had in 1848.[93]

Dramatic news arrived from Paris: the failure of Thiers's attempt to seize the cannons of Montmartre on March 18; the armed resistance of the people of Paris; the withdrawal of the army to encircle the capital; and, finally, the proclamation of the Commune. Limoges's Orleanists immediately proclaimed their support for Versailles, while the moderate newspapers *La Défense nationale* and *La Défense républicaine* merged in order to amplify their opposition to the monarchist threat posed by the new National Assembly. Talandier trumpeted the rights demanded "by our immortal capital . . . which represents the avant-garde of progress." He found nothing unjust in the demands of Paris.[94]

Whereas the Société pour la défense républicaine emphasized the decentralized, municipal aspects of the proclamation of the Commune, the Société populaire applauded the socialist aspirations of the Parisian workers. The quest for municipal autonomy was but the first essential step for the emancipation of the working class.

The events in Paris increased the vehemence with which the Société populaire demanded arms for the Guard and the maintenance of the workshops. When the prefect announced that 6,000 rifles would be distributed in the Haute-Vienne—3,000 in Limoges alone—the wealthy were frightened. Several notables claimed to have received warnings that the Limoges clubs were out to get them, that they had been mentioned at meetings. News of the insurrection in Lyon was received by the Société populaire with shouts of "Long Live the Commune!" and a rendition of the "Marseillaise." On March 21 some 150 people gathered outside the town hall chanting, "We need arms, we are the people; the bourgeoisie has provoked us!" At the same moment a delegation from the radical club implored the Municipal Council to demand that the prefect release the guns to the Guard.[95] The Société pour la défense républicaine called upon the provisional government to "accord to Paris all of the municipal franchises it demands" and attacked Thiers for turning the provinces against the capital. It also called for the armament and review of the National Guard. But, once again, despite the immediacy of the crisis, the municipality had to await the blessing of the central government.[96]

On the thirty-first the council affirmed the closing date of April 5 for the workshops. The following day the prefect authorized a review for the second.[97] But the provisional government ominously announced that the new procureur général would be a violently antirepublican magistrate named Breuilh. Such an appointment augured badly for republicans. There was new talk at the Société populaire of proclaiming the Commune in Limoges.[98]

On April 2 *La Défense républicaine* stated that the majority of the population would proclaim the Commune but limited its conception of the term "commune" to that engendered by the reaction against imperial centralization. The moderate paper carefully distinguished this meaning from any meaning that might be construed as "communist." It asked "the most fervent members of the Société populaire" if the "commune" of Limoges was not "freely elected." Given the "intellectual and moral level" of the population, the paper asked, could the city hope for a more radical Municipal Council, as suggested by another interpretation of "commune?" What frightened these bourgeois republicans was not the "illegality" of revolutions—which seemed to take place in France every twenty years or so—but the powerlessness of the people to take control of their own city. Until the educational and moral level of the Limoges workers was higher, the city should be content with a moderate republic and the right to elect its own council and thus, indirectly, its mayor. Therefore Limoges already had what Paris wanted. The workers should put any thought of insurrection or another meaning of "commune" out of mind.

Both clubs planned meetings for April 2, a day during which rumors of trouble abounded in the city. The Société populaire certainly discussed the awaited armament of the Guard, and probably also whether an attempt should be made to proclaim the Commune in Limoges.[99] Believing that such a step might be taken, the prefect readied the troops. Delegates from the Société populaire asked the Société pour la défense républicaine to join them in a demonstration. They were not warmly received, being reminded by the bourgeois republicans that such an act would be seditious. One military officer warned the workers that the first shots fired would be directed at them.[100]

Yet calm prevailed that day and the following day as well, which surprised the police, in view of yet another postponement of the National Guard review, when the guns would presumably be distributed. That night the Municipal Council agreed that the workshops would stay open as long as any money remained. When the council turned to discuss the elusive review, Dubois argued forcefully that the revolution of September 4 had abrogated all previous laws affecting the Guard. He proposed that the council vote on the demand of the Société populaire that the review take place no matter what the prefect or commander of the military division said. Dubois also allegedly said that, if necessary, the military headquarters be stormed and the guns taken by force, which brought a retort from Ransom that he was inciting revolt. When the vote came on the question of what would have been an illegal review, the moderates won twelve to six. Rebeyrolle shouted that the capitalists were trying to strangle the Republic, to which Talandier replied that the only question was the municipal revolution that Paris had undertaken. At the same time, several people in a group of thirty or so gathered at the place Dauphine were seen wearing red kepi shaped into the *bonnet rouge* of the sansculottes; a red and black flag appeared in the crowd.[101]

On May 6 a train was to leave Limoges carrying troops from the garrison to Versailles. That morning members of the Société populaire marched through the streets toward the station. The troops may have already given some indication that they "did not want to take action" against the Parisians. The workers seemed ready to tear up the tracks to prevent the train from leaving. At the station they found rifles stacked and ready to be loaded onto the trains once the soldiers were aboard. The workers urged the troops to refuse to board; some of those already in the train were singing the "Marseillaise." The stationmaster tried to get the convoy moving, and a few cars were hauled down the tracks, but they were then stopped. By eleven o'clock soldiers and workers were walking back into Limoges together. Some soldiers received vouchers at the *mairie,* while others got them at the hall on the rue Palvézy. One soldier was lodged for that night in an auberge on the route de Toulouse, where he had been led by a man who ordered the innkeeper to lodge him.[102]

At the town hall Rebeyrolle and Dubois proposed that the troops choose between Versailles and Paris. Almost all soldiers assembled there shouted out "Paris." At four in the afternoon some companies of National Guardsmen met to discuss the situation. That evening members of the Société populaire went to the mayor's office for the purpose of discussing whether or not the Commune should be proclaimed in Limoges. They wanted to convince the Municipal Council to deliberate formally on the Paris Commune, but an insufficient number of councilmen were present for any kind of vote. The secretary of the council made it clear that he would not register such an "illegal" deliberation. The mayor demanded to know what the Société populaire meant by a "commune." Outside an officer of the Guard harangued the crowd that had congregated there after leaving the place Dauphine.[103]

A deputation of councilmen and about seventy guardsmen went to see Deplon, the new prefect. Mayor Ransom assured him that there was order in the streets and urged the official to use his influence to obtain a general pardon for the soldiers, who could face the death penalty if convicted of mutiny. Delpon replied that he could only guarantee that the troops would not have to appear before a court-martial, but that simple disciplinary penalties would most likely be meted out if they returned their weapons immediately and turned themselves in.

In the distance the sound of drums called the Guard, and workers soon filled the courtyard of the prefecture. They listened to several impromptu speeches in favor of proclaiming the Commune. Approximately 5 or 6 officers attempted to maintain order, but about 150 guardsmen broke line and ranged themselves on the left side of the courtyard. Someone standing on the stairs cried out, "We are here to protest against the Versailles government!" Others shouted, "We will no longer follow our leaders! . . . Do you want the government of Versailles or that of Paris?" One worker yelled, "If the prefect will not come to us, we will go to him!" Shortly Delpon, who had left the prefecture earlier, returned and three times ordered the outside gate shut, but without success. Two men, one of them almost certainly Dubois, "proclaimed" the Commune. The National Guard offered the prefect no assistance, most of its members having joined the other workers in the courtyard.[104]

Delpon then walked to the place Dauphine, several blocks away, and ordered the cavalry there to disperse the large crowd, which was now shouting for the Commune. As the troops began to clear the place St. Michel, forming four or five groups in double-line formation, the National Guardsmen challenged them with fixed bayonets. The cavalry wheeled quickly around and moved toward a confrontation. A shot was fired from the vicinity of a house owned by a tailor named Thomas, followed by two or three other shots. Rebeyrolle stood near that house, after having allegedly asked a woman standing nearby if she had any gunpowder. A cavalry colonel named Billet, mounted on his horse, was hit, falling mortally wounded on the cobblestones of the place d'Aîne. Immediately, at the instigation of Rebeyrolle, some workers began to construct barricades near the door of St. Michel's and on the adjacent rue Pennevayre and the rue des Prisons. Witnesses, including one jeweler who had been awakened by the shots, heard someone say that the crowd should break into the church and sound the tocsin; another individual heard someone grumble that it was necessary to shoot *ces coquins*—the soldiers. Loyal troops cleared the barricades within several hours, meeting no resistance. Most of the crowd had quickly scattered after the death of Billet. Limoges's very brief Commune was over.[105]

Chamiot, the procureur général and an old republican, met with administrative and military officials and jointly proclaimed a state of seige in Limoges. The Société populaire was immediately closed, its hall boarded up, and the National Guard dissolved. Chamiot, however, did not want the Society for Republican Defense banned for fear of playing into the hands of the reaction that republicans and anticlericals had every reason to fear. The moderate club blamed the Municipal Council for its indecision on the issue of the National Guard review; it expressed a certain sympathy for the workers, who could never, it insisted, remain indifferent in the struggle that would determine the destiny of France. The provisional government would have to "recognize the right of Paris, as well as of other towns, to its municipal franchise." The next day more troops arrived, replacing those whose departure for Versaille had initiated yet another revolutionary *journée* in Limoges. The latter were sent to Agen; it seemed that they could not be trusted.[106]

Were the events in Limoges nothing more than a "decentralized reaction" to state centralization? We have emphasized the demand of Talandier and the Société pour la défense républicaine that Paris—and Limoges—be granted municipal liberties. Almost all important cities in France had joined the opposition to the Empire. For most workers the desire for increased municipal liberties was less important than it was for bourgeois republicans, Orleanists, or even for legitimists such as Louis Guibert. The Société populaire had called for the establishment of a Committee of Public Safety. Yet workers and petty bourgeois accepted decentralization, at least partially, because the financial problems of the city and the conflict between capital and labor had to first be resolved in Limoges, with the issues of national political power left unsettled. Anticlerical measures, the purge of imperial or monarchist officials, and the election of loyal republicans to municipal offices were political goals of both the Society for Republican Defense and the Société populaire. The young Guesde was right when he wrote, in 1877, that the provinces acclaimed "the socialist side of the Commune less than the political side." Corbin, stressing the difficulty of assessing the role of ideology among the Limoges workers during this period, has stated that there were no real socialist demands in the turbulent city.[107]

However, neither the decentralist nor the socialist interpretation of the Limoges events can be completely dismissed. These two interpretations are not mutually exclusive. While exaggerating the organizational and ideological coherence of the movement, the industrialists of Limoges did not simply make up the socialist threat in 1871. We have placed the workers' actions during *l'année terrible* in the context of class antagonism and working-class mobilization that characterized the Empire's last years, as well as the continued industrialization and expansion of the city's working-class faubourgs. The meetings in the salle Palvézy and the *orateur populaire* of the place Dauphine anticipated the sessions of the Société populaire, as well as the hostility toward capitalists during the discussions of the city's financial distress and the bitter Gibus strike. Like the Parisians, the workers of Limoges lacked time to formulate a program. Did minutes exist from the meetings of the Société populaire? If the club had its own newspaper, like its moderate counterpart, we would be able to say more than this. The planned paper *Revendication* never got off the ground. As Jeanne Gaillard puts it, the Communards saw decentralization as "an indispensable stage for socialism in that it would allow them to take over the responsibilities given up by the state."[108] The workers had rejected bourgeois political tutelage, although petty bourgeois leaders like Rebeyrolle attracted support. They saw that the conquest of municipal power could bring serious economic, social, and political reforms. They demanded, among other things, arms for the National Guard; the guarantee of the "right to work" through the maintenance of the municipal workshops, for which strikers would be eligible; the rights of trade associations; and the right of the municipality and the state to put the wealth of capitalists at the people's disposal when the circumstances required. Capital, as Bergeron would insist a year later, was the workers' enemy, forcing them to be "beasts of burden." The state would have to defend workers against the "arbitrary acts" of such manufacturers as Gibus. By forming a *chambre fédérale* that would join the *chambres syndicales* of each trade, workers could gradually defend themselves and eventually eliminate the capitalist from production. This socialism lay, of course, in the future. But the heady period of the Commune was a start; as has been often observed, this made the workers' revolution of 1871 the last of the "old" revolutions but also the first of the new.

Chamiot's attempt to limit the repression did not succeed. The new prefect replaced the republican council with antirepublican conservatives. Three fourths of the workers employed in the municipal workshops were let go immediately, the remainder on April 26. *La Défense républicaine* greeted the proclamation of the state of siege with black-bordered pages. The municipal election at the end of the month left the council with a slight majority of republicans over Orleanists ("liberal independents"), although the Conseil de guerre simply canceled a runoff vote for one seat. As the Communards were being slaughtered in the capital, the fury of reaction struck Limoges. The Conseil de guerre handed down death sentences to Dubois and Rebeyrolle in absentia, since both had fled the city. Twenty-five men were convicted of political crimes.[109]

A Commission of Inquiry into the events of the Commune heard the testimony of leading manufacturers.[110] One by one they indicted the International, although many differed as to the degree of its influence. Two *maîtres de forges* believed that a weaver from Limoges had been won over by workers encountered at the 1867 exposition in Paris. Jean Baptiste de Fontaubert, a porcelain manufacturer, insisted that two thirds of the porcelain workers in Limoges were members: The International worked through the *syndicats,* he asserted, exercising "an absolute authority over its members . . . I am sure that if it ordered members to die of hunger, they would obey." Gibus claimed that the strike against him could only have been a plot of the International. Charles Vergne said that two thirds of his *pâtiers* belonged. The shoe manufacturer Demartial testified that he had seen a small book listing the statutes and membership of the International. Louis Tharaud remembered firing one worker who—although workers in general had been "very discreet" about revealing their membership—"blurted it out when drinking." An employee of the Pouyat porcelain factory asserted that subscription lists openly circulated in the workshops. Most manufacturers cited the arrival of the two Parisian workers; some thought a mysterious lawyer from the capital who came to Limoges in September was involved. One worker admitted that the workers could never have organized themselves without those two porcelain workers, who had "put them on the right path" by instructing them to form *chambres syndicales* that would assume the right to fix wage rates. There was also a rumor that a delegate from the Paris Commune stayed at the Hôtel Boule d'or for eight days early in April.

Other witnesses thought the number of International members had been exaggerated. Leonard Pornin, a shoe manufacturer, did not believe his workers had joined but now took the precaution of forbidding them to read in his workshop. One of his colleagues thought that the only way the working class could be made more "moral" would be to ban political newspapers, clubs, and even cafés. In the cabarets near his factory workers discussed politics while spending their money, particularly those workers "improperly called *artistes,*" that is, decorators, who earned five francs a day. The unskilled workers seemed wiser. In sum, there was no more evidence to assume that the International had three or four thousand members in Limoges, which is what the commission of inquiry claimed, than there was for the absurd assertions that the workers had been paid off by the Austrians and Italians. But the owner of a workshop specializing in decoration who testified that the workers of Limoges shared many of the goals of the international was certainly correct.

The authorities enforcing the "moral order" in France assumed that the International instigated the reconstitution of the *chambres syndicales* in 1872, associations lacking the "security" of wealthy honorary presidents and honorary members. A year after the Commune over one thousand workers had joined the *chambres syndicales,* and Bergeron was again urging the creation of a federation across trades. When enough money had been saved, the *chambres syndicales* would replace the *patronat.* Once again porcelain workers were the leaders. But other trades, too, were active. When a *chambre syndicale* of shoemakers planned a *société anonyme,* the prefect scoffed at their effort. "The members of this organization are all workers who own absolutely nothing and live, for the most part, from day to day."[111]

In the meantime, Colonel Billet was buried in religious and military splendor. The cathedral was draped with rich cloth furnished by the wealthy merchants of Limoges, whose magnanimity had been absent when the city had needed their help.[112] Signs of mourning were strikingly absent in the faubourgs. The newspaper *La Nation française,* published in Paris, began a Limoges edition on April 11, with a monarchist restoration in mind. It recounted alleged horrors perpetrated against Paris by the Communards, noting the "indignation felt by the provinces on the occasion of the riot in the capital." Its editorial of July 14 noted that "Charles Marx, a Jew by birth, originally from the Prussian Rhineland, had put himself at the head of a vast conspiracy which has as its goal the creation of practical communism."[113] The bishop of Limoges launched a campaign to build a new parish near the porcelain factories: The Church of St. Joseph became Limoges's fifth parish.[114] When the Municipal Council refused to give church schools a subvention, the prefect himself allocated part of its budget for this purpose.[115] The butchers held their annual procession of St. Aurélien in peace. The workers gradually returned to their jobs as the economic crisis ebbed; trains soon carried the city's porcelain. A special train transporting eight hundred people to Lourdes presented a marked contrast to the sober gathering of fifteen-hundred workers who followed the casket of Pradeau, a porcelain worker and former *quarante-huitard,* to a civil burial and the Louyat cemetery.[116] Nearby, in a café called Le Petit Musée, located at 46, route de Paris, a hat was passed for the families of those workers who were in prison.[117]

5

Limoges in the Belle Epoque

Roland Duchalard's father moved his family from the countryside to Limoges in 1891 so that the boy and his sibling would benefit from improved city schools. They first settled near the place d'Aîne and then moved to 8, rue Croix Buchilien, near the burgeoning faubourgs beyond the rue Mauvendière. The neighborhood was, in Roland's words, "a little eccentric." He contrasted their large house and garden with the empty lot across from them, the unfinished streets rapidly muddied by rain, and the row of poor houses "badly or inadequately maintained, with gray, leprous facades where the families of workers—porcelain workers or other kinds—took refuge." The young boy quickly became aware that his prosperous family—he described his mother as being "of society" and giving teas in the afternoon—had virtually no contact with the poor who lived on the same street, although they may have both frequented the small grocery store where their street met the avenue Saint-Surin. The reason was simple: Class differences "existed as an insurmountable barrier between those that one used to call 'the great society' and the people. It was then a social convention that had assumed the force of law, and not even the most hardy would have dared to break it."[1]

The family of the poor joiner lived near the Duchalard house. One day the joiner's wife bravely stopped Roland's mother on the street. This in itself was most surprising. She had a favor to ask. Their daughter, who was twelve, was at home dying of tuberculosis. "I see, Madame, that you have a cute little boy. Would you permit him to come to our house to see our little girl, who, alas, has little time left? She speaks often of him and would be happy if she could see him." Roland's mother assented. He went to call on the dying girl, stayed ten or fifteen minutes, and left, convinced that his presence had provided her ultimate consolation. This event, understandably, was one of Roland's most vivid memories. Another was the mounted troops he saw on the way to school during the strikes of April 1905. Had the girl lived, they would have been on opposite sides. She would have been there cheering on the strikers, and he knew it very well.

As the nineteenth century drew to a close in Limoges, urban growth, large-scale industrialization, and class conflict were certainly not new to its inhabitants' experience. But the scale of these changes and the transformation of economic, social, political, and cultural life were surprising, their intensity worrying. The population of the city had increased from just over 55,000 in 1872 to about 84,000 at the end of the century—four times larger than at its beginning. Almost half of the population now depended upon industrial work for its livelihood. Signs of the concentration of capital and industry were readily apparent (see Chapter Six). The place of unskilled and female workers in industry had increased; so had that of the factory. There were twice as many porcelain workers in the city, over 10,500 by 1891, and another 5,000 making shoes—four times the number in 1872. The streets of the faubourgs, where most of the larger factories lay, were jammed with workers rushing to get to work before the bell; they remained quiet until the noonday break for a meal, when the faubourgs again came alive. The imperatives of the manufacturers and their foremen shaped the lives of the workers. The rhythm of work, that is to say, the rhythm of capital, seemed to determine the pace of Limoges and now centered on the periphery of the city. At the same time, commerce also had expanded rapidly. Whereas 1,124 people had paid the business tax in 1859, now there were more than 3,600 *patentés*.[2]

The growth of the city in the 1880s and 1890s continued to fall within the administrative limits of the commune rather than contributing to the development of a series of separately administered communes forming an industrial *banlieue* like the "red belt" surrounding much of Paris. The construction of factories in the open spaces at the edge of the city and the construction of the merchandise railroad station of Montjovis accentuated the expansion of the city's faubourgs. The dense settlement and higher cost of living in the center city encouraged workers to settle in the faubourgs. Here the urban and rural worlds met. The *octroi* had been extended further out in December 1872, despite the opposition of the socialist Vallière, who argued that the poor workers who had lived beyond the *octroi* could only survive by living outside of the customs barrier, taking advantage of slightly lower costs for staples. When the centenary of the *octroi* was celebrated in 1900, much of the land within the circumference of the twenty-three tax posts had been filled in with houses, at least along the central axes leading out of town and the streets connecting them. In 1906 the *octroi* would be extended outward again.[3]

The development of the faubourgs, "ces voies si populeuses et animées," created a natural intersection where the new avenues Poitiers and Tarrade converged with the route de Paris and the avenue Garibaldi, beyond the Theodore Haviland factory. This *rond-point,* the place Carnot, had been named after the Limoges-born president of the Republic, who was assassinated in Lyon in 1895.[4] The Louyat cemetery, once far from the limits of the settlement, now lay at the

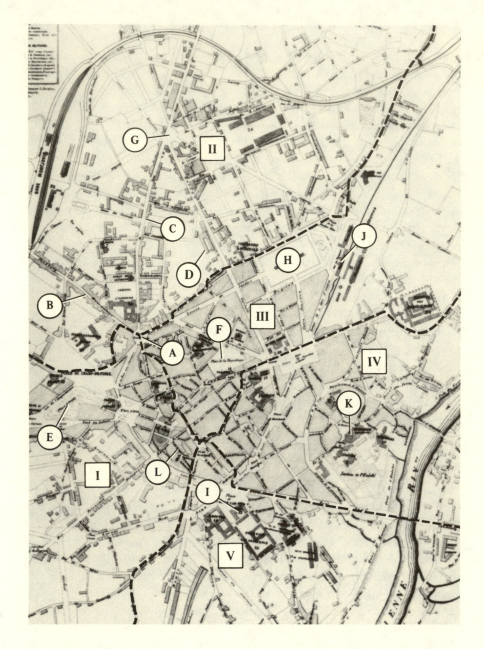

LIMOGES IN 1885

A. place Denis-Dussoubs
B. faubourg Montmailler
C. rue de Paris
D. Factory of Theodore Haviland
E. Jardin d'Orsay
F. place de la République

G. place Carnot (future)
H. Champ de Juillet
I. Town Hall
J. Railroad Station (Gare des Bénédictins)
K. Cathedral
L. rue de la Boucherie

(NOTE: *Roman numerals refer to electoral sections in Limoges [after 1888]*)

edge of the city. It had to be expanded to accommodate the urban overflow at the turn of the century. Four new crematoriums were built in 1894, leading one wag to write that Limoges was indeed a "city of *fours*."[5] The faubourg Montmailler and the route de Paris were now an integral part of life in Limoges, despite a population largely drawn from the rural world; they were now urban enough to be called *rues*.[6]

Limoges was not very pretty—even after the expenditure of over a million francs. The faubourgs had developed according to their proximity to the factories and available land. The radiating roads provided their only apparent harmony, as if they had been planned by someone who wanted to leave Limoges as directly and quickly as possible. If the city cherished one description from bygone years, it was that of a *ville d'art* of enamel and porcelain. The growth of Limoges had been anything but artful. There had been but one planned quarter, that of the investment group Société immobilière. Only one *cité ouvrière* was ever built (inaugurated in 1909), located at the entrance to the faubourg Montjovis, and that single building looked quite out of place among its smaller, flimsier neighbors. Even the relatively prosperous Beaupeyrat quarter to the west, in which a square had been planned, seemed "out of harmony."[7]

Many streets remained unpaved for years, their houses unnumbered, as anonymous as the workers who inhabited them. Most of the houses of the faubourgs had been hastily constructed and were but one or two stories tall; indeed, almost half of all the houses in the city in 1896 (48.6 percent) had only two floors, with 10.9 percent having but a ground floor.[8] The Municipal Council had begun to turn its attention to aligning the faubourgs, particularly where they were encumbered by odd houses obstructing the flow of traffic. Gradually, with the development of such new quarters as Rouchoux, streets were built to link them with the main arteries of the faubourgs. At the turn of the century house numbers and gas lamps followed.[9]

The onrushing growth and industrialization of Limoges also had several consequences for its hinterland. The city and its industries attracted migrants from the department. Limoges was a dynamic urban center in a region that was gradually being depopulated: The 1896 census demonstrated that the Haute-Vienne was the only department in the Center-West that did not decrease in population. Its population had grown by almost three thousand people, but this was so only because of Limoges's five thousand additional inhabitants. The 1901 census reflected the same pattern, with only the Haute-Vienne gaining in population, again because of the attraction exerted by its capital city.[10] At the same time, Limoges's growth engendered a minor agricultural revolution in its surrounding communes. For example, the small, mediocre vineyards began to recede as peasants or tenant farmers brought more land into cultivation. Truck farming and cattle raising developed in response to a larger urban population. Despite the attraction of Limoges, the population of the immediately surrounding communes,

Porcelain workers at the entrance to the Theodore Haviland factory

dispersed in small hamlets and isolated farms, rose with the intensification of agriculture. Births began to regularly outnumber deaths before they did so in Limoges.

The commune of Isle, to the southwest, typified these changes. In 1811 a survey demonstrated that the lands of the commune could barely support the 581 people who lived there. But over the decades rough grazing land and stubble became excellent meadows, the omnipresent chestnut groves gave way to truck farming, and fodder plants and scraggly sheep had been replaced by the Limousin cattle that became the pride of the regional agricultural competitions. The population had more than tripled, although people from Limoges still owned much of the land. In Le Palais, on the north side of the Vienne River, farmers also raised cattle or produced grains for the Limoges market. Yet by the end of the century almost half of the active population in four small factories prepared *pâte* for the porcelain manufacturers. Most of the others worked in agriculture or as domestics in the city. The people of Condat, across the Vienne from Isle and to the southwest, worked in the small factories along the river. Bosmie was known for its truck farming and its "magnificent" horticulture and greenhouses. The consolidation of farmland, an increase in cultivated land, and improved agricultural techniques had increased the yields of wheat, rye, potatoes, beets, and turnips. Some artisanal industry survived in the hamlet of Aigville.[11]

The population of St. Just, also on the Vienne, increased from 907 in 1808 to 1,365 in 1901, but the amount of land cultivated or left as meadows increased even faster, particularly in the last decade of the century. With the exception of a handful of blacksmiths and wheelwrights, virtually the entire active population either produced a sizable harvest of wheat, rye, buckwheat, potatoes, and market vegetables or raised cattle. In Feytiat only about 40 percent of the commune's land had been utilized during the Restoration—no more than in the middle of the eighteenth century. By 1900 most of the land of the commune yielded over 1,000 hectoliters of grains, vegetables, and potatoes, and large herds of cattle fattened peaceably. Here, more than elsewhere in the immediate hinterland, larger plots of land predominated. Twenty-seven people—again, almost all residing in Limoges—owned three quarters of the land, with sixteen people owning two thirds of the latter. In the ancien régime the land had been the property of the clergy and officials of the *généralité;* like the latter, the new owners still sent agents out to oversee their property. Sharecropping was common both on large- and middle-sized plots; some sharecroppers owned a little land but could not make ends meet. Here, also, there was more pastureland. Industrial workers included only some building workers, wheelwrights, blacksmiths, and gasket makers (producing a gasket called *ballo* in patois, with the sixty-nine workers known as *ballaires*). The population had almost doubled, from 721 in 1806 to 1,303 in 1901, despite the migration of many young single women to Limoges during the middle decades of the century. Now entire families seemed to be on the move, and more than half of all boys called to military service entered the factories of Limoges, returning home only on off days rather than remaining in Feytiat as sharecroppers and day laborers. The growth of Limoges had transformed the surrounding communes, as it had the life inside the city; it had not been all that long since the owners of the marginally productive land of Panazol, to the northeast of the city, complained that wolves were feasting on their sheep.[12]

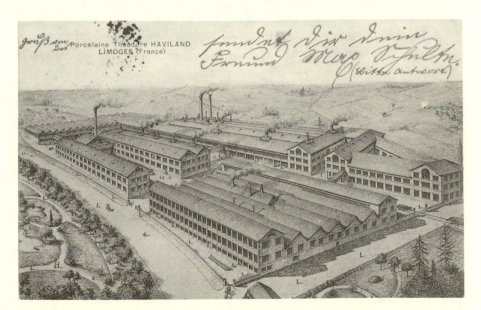

The Theodore Haviland Factory—a contemporary view

The faubourg de Paris

Fin-de-siècle France was the so-called "belle époque," the good old days associated with what Roger Shattuck calls the "atmosphere of permanent explosion in artistic activities" of the avant-garde of modern culture: festive banquets, the great exposition of 1900, and the heyday of boulevard life and the café concert. Paris "knew only that it was having a good time and making a superb spectacle of itself." France, particularly urban France, seemed to celebrate progress in every realm and looked forward excitedly, even frenetically, to the dawning of a new century. Limoges shared this sense of exhilaration. In 1900 *limougeauds* viewed the proliferation of voluntary associations as a sign of progress in their city. There was more to do in the city, more distractions available to those people with the time and the money to enjoy them. The bustle of associational activity, the development of Limoges as a major railroad center, and the expansion of its industries gave the capital of the Limousin a new sense of importance. While not considered one of France's major centers of tourism, it attracted a congress of office clerks, another of *aliénistes,* and hosted regional flower and dog shows. One man imagined *trains de plaisir*—such as those that frequently left Limoges to visit more exotic locales—bringing eager visitors to the city to spend their money, perhaps in one of the city's four department stores. The Hôtel Central opened a fashionable *grande taverne,* while a competitor sent a bus to pick up arriving passengers at the station.[13]

Voluntary associations encouraged a variety of sports, including biking, football, track-and-field events, and—after these exhausting activities—drinking. The hundred members of the Limousin Sports Club could be found in a café on the place Dussoubs. The Association des touristes limousines, founded in 1894, brought biking enthusiasts back from the department's bumpy roads to a café on the Champ de Juillet. Their competitors from the Limousin Athletic Club could be recognized by their black and white racing uniforms. In 1892 three gymnastic societies had enrolled over eighteen hundred members: the Société gymnastique et de tir (1881), the Patriote limousin (1886), and Défense (1893). At the turn of the century sixteen gymnastic and shooting clubs outnumbered the eleven other sporting groups. Among the latter, the Union athlétique limousin (1900) encouraged hiking, and the Société de l'aviron et de la voile (1887) organized "nautical exercises," while the Club nautique sponsored modest regattas on the Vienne for its several hundred members. The Véloce Club (1888) held a race of a hundred kilometers, which drew spirited competition from the rival Union vélocipédique limousin (1890), with its motto "Encore plus vite!" The Société des sauveteurs now challenged the old *ponticauds* for the title of "Kings of the Vienne." Members of the Steeple Chase Club could now be seen bounding over the hedges of the rural Limousin, probably to the amusement of those country folk fishing in the small streams and lakes, picking mushrooms, or gathering chestnuts.[14] There was lots more to do in the belle époque.

Balloons, telephones, and finally (in 1898) automobiles caught the imagination of the city. Charles Haviland purchased one of the first automobiles in Limoges. The Société aérostatique launched balloons, while the Association colombophile— les courriers de Limoges sent pigeons into the air, one of which reached Brussels in ten hours. The Nouvelles Galéries discovered the balloon ascents were a good way to advertise their business. Like the railroad forty years earlier, the tramway emerged as probably the most visible symbol of urban progress. The first two lines, from the rue Baudin to the rond-point Garibaldi (later Carnot) and from the station to the *école normale,* attracted throngs of curious riders on inaugura-tion day (June 6, 1897). Despite many minor accidents, beginning on the very first day, the trams were a great success. The *Almanach Limousin,* although com-plaining of the "unworthy" comportment of the new riders, who pushed and shoved to get aboard, boasted that "thanks to the tramways, our city now has the same physiognomy of great cities; the life and the movement of its thorough-fares now seem greater than ever." The socialist newspaper *Rappel du Centre,* on the other hand, emphasized the egalitarian dimension of the tramways, which served the faubourgs: "Drelin, drelin, c'est le tram qui passe, ici l'égalité, point de place de choix."[15]

Yet despite the sporting clubs and the tramway, the belle époque, in the usual sense of the term, bypassed Limoges—and the city knew it. The culture of the avant-garde, discussed by Shattuck in his fine book *The Banquet Years,* had no apparent impact on Limoges.[16] The gaiety of the *grands boulevards* of the city of light seemed far away indeed, as it did for the *bidonvilles* and grim suburbs of the capital. Several balloon ascents did not constitute a belle époque, nor did a banquet celebrating the hundredth anniversary of the *octroi,* or the arrival of the heralded Barnum and Bailey circus in 1902. Café concerts in fin-de-siècle

Limoges did not fare any better than their predecessors. These had been little more than lairs of prostitution, such as Chez Gane, until one of those "lyrical artistes" blew the whistle on the place in 1886 after being forced to pay large sums of money to the owner, who told her to bring *bons types* back for some business.[17] For those citizens "not satisfied with the pleasures of the hearth, moonlight walks under the trees of the Champ de Juillet," or Limoges's 313 existing cafés and cabarats, a café concert made another try. The casino opened its doors in January, 1901, and the eager population at first came in droves, although some people complained that the audience could not understand the dialogue of the presentations because it was in patois, which only the workers knew. There was still much that seemed rural about Limoges, such as the hair fair, where peasant girls from the region sold up to 350 kilograms of their hair to merchants.[18]

Fin-de-siècle Limoges retained its reputation as a place with a population that was *froide*. The bourgeoisie, having closed its shops at the end of the day, rarely left the quiet sanctity of home. However, the 240 members of the Cercle de l'union on the boulevard Fleurus paid dearly for such distractions as reading, whist, bridge, drink, and conversation among the "aristocratic element of Limoges and the department, or great industrialists and merchants, retired or still active." In the 1880s large sums had sometimes been lost in a single night; now the stakes were more modest, with politics the basic theme of their discussions. The Cercle Turgot, once known as the Cercle des jeunes gens, joined 200 bourgeois, principally drawn from the world of commerce.[19] But their solemn gatherings could hardly have been confused with the humorous, youthful, and irreverent culture of the so-called "banquet years."[20]

Limoges illustré, which recorded the highlights of social, cultural, and religious life in the city, found little to relate. The bimonthly review complained that Limoges remained a sad place, citing, among other things, the lack of serious dancing (as opposed to the *bals de société*) as an example of cultural impoverishment. Sounding very much like J. J. Juge early in the century, the journal criticized the public's taste for luxury. Dances had become too complicated, such as "Le Cake-walk" (also known as "Le Kangourou"), imported from America, it was commonly assumed, by way of Paris. For the author this dance evoked "the image of a poodle forced to walk on its hind legs. There are no precise rules; it marks the triumph of personal improvisation!" If the middle classes did not like to dance anymore, especially like *that,* they enjoyed singing immensely, and the various local singing societies and visiting groups continued to draw crowds, particularly the Enfants de Limoges. But Camille Jouhanneaud's complaint in the retrospective article "Limoges, fin de siècle," published in the *Almanach Limousin,* insisted that his city had little intellectual or social life. The Société philharmonique had closed its doors. He blamed this on the lack of an aristocratic tradition in the "ville de travail et de traditions bourgeoises." While denying that his city had ever been as morose as was commonly believed, he feared that Limoges would become one large factory.[21] It now sounded like an old story.

Walking back from the faubourgs, a quick stroll through the old city revealed a changed iconography. Earlier in the century visitors had noted the number of statues of the Virgin Mary and the saints as a sign of the close relationship between the Church and the city: Notre-Dame-du-Pont, Notre-Dame-du-Battoir, Notre-Dame-des-Paresseuses, and Madame-des-Touchoux, who, it was believed, would marry off girls who offered her hairpins. Hippolyte Ducourtieux, a Catholic printer, proudly counted two hundred statues still standing in 1864, many in niches and on streetcorners. By 1900 almost all were gone, victims of the anticlerical sentiments of the municipality and the workers as well as of physical changes, such as new streets like the rue de l'Abbessaille along the Vienne, the rue de Tourny, the rue du Verdurier, and the *champ de foire*. One *calvaire* had fallen victim to a municipal decree. By the turn of the century, Hippolyte Ducourtieux's son, Paul, claimed that religious sentiments were concentrated in the butchers' quarter. And, it seemed to some, perhaps only in the butchers' quarter, which treasured the statue of Notre-Dame-la-Pitié. A large crucifix also stood near the avenue Baudin to the east. St. Joseph's Church, built on the rue de la Fonderie in the late 1870s with the goal of "moralizing" the factory population, had become much more of an object of contempt for the workers in the faubourgs than a place of reverence intended to bring them back to the Church. When the municipality of Limoges refused to allocate any money, the bishop raised funds from those families whose piety equaled their wealth. But the new church parishioners, like those of Limoges's other new church, Sacré-Coeur, located beyond the place des Carmes, were both poor and few in number.[22]

The waning influence of the Church in private life encouraged the secularization of public life in Limoges. The de-Christianization of the population (see Chapter Three) continued, a process documented by quantitative sources. The qualitative evidence is equally striking. Most Catholics in the Limousin were baptized, married, and buried in the Church but otherwise seemed largely unaffected by its teachings and practices. What religious beliefs had been maintained sometimes seemed little more than superstition and the "mad beliefs" emphasized by a recent historian.[23]

Monseigneur Duquesnay, bishop of Limoges during the years following the Commune, lamented the fact that "it seems as though evil [had] triumphed" in his diocese.[24] Subsequent pastoral letters declared that "the danger for the majority of our population is not yet impiety but rather indifference, the incurable apathy, the complete and total abandonment of religious duties . . . it is a universal defection" from the Catholic Church. The missions of 1874 stirred up more resentment than enthusiasm. Those of 1886 were even less successful. At the same time, vocations for the priesthood in the Limousin continued to decline; between 1835 and 1880 only 53 priests were ordained, and the number of priests in the

Haute-Vienne fell from 259 in 1870 to 235 in 1900. Their flocks were also smaller. By 1900 8 percent of the children born to working-class families in Limoges—the most likely group to delay baptism—were never baptized at all. By 1914 that percentage had increased to roughly 34 percent. During that same period the proportion of civil burials grew from 6.8 percent in 1900 to 11.8 percent in 1914; civil marriages grew from 18.5 percent to 39.5 percent at the outbreak of World War I.[25] Table 5 summarizes these trends.

TABLE 5   Rise in De-Christianization in
the City of Limoges

year	nonbaptized children	civil burials	civil marriages
1899	2.50%	5.75%	14.00%
1901	8.00	6.85	18.50
1904	19.20	18.00	32.80
1907	25.00	22.90	48.50
1910	21.25	27.25	30.50
1914	33.90	11.80	29.50

Source: R. Limouzin-Lamothe, Le Diocèse de Limoges du XVIe siècle à nos jours (1510–1950) (Strasbourg, 1953), p. 246.

The Church's work appeared counterproductive. According to one local historian, there seemed to be some truth to the contention of a Protestant brochure that being saved, in the eyes of the Church, amounted to a series of "sins redeemed by penance, penances redeemed by indulgences purchased with money."[26] (Protestants, too, made little headway, winning no more than a handful of converts in Limoges and a few more in several villages in the arrondissement of Bellac.) In 1875 Bishop Duquesnay had baldly identified the political interests of the Church with the ruling classes: "Without a doubt, we, the priests, would be the first victims [of a revolution] . . . but you, the bourgeoisie of our cities, you, the prosperous landowners of the countryside, you merchants and manufacturers, all of you who own something and have an interest in the conservation of order and freedom, you are threatened by the same enemies." These enemies included "proud and lying science." In 1877, the year of the seize mai crisis, he invoked "the principle of infallible authority that requires total and unswerving submission."[27]

Another successor, Bishop Renouard, antagonized radicals and socialists alike when, in 1892, he made a point of insisting that men were not born equal.[28] The identification of several powerful manufacturers and merchants with clerical royalism did not help the image of the Church. The Masons and the active group of freethinkers aided the spread of anticlerical values.[29] Anticlericalism was a ground swell of popular emotion even more than it was a practical political campaign (the outline of which will be traced in a subsequent chapter) against the enemies of the Republic. As the crosses and statues disappeared from the public thoroughfares, few *limougeauds* cared to put them back up. The crowds opposing the religious processions of the early 1880s far outnumbered those participating in them.

While the Municipal Council expressed no interest in the needed repairs to the cathedral and the churches of Limoges, the new town hall proudly symbolized the secular city. The tasks of administering a large city had not been easily accomplished in the old wooden structure built in the late 1830s, which was inadequate in size and had poor lighting. There had been but one room of normal size, and that was almost totally taken up by a large table covered with green velvet. Almost every official communal function took place there, from council meetings to marriages. The new town hall was inaugurated on July 14, 1883. It looked suspiciously like a *bon marché* copy of the Hôtel de Ville in Paris. Couples being married in the *salle de mariage* could gaze at an allegorical scene painted on the ceiling—portraying the virtues of temperance, sweetness, fidelity and, *malgré tout,* chastity—the work of an artist with the wonderfully appropriate name of M. Urbain Bourgeois. Two splendid porcelain vases decorated the first floor of the imposing building.[30]

Limoges, *ville du travail, la ville rouge.* How did the traditional quarters, trades, and customs fare in new Limoges? The old quarters of Naveix and Abbessaille had changed. The inauguration in 1881 of the railroad along the Vienne River to Eymoutiers practically finished off the old port of Naveix. The shift to coal

View of the Abbessaille quarter

Washerwomen working beneath the Pont St. Etienne

as fuel for porcelain kilns had already cut deeply into the available river work. The *ramier* of the Pont St. Etienne gradually fell into disuse until it was finally dislodged by the water and carried away.[31] The *ponticauds* still used flat-bottomed boats, but far fewer of them found work. Laundresses still toiled along the banks of the river, but a steam-cleaning plant had reduced their number and cut into the business of those who remained. They no longer went around to their clients once a year with a wine bottle to be filled—the *pintes des blanchisseuses* had disappeared. The traditional festivals of that quarter had become the object of a certain romanticization by contemporary folklorists and historians. The last of the town criers could still be seen walking up the hill of the old faubourg of Sablard and across the Pont St. Etienne.[32]

Eugen Weber has described the disappearance of "rural" traditions and customs during the first decades of the Third Republic.[33] To what extent rural life was definitively transformed by a victorious urban culture is debatable. Traditional urban customs persisted until late in the century in the old Abbessaille and Naveix quarters. Early in this century the juvenile king and queen still led the annual procession of the *ponticauds*. But they went around in an automobile, followed by such floats as a Venetian gondola and a representation of the relatively recent Eiffel Tower, which few *limougeauds* and probably no one from the quarter had ever seen. The gardeners of the *banlieue* still marched in procession to the modest Church of Ste. Marie with fruits and vegetables on the feast day of St. Fiacre, but the event practically went unnoticed, even by the police, who were supposed to look out for such things.[34]

Carnival, too, while never very boisterously celebrated in cold and reserved Limoges, was different. The street burlesque of the Pont Neuf quarter had disappeared. No longer were local offenders of popular justice mocked; instead, masks of President Kruger of South Africa and other political figures turned up. Carnival had once filled up the streets of Limoges and even the esplanade of the Champ de Juillet; but each year there were fewer revelers. There seemed to be something ironic about the "charming domestic gatherings of bourgeois families" for this occasion. They paid photographers to take carefully posed pictures of their children dressed as powdered marquis, exotic Egyptians, or mysterious Persians, while *le peuple,* having shed their masks, marched through the streets in *cortèges populaires* expressing their own sense of popular justice, once limited to free expression only during Mardi Gras. Now marches left the Bourse du Travail and, aside from May Day, followed not the usual calendar but the timing of elections and strikes. Another traditional celebration, the *fête de boeuf,* had moved inside to the splendid hall of the Hôtel Continental, which was enjoyed by the elite of Limoges. The fair of St. Loup in May was now little more than a vast commercial exchange. The peasants flocked to the place d'Orsay, as before, to sell their produce and animals, but they no longer remained after their business had been transacted to drink, sing—and, occasionally, to have their pockets picked. They still liked to dance, but not in Limoges.[35]

The experience of the butchers and their encounter with the changing city reveal something, I think, of the passing of the nineteenth century. Contemporaries of all political persuasions were fascinated by the juxtaposition of the butchers—their traditions and their quarter—with the new city. What a contrast between the rue de la Boucherie, with its tiny chapel and statue of the Notre-Dame-la-

R. Harari

LIMOGES - La Rue de la Boucherie

The rue de la Boucherie

Another view of the rue de la Boucherie

Pitié, and the industrial faubourgs, "populated with factories that stretch without end."[36] Adrien Delor, a Catholic priest, bemoaned the anticlerical and socialist passion of the working class. One of his friends, the Marquis de Moussac, wrote reverently of a simple leather dresser from the center city who, sharing the religiosity of the butchers, went into the faubourgs and *banlieue* of Limoges to preach the catechism. He found few who listened. But Delor and the Marquis de Moussac both took pride in the fact that all was not lost in Limoges. "What a remarkable contrast," Delor noted, "between the *moeurs* and traditions of the butchers of our city and the unfortunate populations attached to the local industries! On the one hand we find the hatred of religion, on the other respect and love for God." He lamented the absence of workers from religious ceremonies; the butchers, in contrast, auctioned off some of the prize places in ceremonies and used the proceeds to embellish their chapel. Like his mentor Frédéric Le Play, Delor claimed to have discovered "a pearl of the Middle Ages" in the rue de la Boucherie:

> If one does not go to the butchers' quarter to find lessons in grammar or delicate language, one does find honest work . . . Confined to a special quarter, they have until now resisted the invasion of modern ideas. At a time when the very existence of society is universally threatened, where the question of work is posed as the most terrible problem, would it not be useful to establish, by the example that we find under our very eyes, the conditions absolutely essential for social peace?

For Catholic writers, then, the butchers, who had "shown themselves wise by abstaining from certain innovations, such as the department stores," were models for the workers to imitate.[37]

Were these Catholic writers correct in assuming that the butchers' quarter had remained unchanged while large-scale industrialization transformed the city around them? The quarter had, in fact, been affected in several significant ways. The physical expansion of the city helped erode the virtual monopoly that the 5 clans had held in the meat trade for centuries. For this Abbé Delor and the Marquis de Moussac could blame the recently developed faubourgs that housed most of the industrial workers.[38] The butchers' families lost their long-standing agreement with the municipality, which made it much easier for outsiders to get into the business. Whereas in 1877 only 4 butchers resided outside of the quarter, by 1892 12 of the 86 butchers lived in other sections of the city. By 1903 15 butchers were dispersed throughout the city. But more than the locus of the trade was changing. In 1857 all of Limoges's 60 butchers were from the clans. By 1862 only 3 newcomers had appeared. Yet in 1877 18 butchers were outsiders and 14 of these lived in the traditional quarter; some had even married into the clans. By 1903 more than half (64 out of 127) of Limoges's butchers were not from the fabled families, although some were related by marriage. But even the latter fact indicated that the old neighborhood was not the same, although it retained much of its appearance and odor. Census takers found a smattering of other trades and occupations there. In 1876 there had been 5 heads of household who were not butchers (a barber, a joiner, a *propriétaire* and 2 grocers); the 1906 census revealed only 7 out of 57 households not headed by butchers (a shoemaker, a grocer whose shop doubled as a café, a *propriétaire,* a carpenter, a cutler, a day laborer, and one man without a listed profession). Four others were obviously identified with the street's traditional trade: the widow Malinvaud, the widow Pouret, Marie Cibot, and a laborer at the slaughterhouse. Yet 15 of the 57 heads of household were not of the clans, including (to repeat) 8 of the butchers.[39]

More than any other occupational group in Limoges, the butchers were natives of their city, having traditionally *all* been born there. Indeed, as late as 1906 only two of the butchers had not been born in Limoges. Both were from outside the families. Pierre Cibot's wife was from the department of Haute-Vienne, but not its capital, which was also unusual. The butchers' domestics had not necessarily been from Limoges; most of the ten listed as residing with them were from Haute-Vienne, but not Limoges. They were included in the religious celebrations of the trade in the neighborhood but could not participate in the activities of the old corporation. The cutler Chapius, from the Haute-Saône, must have seemed like an oddity on the street. But he soon was in the company of several other newcomers.

The censuses also reveal some of the changes among the butchers' families that their patriarchs were not happy to see. A few second sons, as has already been suggested, moved away to set up shop outside the quarter. Some other sons and daughters married outside the community. Some sons who had been to school refused to take over the family business and adopted other occupations. In 1903 eleven Cibots, nine Plainemaisons, eight Malinvauds, six Pourets, four Parots, and two Juges did something else for a living. Some contemporaries believed that the butchers were having fewer children than before, but the number of children in the butchers' families and the size of the neighborhood had often been wildly exaggerated (eight hundred people in the quarter, with an average of six children per family, according to myth). The decline in the number of children, though not abrupt, was noticeable all the same.[40]

The butchers' associations had even been forced to submit to the bureaucratic requirements of the French Republic. The 1884 law governing associations brought them to the prefecture, where they had to wait in line, like everyone else, to "regularize" their corporation by drawing up legal statutes that would have to be approved by the government. The Syndicat professionel de la boucherie, recognized in 1891, henceforth had the formally stated goal of "creating relations and links of fraternity among members." The general secretary of the *syndicat* represented the butchers in their dealings with the town. The corporation was legalized in the fall of 1887; the fifty-five heads of the families elected four syndics, among whose duties was the enforcement of the rare fines for violation of traditional agreements governing the practice of the trade. Four overlapping organizations resulted from the legal shuffling required by the hated Republic: the *syndicat* of the master butchers; the corporation; the confraternity, whose chief task was the upkeep of the chapel; and the *cercle* of St. Aurélien, which soon moved from the tiny upstairs chapel to the nearby rue Croix Mandonnaud, where pictures of Christ and the Virgin Mary overlooked a billiard table. The first syndic of the confraternity of St. Aurélien also presided over the *cercle* and the *syndicat*. Only the corporation included butchers and domestics from outside the families. Even then the syndic's relations with the municipality were not necessarily cordial. They resisted municipally decreed changes in the regulation of the slaughterhouses; on one occasion a syndic was forced to leave the slaughterhouse by a policeman whom he had threatened. In 1892 the municipality seemed to side with the public, which protested the high price of meat.[41]

Although one wag had commented that it would take "a new Hercules" to clean up the street, some improvements in the physical appearance of the rue de la Boucherie could be readily seen. The butchers had accepted—even petitioned for—the paving of their street and the institution of electricity. After the Revolution of 1830, the new municipality had ordered a plan for aligning the street, but the project seems never to have left the drawing-board stage, and the document itself was subsequently lost. The municipality hatched another such "plot" against the butchers in 1876, ordering the town architect to prepare a map of the quarter that would identify several houses and facades of buildings that could be eliminated in order to widen the street to ten meters, thus bringing more air and light into the neighborhood while facilitating the flow of shoppers. Cibot *dit* le Pape protested vigorously, claiming that cutting back his shop would ruin his business;

his sobriquet suggests that he may have been used to getting his way. In the end the street was widened, but most of this plan, too, remained on the drawing board. The municipality had, however, succeeded in forcing the butchers to remove commercial stalls from the street in front of their stores, which had greatly contributed to congestion. After 1885 the butchers' fierce dogs, which had terrorized adjacent neighborhoods, were no longer permitted to run free at night.[42]

Anticlerical decrees aimed at religious processions were even more traumatic, sparking bitter resistance from the neighborhood whose major events were the celebration of their saints' days and, above all, the Ostensions. In 1876 Ostensions—held when Marshall MacMahon was contemplating a monarchist restoration that would have pleased the butchers enormously—saw 230 relics carried through the streets of Limoges in 92 *reliquaires*. The butchers played their traditional prominent role in the majestic, colorful ceremonies. Until 1880 there had been complaints, but no organized opposition to the celebration of religious fetes, although for reasons of safety, the ritual fusillade of the butchers was banned. But that year the anticlerical tide of the radicals carried the day.[43]

Limoges's Radical mayor, Pénicaud, citing petitions against the butchers, banned "exterior religious ceremonies, known under the name of processions, . . . in the streets and public places of the commune." The butchers vowed not to yield, informing the mayor, "We had them before you; we will have them after you." Fearing trouble, Pénicaud called the syndics of the butchers' corporation to the town hall; his assistant explained the motivation for the decree and defied the "princes of blood" to find a priest who would dare join them in the procession. The chief syndic of the butchers informed the mayor by letter that they intended to proceed as usual, with the assistance of Abbé Bouillard, of the parish of St. Pierre.[44]

On the morning of May 16, 1880, the feast day of St. Martial, thousands of people crowded into the quarter and its adjoining streets to see if the butchers would dare defy the police. The crowd seemed hostile to the butchers. An eyewitness sympathetic to the smocked warriors of religion (who later published a pamphlet describing the events) depicted the crowd with the fear and loathing of Hippolyte Taine: "I saw the hideous mob that ran through the town during the evening of April 4, 1871 [the night of the ill-fated attempt to proclaim the Commune in Limoges]; I believe that I found it again on May 16, 1880, at the doors of the chapel of St. Aurélien. Yes, all of the depraved and worthless people of the city, indeed, all of the usual people who attend civil burials . . ." He criticized the municipal police for not clearing these "freethinkers and rakes" from the tiny square before the holy chapel.[45]

The central police commissioner entered the sacristy of the chapel and informed the priest of the "terrible responsibility" he would assume if the procession took place. Undaunted, Abbé Bouillard announced, "Messieurs les bouchers, we are going to have a procession that will supersede all decrees, in this sad era when only vice and scandal seem to have the right to establish themselves in our streets and at our public places. We will have our procession, but a procession in which the venerated relics of our august protector [St. Martial] will not fall victim to the insults of a vile populace. The relics will remain in the sanctuary." Leaving the chapel by the small door to the sanctuary—the main door being blocked by the crowd—the butchers formed what their fervent admirer called "an invincible phalanx." They were greeted with some shouts of "Long Live the Republic" and "Well, St. Aurélien stayed in his little prison!" The butchers answered with their own insults in patois, marching first to St. Michel and then to St. Pierre, where the members of the prosperous Confraternity of the Holy Sacrament ("bourgeois and notable men," in the opinion of the humble eyewitness) awaited them. A girl's choir sang, "Aux mauvais jours de la Patrie, nous saurons, comme autrefois, même au péril de notre vie, défendre et garder notre croix."[46]

The police let this procession pass through the streets, but it was to be the last one of the century in Limoges. Henceforth, despite angry letters from the bishop and complaints that the ban on processions cost commerce dearly, the butchers had to carry the relics from church to church in a closed wagon. The faithful straggled behind the wagon in twos and threes to avoid being arrested for participating in a procession. In 1890 the police intervened to silence some musicians who were following the crowd. Seven years later a number of women sang, "Nous voulons Dieu, c'est notre Père," thereby defying the municipality. Henceforth the police carefully noted which houses—in addition to those on the rue de la Boucherie and around the chapel of St. Aurélien—were decorated on religious occasions. In

Edition du Courrier du Centre, Limoges

LIMOGES. - Les Fêtes de Jeanne d'Arc. - 10. - Rue de la Boucherie

The festival of Jeanne d'Arc being celebrated on the rue de la Boucherie

The place Denis Dussoubs, with the statue of the local hero

1897 nuns led the students from the rue des Vénitiens to St. Pierre with a banner. Plainemaison *dit* Polka carried the flag of the butchers' confraternity during the last Ostensions of the century. For the first time in twenty years some butchers fired off pistols and rifles in celebration. The police took note of the incidents but did not intervene.[47]

The butchers continued to prostrate themselves before the relics of St. Martial and to illuminate their street on certain holy days, particularly on the feast day of their corporation; but the lights were gradually going out all around them. Surrounded by anticlericalism, they found some consolation in the fact that the pope had asked about their corporation when receiving Malinvaud Mantoue in 1890, naming the first syndic to the Order of St. Gregory the Great. The circle of St. Aurélien claimed the widow of General MacMahon as an honorary member. State officials suspected the butchers of maintaining links to royalist causes. Indeed, they occasionally turned up at royalist meetings. When Adrien Delor compared them to the intransigent *chouans* of the Vendée, the analogy could not have pleased the republicans. In 1891 they declined an offer from Mayor Chénieux to dine with Sadi Carnot, noting that such an act might jeopardize their "right" to greet French monarchs in the future. Neither the prefect nor the mayor attended their reception following the now subdued Ostensions; the bishop never failed to appear, while invariably being "out of town" during the secular celebration of July 14. Ultimately Marshal Pétain proved more to their taste; the butchers presented him with the keys to the city during World War II.[48]

The most graphic evidence that Limoges was changing all around the butchers occurred in December 1896, when the fifty-five *garçons* employed by sixteen of the butchers to work in the slaughterhouse went out on strike. They demanded

an end to Sunday afternoon work (the butchers seemed to have effectively separated their own religious convictions from their attitude toward work on the
Sabbath by their employees), a small raise in salary, and insurance against accidents. The butchers, as always, formed a common front; the absence of their
workers would deprive them of their Sunday afternoon strolls with their wives.[49]

The slaughterhouse became the scene of what could only have been a thoroughly disagreeable event for the butchers: Some of their employees urged those
still working to follow them back to town, where they walked through the streets
while smoking cigarettes. They were followed at a distance by the police, who
seemed amused by the whole thing. The butchers blamed the strike on one
Rabier, from Paris, who had organized a small *syndicat*. They decided not to
respond to the demands of the *garçons*, particularly as their employees were meeting at the Bourse du Travail and accepting advice and money from the Fédération des syndicats. The rumor coming from the Bourse had the *garçons* planning
to establish a cooperative *boucherie*, which would threaten the butchers, who already feared that the cooperative L'Union might succeed in taking away some
of their customers. But a few of the *garçons* already seemed on the verge of giving in. When the army sent soldiers to work for at least one butcher, joining
strikebreakers brought in from the countryside, the strikers' resistance revived.
Malinvaud *dit* Mantoue announced that the butchers would make no concessions;
some had already indicated that those who struck were never to be permitted to
return.

Despite preliminary plans for a cooperative *boucherie,* gradually the *garçons*
swallowed their pride and asked the butchers to take them back. The strike was
over by Christmas. Several of the *garçons* started a cooperative, but it was short-
lived, and they left town.[50] The rue de la Boucherie had never seen anything like
it before. It was a sign of the times.

In the early years of the Republic, the era of dramatic representations and
stately busts of Marianne, the Municipal Council had moved to create a public
iconography that would reflect the city's political evolution and its place in the
avant-garde of republican socialism.[51] Aside from one mediocre figure of Marshal
Jourdan, Limoges, which prided itself on being a *ville d'art,* had no objects of
artistic interest on public display.[52] The municipality was embarrassed to have to
borrow several Gobelin tapestries when the President of the Republic paid a visit
in 1891. In 1881 the council had voted to commission a bronze statue of Adrien
Dubouché, founder of the porcelain museum, but the government refused to provide financial assistance. Finally the administration of Emile Labussière, who had
been elected as a Radical in 1892, took action. Denis Dussoubs had symbolized
the faithful militance of Limoges for the democratic and social Republic; it will
be remembered that he had died protesting the coup d'état of 1851. The place
Dauphine/Liberté, that modest, circular intersection where the two most important faubourgs met the central city, seemed the ideal location for such a statue.[53]

It appeared to separate the faubourgs from the central city, placed there as if to guard and protect them.

The statue was to be an emphatic celebration of the city's past. The work of its sculptor, Léon-Rouselle Bardelle, pleased the Minister of Public Instruction, whose office contributed one third of the cost (fifteen thousand francs) of the statue, the rest being covered by private donations.

> The artist has represented Denis Dussoubs standing atop a barricade, his right arm raised toward the sky in a gesture of energetic affirmation, his left hand nervously touching his chest, appearing to shout the supreme cry, "Long Live the Republic!" I find the movement truly beautiful, and I find in the figure a passionate and superb élan.[54]

The inauguration of the statue of Denis Dussoubs in 1892 was a splendid occasion for Limoges's radical-socialists. The day was sunny, the place Denis Dussoubs resplendent in tricolor. The prefect, as well as members of the General Council and the Municipal Council, sat on a large reviewing stand, and by two thirty in the afternoon the entire area was full. Daniel Lamazière, who had been elected deputy in 1849, described Dussoubs as a martyr who was devoted to social justice. Louis Mollat, another old *quarante-huitard,* recalled that Dussoubs had been a republican because he had found the Republic consistent with human dignity, progress, and universal peace; he had become a socialist because "the mass of the nation was sacrificed to the interests of a small minority." The French Revolution had abolished the rule of the aristocracy, but the ninth of Thermidor had cast "the mass of the population aside . . . and the laws that followed were made exclusively in favor of the privileged class." The Revolution of 1830, despite being the work of *le peuple,* had only consecrated and consolidated this usurpation by the wealthy of France's revolutionary heritage. Nothing had been done for the proletariat. Labussière, spokesman for Limoges's revolutionary heritage, stressed that Dussoubs's work had to be completed. France had a republic, steam engines, even electricity, but it did not have social justice. That night the mayor presided over a banquet in the salle des conférences, where those gathered toasted the unity of socialists in the next municipal election. The statue of Denis Dussoubs remained a symbol of socialism in the city until the Germans destroyed it during World War II.[55]

Two monumental fountains (one built on the place de la République in 1893 and the other constructed in front of the town hall the following year), several busts, and a number of other statues completed the expanding iconography of the Republic. A statue of Sadi Carnot was inaugurated three years later at the carrefour Tourny. The project had been begun by the "Opportunist" municipal administration before the election of Labussière in 1895. Some socialists vowed to boycott the ceremony, as the clerical and royalist faction had made a point of ignoring the inauguration of the Dussoubs statue five years earlier. But the mayor joined the prefect in making patriotic speeches, avoiding, of course, all reference to the story that Carnot had been elected to the largely ceremonial post by his colleagues in the Chamber of Deputies, who followed Georges Clemenceau's mean-spirited advice, "Vote for the stupidest, vote for Sadi!" Nonetheless, an imposing crowd turned out for the occasion to watch Limoges's musical societies march by the statue and to voice its discontent when an orchestra hired for the ceremony failed to appear. The anarchists groused about the irony of Labussière, now a socialist deputy, unveiling a statue of the President of the bourgeois Republic. But at the end of the day Limoges had another secular, republican statue.[56]

A monument honoring the *mobiles* of Haute-Vienne, who fought during the Franco-Prussian War, was erected at the corner of the avenue de la Gare and the place Jourdan; it became a moment of political triumph for Labussière and completed the republican iconography. The socialist mayor of Limoges stole the thunder from the nationalist right when Alexandre Millerand, the socialist minister, arrived for the inauguration in 1899. The monument had long been planned and was often postponed. Donations trickled in, but the city's wealthy merchants refused to part with their money—a reflection of their attitude during the Franco-Prussian War. Millerand's invitation to visit Limoges touched off a political stir. The clerical newspaper *La Gazette* raged against the idea of a socialist minister presiding at a patriotic ceremony in memory of fallen French soldiers. Socialists, however, could accept a memorial to the *mobiles* funded by contributions from the local population after the fall of the Second Empire without compromising their antimilitarism. At the same time, some Guesdists balked at the thought of inviting a reform socialist to sit in bourgeois cabinet meetings with Gallifet, the Minister of War, a henchman of 1871.[57]

Millerand's visit provided the socialist municipality of Emile Labussière with the opportunity to affirm his town's identity. It also presents us with an opportunity to formulate another interpretation of the notion of the belle époque and Shattuck's "banquet years." *La Rappel du Centre* acclaimed the arrival of the minister in the "valiant industrial city." The Bourse du Travail eagerly awaited its friend, the "first minister who loves the proletariat." Fifteen hundred people welcomed Millerand at the Gare des Bénédictines at 3:45 A.M., shouting, "Vive la République!" and "Vive la sociale!" A few hours later the *fanfare* of the Bourse accompanied Millerand and several thousand people on his tour of the city.[58]

The inauguration followed a *déjeuner populaire* at the town hall: Gathered in ranks were the surviving members of the *mobiles,* the *fanfare* of the Bourse, the Société des sauvteurs, a small group of retired sailors, and the gymnastic societies. The nationalists did not appear; the opposition of a group of army veterans was shouted down by the delegates from the unions and the Bourse gathered behind a red flag. The staff from the nearby offices of *La Gazette* and the officers standing outside their clubs could only glower at the tricolor and red flags seen at the ceremony.

Millerand, who must by then have been exhausted, was taken to the Bourse, where ten thousand people awaited him. Labussière and Edouard Treich, the general secretary of the Bourse, welcomed the minister on behalf of the city's workers. The president of the Cercle démocratique des travailleurs and the general secretary of the cooperative L'Union also spoke. Next followed a dinner at a hotel, a *punch populaire* at the town hall, and a short speech by Millerand. After about twenty hours of events, the minister's long day was over. The *fête socialiste* ended at midnight. Millerand left for Paris the next morning.[59]

Did such organized, festive, collective expressions of municipal political commitment represent the ellusive belle époque in fin-de-siècle Limoges?" The "red city" certainly was not part of the "prosperous and complacent France" against whose bourgeois image the cultural avant-garde gathered together in solidarity. And yet one can argue that the manifestations of popular political culture had not only the same enemy—the prosperous and complacent bourgeoisie—but were expressed in some of the same exhilarating forms of collective sociability, celebrating the thrill of new ideas and the belief that Limoges was on the threshold of a new era of social progress. There was at least one important difference, of course. Whereas the cultural avant-garde struck out for, indeed represented, the rejection of the dominant culture of the bourgeois Republic, a sentiment with which Limoges's workers could have easily agreed, the city's socialists celebrated the collective consciousness of the working class. Was the energetic affirmation of the city's working-class and socialist identity the popular equivalent of the "banquet years"? Shattuck identifies the beginning of that period with the gigantic state funeral for Victor Hugo in 1885.[60] Appropriately, when the municipality in Limoges sent a delegation to the funeral and renamed the boulevard de la Poste aux chevaux the boulevard Victor Hugo, it celebrated him first and foremost as a political hero. If Limoges witnessed a few avant-garde banquets, innumerable political banquets and *punches populaires* took place at the *mairie* and the Bourse du Travail. Throughout France, the extent to which the high culture of the avant-garde filtered down to ordinary people is questionable. The culture of class conflict, in contrast, was embedded in the everyday life of ordinary people in Limoges and, I suspect, elsewhere. Its vibrancy underlay the extraordinary decade (1895–1905) of economic, social, political conflict. In 1895 the socialists assumed municipal power in Limoges and established the Bourse du Travail. The Bourse du Travail sustained a wave of strikes that year, the same year the Congrès Fédérative created the Confédération Général du Travail after preliminary discussions in the café of Edouard Treich, who became the general secretary of the Bourse du Travail. Socialism and syndicalism seemed wedded, two arms of working class mobilization for municipal and, ultimately, national power. A remarkable convergence of daily life and political and social contention occurred. At long last Limoges found its municipal identity. Denied the title of *bonne ville* during the Restoration (a rejection noted even at the end of the century) and over-whelmed by the imperatives of the centralized state during the Second Empire, Limoges gloried in the title of *la ville rouge*. The collective memory of past struggles helped shape an awareness of class politics and popular ideology during the fin-de-siècle period.

This important subject will be treated in greater depth in the final chapters. Here it suffices to say that the manifestations of this popular political culture were dizzying in their variety as the century approached its end: speeches on behalf of the Republic of Transvaal, featuring a free concert by the Fanfare de Limoges; the *fête de bienfaisance* of the Cercle démocratique; a talk on "collectivism" by a delegate of the Parti ouvrier français; the commemoration of the fiftieth anniversary of the establishment of the mutual aid society of leather workers, La Fraternelle; "thunderous applause" for a lecture presenting a historical account of class struggle; the *fête de bienfaisance* of the Cercle démocratique des travailleurs; a May Day celebration during which four thousand people attended a concert; and so on. That same heady year a strike against the printers of the clerical newspaper *La Croix* brought crowds into the streets in support of the workers. The municipal elections generated numerous section meetings and bright red and purple posters denouncing the alliance of the clerical party and the bourgeois *progressistes* of Dr. Chénieux. These bright *affiches* reminded voters of the success the socialist-dominated municipality had had in providing physical improvements to the long-neglected urban infrastructure: the destruction of the sordid Viraclaud quarter in preparation for the building of a new prefecture and post office; the opening of the tramways, facilitating the communication of the faubourgs with the central city; and the laicization of education and charities of Limoges. The presence of an unhealthy and dangerous asylum for terminally ill tuberculosis patients sparked demonstrations against this institution, which was owned by a wealthy and pious widow. The working class, long denied access to meeting places and confined to the periphery of the city, now marched through the streets of Limoges on May Day, filling the Cirque and the Bourse du Travail in order to listen to speeches. Politics infused the rituals of fireworks and *bals populaires* on July 14 and at the Bourse, the *punch populaire* of the balloon ascent, and even the release of the homing pigeons of the Société colombophile. One anticlerical rally drew three thousand people to the Cirque. Jules Guesde told a crowd of about the same size that the socialist party could only take power when the means of production had been socialized, but that a unified effort for reform could bring concrete results. One only had to look around Limoges to see that this was the case. *Le Rappel du Centre* trumpeted this period of increased proletarian consciousness. The *fêtes populaires* were political. They celebrated consciousness, organization, and militancy.[61]

The *fête de la muse* in 1903 was advertised as the "triumph of the humble." The search for a beauty queen had been narrowed to a *décalqueuse* from the proletarian faubourg of the rue de Paris, a female shoemaker from the Monteux factory, a woman employed by one of the printing companies, a seamstress, and a final entry "from the small town of the Haviland factory." The upper-class judges wished them well and, in a pointed reference to the turbulent years of the turn of the century, hoped they would enjoy "a life free of conflict, sanctified by work and the peace of love." This was not to be.[62]

6

Large-Scale Industrialization and Political Organization, 1871-95

In 1878 Gérald Malinvaud, president of the Société des sabotiers, modestly withdrew his name as a candidate for election to the Limoges Municipal Council despite the urging of his friends that he should run. "The moment seems inappropriate," he said, "for a simple worker, even one motivated by the greatest courage and unselfishness, to be able to work effectively for the ideas that you would like to see realized and, alone on a large Municipal Council, to do everything that would be expected of him." But he promised that he would do all he could "to advance the causes that concern the proletariat" as a delegate to the congress in Lyon.[1] Three years later six workers were elected to the Limoges Municipal Council. In 1895 Limoges joined the ranks of France's socialist municipalities, with workers occupying more than half of the council seats. In step with the growth of the city, the continued concentration of large-scale industry, and the development of workers' associations and political militancy, Limoges's evolution seemed complete.

Reflecting on the 1878 centenary marking the death of Voltaire, one local writer predicted that in 1978 people would laugh at the heated discussions in Limoges about the lingering influence of what he called "the clerical coterie"—which was restored to a position of influence by the government of the "moral order" after the Commune—from whose grasp France and his city would long since have been delivered. For this republican, there would be no greater evidence of the extent to which clerical influence was still powerful than the attacks by the Church on Voltaire, the "free genius of France, symbolized by the most illustrious representative of the eighteenth century." But time and the city of Limoges were on the side of the republicans in their struggle against the "men of the past" and their "clerical party."[2]

The Republic easily found roots in Limoges long before the resolution of the *seize mai* crisis in 1877 and the national republican electoral successes of the early 1880s. Since the July Monarchy Limoges had never ceased to be republican. The local monarchist newspapers in the mid-1870s (*Journal de la Haute-Vienne,* which began publication in 1874, and *La Haute-Vienne,* its successor, which began in 1876) found little support for the Church, the army, and General MacMahon. Before the 1876 municipal elections the monarchists discussed urban improvements that might impress a new sovereign, but the results of the balloting left the conservative newspaper with little hope.[3] *La Haute-Vienne* published its last issue on May 31, 1876, remaining "Catholic, royalist, and French" to the bitter end. A successor, brought in to support MacMahon, survived only four months (until the *seize mai* crisis).[4]

A small group of royalists had tried to curry favor among the workers after the Commune. Believing that "social disunity was the consequence of lost faith" and that God had punished France, several wealthy royalists organized clubs that they hoped would help workers recover their faith.[5] The Cercle St. Joseph, established in 1871, created a *caisse de famille,* offered members approved books and games, noted attendance at mass and vespers (thus determining each worker's standing in the club), and formed a committee to recruit new members. Yet despite one of the founder's contention that "faith is more lively among the working class than is commonly believed," the club's quest for a thousand members fell embarrassingly short: There were only twenty members in 1871 and thirty-one in 1874. The Cercle catholique d'ouvriers found only about twenty more.[6] The Cercle de la jeunesse had more honorary members than its twenty-eight workers; the rest were shop employees. Not even the bishop's own club, the Cercle St. Etienne, with a fund for the sick and a *buvette,* could attract more than thirty members, most of whom lived within hailing distance of the bishop's palace.[7] The police did not even bother to list these clubs among Catholic organizations—the St. Vincent de Paul Society and a Comité des écoles libres—existing in Limoges in 1882.[8] An incident in 1878 was revealing: About seven hundred people, mostly workers, interrupted a procession to the newly constructed Church of Sacré-Coeur with shouts of "Ça ira!" and "La Marseillaise," neither of which was music to clerical and royalist ears.[9]

The Municipal Council worked actively for republican education and against the Church, agreeing with Gambetta that the real enemy—even the real "International"—was clericalism.[10] Something also had to be done to improve Limoges's schools and make them workshops of republicanism. In 1873 inspectors had found little to please them; in one congregational school for girls "instruction was unorganized"; the congregations seemed to teach only "religious obligations and meaningless and useless facts." One school "in terrible condition, dark, smelly, and cramped," seemed typical. Inspectors complained about "the Limousin accent that the teachers themselves lose only with difficulty." The municipality created boys' schools in the faubourg Montmailler, the quarter of Pont Neuf, and that of Chinchauvaud at the northern edge of the city; the older schools received books for poor children—who were in the majority—and the school of Ste. Marie sported new latrines.[11]

The municipality refused to approve funds for congregational teachers in 1877. When all of the candidates of the Comité central républicain were elected in 1878, having made opposition to the "government of the priests" their rallying cry, the new council ended all instruction by religious orders in public schools. Within several years all of the boys' schools had been laicized in order, in the words of the council's *rapporteur,* "to save the young generation of *le peuple* from the clutches of ignorance and superstition." By 1882 the four remaining congregational schools for girls were taken over the same year that the council voted to suppress the remaining convents.[12]

The militance of the workers that had characterized the 1868–71 period subsided in the wake of the repression. The language of the surviving workers' associations was quite moderate—at least in public. L'Initiative, the porcelain workers' *chambre syndicale,* ended its blacklisting of the Gibus and Redon company, against whom the strike of January 1871 had taken place; two of the association's officers had continued to work for the company. The gesture was meant to demonstrate that the workers "do not want a war" with their employers and were not trying to provoke strikes.[13] There were but six *chambres syndicales,* five for porcelain workers and the shoemakers' La Solidarité.[14]

The association of decorators, established in February 1870, assumed responsibility for "watching over the moral, intellectual, and material interests of the profession" by calling to the attention of elected political representatives possible reforms "that could enhance the progress, prosperity, work, and well-being of the worker." One of these goals was to "maintain and raise wages by every legal means that the union will judge to be necessary and fair." This association of 150 workers (whose members had to be 21 years of age and have worked as decorators for 5 years) sought to assure the apprenticeship of the sons of members, provided a placement service and a professional library, and oversaw the contractual agreements so that apprentices "would receive such information that they might become not only good workers but also honest citizens." Any member of "recognized immorality" could be expelled. In some ways these *chambres syndicales* resembled the *compagnonnage* without the mystic trappings. Yet L'Initiative, accused by the police of having ties to the International, promised in its statutes to aid workers of other trades as much as possible when they were out of work. Though overwhelmingly limited to skilled workers, these *chambres syndicales* at least helped solidify the sense of dignity of labor and fostered a commonality of vulnerability and mutual assistance.[15]

These *syndicats* could call a strike and distribute funds to strikers, but they had little money (458 francs for 240 decorators in June 1872). During the 1870s La Conciliation—which was also the name of a workers' association—remained the theme of these organizations. Only two strikes by turners (one in 1872 and another in 1873) disturbed a decade of labor quiescence: bowl turners won a small raise in the first case and plate and saucer turners lost the same demand in the second strike against the Touze Company. The police blamed the union for prolonging the strike after most workers wanted to return. Searches of the houses of militants revealed that there was communication with workers in other porcelain centers but not the suspected links to the International.[16] In the 1873 strike the turners were unable to convince those colleagues working for other companies to join them; furthermore, some of the saucer turners returned to work, leaving the plate turners alone. Workers shouted "Long Live the Social Republic!" in the streets, but when the manufacturers threatened to shut down the entire industry on September 25, the strikers capitulated.[17] The "coalition" of employers was technically illegal, but the prefect considered that it would be "deplorable" to enforce the law in this case because they were resisting the action of their workers.

Some skilled workers still look to producers' cooperatives to emancipate themselves from the capitalist system. Led by the omnipresent Bergeron, in 1874 the *chambre syndicale* of the porcelain painters hoped that its members would "cease to be exploited labor" once it had achieved the goal of five hundred members and five thousand francs in capital. These "freethinkers and, above all, socialists," in the words of the police commissioner, had a tradition of working together in small shops that helped shape their dream. But most were workers who, despite their skill, "live from day to day," including Martial Aragon, an activist during the Empire's last years, and Jean Treich, a porcelain worker. Their plan failed.[18] The cooperative vision was alive more than ten years later (1889) when the workers of L'Initiative discussed the possibility of raising several hundred thousand francs by undertaking a loan and selling shares. These workers, "the hardest-working part of the population," had no other resources than their labor and consequently abandoned the project.[19]

A consumers' cooperative did have a major impact in Limoges. One such cooperative had failed after a brief existence in 1865, and several others were still-born in the early years of the Third Republic.[20] But two others begun by porcelain workers and decorators in two factories managed to survive. Le Progrès and L'Epargne joined after 2 years, with 45 members and a capital of 450 francs. In 1885 the cooperative L'Union sold flour, sugar, coal, and coffee from a rented building at reduced prices to its 417 members; it had 5 branch offices and a warehouse on the boulevard de la Cité. It also sold wine, lingerie, cloth (sending buyers to Roubaix and Sedan), and shoes, principally the sabots and *galoches* furnished by the producers' cooperative La Conciliation. Two years later, with 1,325 members, L'Union added a bakery that produced (and delivered to homes) some 110,000 kilograms in that year alone, and almost twice as much by 1900. Each year L'Union paid dividends, usually about 10 percent of the total sum expended that year by members. In 1893 the cooperative purchased an abandoned porcelain factory some 5,000 square meters in size. It was inaugurated with an enormous fete in December 1894.[21]

It would be easy to dismiss L'Union as nothing more than a cooperative, little different from other large capitalist enterprises and without political relevance. In fact, L'Union became a political issue, helping to define differences between workers and capitalists, the faubourgs and the commercial districts, socialists and bourgeois republicans. As L'Union undersold local merchants, it attracted the wrath of commercial associations, particularly the Taxpayers' League and the League of Commerce. In 1892 these conservative organizations launched a bitter campaign against L'Union, demanding that the Minister of Commerce tax the cooperative. These organizations told workers that L'Union compromised their true interests, making it impossible for them to ever rise to the status of shopkeeper because the cooperative would drive them out of business.[22] L'Union therefore faced the opposition of the Opportunists, led by Dr. François Chénieux, who depended upon commercial electoral support.

L'Union became identified as a group opposed to capitalist interests and, at the same time, as contributing to the welfare of workers. Most of its administrators were socialists.[23] Politics inevitably entered its celebrations. Its halls were used for political meetings. Socialist workers were its constituency. L'Union helped underscore the perception that capital—the department stores and wholesale merchants, as well as employers and their representatives—were the workers' enemies.[24] Some at the Bourse contended that L'Union was irrelevant to the struggle of workers, but the workers of Limoges believed that it offered at least a glimpse of a socialist society without capitalist middlemen.[25]

The late 1870s saw a revival of workers' associations, for between 1876 and 1884 twelve new *syndicats* were formed. By the latter date 28 percent of the porcelain workers were organized, including *useurs de grains,* polishers, *gazetiers,* and some day laborers. Other trades that followed suit included sabot makers, cabinetmakers, carpenters, typographers, stonecutters, barrel makers, carriage makers, house painters, and musicians. A police report submitted to the prefect of police in Paris at the time of the Marseille congress of 1879, however, asserted that five of the associations were "very revolutionary, socialist," including the porcelain workers' L'Initiative and the shoemakers' La Solidarité. Yet these *chambres syndicales* demonstrated almost no cooperation or militancy. Even within the trades no strikes occurred until 1882, almost ten years after the previous strike in the city. One hundred and fifty carpenters struck for one and a half months in the summer, gaining a slight salary increase; two brief walkouts by twenty *useurs de grains* ended in defeat when the polishers, whom the *useurs de grains* had always treated as inferior, refused to join them.[26]

In November 1882 a strike of some significance occurred. The turners of several porcelain factories walked out, demanding uniform piece rates in every manufacture, particularly for some of the newer, larger items not covered by previous agreements. Some employers announced that they would pay more, but most refused, including several who reneged on a hastily arranged agreement. Several hundred turners soon went out on strike. They held out for several months, supported by contributions from workers in other porcelain centers. The Municipal Council voted thirty thousand francs in assistance to aid those workers—some five thousand by the end of January 1883—laid off because of the strike.[27]

Some of the manufacturers accused German and British competitors of financing the strike in order to ruin the Limoges industry. Most of the strikers, it seemed, specialized in the small cups and certain other items that the German companies produced. The employers vowed to hold out as long as necessary for fear of "seeing the seeds of socialism planted in Limoges." Two workers elected to the Municipal Council, Boudaud and Roulhac, already demonstrated "collectivist doctrines." One of them called for a federation of all *syndicats* to aid strikers. Circulars from the strike committee had turned up in Paris, and contributions had come in from the British trade unions. Roulhac himself had been to Paris, supposedly to "explain" the strike to the "Parisian committees." Furthermore, a socialist named Chabert was back in town. In 1879 this Parisian worker had come to Limoges to urge the alliance of the proletariat with progressive factions of the bourgeoisie in a "war on capitalism." He had peppered his speech with "workshop expressions." Now, on January 12, 1883, he had returned, escorted by twelve men—"all well dressed." After meeting with strikers, he delivered a thunderous oration on "the bourgeoisie and the proletariat," calling for a social revolution against the former. A couple of days later a boisterous audience of one thousand listened to a member of the strike committee denounce the bourgeoisie as "thieves and liars," not the kind of talk the manufacturers wanted to hear. The strike held the interest of the public for its duration. The new moderate republican paper *Le Petit Centre* discussed "strikes and public opinion," and conversation was focused on the new machines in the industry and on foreign competition.[28]

Despite winning a 10 percent raise (they had originally asked for 25 percent), the workers ended their strike in defeat. The *hommes du four,* who earned only 1.75 francs a day, and the *retoucheuses,* who made only 1.20, refused to support their comrades, who took home between 5 and 6 francs a day. The resources of the union having been virtually exhausted, the strikers received only 1 franc a day in assistance. They finally accepted arbitration by the president of the Conseil des prud'hommes. The prefect noted that the "antagonism of the workers against their bosses has not lost any of its intensity and will reappear." The defeat was damaging, particularly as an economic crisis soon hit the industry, accentuated by a rise in American customs duties on porcelain. L'Initiative had spent over 17,000 francs on the strike and went into debt; the number of members fell from over 1,000 in 1876 to about 200 several years later.[29] If anything, the strike's failure confirmed the difficulty in getting porcelain workers of different occupations to support each other in a crisis situation. It also caused the manufacturers to revive the Union des fabricants. The discouraging economic situation and the unity of the manufacturers contributed to the "crisis of syndicalism" in Limoges, which lasted from 1883 to 1892.[30]

Seeing the lack of solidarity among workers of different occupations and industries during the turners' strikes, but convinced that the interests of all workers were identical, in January 1883 a Union fédérative des chambres syndicales attempted to unite the existing workers' associations "to support and to fortify the Republic" behind demands for legislation that would aid the workers "of the cities and the fields . . . the masters of the destiny of the nation." Each member union (or cooperative) would send two delegates to serve on the federal council. Acknowledging the struggle between capital and labor, the Federation would "take into consideration all useful measures to study the general interest of the workers" and to "study the practical means necessary to achieve the moral, intellectual, and material improvement of the workers, as well as the legitimate satisfaction of their needs." No strike was to be called unless the union had explained its action to the Federation, which would attempt conciliation. If that failed, the Federation would support strikers "morally and materially." But, in truth, the Federation existed only on paper. Weakened by the turners' strikes, the "crisis of syndicalism" struck Limoges. Only six unions were left in 1890, and L'Initiative had but 130 members.[31]

Between 1883 and 1893 only five short strikes occurred in Limoges, none of which were of any importance. Three were by shoemakers (sabotiers, in one case), and one each by blacksmiths and typographers. Only the 1886 strike by blacksmiths and that of the sabotiers in 1889 succeeded.[32] The lack of strikes attested to the economic crisis, depriving workers of resources to sustain a strike and of any leverage against their employers; it also attested to the decline of union strength in Limoges.[33] Yet, as the porcelain industry was being transformed, technological and organizational changes in the industry helped generate worker resistance.

In July 1891 Charles Haviland boasted to Léon Bourgeois—on the occasion of the latter's visit to Limoges as Minister of Commerce—that "one does not have to dream of providing the [porcelain] industry with a force of artisanal workers."[34] A reduced number of artistes en porcelaine—hardly anyone called them that anymore—still found work decorating objects submitted as special orders, touching up the decals or edges of plates, or creating the original models for the pieces to be produced. Female décalqueuses had replaced most of the deft painters in the decoration workshops, many of which were now owned by the manufacturers themselves. Machines accomplished many of the tasks of other skilled workers.

By the end of the century the porcelain industry was characterized by large-scale production in factories. Most of the smaller factories in the region had closed down completely or had moved to Limoges. All porcelain produced by the 4 remaining manufacturers outside of Limoges—including one in nearby Bourganeuf, in the Creuse—was decorated in Limoges. The shift from wood to coal as a source of fuel was complete and it was no longer an advantage for the smaller manufacturers outside Limoges to be closer to the forests. Proximity to the Gare Montjovis was paramount. Signs of industrial concentration were everywhere: The factories, the number of kilns, annual production, and the workforce employed had increased rapidly. The number of porcelain factories in Limoges had remained quite constant—32 in 1870, 35 in 1882, 29 in 1890, and 34 in 1900—but the number of workers employed had jumped dramatically, particularly after 1895. In 1892 some 5,246 porcelain workers labored in 32 factories. By 1905 there were approximately 13,000 porcelain workers in 35 factories, representing some 40 percent of the approximately 32,000 workers in the city. The livelihood of about 30,400 people was directly dependent on the production or decoration of porcelain, without taking into consideration the shopkeepers, who depended upon working-class clients. The number of kilns had risen only moderately despite the expansion of the industry. There were 122 kilns in 1907, the average being much larger in size than the 86 in 1882. At the time of the Franco-Prussian War any factory employing over 100 workers represented a sizable industrial concentration—even in working-class Limoges. By the turn of the century Charles Haviland employed over 2,000 workers in his giant factory, with its 15 kilns, on the avenue Garibaldi; his brother, Theodore, employed over 1,000 workers on the avenue de Poitiers. Between them they accounted for more than one third of the porcelain business in the city; the four largest companies combined accounted for half of all production in Limoges. Over 20 manufacturers employed more than 100 workers. Between 1896 and 1900, the number of porcelain workers doubled.[35]

There was another significant sign of industrial concentration, namely, capital within the industry. Whereas in 1870 some 44 decoration workshops existed separately from the factories, only 18 operated independently in 1905. More and more *fabricants* followed the example of the Havilands, who had been the first to combine production and decoration in one factory during the Second Empire. In 1904 1,200 workers labored in the kaolin quarries of the department and another 6,400 prepared the *pâte* for production.[36]

Technological advances lay behind these changes, enabling the industry to recover from the major slump of the mid-1880s, when only about 3,200 workers remained employed; these crises were largely exacerbated by American tariff policies. Here, as before, the Havilands led the way. The critical transition from wood to coal-fueled kilns has already been noted. Coal proved to be a much more efficient source of fuel, cutting by more than half the tonnage of fuel required for each batch, or *journée*. By 1900 only a fifth of the ovens were fueled by wood, producing less than 10 percent of the *fournées,* these specialized in certain colors (such as cobalt blue) and luxury items. The number of steam engines had risen from 264 in 1889 to 580 ten years later.[37]

These major technological changes reduced the dependency of employers upon skilled labor, enhancing the standardization of production. At the same time, the industry satisfied changes in consumer taste for porcelain, particularly in the United States. No development was more important than the introduction of the decoration of plates by impression and, above all, the continued development of a process of chromolithography that largely replaced hand painting. By the end of the 1880s all of the largest companies did their own decoration. Henceforth decoration, too, could be standardized while still permitting up to fifteen different colors to be used at once. Once the "model" had been created, enhanced by improvements in the application of colors, female workers—paid far less than the highly skilled *artistes en porcelaine* had earned—could put the mass-produced decals on the plates. A second baking followed, usually in long, new *moufles* with the unfortunate name of *crématoires.* By 1907 only 7 percent of the porcelain produced in Limoges was the plain white product once à la mode. Yet it is important to note that the introduction of these techniques did not erode the reputation among consumers that first-quality porcelain, though standardized, had as a luxury item, although the price of fine porcelain fell. The demand for the finest porcelain remained high. Limoges porcelain captured prizes in the expositions of 1889 and 1900. While the industry was still vulnerable to any economic crisis that lowered the demand for luxury items, the manufacturers were eager to reduce their labor costs by eliminating some skilled workers. The *décalqueuse* earned but one fourth of the salary of an *artiste en porcelaine.* Besides the porcelain painters (some of whom stayed on to paint the edges of plates with gold or to touch up the plates), the number of skilled *fleuristes, figuristes, chiffreurs,* and *fileurs* dwindled. Between 1884 and 1901 the percentage of female workers in the industry increased from 24 to 35 percent. By the end of the 1880s all of the largest manufacturers did their own decoration at the factory. Eight produced their own decal sheets. The skilled painters, once called *Messieurs les artistes* by the proletarian kiln workers, had largely disappeared.[38]

There were other timely technological advances as well. The kilns were now twice as large in diameter as before (up to 8 meters), and the introduction of the *flamme renversé,* replacing the old direct-flame method, permitted the even distribution of heat, thereby facilitating standardization. By 1900, 60 percent of the *fours* were heated in this way. Several new machines contributed to a certain uniformity, including several kinds of mechanical presses for the operation of *moulage* for all flat pieces of porcelain. The Faure plate machine, first put into limited use around 1870, also contributed to a high degree of standardization. One worker could now turn out some 8,000 saucers in about 15 working days, compared to some 1,500 earlier. One *tourneur* with a single assistant could send along between 450 and 500 plates per day—about 5 times more than before. Despite the increase in productivity, the number of *tourneurs* was considerably reduced; both the number of apprentices and the length of apprenticeship also declined. Steam engines had almost completely replaced the foot pedals used by the *tourneurs*. Improvements in casting (*coulage*) added to the durability of complicated pieces, such as extremely thin plates with fancy details in their shapes or particularly large and cumbersome pieces that had previously required considerable skill and attention from the turners. The *moules* were now almost all produced by machine, although *modeleurs* created each model. A German chemical discovery—a mixture of *silicate de soude* and *barbotine*—improved the *moules,* which previously had to be dried after each use and could only be used for a short time. By 1900 the *gazettes* were also being produced by machine. Another machine invented around 1875 replaced the workers who crushed and worked the kaolin with their wooden sabots (an operation consequently known as *marchage*), and improved the presses; the *pâte* was of more uniform quality and was therefore less subject to breakage in the kiln. Concentration of capital, mechanization, standardization, larger factories, larger kilns, more workers, reduced skill, and industrial discipline were the key developments in the porcelain industry. Keeping up-to-date in the industry required considerable capital. Three plate machines alone cost anywhere from 1,200 to 1,500 francs. Labor still accounted for between 40 and 50 percent of the manufacturer's total costs. In addition, only about 12 of the company buildings were owned by the employers; rent added between 2,500 to 3,000 francs a year to a company's total expenses. The larger companies prospered: The Havilands helped drive out some smaller manufacturers, or at least forced them away from the production of the most lucrative items, namely, dinnerware and café service. All of these costs adversely affected workers' salaries.[39]

Limoges's second industry, shoe manufacturing, also owed some of its rapid growth to mechanization after 1880. Whereas the number of porcelain workers had increased 260 percent between 1870 and 1905, the number of shoemakers had grown almost twice as fast, increasing by 500 percent (from eight or nine hundred to about four thousand shoemakers). Until the 1890s the industry remained semiartisanal, with each worker making shoes from the first step to the last, often working at home. Even the largest manufacturer, Monteux, employed three hundred home workers among his seven hundred workers. But an import from the United States gradually revolutionized production, destroying the artisanal base of the industry (the exclusive nature of the trade having long since disappeared). Around 1900 the Goodyear machine took over most of the tasks previously done by hand. Here, too, an influx of female workers into the industry had been marked. In 1905 four thousand shoemakers worked in Limoges, most of them in eighteen factories, where foremen had become a fixture.[40]

More than ever, porcelain and shoemaking, dominated the economy of Limoges; the crises of those industries became those of the city. More than half of the workers in Limoges (some fifteen thousand worked in other industries, two thousand in printing, and more than one thousand in the building trades supported by the expanding city) were involved in the production of porcelain or shoes. Yet industrial concentration did not in itself generate militancy. The wide range of occupations within Limoges's most important industry and concomitant differences in levels of skill and remuneration mitigated against effective collective action, this despite the porcelain workers' long tradition of organization. Some thirty-seven different occupations remained in the industry, with daily wages ranging from under three francs for common laborers to as much as eight and even ten francs for some of the remaining decorators.[41]

On the other hand, the concentrated factory production created miserable conditions and resentment against employers and foremen and accentuated the development of working-class faubourgs that provided a base for the militancy of porcelain workers. These changes help explain the evolution of workers' associations from mutual aid societies, which avoided strikes wherever possible, to aggressive organizations, a transformation that began in the early 1890s.

The foreman became a symbol of capitalism. The *patron,* now often a distant figure—Americans, in the case of the Haviland brothers—owned the factory, but the foreman enforced discipline. He or she became the most visible target of strikes.[42] At the same time, unhealthy working conditions within the factories characterized the porcelain industry, making discipline a major issue. The *hommes du four* were exposed to stifling heat for extraordinarily long shifts and, at least partially as a result, suffered high rates of alcoholism. Saturnine poisoning afflicted those in the decoration workshops, as well as polishers and *useurs de grains;* chemicals, powders, fragments of granite and silex, toxic dust, and particles of enamel permeated the air. The *poudreuses* were particularly vulnerable. In 1896 one inspector reported that they were recruited from the "most miserable" part of the population; according to one factory director, "a woman comes to seek a job as a *poudreuse* only when she is dying of hunger." High rates of chronic bronchitis and tuberculosis (also linked to inadequate nutrition and poor housing conditions) afflicted porcelain workers. Tuberculosis killed thirty-six of the seventy-five porcelain workers who died in 1887; the following year twenty of thirty such workers who were examined by a doctor suffered from the disease; another survey found that 73 percent of female workers had it. An expert on health conditions in the industry estimated that the average life expectancy (computed from birth) for the male porcelain workers was forty-three but only thirty-eight for females (who were more apt to work in the decoration workshops). Tuberculosis killed one person every forty hours in Limoges. *Phtisie* killed workers who prepared the kaolin into *pâte* in the small and badly ventilated *moulins* near the Vienne River. Some workers were subject to deformation (such as the left leg of *useurs de grains,* who also were particularly vulnerable to disease because they held the *pinceaux* used in their task in their mouths, exchanging them with other workers).[43] Although some *patrons* provided their workers with milk because they thought it would help them resist poisoning, recommendations of the departmental hygiene council—such as the amount of open space for each kiln—seemed to be routinely ignored. The foremen were the chief object of the workers' complaints, preventing the workers from leaving to get fresh air, food, and drink, or to care for their children outside the factory. Small wonder that they referred to themselves as "convicts" at the mercy of the guards of the "prison" boss.[44] Concurrent with the upswing in the porcelain industry, the Union des fabricants posted regulations in most factories. These set the exact hours at which workers were to arrive, threatened them with dismissal if they left during the day, made them collectively responsible for their work materials, and forbade them from bringing alcohol into the factory. Posted regulations confirmed the arbitrary authority of the foreman, who interpreted the rules and could dismiss any worker. Workers reacted angrily to these regulations, which could keep them inside when they were not needed. Several cases of enforcement contributed to the tensions between workers and foremen. In 1896 a worker was denied permission to leave work to see his father, who was critically ill. After work he returned home to find him dead. As *patrons* hired more overseers to enforce regulations in the factory, foremen became particular targets of strikes and protests, being identified as the most obvious representatives—indeed, enforcers—of capitalism.[45]

Outside the factory the workers' living conditions improved only slightly, and then only between 1900 and 1910. Whereas French workers saw their salaries rise faster than the cost of living between 1880 and 1900—particularly during the 1880s—in Limoges the purchasing power of porcelain workers returned to the level of 1882 only in 1904. For a porcelain worker's family to keep up with the cost of living in 1895, his wife or at least one child had to be bringing in a minimum of 1.50 francs a day, assuming, of course, that there were no layoffs. Working-class housing remained generally inadequate. The buildings of the faubourgs were described by a contemporary as "always sad, often badly kept up, lost in some narrow and evil-smelling street; now this is the usual case in those workers' quarters that form the faubourgs of Limoges."[46] Paul Ducourtieux offered this verbal picture to rural people who might not have seen them:

> . . . wooden houses, generally inordinately high and without proportion to their width and to the width of the streets. The alleys are somber and fetid, the narrow stairways give way underfoot; the landings are encumbered with garbage, the rooms poorly ventilated, the walls are bare or covered with old wallpaper that serves as a refuge for a variety of insects. To these powerful causes of insalubrity one must add the piling in of too many people in rooms that are too small.[47]

One study early in this century found that housing conditions in Limoges lagged behind those in St. Etienne, Reims, St. Quentin, and Troyes—all working-class cities. Dividing the lodgings in workers' quarters into such categories as "over-crowded," "insufficient," "sufficient," "large," and "very large," the survey determined that 72 percent of Limoges's workers' lodgings were either overcrowded or insufficient (compared to St. Etienne's 70.5 percent).[48]

These faubourgs sometimes gave people from the fancier quarters the impression of the countryside; roosters could be heard even before the call of the factory bell. The presence of a proletariat and its often presumed "peasant" nature could accentuate this image of chaos and even disorganization. We have, among others, the following contemporary description:

> What a din in the faubourgs! We were awakened before the rooster's call by the interminable noise of carts, the plodding steps of animals and men, the bellowing or bleating of herds, the savage squealing of pigs, all intermingled with rasping peasant voices.[49]

Within Limoges tensions may have existed between the *villauds* and the newly arrived peasant workers, sometimes called *bicanards*. The *villauds,* who considered themselves to be the "real workers," teased their rustic comrades about their lack of humor and joked that they still listened for the call of the rooster and not the factory bell.[50] Rural migrants may have sometimes been seen as competitors for jobs, unwelcome refugees from the archaic countryside.

Yet workers—particularly porcelain workers—shared origins and patterns of residence that contributed to their organizational solidarity as the century ended. Eighty-five percent of the porcelain workers in Limoges were from the Haute-Vienne, most from the southern part of the department. Many still spoke the patois that characterized the region south of Limoges; they must have appreciated Jean Jaurès's toast in patois in 1895. Most of the others were from the neighboring departments of the Creuse, Charente, Dordogne, or Corrèze. With the disappearance of many skilled workers, *porcelainiers* from Paris or the Berry became quite rare and the industry's range of migration grew even narrower. By the turn of the century more than half the porcelain workers had been born in Limoges. In general, the more skilled the occupation, the higher was the percentage of workers from the city: 86 percent of porcelain painters, 56 percent of *ouvriers en porcelaine,* and a little less than 50 percent of the day laborers. Of the 1,426 employees of Theodore Haviland in 1906, 894 (62.7 percent) had been born in Limoges, 397 (27.8 percent) had been born in the Haute-Vienne or elsewhere in France, principally the Corrèze (26), Charente (23), Dordogne (20), Creuse (16), Gironde (8), Cher (6), and the Puy-de-Dôme, Allier, and Seine (4 each). Within the department the industry continued to draw workers from the southern hinterland.[51]

The range of migration may also help explain the relative militancy—or sometimes the lack of it—in other industries. A greater percentage of workers not in the porcelain industry were born outside Limoges.[52] Kathryn Amdur makes the important point that the influx of young, female labor in the shoemaking industry, replacing middle-aged artisans, may have weakened the militancy of workers in that industry. Of the workers employed by Monteux in 1906, whose factory was the largest and arguably the most radical, 68 percent had been born in Limoges—a much greater percentage than for the industry as a whole. Shoemakers, although less organized, contributed to the radicalization of the Limoges working class.[53]

Whether or not migrants to Limoges had prior industrial experience in the defunct factories of a number of small towns, their entry into *le milieu ouvrier* of Limoges was apt to be definitive. They settled in the faubourgs but returned home often to work the harvests during layoffs in Limoges, or to partake of the rural pleasures of the Limousin. The workers helped make the socialist politics of the city those of the countryside. As one historian of the 1905 strikes has noted, "the links between the working population of the city and the rural population were numerous and exchanges were incessant."[54] Furthermore, the militance of the city helped draw migrants into the popular culture of political conflict that, after 1895, centered on the socialist municipality and the Bourse du Travail. Porcelain workers, representing the highest percentage of workers born in Limoges, may have led the way, but many migrants followed. The development of the porcelain and shoe industries during the 1880s and early 1890s resulted in a marked acceleration of class consciousness in Limoges that, by the early 1890s, had been channeled into political and economic action.

The left shaped political and public life in Limoges. The city embellished its reputation as *la ville rouge,* preparing the way for the socialist municipality (1895–1905). In each legislative election the left received more than 50 percent of the votes in Limoges, the only exception being the election of the Boulangist Le Veillé in 1889, when some workers saw the general as leading them down the road to socialism. In 1885 the Haute-Vienne was the only one of ten departments to elect a deputy from the far left, Planteau, a porcelain painter. The 1898 legislative elections confirmed the victory of socialism in Limoges.[55]

The political evolution of the city was confirmed in the municipal elections held between 1878 and 1888. First, the numerical predominance of the workers guaranteed victory for the radical republicans, particularly when voting was by the *scrutin de liste,* that is, with everyone able to vote for candidates on a single list for the entire city, which was the case from 1880 until 1888. After another Radical success in the latter election, the conservative departmental General Council returned to the system of balloting by section, or district, that had been in place from 1870 to 1880, thereby partially eliminating the workers' numerical advantage in the city. Second, whereas Gérald Malinvaud had modestly refused to stand as a candidate in 1878, eight workers were elected to the municipal council in 1881, six of whom were porcelain workers elected from a list of thirty-two candidates selected by a Comité des corporations ouvrières and a number of bourgeois radicals.[56] Working-class representation on—and eventually domination of—the Municipal Council was never again problematic. In 1904 nineteen of the thirty-six councilmen were workers. Third, facing a working-class challenge for control of the city, the bourgeois moderates, the Opportunists (or, as they became known in the 1890s, *progressistes*) rallied their forces. In 1878 moderate candidates contended that any preoccupation on the council with the question of the working class constituted "politics," which they contrasted with the "real" interests of the city. In 1884 the "independents" chosen among industrialists and merchants promised to "occupy themselves with the business of the city and not with politics." The Radicals, however, emerged with a majority. The principal issue that divided the latter from the Opportunists was their attitude toward the working class; the former, who were populists, demanded reforms and accepted the workers as allies in their struggle against clericalism. The Opportunists soon put their anticlericalism out of mind and allied with the monarchist and clerical faction. In the election of 1886 the candidates of the Alliance républicaine (Opportunists), mostly merchants, demanded that commerce and industry be properly represented on the council, and that the "sterile and useless discussions on the council be replaced by discussions about business." Before the elections of 1888 the bourgeois "independent republicans" challenged the Radicals, who demanded an "improvement in the situation of the working class."[57]

Finally, working-class political contention politicized public life in the city. The municipal elections were hotly contested; they were preceded by crowded, boisterous meetings, accompanied by colorful *affiches* and newspaper accounts, and were followed by demonstrations of joy or contempt. These elections seem to have aroused the passionate interest of citizens more than national elections. At the same time, the political clubs that developed in the 1880s and newspapers helped keep ordinary people aware of the ideological as well as practical implications of their choices. Municipal politics mattered.

The political clubs that began in the 1880s became virtual political parties by the end of the century. Before the 1881 election a group of anticlerical republicans formed a club, the Cercle démocratique des travailleurs. Its stated goal was to bring middle-class and working-class republicans together "by daily contact . . . workers with tools and those with pens, from the workshop of those from the office, who until now have been kept too far apart by their different occupations and habits."[58] Maintaining a reading room and sponsoring "family discussions" of political issues, this club came under the influence of Emile Labussière. The latter was born in 1853 in Bénévent l'Abbaye, in the Creuse, the son of an *ouvrier maçon* and a seamstress. He moved to Limoges, becoming a public works entrepreneur, and joined the Cercle démocratique. He quickly won a political following and was elected as a Radical to the Municipal Council in 1886, after the resignation of the minority of twelve Opportunists. The following year, the pre-

fect dismissed Tarrade, the Radical mayor, who had reduced the budget of the recently laicized Bureau de bienfaisance, after accusing its director, an Opportunist,
of financial mismanagement. The entire Municipal Council resigned in protest,
forcing a new election in which not a single candidate of the Opportunist Alliance
républicaine was elected. When Tarrade died, Labussière became mayor of Limoges. He was elected to the Chamber of Deputies in 1893 and again in 1898.
Henceforth the club followed Labussière's own political odyssey from a Radical to
a reform socialist, planning electoral strategy in the national and municipal elections and contributing to the mass politicization that marked the century's last
decade.[59]

In 1892 the Opportunists won a narrow majority (nineteen seats to seventeen),
although they trailed in the total popular vote. Three years later Labussière defeated the Opportunist leader, Dr. François Chénieux, in a bitter struggle for a
General Council seat representing the north, or urban, canton of Limoges. The
Opportunists resigned, provoking a pivotal election for a new Municipal Council. In preparation for this crucial election Labussière demonstrated one of his
most salient personal characteristics and the source of his popular appeal: his ability to engineer compromise and inspire unity among socialists. In this he resembled Jaurès, whom he would welcome to Limoges on several occasions. The general secretary of the Cercle démocratique was Léon Betoulle, the correspondent
for *La Dépêche de Toulouse,* a paper greatly influenced by Jaurès. The Cercle
démocratique gradually changed from a club of Radicals to a club of radical or
republican socialists. By 1895 Labussière was calling himself a socialist, and the
Cercle démocratique had become the center for reform socialism in Limoges.[60]

If the republican socialists were the heirs of the *quarante-huitards* and the socialists of 1871, their rivals, the bourgeois Opportunists or *progressistes* had descended from the Orleanist *juste milieu.* The "faubourg St. Germain" of Limoges
was the Cercle Turgot, to which many of the city's wealthy businessmen (Dr.
Chénieux's patients) belonged, as did clerks and employees easily frightened by
"the socialist menace."[61] Their political wing was the Cercle républicain de la
Haute-Vienne, formed in 1887 to counter the Radicals and surviving in the hope
of fending off the socialists. Five years later the *cercle des pommes cuites,* as its
detractors called it, had four hundred members, presided over by Dantony, Chénieux's deputy mayor.[62] The basis of the Opportunists' political platform continued to be social order. Their support came from the largely commercial quarters of the center city that feared both socialism and syndicalism. This led them
to an easy electoral accommodation with the clerical party (such that the socialist
sometimes referred to Chénieux as "virgin and martyr" and claimed that he and
his friends served up clerical delicacies at their annual banquet).[63]

Allemanist socialism followed both Jean Allemane and the strike of 1882–83 to
Limoges. Twelve workers, several of whom had been involved in the lengthy
strike by turners, met in a café on the avenue Garibaldi, in the shadow of the

Haviland factory. Their leaders had met with Allemane during his visit to Limoges in 1881. They drafted a preamble for what they called the Socialist Federation of Haute-Vienne, which echoed Abbe Sieyès: "What are we? Nothing. What do we want to be? Everything." Jean Thabard, a porcelain painter on the Municipal Council, and Gabriel Collet, a *mouleur* who owned the café, had welcomed Allemane to Limoges. They now called themselves socialist revolutionaries, emphasizing political action but distrusting bourgeois radicals. They formed a club "for the propagation and the defense of the interests of the proletariat" and created a program of *études sociales* to attract workers, but they remained a small group composed of porcelain and shoemakers. After one member barely escaped prosecution for running off with the strike funds of his *syndicat,* the club showed few signs of life until 1893. Léonard Boudaud, a *couleur de moules* and also a councilman, had run for a seat in the Chamber of Deputies in 1889 as a "scientific collectivist" against Périn, Le Play, and the Boulangist Le Veillé. Easily defeated, he worked to reconstitute the Avant-garde as a study group and a center of propaganda, assisted by Ferdinand Tabaton-Tuilière, another porcelain painter, Léonard Neveu, a porcelain polisher, and Jacques Tillet, a *mouleur.* Allemanists retained close ties with the unions; both Neveu and Tillet were officers of their *syndicats.*[64] The Avant-garde celebrated the first May Day 1890 in Limoges after announcing that its members would refuse to work that day. They held a *punch populaire* the following year in Collet's café, located in the faubourg de Paris, attended by thirty-nine militants, a number not far below their total strength.[65] After trying to revive the club on a somewhat broader base as the Cercle de l'émancipation du parti ouvrier Limousin (which the Minister of the Interior refused to authorize), little more was heard of the Avant-garde until 1892. In that year Tillet and Tabaton-Tuilière were elected to the Municipal Council, demonstrating some Allemanist support. But when the Allemanists refused to join the republican-socialists in an alliance against the *opportuno-monarchistes* the following year, their influence declined sharply and their candidates received an average of only 150 votes in the three sections in which they entered candidates.[66] When the Avant-garde started a *groupe d'études sociales* in 1896, only one person came. In 1898 the group seemed almost to repudiate Allemanism, for Boudaud admitted that his policies had failed. While adopting the new name of Ni Dieu, ni maître, the Allemanists moved closer to Guesdism.[67]

When he visited Limoges in 1886 and 1894 Jules Guesde found support even before there was a Guesdist club there. Some "revisionist socialists" had supported the republican socialists, unlike the Allemanists. Guesde's influence may date back even further; early in 1879 Malinvaud wrote a Parisian socialist, "I absolutely need the address of Jules Guesde for some very serious business that I will put to you when you have replied to me." In 1893 a delegation of sixty Guesdist workers marched to the town hall and left a list of demands on behalf of the *chambres syndicales,* which were first read on the steps by Hummel, the shoemaker. The petition "recognized that among the ruling class there are men of heart who, in many circumstances, have defended the proletariat; but it may also be recognized that, almost always, these men have not had the energy to go far enough." It attacked "capital, the absolute master of humanity, which generates, by its goals and caprices, so many perturbations in social life, that one can now see entire cities, once flourishing and full of life, fall, in a single day, in the most complete misery because it pleases industrialists to move away." The Guesdists made a special plea for the unemployed, asking that "certain industrialists"—namely, the porcelain manufacturers—be forced to stop their "unrestrained production," and that the eight-hour day, a minimum wage—to be enforced by a new federation of unions or the municipality—and retirement pensions be established.[68]

The following year Guesdists demanded the legalization of the International (the strains of whose hymn echoed through banquet halls during May Day celebrations), the establishment of a Bourse, and other demands. Here shouts of "Long Live Denis Dussoubs!" and "Long Live the Commune!" attested to some continuity between the socialism of nineteenth-century revolutions and that of the 1890s. But most of the population greeted May Day with simple curiosity, at least at first, if not with indifference.[69] The Guesdists lacked a formal organization in Limoges until the establishment of the Cercle de l'union des républicains socialistes in 1896.[70]

The anarchists, too, formed a club in the politicized nineties. The police easily assessed the numbers of anarchists in Limoges because all of them turned up at political meetings or stood outside distributing propaganda. A Parisian anarchist, Alexandre Tennevin, who had joined Louise Michel in organizing the first May Day in Paris, established the club La Jeunesse libertaire in Limoges in 1894. Following his departure for the capital the next year, some thirty people were still members, but they rarely met. The club barely survived the arrest of several members in 1896 for passing counterfeit money. Théophile Beaure, whose brother, Armand, had been implicated in that scheme, kept the group going. Jules Bocrian, a porcelain worker, gradually assumed leadership of the group, which met once a week in a café. But police counted only four militant anarchists in Limoges at the time of the wave of anarchist bombings in Paris.[71]

Can one say that any kind of anarchist tradition existed in Limoges? One local historian claimed that the attempted insurrection of April 4, 1871, was partially inspired by anarchists, but no evidence at all exists to support such an assertion.[72] Anarchist sentiments may have been found among some home workers, particularly shoemakers. Strong antistate sentiment survived the Bonapartist experience of the Second Empire and the centralized repression that followed.

Thirty-nine anarchists celebrated their version of the Commune in 1893 by listening to Tennevin attack "the pseudo-Republic that we have suffered for twenty years" and denounce Guesde for wanting to turn France over to new masters of a different political stripe. One anarchist called Ravachol "this great citizen who will be honored as a benefactor of humanity." In 1894 the anarchist François Le Minez passed through the city, eating a simple meal, the police noted, at a restaurant across from the town hall, where he received a little money to help him get to nearby Pierre Buffière. A number of anarchists were "massed in a corner" during a socialist speech in April 1895. In 1897 Henri Dharr, editor of *Au libertaire,* won few disciples when he told an audience of three hundred that universal suffrage was the greatest crime of the century. When interrupted by people demanding to know how an anarchist society could be established, he replied that the answer would be the subject of future talks.[73]

The 1888 election marked a turning point in the city's political evolution because it was the first in which workers ran for municipal office as socialists. It was contested in five electoral sections, as ordered by the departmental General Council. Voting by section made an alliance among the left imperative. But the Allemanists first declared that as "revolutionary socialists" only the international goal of the socialization of the means of production could lead to a true communist society in which "each according to his means would receive according to his needs." The working-class socialist party thus would remain aloof from bourgeois political parties. Emancipation "could only occur through revolutionary action." Political power might be achieved at the municipal, departmental, and even national levels, but not at the expense of compromise. The Allemanists therefore entered candidates in several sections on an anticapitalist and antistate platform, calling for, among other demands, the ratification of the deliberation of the Municipal Council by the people and not the prefect, the abolition of the position of President of the Republic, the guarantee of municipal work for workers during economic crises, and assistance for those on strike.[74]

The Radicals and republican socialists, on the other hand, agreed on the necessity of working together. They called for the establishment of a Bourse du Travail, assistance for workers, street repairs in proletarian quarters, and a greater tax on property, the abolition of the senate, the return to voting by list, and, in addition, to a wide range of anticlerical measures. Even though the Allemanists did not join the Radicals and the radical-socialists, the Opportunists (who called themselves "independent republicans") needed support from the conservatives. The clerical *La Gazette* at first wanted no alliance with republicans of any shade, even those who were as socially conservative as they were; it continued to taunt the left with a regular column on "working-class agitation." But the strength of the left frightened them into an alliance with the Opportunists, whose platform called for a careful study of the workers' living conditions but warned against "sterile demands." The monarchists ran their own candidates only in the first and third sections but supported the Opportunists in those districts on the second ballot and in the other sections.[75]

The alliance of Opportunists and monarchists gave them a strong minority consisting of 15 of the 36 seats on the council—but not victory. The Allemanist candidates, 10 of whom had run in one section, did badly; their leading candidate, Neveu, received only 159 votes, which was far below the 1,146 received by the last qualifying candidate in that section. In the second section—essentially comprising the northern faubourgs—5 workers were elected but no Allemanists, with Neveu receiving only 372 votes.[76]

Despite a relatively light turnout this municipal election demonstrated the division between, on the one hand, the proletarian sections associated with large-scale industrialization and the recent growth of the city and, on the other, old Limoges. The *opportuno-monarchistes,* as the left dubbed them, swept the fourth section, which centered on the cathedral and the old Cité ("en chauffant sérieusement les Naveix, les curés pourront peut-être obtenir un succès" claimed a Radical electoral poster). The eight councilmen elected from that section included a number of prominent industrialists and merchants, among them the porcelain manufacturer Sazarat. Here the alliance with the conservatives helped the Opportunists. In the third section, which included much of the central commercial district, the place de la République, and the Champ de Juillet, the Opportunists won four out of five places. Two merchants, including Dantony, Chénieux's right-hand man, led the way. In the first section, also part of the old commercial city, including the place de la Motte and the butchers' quarter, only two Opportunists were elected, for the route d'Angoulême and the ancienne route d'Aixe on the periphery provided workers' votes for the left. In the second and fifth sections the left was swept to victory, as expected. Labussière led the voting in the second section, followed by a lawyer and two workers. The image of this second section, which included the rue de Paris and the faubourgs Montmailler and Montjovis, sketched by a Radical publicist in a spoof on voting by district was accurate: porcelain workers in rural outfits with factories behind them. In the fifth section, which included the avenue and faubourg Pont Neuf, three Radicals were elected, giving the Radicals and republican socialists twenty-one seats.[77]

In 1892 several deaths and resignations necessitated a by-election for new councilmen. The tone of this election was noticeably sharper. The brief flirtation of some workers with General Boulanger in 1889 had ended. More Radicals were now calling themselves radical-socialists, demanding a Bourse du Travail and a government that would "offer the workers more than simply promises."[78] The monarchist and Opportunist press had launched a vigorous campaign against the unions and their role in the shoemakers' strike; the clerical party demanded the return to the streets of religious processions. *Le Petit Centre,* the voice of the Opportunists, took aim at the "socialist threat," now frightened by the specter of May Day demonstrations. The paper lambasted those who wanted to overthrow the "present social state," particularly those "ridiculous" bourgeois who joined the workers. One could now read scrawled on the walls "Long Live the Proletarian Republic!" *Le Petit Centre* bravely asserted that there were no more classes in France since the Revolution of 1789. There had been, one had to admit, a dominant "caste" during the July Monarchy, but the rights and privileges that stemmed from money no longer existed because of the fusion of the old classes into "what one calls today the French people." A month before the election the moderate paper had warned that republicans were confronted by their "hereditary and implacable enemy: reaction." But by the time of the election *Le Petit Centre* had eagerly joined the monarchists.[79]

The election ended the left's majority, since the Opportunists held nineteen seats, as compared to seventeen held by the old majority (two of whom were Allemanists). The left swept the proletarian quarters, as expected, but lost seats in the other sections in the wake of a campaign by the right to raise the specter of a red peril. Twelve of the thirteen candidates elected on the first ballot were Radicals and radical-socialists, but the sectioning of Limoges brought the Opportunists victory in much closer elections in the first, third, and fourth sections on the second ballot. The Opportunist victory inaugurated three years of bitter contention within the council, with Dr. Chénieux, who was no friend of the workers, elected as mayor and Dantony as his deputy.[80]

During the Chénieux administration—and at least partially because of it—workers' associations became more aggressive. The number of unions increased from 8 in December 1890 to 21 at the end of 1893, including the Chambre syndicale des ouvriers et ouvrières de la cordonnerie de Limoges. In 1893 several militants organized a Federation that joined ten of the twenty-three *syndicats* in the city. This Federation, like its ephemeral predecessor ten years earlier, announced it would follow a policy of conciliation rather than seeking conflict. But each *syndicat* was free to strike on its own and then notify the directing committee of the Federation, which would include the general secretary, treasurer, their assistants, and one delegate for each union. The Federation sought to assume responsibility for the interests of workers, representing and negotiating, where necessary, for them.

Edouard Treich served as general secretary of the Federation. The son of a porcelain worker active in L'Initiative twenty years earlier, he had left Limoges to work in Paris and then, briefly, in Barcelona, as a turner.[81] Upon his return Treich worked for the Blanchard Company on the rue de Paris, and had been active in the revival of the *syndicats* in the late 1880s. He managed to set up a small café on the rue de la Fonderie, which joined the rue de Paris and the faubourg Montmailler. It was in the Treich café that the workers drew up statues for the Federation.

Treich, a Guesdist and a member of the Municipal Council, believed that the unions could serve as a foundation for political action. The treasurer of the Federation, Aristide Hummel, a shoemaker, was also a Guesdist and served on the Municipal Council. The other militants represented a cross section of the working-class population: Jacques (or Marcelin) Rougerie, a typographer; Martial

Ruby, a socialist tailor "with no other resource," the police determined, "than the product of his labor"; the Allemanist Neveu, rue des Petites Carmes, had worked for twelve years in one of the Haviland factories; forty-three-year-old Jean Issanchou worked for the Monteux Company; his son was a porcelain painter.[82]

The fledgling Federation faced several immediate problems. Its daily newspaper, *L'Express du Limousin,* ran out of money, became a biweekly, and then folded. Furthermore, the member *syndicats* still lacked a regular meeting place, which contributed to the lack of cohesion when the Chénieux council rejected the proposal to establish a Bourse du Travail. Yet the Federation and the increasing number of *syndicats* did contribute to a more aggressive mood among workers and an increase in strike activity by 1893. A strike of 6 typographers against the Plainemaison Company in April was meant to protest the use of lower-paid female workers. It was backed by the *syndicat.* After attempts at conciliation and arbitration failed, the strike finally faltered, with the *patron* insisting that he could pay whom he wanted what he wanted. When *monteurs* working for the Blanchard Company walked out to underscore their demand that a foreman be fired, the *chambre syndicale* obtained a compromise settlement from the company. A 2-week strike of porcelain workers in the fall succeeded in securing a raise because of the financial support of organized workers in other trades. The following January the shoemakers' union orchestrated a 3-day strike of *finisseurs* who opposed a reduction in the piece rate and the firing of a foreman who assessed and paid for the work of home workers; he was accused of giving out work to the orphanage at Mas Eloi, bringing about a reduction in the piece rate. Hummel, who had once worked there, organized the strike at his new company, and *L'Express du Limousin* announced the intervention of the Federation. The workers returned after the company agreed to return to the old rate for some items, but the foreman—a sign of the times—stayed on. In April 1894, 60 *plâtriers* won a raise after a brief strike instigated by the union. The same month the Federation negotiated with the owner of the Café de l'Univers, whose 6 waiters had struck because he insisted on keeping their tips. These strikes were not all successful, but we can see what the manufacturers saw: that the increase in unionization and the creation of the Federation seemed to generate a new momentum for workers in Limoges, joining twenty-three *syndicats* and 1,408 workers at its inception.[83]

The year 1895 marked a new stage in the political and social evolution of Limoges. Assisted by a new paper, *Le Rappel du Centre,* Labussière defeated Chénieux in a race for the General Council seat from Limoges. Eighteen Opportunists resigned from the council in order to provoke an election. At stake was the proposed Bourse du Travail, which Chénieux's council had effectively blocked. The election brought a sweep for the united socialists: twenty-one radical- or reform socialists, nine Guesdists, and six Allemanists were elected. Limoges, with Labussière again elected mayor, became a socialist municipality. In September

1895 the Confédération générale du travail (C.G.T.) was established in Limoges, at the seventh congress of the Chambres syndicales, groupes corporatifs, fédérations, and bourses du travail. Some of the preliminary work for that historic event occurred in Treich's café on the rue de la Fonderie. Labussière presided over a banquet for the delegates and offered a fete in their honor. The C.G.T. launched a new era for French workers. On December 11, upon the formal recommendation of a committee chaired by Pierre Teissonnière, the council unanimously voted to establish a Bourse du Travail.[84]

The municipality agreed to purchase a factory building on the avenue de la Gare—which ran between the place Jourdan and the Gare des Bénédictins—to house the Bourse du Travail and the city's thirty-two *syndicats*. The city would provide furniture for the two-story building—which included two sizable halls, a kitchen, an office, and the lodgings for the general secretary and a concierge—and to make needed major repairs. In addition, an annual municipal subsidy of six thousand francs would pay the rent (twenty-five hundred francs), heat, light, and general upkeep of the Bourse du Travail for a minimum of fifteen years.[85]

The Bourse would: "(1) attempt to find jobs for workers of both sexes without distinction of trade; (2) enhance and develop the organization of trade associations; (3) organize the efforts of salaried workers to improve their material situation, assure their independence, and elevate their intellectual and moral level; (4) keep statistics on the work situation in various regions, particularly in this region; (5) revive the manual arts, which are in the process of disappearing, as a result of the division of labor, with professional courses and apprenticeship competitions; (6) and, finally, provide an information service for everything of interest to the workers."[86]

In order to fulfill the dictates of the 1884 law on associations, the statutes asserted that "the Bourse will remain completely outside of political and religious questions." Likewise, the municipality would not become involved in the operation of the Bourse. But how would the various unions be represented? By how many delegates? Treich wanted the ratio of delegates to be one for every hundred workers in each occupation, which would have left porcelain workers in a dominant position vis-à-vis the other occupations. Hummel opposed this.[87] Finally it was agreed that four delegates would represent each union on the general committee of the Bourse (and serve as the directing committee of the Federation). One delegate from each union would serve on the Bourse's executive committee for one year, with the possibility of reelection. This committee would represent the Bourse before the municipality. But since both bodies met infrequently (four and twelve times a year, respectively), the positions of general secretary (Treich) and treasurer (Hummel), both of which were salaried, became crucial. Treich therefore was the most important figure at the Bourse, being responsible for all official correspondence, reports, and the operation of the placement bureau.[88]

The municipality turned over the building to the Bourse on March 11, 1896. The Bourse began operation with the enthusiastic support of the socialist municipality and the working class. Hummel was ecstatic. "Finally Limoges has awakened under the protection of triumphant socialism! Long live emancipation! Down with the two-faced reaction of the tricolor!"[89] The Bourse, representing thirty-five *syndicats* and more than five thousand workers, as well as thousands of nonunionized workers indirectly, would not remain independent of political life. Treich, Hummel, and Pierre Teissonière served on the Municipal Council. The Bourse itself became a political issue, opposed by the Opportunists and the monarchists. Strikes became inextricably interwined with the political life of the city. The year 1895 brought a wave of nine strikes even before the Bourse had opened its doors. Economic, social, and political conflict now seemed to merge with everyday life in belle époque Limoges.

7

"De la gare à la conférence contradictoire": Popular Politics and Strikes During the Socialist Municipality, 1895-1905

On May Day 1896 the *grande salle* of the new Bourse du Travail was gaily decorated with tricolor flags and red paper hangings, with twisted fillets of the socialist color behind the tribune. In the center stood a large bust of Marianne, adorned with a tricolor sash. Two tables covered with red cloth were placed on each side of the tribune, and the town hall was supplied with enough chairs and benches to accommodate a thousand people. The inauguration of the Bourse du Travail coincided with the critical municipal elections that would take place the same week. Emile Labussière urged workers to vote for the socialists on May 3.[1] The political theme of Labussière's speech symbolized the close ties between economic and political action in Limoges during the years of the socialist municipality.

The elections of 1896 shaped political life in Limoges for the next decade. Fearing a socialist sweep, Opportunists and clericals joined forces again, generating meetings and speeches in which virtually the entire city seemed to participate. Candidates of the conservative alliance accused the Bourse of using municipal funds to foment strikes. They appealed to those citizens "who want to turn back the men of disorder." A vote for the Chénieux list would, in their eyes, be a vote against the "collectivist barracks" that would follow the victory of socialism in Limoges. Such talk appealed to the League of Commerce and Industry, as did their demand that the consumer cooperative L'Union be taxed, that there be a reduction in the tax on "hygenic drinks"—including wine—and that there be "freedom" of unions to meet outside the Bourse du Travail (an ironic twist, since the Opportunist administration had made it difficult for unions to meet anywhere). A militant Catholic priest, Abbé Marévéry, offered his support to the Opportunists and asked his followers to tone down their religious appeals in order not to antagonize those socially conservative bourgeois constituents who also happened to be anticlerical. He led a committee "for social defense" and sent Ché-nieux a list of some fifteen hundred names of conservatives who had abstained from voting in the last election. Marévéry called for the city to rally to the old virtues of "country, family, property, and the Church" against the socialists.[2]

Labussière urged voters to examine the record since the socialist municipality came to office eight months earlier. While maintaining a budgetary surplus of almost two hundred thousand francs, the municipality had kept its promises, establishing the Bourse du Travail, providing more money for schools and day nurseries, beginning work on the Viraclaud quarter, extending electrical service, and expediting the construction of the tramways. At the same time the socialists tried to counter—apparently with some success—the Opportunists' appeal to the middle class by asserting that the workers were the clients, friends, and allies of shopkeepers against the wholesale merchants and department stores. The Opportunists pledged to carry out their own urban projects, appealing to the interests of the commercial quarters; the socialists claimed that their opponents emphasized the construction of the long-awaited rue Centrale, which would benefit the predominantly bourgeois quarters at the expense of the faubourgs. The bourgeois republicans appealed directly to the Ligue du commerce et de l'industrie, claiming that the reelection of the socialists posed a threat to the economic interests of Limoges. As for the Guesdists, they were less concerned with the tramways than were the radical-socialists, since most workers lived within walking distance of the factories and the Viraclaud quarter. They demanded an improvement in street-cleaning services available to the faubourgs, better housing for workers, cheaper seats in the theater, greater economic and medical assistance for the poor, and salaries for municipal councilmen so that more workers could afford to seek elected office.[3] But the Guesdists and the radical-socialists agreed fundamentally, promising, "If we are elected, we will do what has been accomplished in Roubaix and Montluçon and will work for the well-being of the working class."[4]

The Allemanists, however, again debated the merits of a socialist alliance. They refused to support socialist candidates who were not workers, as well as Treich, whom they accused of personal ambition and of pushing the Bourse toward independent political action. One meeting of the Avant-garde electoral committee degenerated into a fight over the question of joining the other socialists. Finally the Allemanists agreed to support socialist candidates in the fourth and fifth sections on the second ballot if their candidates were eliminated on the first ballot, which they would surely be.[5]

Workers filled the cafés and public school halls, such as in the second section, where 600 people gathered in the *école maternelle,* ancienne route d'Aixe. Workers' associations gathered to hear the *professions de foi* of the candidates; two Guesdists asked 150 building workers in the salle des conférences for their support, and 80 day laborers welcomed other candidates before discussing ways of attracting more laborers to their fledgling organization.[6] Incumbents eagerly defended their records and aspiring councilmen made promises. The decentralized popular democracy of 1793, 1848, and 1871 seemed to have revived. Léon Neveu discussed his record with 300 workers on May Day. He had voted against municipal funding for the theater because he thought that "such projects insult the public." He had also opposed support for the racetrack, "because the subvention . . . implies that the improvement of the breed [*race*] of horses should come before the development of the human race!"[7] Here his logic seemed impeccable, but he also had to explain to workers why he had joined the hated Chénieux in opposing aid to the mutual aid societies.[8] Not surprisingly, Neveu did poorly in the election.

Limoges's revolutionary heritage informed many of these meetings. One speaker reminded his audience that the revolutions of 1789 and 1830 had unseated the aristocracy, only to hand power over to an equally oppressive bourgeoisie, now identified with Dr. Chénieux, the leader of the conservative bourgeoisie that had ruled Limoges since the Revolution of 1830.[9] Municipal elections, socialists believed, were, "above all, the foundation of the social edifice"; workers could dethrone the bourgeoisie in Limoges. Chénieux represented the interests of the *juste-milieu, les gros,* the wealthy industrialists, wholesale merchants, and the department stores. His enemies claimed that the doctor had built up a prosperous practice treating only the illnesses and diseases of the wealthy. At the same time, he accepted a salary at the small medical school. The socialists accused him of lacking sympathy for the poor, who were ill, and of saying, "What do you want? . . . people who live like that are used to being sick and we should just leave them alone."[10] In 1892, it was said, Chénieux had turned away a poor woman about to be thrown out of her rented apartment. When the woman, who had four or five children, asked him for help, he allegedly replied, "Madame, it was not I who forced you to have that many children." Furthermore, he had "insulted" the workers by refusing municipal funds for the 1895 corporative congress, refusing to open municipal workshops in 1893–94, and allocating the derisory sum of only three hundred francs to assist workers laid off during the porcelain strike of 1893. His medical colleague and political enemy, Dr. Raymond, reminded one faubourg audience that Chénieux had supported the "brigand" Napoleon III even as the latter was "strangling the Republic." Limoges's role in the Second Republic had, after all, been immortalized by the statue of Denis Dussoubs, martyred while resisting the coup d'état. Chénieux seemed to be "the candidate of the priests, the reactionaries, and the butchers; [the latter] celebrated the election of their good friend Chénieux [in 1892] in a particular fashion. By eight o'clock, the men and women of the picturesque quarter awaited the election results impatiently." Now Chénieux refused to participate in the popular political forums that the workers loved, such as a meeting in the salle des pénitents blancs, filled with those Chénieux had called "the dregs of society," who had celebrated his defeat long into the night the previous year.[11] Such gatherings inevitably ended with shouts of "Long Live the Social Republic!"—not the sort of thing Chénieux wanted to hear.[12]

The election took place in an intense atmosphere hitherto unseen in a municipal election in Limoges. Since demonstrations against Chénieux had followed the elections of 1895, the prefect mobilized gendarmes, four squadrons of infantry, and even the artillery. He left the telephone lines open to Paris. The entire city awaited the results of the first ballot. Workers filled the streets and the café. The socialist candidates emerged with a strong majority, with twenty-four of the council's thirty-six seats (fifteen radical-socialists and nine Guesdists). Thirteen workers were elected from the proletarian second and fifth sections, as well as from the largely mixed fourth. These men would represent the world of the faubourgs (four lived on the avenue Garibaldi, while others lived on the faubourg de Paris, the avenue Armand Barbès, the rue de la Fonderie, and the chemin du Petit Treuil).[13] Opportunists were returned in the two most bourgeois sections: the first, the fief of Chénieux, and the third, where all six Opportunist candidates were elected. Table 6 graphically illustrates the election results:

TABLE 6   The 1896 Municipal Elections

Section	First Ballot	Second Ballot
First	four *progressistes*	two *progressites*, and three socialists
Second	ten socialists	
Third	six *progressistes*	
Fourth		seven socialists
Fifth	one socialist	three socialists

Source: 3M 438 and 442.

As Treich put it, "universal suffrage has indicated what the people want: that the proletariat can finally participate in the leadership of city business."[14] The socialist majoriy reelected Labussière as mayor. Labussière's mandate was confirmed with a convincing victory over Chénieux in the 1898 legislative elections. Backed by the faubourgs, but not the conservative central districts, a cortège of three thousand people celebrated with shouts of "Down with Chénieux!" But the presence of twelve Opportunists—one third of the council—invariably generated bitter division and heated debates during the four years of the council. At the same time, the political mobilization of the workers generated continued bourgeois resistance. During the belle époque public life and collective political conflict converged.

Public political meetings were one salient manifestation of the political awakening of Limoges workers in the fin-de-siècle period, which was marked by the largest turnout of voters in municipal elections yet seen. Political life moved from the small clubs located in the back rooms of cafés into the larger meeting halls and the Bourse du Travail. When Jules Guesde visited Limoges in 1894, his followers had to rent the Antignac hall in the Café de Paris because Chénieux refused to allow him to speak in the municipal theater. Workers heard him emphasize the practical possibilities of municipal power and condemn the deadly anarchist bombing of the Café Terminus in Paris: The "socialist bombs" would be "syndicalist organizations preparing a revolutionary army," and simple ballots would "ensure the triumph of the social Republic."[15] In the socialist municipality the political meeting became a way of life as workers escorted distinguished visitors such as Guesde "de la gare à la conférence contradictoire" ("from the railroad station to the political debate"). The rhythm of such political meetings, which served as political schoolhouses—the parliaments of the people—partially depended on national and municipal elections and the visits of national political leaders. Yet the meetings did not stop when the elections were over; they often featured local political figures, such as Labussière, Treich, Teissonnière père and fils, and Abbé Marévéry, or municipal councilmen reporting back to their constituents. All such occasions gave ordinary people an opportunity to choose among a variety of ideologies and to influence the way the city was run. These events helped draw average citizens into political life, a fact whose importance cannot be underestimated.

Several thousand people singing "La Carmagnole" and "La Marseillaise" and shouting "Long Live Denis Dussoubs!" welcomed Jean Jaurès to Limoges following the 1895 municipal elections. After escorting the socialist leader to the *salle,* they heard Jaurès call the republican government "merely an instrument in the hands of the capitalist class." The arrival of the Abbé Marévéry was greeted with "shouts, animal sounds, and torrents of whistles." The prelate then challenged the conclusions of Jaurès, who later visited the Cercle démocratique, offered a toast in patois that evening at a banquet, and visited the statue of Dussoubs.[16]

Abbé Marévéry had risen spontaneously to speak at the meeting. Other meetings, specifically *conférences contradictoires,* featured speakers who had been invited to debate the principal orator. Several months earlier such a meeting had pitted Lefèvre, a Parisian municipal councilman, against Marévéry in a debate on French history. The confrontation drew a packed house, including municipal councilmen and members of the Catholic clubs. What *Le Rappel du Centre* called a stimulating and "completely courteous discussion" followed Lefèvre's speech; the audience provided an astonishing lesson for those who claim that public meetings inevitably degenerate into a tumult."[17]

The *conférence contradictoire* contributed to—in Limoges but, I suspect, elsewhere as well—the first great wave of spirited popular debate and participation since the Commune, when the public meeting movement, encouraged by the law of June 18, 1868, helped sound the death knell of the Second Empire. The Antignac hall, the Café de Paris, and the Chalou hall, on the rue de Paris, became the workshops of popular democracy and municipal socialism.[18]

The social Catholics, whom we will discuss in greater detail later in this chapter, challenged the socialists in the *conférences contradictoire,* while the Opportunists or *progressistes* stayed away from these smokey halls of working-class political mobilization. Abbé Marévéry, who frequented these meetings, was described as "alone against the crowd" by the Catholic newspaper *L'Univers,* suffering "attacks against the bourgeoisie, cries of hatred against the Church" orchestrated by Jaurès, "the prophet of vengeance." When he visited Limoges, Vaillant expressed surprise at seeing "men dressed in the cassocks of the past" at such meetings, particularly in anticlerical Limoges.

A *conférence contradictoire* held in December 1899 seems typical. An overflow crowd heard Marévéry attack collectivism while maintaining that workers should be paid an adequate salary. He was followed to the rostrum by a porcelain painter named Ribière, who lamented that workers' salaries had declined since 1789 but claimed that collectivism was not the answer to the workers' plight. The Guesdist militant Chauly then took to the floor to defend collectivism: All capital, he insisted, should be nationalized, with the State the only employer. This brought Abbé Desgranges into the debate who argued that collectivism of any kind could lead only to "tyranny and the end of freedom." Yet despite the ideological distance that separated the speakers, the session ended, again, in what was described as "a courteous exchange between Abbé Marévéry and several workers on the same theories." In 1900 some three thousand people listened to a similar debate at the Cirque on a Sunday, while the *fanfare* of the Bourse de Travail played "L'Internationale" in "one of those beautiful and imposing socialist events to which the worthy workers of our town are now accustomed."[20]

Abbé Desgranges accepted the necessity of engaging in the political rituals of the Church's bitterest enemies "in order to repulse their insults and counter their maneuvers, to expose their audacity with unrelenting rsistance, to dissipate their most virulent prejudices and thus attenuate their hostility."[21] Winning conversions to Catholicism in this missionary country seemed impossible, but the activist priests were willing to try. Desgranges and Marévéry therefore stood in their black cassocks among the workers, dressed in their blue work clothes, many of whom had certainly not been in church since they were baptized and were too young to walk out on their own. Desgranges acknowledged the difficult beginnings of such encounters, "the violent obstruction, gross interruptions, the physical toll of prolonged discussions for four or five hours, the confrontations at the exits, and the perfidious accounts [in the newspapers of what had happened]." The priest was an expert and an authority on *conférences contradictoires,* having participated in some twenty-one hundred of them throughout France. Limoges was the center of his struggle, with the *conférence contradictoire* serving as his forum, too.[22]

Despite the rhetoric and verbal fireworks marking the heated encounters between socialists and priests in the somber halls of Limoges, there is not a single report of physical violence. Desgranges could only recall twelve occasions (out of more than twenty-one hundred) when troublemakers had to be expelled from the hall, and only three times did the crowd force him to stop speaking. Desgranges tried to create the most advantageous physical environment possible for the meeting, which was no easy task since socialists numerically dominated virtually every audience. An 1881 law required that a *bureau* of at least five people preside over every such public gathering, which normally included a president, a vice president, and an assessor to ensure order. Frequently the audience elected this *bureau*, most frequently by acclamation, a tradition dating back to the French Revolution. For a *conférence contradictoire* sponsored by Catholics, the composition of the *bureau* could not be left to popular acclamation. Thus Abbé Desgranges tried to constitute a friendly *bureau* and inform the prefecture of its composition the day before the planned meeting. One of the responsibilities of the president was to draw up the *ordre du jour,* which usually constituted the subject of the principal speaker's talk, approved by acclamation at the end of the meeting. In the face of almost certain hostility, a sympathetic or at least neutral president could help the priest "introduce certain timely ideas to the forum of public opinion, or make known demands to public authorities."[23]

Before discussing the experience of the socialist municipality, we should first see how the other contenders for political power—in addition to the Opportunists—fared during the period: the right-wing parties, both royalist and social Catholic, and their electoral allies; the related nationalist groups, the anarchists, who were allied with no one; and, above all, the Allemanists and Guesdists.

The right-wing parties found no more support after the 1895 elections than before, although they were useful to the Opportunists in the municipal elections. The Catholic press provided the principal political resource of the right. Until 1881 the region's only Catholic newspaper was *La Semaine religieuse,* which provided a tedious summary of religious information that was read by the clergy and a few pious laymen. In 1881 Louis Guibert, editor of the *Almanach Limousin,* opened the offices of *La Gazette du Centre* on the place Jourdan. At the turn of the century the monarchist newspaper sent several thousand copies of each edition into the Center region of France. By then *La Gazette du Centre* had a friendly rival, a local edition of the Assumptionist newspaper *La Croix* that matched its circulation. Abbé Ardant, the scion of an old Bonapartist family of printers, directed the virulent anti-Semitism of *La Croix* at the rural masses of the Limousin. Its crude language ("toutes ces crapules de juifs et de francs-maçons qui ne valent pas les quatres fers d'un chien") contrasted with the pompous sarcastic tone of Guibert's more dignified *Le Gazette du Contre.*[24]

But even the press could not generate successful political organizations and mass support. A Comité républicain national ouvrier, orchestrated from Paris and coordinated locally by a rascal named Ferraud, had helped elect Le Veillé to the Chamber of Deputies as a Boulangist in 1889. Following the workers' brief Boulanger infatuation, the Boulangists of the Ligue des patriotes had no influence on municipal elections because of their antirepublican stance. A nationalist weekly, *Le Tout Limoges,* ceased publication in 1892 after a brief appearance of less than two months. The Dreyfus affair, however, revived royalist and nationalist activity. It breathed some life into the Cercle St. Joseph, led by Chabrol, a lawyer whose son served as general secretary of the Jeunesse royaliste. A wine merchant named Gardelle was also active in the club. In 1897 a former secretary to Déroulède arrived from Paris with the hope of reviving the Ligue des patriotes, but despite the presence of a number of gymnastic societies he had no success.[25]

In 1898 Comte Etienne de Montbron, de Villelume, and the other patriarchs of the Limousin's old royalist families arrived from their country châteaux to find allies in the godless city. Habit, far more than hope, brought them together. A small audience of clerks and employees from the stores and offices of a few bourgeois royalists heard an Orleanist lawyer from Paris assert that a monarch would have prevented the current crisis in the porcelain industry, presumably by buying lots of plates, because kings dearly loved workers. He bravely promised that "when Philippe VII comes to visit Limoges, he will be received by the oldest corporation of workers—somewhat bourgeois, if you will—the butchers!"[26] Some two hundred unemployed workers were lured to another meeting with promises of money, drinks, and cigarettes. The following year the government prosecuted the Jeunesse royaliste, in conjunction with the move against the rightist leagues in the capital.[27] De Montbron was convicted of membership in an illegal association and was fined eighty francs, which he could certainly afford; Chabrol fils had to pay twenty-five francs, which may have put a modest strain on the family business. The prefect mentioned Chabrol as the only person in Limoges who might pose an active threat to the Republic.[28]

The remnants of the royalist group formed the Ligue anti-sémitique ou nationaliste with the financial support of one Comte de Bony from the commune of St. Priest Ligoure. They, too, believed their time had come during the Dreyfus affair. Barbou des Courrières, a young editor of *La Gazette du Centre,* aided by Le Veillé's wife, tried in vain to organize a newspaper and a demonstration against Dreyfus. Members gathered at the Café de la Poste to send congratulations to nationalist deputies elected in Paris. Yet they admitted that their propaganda efforts had and would continue to come to nothing. Limoges was "le fief des socialistes dreyfusards."[29]

Indeed, the Dreyfus affair helped bring the left together in Limoges. There seemed to have been little public discussion of the arrest and trial of Dreyfus until the imprisonment and suicide of Colonel Henry. But after that dramatic turn of events police estimated that 80 percent of the workers talked about the *affaire* every day, contrasting this with the seeming indifference of the rural population.

The vast majority supported Dreyfus in Limoges. The Ligue nationaliste held meetings in 1899 and 1900, and Abbé Marévéry, angered by Déroulède's arrest, brought in an anti-Semitic speaker. A clerical organization distributed anti-Dreyfusard literature, but the reaction in Limoges to the Dreyfus affair demonstrated the right's lack of support.[30]

When the national threat to the Republic became apparent, the socialist political clubs formed a joint Vigilance Committee for the Defense of the Republic; they had worked together for the election of Labussière to the Chamber of Deputies in 1898. Public opinion stood solidly behind the effort. Over three thousand people attended the first general meeting of the committee. The remaining events of the *affaire* unfolded calmly in Limoges, with only very minor incidents. The population evidenced more anxiety over the municipal elections and strikes in the city than with the course of the Dreyfus affair at the time of the verdict of Rennes.[31]

By 1901 the Catholic right appeared to have abandoned hope for a monarchical restoration; it now awaited a "strong man" who, in the opinion of one nationalist, "knows how to make himself obeyed . . . the French are a people who have always needed to be guided. Kings are no longer in season, but there is always dictatorship . . . the only cure for this country from the evil that afflicts it." The anti-Semitic nationalists founded another organization the following year, the Section Limousin de la patrie française, led by Auguste Sautour, an abrasive accountant whose brother worked as a foreman for the Charles Haviland Company.[32]

But the old patterns of rightist political activity still persisted. The patriarchs of the ancient families would arrive from their châteaux—de Montbron from Montbron, de Villelume from Tharaud, in Sérilhac—go to mass (never missing January 21, the day on which Louis XVI had been executed in the year 1793), attend a banquet with the Chabrols, and listen, in the company of several porcelain manufacturers and an occasional butcher, to assorted denunciations of the Republic, Jews, Masons, and the Bourse du Travail, shouting "France for the French!" at the evening's conclusion.[33] They had to content themselves with some support from the surviving Catholic clubs and the Ligue du commerce et de l'industrie, some of whose members shared their hatred of "hoarding Jews" who were taking over "every branch of commerce." But the right remained isolated from the general population. Its banquets and celebrations took place inside rented hotel dining rooms, with guards at the door, not in the crowded café halls or in the streets of Limoges. Royalists and nationalists counted only about a hundred active supporters in *la ville rouge*.[34]

The social Catholics shared anti-Semitism and antipathy for the socialists with the royalist right, yet social Catholic priests believed that poverty was a cause and not merely a result of the demoralization that accompanied the workers' abandonment of the Church. Without offering a critique of capitalism itself, they insisted that Limoges's industrialists paid insufficient attention to the workers' material needs. They believed that a return to religion would encourage a sense of solidarity between employers and workers. This took Marévéry and Desgranges into the world of the *conférence contradictoire,* as we have seen.

Marévéry, born in 1867, had grown up on the faubourg des Arènes, an eyewitness to the poverty of the proletariat. Vicar of the Church of St. Pierre, this small, intelligent, severe, and combative priest hoped to establish new associations that could truly moralize workers and thus lure them away from parties of the left. He wrote regularly in *La Croix* under the pseudonym Marlyou. The anticlerical prefect Monteil claimed that Marévéry ran the entire diocese. But while the bishop hobnobbed with blue-blooded royalists, the priest entered the *milieu ouvrier* in search of converts. The industrial faubourgs were his missionary area.[35]

Abbé Jean Desgranges understood something of the origins of strikes in Limoges. "The tasks foisted upon each worker are becoming more and more mechanical and monotonous. Imagine, therefore, what goes on in the soul of a worker who, from January 1 through December 31, for thirty or forty years, turns the same saucer or embellishes the same plates." Small wonder, then, that so many workers were vulnerable to "all the contacts and all of the promiscuities engendered in urban areas." Large-scale industrialization had isolated the worker from "beneficial" relationships, particularly as the employer had become a distant figure.[36] Desgranges claimed that the Republic remained nothing more than "a cruel development" without better educated and responsible workers. Like Marévéry he believed that only religion could bring employers and workers together.[37]

A third social Catholic militant, Abbé Ardant seemed the least "social" Catholic; without question he was the most caustic and violently anti-Semitic. "All for God and for France and nothing for the Jews, who deserve to be attacked!" he shouted at a meeting in April 1900. Young Frenchmen had to be protected by the Church from ideas, namely, socialism, imported from outside France, the inspiration of the German Jew Karl Marx. In 1903 he thundered that the congregations had to defend the Church "to the last cartridge."[38] Desgranges and Marévéry shared his beliefs, with the former asserting that France should recognize its real enemies, Jews and socialists.[39]

In 1891 the social Catholic priests created the Secrétariat du peuple, overseen by six nuns, offering workers lectures, discussions, Catholic books, and legal and medical advice. Members of the Catholic Cercle d'études, shopkeepers, clerks, teachers from the few remaining *écoles libres,* their pupils, and a few prosperous workers heard talks on topics like "Savings and the Working-Class Family," "Rest on Sunday," "Anarchism," and "The Inquisition." Abbé Marévéry used the Secrétariat du peuple to try to rally support against the socialists before the 1896 election; the priest pored over electoral lists in search of voters eager "to conserve the bases of society, religion, family, property, and patriotism," and who awaited legislation ensuring that Sunday remain a day of rest and imposing heavy taxes on the department stores and L'Union.[41] In June 1899 the three priests also founded a club for social Catholic propaganda.

How did the city's handful of anarchists fare in the belle époque? They sponsored two speakers in 1897. Sébastien Faure spoke to a sizable crowd of 1,000 people, the vast majority of whom were not anarchists but had turned out, as with other speakers, to consider what the latter had to say. The crowd was perhaps swollen by the publicity surrounding a number of recent fires set on the property of a local magistrate and popularly attributed to anarchists. The visit of Broussouloux demonstrated the problems anarchists confronted. The Antignac hall, rented for 24 francs, was the scene of his diatribe against the clergy. The take at the door was 47.50 francs, suggesting an audience of 95 if they paid 50 centimes apiece at the door. But the café owner was angry because the audience had not bought a single drink (in fact, half left during the talk). He refused to rent the hall to the anarchists a second night. The modest take had to cover another rental of a café hall and posters advertising the next talk, "The Crimes of Religions," as well as partially offset the speaker's expenses. Broussouloux delivered his lectures in the Café de l'Univers and the Café de Paris (whose hall cost five francs more to rent). The final talk had been advertised as an "evening for the entire family," although few women attended; a few songs and *monologues* concluded the event. But the receipts were barely sufficient to send Broussouloux to Nevers, his next stop. He complained about the paltry sum, even when the Limoges anarchist leader Beaure assured him that everyone had "given, each according to his means." He left Limoges with a third-class ticket.[43]

Two years later, while the Dreyfus affair captured the headlines, anarchists sponsored two lectures by Séraphine Pajuad. About four hundred people heard the speaker defend Dreyfus and attack anti-Semitism while, at the same time, stressing the uselessness of electoral participation. Of the three hundred who attended the second lecture, the police estimated that about thirty were anarchists. The rest had come, as in 1897, because they were curious, or to listen to Treich attack the anarchists' conclusions. Thirty anarchists out of a population of thirty thousand was not a good showing. They were seen distributing propaganda outside political meetings or "massés dans un coin" inside the hall. In the words of the prefect in 1896, "the anarchists are few here and not at all listened to." Deprived of a significant following, the *beaux gestes* of the anarchists were limited to verbal attacks against all kinds of authority and the defacement of the statue of Sadi Carnot, assassinated by the anarchist in Lyon, with the slogan "Vive l'anarchie!"[44]

Limoges may have earned its reputation as *la ville rouge,* but it was far from being a "fief of Guesdism," as it is described by Claude Willard.[45] The Guesdist candidate in the 1898 legislative elections received only 2.5 percent of the vote in the Haute-Vienne; in the contest for Conseil d'arrondissement in 1901, the Guesdist candidate claimed 2.7 percent of the vote in the Limoges district. In

1902 Chauly, a Guesdist running for Labussière's seat in the Chamber of Deputies, received only 760 votes to the mayor's 12,700. And in 1904, 5 Guesdist militants were handily defeated when they ran in the municipal elections against the reform socialists.[46]

Guesdist organization came to Limoges after Guesde already had followers there. The Cercle de l'union des républicains socialistes was founded early in 1896 by Treich, Emile Teissonnière (a *mouleur*), Jean Rougerie (a shoemaker and official of L'Union), and Coussy. All four had left either the radical-socialist Cercle démocratique or the Allemanist Avant-garde. At its first meeting sixty people gathered in a room on the second floor of the Café de France, place de l'Hôtel de Ville, with the municipal elections in mind. The first public meeting occurred in a school on the ancienne route d'Aixe, hoping to draw the workers of the faubourgs. A year later six hundred people attended the *fête de famille* that inaugurated a room in the Café de Paris. Teissonnière served as the general secretary of the club, but the task of presiding over meetings passed from member to member. The club maintained a small library that received the major political newspapers from Paris and the region. Anyone could join if sponsored by two members and upon receipt of the yearly fee of five francs. At the same time, Treich's leadership of the Bourse du Travail as general secretary, reaffirmed in 1897 by twenty votes, with only two abstentions, helped maintain Guesdist strength as well as the alliance with the reform socialists.[47]

Some of Willard's generalizations about the role of the Guesdists in the evolution of French socialism ring true for Limoges. More than any other group, the Guesdists functioned as a political party. Their club met more often than the Cercle démocratique between elections. The Guesdists acquainted many workers with the fundamental tenets of Marxism. However watered down and simplified, workers absorbed something of the historical origins of capitalism and of class conflict, which explained the realities of their world. At the May Day celebrations of 1896 available books and pamphlets included Marx's *Communist Manifesto*, Paul Lafargue's "Le Communisme et L'Internationalisme," as well as Guesde's "Problème et solution: Les Huit Heures à la Chambre." Guesdist newspapers aided the ideological education at Limoges workers. *La Bataille sociale, Le Socialiste de la Haute-Vienne,* and *L'Avenir* in turn presented *un marxisme sommaire.*[48] After the acrimonious split within the Guesdist camp, which began in 1898, and following frequent ideological and tactical battles with the reform socialists, the Guesdists published a translation of Karl Kautsky's analysis of the differences between revolutionary socialism and reformism. The orthodox Guesdists seemed to have combed Guesde's writings in the hope of finding support for their position against the reform socialists.[49]

Jules Guesde's visits to Limoges helped build up his political following. Docteur Fraisseux, a militant from Eymoutiers, later recalled that in the Haute-Vienne Guesde appeared as "both the prophet and the law" for many socialists: "For us he was the incarnation of the Revolution—we were nourished by his writing, his speeches, his articles." Fraisseux recalled with pleasure the evenings devoted to reading and discussion. In the midst of the poverty of the workers and the bitterness of class antagonism, "Marxist theory of scientific socialism seemed clarified, justified, and consecrated, right before my eyes." As a young apprentice of socialism, "capitalist society appeared to me like an edifice, a fortress, built upon two pillars—clericalism and militarism. And I told myself, 'We must first demolish the two supports, and then the fortress will collapse by itself.' "[50]

Guesdist militants were most likely to emerge from the *milieu ouvrier,* especially skilled porcelain workers. Of the nineteen active Guesdists, all but four were workers; eight of them were porcelain painters. All ten of the leading Allemanists were workers, eight of them in the porcelain industry. Reform socialists, on the other hand, included leaders of mixed social origin: Of the sixteen militants, six were indisputably bourgeois, including the journalist Pierre Bertrand.[51] The Guesdist Jean Parvy, born in 1876, was the son of a sharecropper living on the outskirts of Limoges. He moved to the city with his father when the elder Parvy found work as a municipal paver. Parvy left school at the age of twelve to become an apprentice porcelain decorator; he joined the union at the age of sixteen, but four years later lost his job after striking. He became secretary of the Limousin section of the Parti ouvrier français in 1902 and later served in the same capacity for the Fédération du parti socialiste de France. His friend Adrien Pressemane also left school to become a porcelain painter. As a young man he "studied to satisfy his thirst for knowledge, which made him a cultivated autodidact through extended reading and a systematic analysis of economic, social, and political problems." Joining the union and the radical-socialist club, he moved into the Parti ouvrier and then the Parti socialiste de France. As a writer he reached the urban and rural poor alike, thanks to "the vigor of his thought, the richness of his phrases, a commanding logic, effective presentation, a kind of controlled but mounting emotion, a melodious voice, somewhat singsong, nuanced, marked by a Limousin accent that distinctly separated his words." Léon Blum later paid tribute to "the lyrical power of this great popular orator."[52]

For porcelain workers like Parvy and Pressemane the attraction of Guesdism lay perhaps as much in its commitment to political action as in its promise of the inevitable victory of socialism. Guesde had written that "If someday the workers, the unfortunate, the disinherited, all those who suffer in contemporary society, all of those who are exploited and downtrodden, learn to affirm their will by dropping their votes into the urn in order to end all of the miseries, all of the suffering, all the injuries they suffer in bourgeois society, bourgeois society will be all but finished."[53] Treich believed that "political and economic action, wisely combined, can and should lead to a change in the present social state, and, until the contrary is proved, all militants desiring to lead the proletariat to power should employ this wise and reasonable tactic."[54] Yet why, in working-class

Limoges, *la ville rouge,* did the Guesdists remain a minority party within a socialist camp?

Guesdists in Limoges remained somewhat ambivalent about the purpose of municipal political contention. Guesde "did not believe that socialism in towns and cities was the first step in a successful movement for municipal autonomy. For him the Commune was a training ground for electoral participation at the national level. It prepared workers for the eventual seizure of state power by means of the vote."[55] Municipal elections provided a splendid occasion for political propaganda. This ambivalence about the possibility and desirability of local power as an end in itself sometimes did not serve the Guesdists well. They were convinced that socialism was impossible in a country with a powerful central state apparatus acting on behalf of the capitalist class. In Limoges the Guesdists were forced to ally themselves with the reform socialists in order to defeat the combined forces of the bourgeois Opportunists/*progressistes* and the much smaller antirepublican clerical party. Participants in a limited form of municipal socialism, they found themselves supporting tangible measures of reform for which the reform socialists received the lion's share of the credit. The Guesdist newspapers emphasized ideological issues, while *Le Rappel du Centre* and its successor, *Le Réveil du Centre* considered municipal questions. Yet the reform socialists also claimed Marx (and sometimes Guesde as well) as their own.

Furthermore, because the reform socialists dominated the municipality (and had the support of Treich and other moderate Guesdists), the Guesdists were far less successful than their counterparts in the North, the Allier, and other strongholds in merging their political organization with the mainstream of working-class life. The most important *fêtes populaires* were associated with or commandeered by the municipality, May Day being the obvious example. The reform socialists were in a far better position to capitalize on the city's tradition of local political initiative and revolutionary action (represented by the *bonnet phrygien* in *Le Rappel du Centre* and by the statue of Dussoubs), in contrast to the centralized and authoritarian impulse of the orthodox Guesdists. Both the reform socialists and the Guesdists claimed and celebrated the anniversary of the Commune, although that event was more firmly grounded in the mythology of the Guesdists. The municipality stood in opposition to the "two pillars" of capitalism, as identified by Fraisseux, namely, the Church and the army. The concrete steps taken by the municipality against the Church won many workers over to the practical possibilities offered by municipal power. Even in 1904, when Labussière was denounced by militant Guesdists, Pressemane stood with the mayor at a giant anticlerical rally, one that benefited the reform socialists. Likewise, the Guesdists did not have a monopoly on the well-known antimilitarism of the Limoges working class, particularly after 1900, although they were more identified with public demonstrations of that sentiment, such as *punches* for departing conscripts and antimilitaristic propaganda.

Not until 1903 did militant Guesdists really control the Bourse du Travail. Until then the close ties between socialism and syndicalism in the city had worked to the advantage of the reform socialists, aided by Labussière's considerable influence and the tangible accomplishments of his administration. The Guesdists profited from their virtual absorption of the Allemanists in 1898. Yet they never recovered, as they were the first to admit, from the Millerand crisis, which clearly defined the ideological distance that separated them from the reform socialists and accentuated the personality conflicts between Treich and Teissonnière. Certainly the fact that the Dreyfus affair and the elections of 1898 brought socialists together did not diminish the tensions between the Cercle démocratique and the Guesdist club, which expelled a so-called "spy" for the reform socialists from a meeting in 1898. Bitter relations persisted within the Guesdist camp between Treich, Labussière's ally, and Teissonnière, who joined Guesde himself in blaming Treich for politicizing the Bourse du Travail.[56]

Millerand's decision to join the ministry of Waldeck-Rousseau in 1899 deeply split the ranks of socialists. Teissonnière and the orthodox Guesdists castigated Millerand and his supporters, while Treich joined the republican socialists in applauding the first socialist minister. Teissonnière accused Treich of trying to undermine *La Bataille sociale* and subverting the autonomy of the *syndicats* while forcing the Bourse's moderate line upon them. Treich joined Labussière in Paris, where they represented the thirty-six-member *syndicats* of the Bourse at the congress in Paris in 1899, where they thanked Millerand for accepting a ministerial post.

But there was to be more. In January 1900 Treich's opponents claimed that he had helped a Parisian insurance company, Le Chômage, contract some fifteen thousand francs' worth of business in return for a sizable kickback—some said as much as twelve thousand francs. Teissonnière alluded to the disappearance of some money from the Bourse several years earlier, the implication being that Treich had taken it. Confronted at a meeting of the club, Treich became "very pale," in the words of the omnipresent special police commissioner. He first denied receiving any *pots du vin,* as well as being guilty of any wrongdoing related to the disappearance of funds. His enemy pressed on, shouting that Treich was "unworthy" of the club and demanding an answer of yes or no as to whether he had received any money from the insurance company. Treich weakly replied in the affirmative. He was through. On March 1 the "jury of honor" constituted within the Guesdist club found Treich guilty. In the meantime he had further antagonized his enemies by praising Millerand. Teissonnière demanded that the club decide whether it would follow his Guesdist line or that of Millerand and Treich. By secret ballot the members voted forty-nine to thirty (with two abstentions) to follow Teissonnière. Treich left the hall with his followers.[57] The split was as public as it was complete.

Because of a truce between the quarreling socialist groups, the Guesdists supported the successful referendum on the first five years of the Labussière adminis-tration. Publicly the split was ignored during the election of 1900. A committee of "socialist concentration" representing reformists, Guesdists, and Allemanists met approximately twenty times to draw up a common list of candidates. A final stormy meeting resulted in a combined list of socialist candidates.[58]

Once again Chénieux asked for the support of the clerical party against the socialists, blaming the Bourse for strike agitation: "This year," Chénieux's party claimed with irony, "the municipal elections are of capital importance!"[59] *La Rappel du Centre* extolled the fact that the city was living through "a period of remarkable increase in proletarian consciousness" and underlined the significance of the election in fulfilling Limoges's role in the emancipation of workers. In contrast, the *progressistes* defended private property as a fortress of good besieged by the workers. But they did not even bother to send candidates to the electoral meetings in the proletarian sections, where socialists appealed to the workers. In the fifth section, along and across the Vienne, the socialists promised to forge a new street, establish a new school for boys near the town hall, put street lights in the hamlet of St. Lazare, prolong several rural paths, and, in short, attend to the needs of "the valiant population of the bridges, so essentially proletarian." The tone was different in the conservative sections, such as the first, where the butch-ers listened to Abbé Ardant denounce the socialists. When one worker did speak at a meeting sponsored by the Opportunist-*progressiste* club, it was considered newsworthy by the socialists, who described him as "a drunken dupe"; in fact, the police reported his incoherence.[60]

Socialist candidates were returned in 4 of the city's 5 sections, perhaps aided by written appeals to the workers and poems in patois ("Au electour de lô proumièro seccê!"). In the second election—the "Belleville of Limoges"—the porcelain painter Millet finished with twice as many votes as the leading "anti-collectivist," a wood merchant named Lamaison. The leading *progressiste* finished more than 400 votes behind the last socialist elected in the fourth, and 175 votes behind in the fifth. A second balloting was required only in the first section, and there, too, the socialists were victorious: Tabaton Tuilière, Faure, and Teissonnière, the last having finished 50 votes ahead of Chénieux on the first round. Five *progressistes* were returned in the bourgeois third section, all on the first ballot: Tarnaud, who owned a printing company; Dantony, wholesale merchant and former deputy mayor under Chénieux; Desvalois, *métreur;* Pinton, another whole-sale merchant; and Sonnet, a retired army captain. With reform socialists hold-ing 23 seats of the socialists' 31, the reelection of Labussière was a foregone conclu-sion. The mayor urged the socialists to put aside their recent quarrels and return energetically to the administration of their city. The 200 people who attended the first meeting of the council, "mostly workers" in the words of the police, "the habituées of the Bourse du Travail!" shouted, "Long Live the Social Republic!"[61]

The election over, Treich lost little time in beginning another club, the Cercle d'unité socialiste, which adopted virtually the same statutes as the Cercle démocratique. It named Labussière honorary president, quickly enrolled 250 members, and planned branches in other towns in the region. The reform socialists thus emerged from the split and the election greatly strengthened. In October the new club rejected a general strike as an immediate tactic while accepting its possible use in principle. The Guesdist club, on the other hand, was now stronger, its ideological stance firm. There was more propaganda and talk of strikes and revolution. The writings of Marx and Engels appear to have circulated widely. On May 26 the 9 Guesdist and Allemanist councilmen had inserted into the minutes a declaration that economic emancipation of the working class was more important than the organization of a political movement, and that international emancipation was the goal of socialism and would be complete only when the means of production had been placed at the disposition of all ("chacun donnant ses forces, recevra suivant ses besoins d'après les moyens de la collectivité"). With this in mind, the conquest of political and administrative power would serve as a means of proletarian emancipation, justifying alliances with other socialist groups to defeat the union of bourgeois and clerical parties. By the end of June 1900 the Guesdist club was meeting jointly with the successor of Avant-garde, Ni Dieu, ni maître, although the two groups agreed to maintain a separate identity. Guesde himself came back to Limoges in December and responded to Labussière's criticism of the split, engendered by the Millerand crisis, with an attack on the mayor. Treich left Limoges early in February 1901, having accepted the post of *receveur buraliste* in Versailles, which his enemies contended was a payoff for his services to the bourgeois republic.[62]

With Treich's departure the Bourse gradually fell under the domination of his enemies.[63] The Guesdists began another newspaper in 1901, *L'Avenir,* which proclaimed itself "a free tribune for all socialists who refuse to abandon their ideals and who accept collectivism or communism . . . so little known by workers of our region." *L'Avenir* demanded that the Bourse stick to economic issues. That same year Teissonnière stated that the Allemanists and Guesdists could march toward the same revolutionary goal. But the newspaper went out of business on April 4, 1903, citing a lack of interest among the proletariat. Its final editorial bitterly recalled "the treason of Millerand." Guesdist gatherings seem to have been infrequent thereafter, although some five hundred people listened to Guesde in 1903, shouting, "Down with Labussière!"[64] *Le Socialiste de la Haute-Vienne* took up the struggle against the reformists and their newspaper (*Le Rappel du Centre* and then *Le Réveil du Centre*) in October 1903, with Pressemane stressing the principles of the Parti socialiste de France: opposition to the bourgeois state; and reforms, but without any compromises with the bourgeoisie. The Parti socialiste de France, joining Guesdists and Allemanists, sponsored *punches* for conscripts at its headquarters, 31, rue de Paris, and sold antimilitaristic postcards. But despite its claim of eight hundred members and some growth since

1899, "when we were few and were betrayed by the Judas of socialism," the Guesdists remained a vocal minority within the socialist movement, with but four representatives elected to the council in 1904; that election once again assured the domination of the reform socialists. Furthermore, the Guesdists themselves never really completely distanced themselves from reformism. Emile Teissonnière thus wrote in *L'Avenir* (June 1902) of a "revolutionary conception of partial reforms" to protect workers "The revolutionary socialists have always formulated, along-side their high communist or collectivist ideal, a series of demands known as im-mediate: On the side of a maximum program [goes] a minimum program."[65]

Decentralization was consistent with the political program of Limoges's reform socialists, at least partially because of the experience of the nineteenth-century revolutions, whose popular movements confronted and ultimately fell victim to the centralized state. But other positive traditions of democratic socialism were also important, with origins in the direct democracy of the clubs and sections of the French Revolution, the Revolution of 1848, and the Commune of 1871. Before the election of the Labussière administration, in August 1895, *Le Rappel du Centre* promised that the socialists would defend "Limoges travailleur et ouvrier contre une administration préfectorale réactionnaire." The reform socialists of 1895–1905 demanded a level of decentralization and autonomy incompatible with the bourgeois republic. They were doing more than simply resisting the agents of the state—the Ministry of the Interior, the prefects, and the special police com-missioners: They believed they were taking concrete steps toward building a so-cialist world.

Following over a century of manifestly increasing centralization, it was not sur-prising that the law of April 5, 1884, on municipalities severely limited the au-tonomy of the commune. Although the mayors of even large cities were to be elected by the Municipal Council, Limoges's socialists soon discovered that "even the simplest municipal acts [were] subject to a thousand vexing formalities."[66] In 1898, for example, *Le Rappel* demanded a change in Article III of the law so that each commune "could occupy itself, without any limitation or reserve, with all questions that concern it, no matter what they are." Decentralization was one of Labussière's electoral themes against Chénieux in 1898. The socialists wanted the mayor to have the power to appoint and dismiss all municipal officials with-out the prefect's approval, to have complete control over the operation and utiliza-tion of the tax revenues from the *octroi*, and to be able to undertake loans and extraordinary expenses without the approval of the President of the Republic, the prefect, and the departmental General Council. Undertaking a loan of six million francs to carry out many essential public works projects turned out to be a night-marish quest for a variety of official approvals from on high. Each municipal deliberation had to be approved by the prefect and could be declared invalid. The newly elected council quickly experienced this when the prefect annulled a coun-cil decision to give one thousand francs to the families of striking cabinetmakers in October 1895. On July 27, 1896, the council voted to give the mayor, deputy mayors, and councilmen annual salaries of four thousand, eight hundred, and six hundred francs, respectively. Such remuneration was intended to encourage workers to run for office by freeing them from dependence upon their factory wages and giving them time to occupy themselves with time-consuming tasks of the municipality. But the prefect simply invalidated the council's decision. The council could only reimburse members for expenses incurred in connection with their duties.[67]

An incident that occurred in 1897 exemplifies another dimension of the same conflict. Two municipal policemen purchased a wreath of honor for the mayor. Such homage to a socialist mayor enraged the prefect and Chénieux, who quarreled incessantly with his enemies at council meetings. What would happen, Chénieux asked, if the general strike occurred? Who would keep order? It was commonly believed that Chénieux had used the police to spy on the *syndicats* and the political clubs. Labussière, on the other hand, had hired unemployed and blacklisted workers for the police force. The prefect dismissed the two policemen, but the municipality found them other work. The special police commissioners attached to the railroad station, where they could keep track of the comings and goings of political enemies, reported to the Minister of the Interior and to the prefect. So did police spies, such as one Pasteur in 1897, reporting on Treich. The municipal police, in contrast, were under the orders of the mayor. Such a situation, in a city torn by strikes, inevitably led to tension between the socialist municipality and the central government. For example, in 1898 *Le Rappel du Centre* accused Prefect Couppel de Lude of aiding Chénieux by eliminating workers from the electoral list by raising questions of their residence.[68]

Before the elections of 1900 the socialists listed decentralization among their most important demands. "L'affranchissement de la commune qui devra avoir son autonomie, c'est-à-dire être maîtresse absolue de son administration, finances, et police." Its concrete plan of action emphasized local initiative and the rights and duties of local citizens to look after their own business and fulfill their city's destiny. In 1896 a *fête populaire* celebrated the Commune at the time of Viviani's visit, and *Le Rappel du Centre* offered its readers "Scenes from the Commune," presenting a historical perspective on decentralization.

More municipal autonomy, the socialists believed, would enable them to improve their city. There was hope: "Limoges, asleep for a long time, is awakening from its slumber and, following the path of the municipality, is growing and being embellished every day."[69] The council was therefore quite busy, meeting 79 times during its first 4 years, appointing 191 special committees, considering more than 1,800 items of business, and listening to over 1,600 reports. It set out to affirm the identity of the city as a socialist municipality. The newly elected council adhered to the group of socialist municipalities in France, sent money to the Carmaux strikers, and in 1900 allocated funds to print 3,000 copies, to be distributed to students, of the account of the death of Denis Dussoubs on the barricades after the coup d'état of 1851. *Le Rappel du Centre* kept readers abreast of the struggles of other socialist municipalities by initiating a series in 1900 entitled "La Conquête des municipalités," paying homage to Jean Dormoy, mayor of Montluçon, after his death in 1898, and criticizing the central government.[70]

The socialist municipality thus set out to shape the city in its own image. The anticlerical legislation of the early 1880s had left its mark on the eager city. The Oblats, Jesuits, Marists, and Franciscans had all been expelled in 1880, the latter losing their posts at the Louyat cemetery, a private company having been engaged to haul bodies out the rue de Paris. "The coming of the social Republic," the municipal commission had added confidently, "will be the end of all religions."[71] Labussière's administration moved to remove the remaining traces of the city's religious heritage, undertaking what might be described as a secular, socialist exorcism of the perceived "pillar of capitalism." Here, too, the socialists built upon the anticlerical tradition of the Radicals, who had, as we have seen, banned religious processions in public and ordered the removal of a *calvaire* from one street, leaving the nearby butchers' statue alone.[72]

Thereafter the Ostensions took place without their characteristic colorful and boisterous processions. The relics were transported from church to church in closed wagons, without music or banners. The faithful had to walk in small groups to avoid being arrested for participating in a procession.[73] The briefest appearance of any religious group in the streets brought an immediate protest at the council meetings. When Teissonnière observed "nuns accompanying a saint— I have no idea which one—carried by young girls" in May, 1891, and spotted religious banners in June, he demanded to know the identity of the saint who "enjoys the favor of the police." Fifty girls between the ages of ten and twelve, not an imposing force, were celebrating the Fête Dieu by carrying banners from their school to St. Pierre.[74] In 1890 and 1894, petitions asked permission to celebrate publicly the 900th anniversary of the "miracle des Ardants," which had once lifted a plague: but the decree of 1880 was affirmed, despite Louis Guibert's glowing description of such events in the *Almanach Limousin:* "Nothing is more magnificent than the arrival of all of the Bishops, mitres on their heads and crosses in their hands, walking past the assembled crowds of faithful who are bowed respectfully before their blessing . . . there is nothing richer, nothing more picturesque."[75]

The socialist municipality did not agree. In 1897 the *Almanach Limousin* sadly noted the absence of "the processions that once had so much color, contrast, and life that the populations saluted with joyous shouts." Only a modest number of houses were illuminated, in contrast to the days of manifest piety in old Limoges, notably on the rue de la Boucherie. Plainemaison *dit* Polka, who had paid a tidy sum for the honor of carrying the flag of the corporation, led the butchers, who ignored the police and fired their pistols into the air in celebration. Afterward they sent a warm telegram to the Duc d'Orléans, under whose reign religious processions would surely return.[76]

Evoking the memory of the city's tradition, the council changed the names of many streets, again following the lead of the Radicals. By the turn of the century the avenue du Crucifix had become the avenue Garibaldi; the place du Séminaire was now the place Auguste Blanqui; the boulevard Ste. Catherine became the boulevard Gambetta; the rue Ste. Catherine was renamed the rue Jeanty Sarre (another victim of 1851); the boulevard des Ursulines was called the boulevard Louis Blanc; the rue St. Esprit was renamed the rue Victor Hugo; the rue du Collège was now the rue Georges Périn; and the faubourg de la Boucherie became the rue Raspail. The *Almanach Limousin* protested. If the council insisted on such "unfortunate" names, they should be applied to streets in the faubourgs. Given the social composition of the faubourgs, this might have been reasonable, but it would have deprived the council and the majority of anticlerical citizens the opportunity to celebrate a victory over the Church. Monteil, the anticlerical prefect, willingly approved many of these changes. In 1905 the *Almanach Limousin* again protested what it called the "ravages of vandalism," the result of a "war without mercy" waged by socialists against the identity of old Limoges, still eager "to give [more streets] the names of several obscure heroes of the Revolution [of 1848]." Now there was discussion of changing the name of the boulevard St. Maurice—which lay where the old Cité walls had stood, not far from the cathedral—to the boulevard Emile Zola. This ultimate insult to the Church seemed to be the final straw. Treich, supporting the red flag in 1898, had said that "for too long a time the enemies of the Republic thought themselves the masters of the streets; the streets no longer belonged to the people." Now, emphatically, they did.[77]

The municipality also moved against the remaining church-influenced institutions. During the Republic's first decades the laicization of the hospital had been considered less urgent than ending clerical influence in the schools, the most obvious targets for antirepublican subversion. In 1899 Treich led the fight to laicize the hospital, claiming that the nuns cared for the sick only seven hours a day, reading or praying the rest of the time. He even blamed them for the death of a child in 1895. The workers resented being cared for by nuns, who encouraged them—even forced, he said—to say prayers. Only reactionary newspapers could be found there. Doctor Raymond asserted that the sisters had ignored the medical progress of the last twenty years, refusing to follow rules for antiseptic care, assist at operations on men, or treat uterine infections or syphilis. The Opportunists, electoral allies of the clericals, defended the sisters with such fervor that Treich accused Chénieux of "speaking in Jesuit."[78] The laicization measures passed easily in January 1899. Three years later the municipality voted funds to create a lay school to train nurses and orderlies and to build a lay orphanage on the outskirts of the city, at Mas Eloi.[79]

The laicization campaign culminated in a controversy over a private asylum for tuberculosis victims. Madame Noualhier, from the old Bonapartist family, operated a notoriously unhealthy sanitarium. Most of the patients were brought in from Paris. Neighbors complained. In 1900 the mayor, the departmental council of hygiene, the medical school, and army doctors demanded that the institution be closed in the interests of public health. Ten thousand people signed a petition against the asylum. Backed by the royalist right, Madame Noualhier refused, answering her critics with "Death will surprise you!" There followed a series of large and regrettably tasteless demonstrations against "the asylum of those condemned to death" and against Louis Guibert, the editor of *La Gazette* and Madame Noualhier's ally. One procession followed a man carrying a black banner emblazoned with a skull and crossbones. Another took on some of the dimensions of the old charivari, with marchers making "rough music" with pots and pans, Venetian lanterns, and banners with unflattering references to Madame Noualhier. A crippled man was hauled to her door in a wagon. Finally, on August 16 Labussière closed the asylum by municipal decree. The Conseil d'état eventually overturned the mayor's action after Madame Noualheir's appeal, but by then she had moved to Paris.[80]

Signs of the secularization of the city appeared as the century ended. For the first time the public could stroll through the bishop's garden. A municipal decree in 1901 stilled the church bells at night; Beaulieu, the socialist who proposed the measure, argued that the Carmelite sisters were "voluntarily separated from the world and morally dead so far as society is concerned by virtue of their vows."[81] Limoges now had many clocks that told the time; so did the factory bells. The Libre Pensée club established an annual prize of ten francs for boys and girls "who have obtained the most points for antireligious moral and civic instruction." Municipal employees had to send their children to lay schools, and teachers who brought religion into the classroom were called on the carpet. In 1901 the council congratulated Prefect Monteil and the academic inspector for their anticlerical efforts.[82] Municipal politics had certainly changed since the Second Empire, when one mayor had asked the priest of the city to pray for better weather![83] There were, to be sure, small, ugly incidents from time to time: Churchgoers insulted on a Holy Thursday; children hurling rocks at a priest; freethinkers disrupting the benediction of the body of one of their comrades—whose family claimed he had undergone a deathbed repentance—followed by an unsightly brawl over the poor man's grave at the Louyat cemetery.[84] The laicization campaign culminated in a giant *fête scolaire laïque,* held in June 1904, which began with a speech and a concert at the Cirque in the morning, followed by a parade of eight thousand people celebrating, among other accomplishments, lay night courses for adults and the *université populaire* recently established in the faubourgs. Louis Guibert did not live to see the event that would have outraged and saddened but not surprised him. Limoges had become a vastly different city from the one whose religious history he had so carefully studied and described at the very time when religious attachment seemed to be a thing of the past.[85]

With a six-million franc loan, the municipality worked to transform the old city, bringing light to the Verdurier quarter and sidewalks to others, completing the tramways, building a *cirque,* and expanding the sewer and water system into the faubourgs, including the aqueduct of Aiqueperse. Labussière's mandate had been to improve Limoges: "Limoges qui pue" had been the headline of one critique of the Chénieux administration offered by *Le Rappel du Centre* before the 1895 elections. One of the first acts of the council had been to purchase the land that made possible the creation of a road linking the rue Montmailler to the rue de la Fonderie.[86]

The Viraclaud quarter had resisted improvement for decades. Having no sewer system, the quarter also possessed a number of relatively small and poorly constructed houses that lacked even *fossés d'aisance.* The houses in the quarter had lost about 50 percent of their value since the middle of the Second Empire. Several of its streets were nothing more than alleyways two meters wide. A report on the health of the city gave officials considerable cause for alarm: the Viraclaud's mortality rate was 20 percent higher than the rest of Limoges. Then there was the related problem of prostitution (indeed, two of the deaths cited had been from syphilis). Of the more than four hundred people who worked in the neighborhood, over one hundred were prostitutes. By the last count—in 1879—there had been seventy-four prostitutes working in seventeen houses in the city, with another eighty-nine registered with the police as working independently. Whereas the estimated number of "clandestine" or unregistered prostitutes had been about two hundred, now there seemed to be more of them than ever in the larger city.[87] What was to be done?

In 1887 the city's idea was to push prostitution into the faubourgs, to the peripheral quarter called Hautes Coutures or Le Clos Chardon, centering on the rue Beaupuy, to the north and beyond the Montjovis station. The police had called in the madames and informed them that they would have to move. A year later people living on streets adjacent to Viraclaud had complained that nothing had been done. The administration would tolerate Viraclaud's principal activity, but new *maisons de tolérance* would not be welcome. Labussière's first council had declared that other projects—notably the tramways and the aqueducts—were more pressing. The socialist municipality turned its attention to Viraclaud. In 1898 the expropriation of houses in the quarters began. A year later much of the old, tottering quarter came down. The new century brought a new quarter, this one administrative. The rue Centrale—now the rue Jean Jaurès—awaited since the Second Empire, was ultimately cut through the center of town, linking the place Manigne, near the town hall, with the place Dussoubs and the rue Montmailler. This street led to the new post office, prefecture, and departmental archives. The paving of the rue des Combes helped lend a more favorable image to the streets that remained on the fringes of what had been Viraclaud. Well dressed *fonctionnaires* replaced drunken soldiers, boisterous youths out for their first adventures, and unemployed common laborers in the vicinity. Some of the *maisons de tolérance* disappeared, while others moved to different quarters of the city. Whereas the moderate bourgeois administration of the mid-1880s had tried to push prostitution into the working-class faubourgs, the Labussière municipality cleaned up the Viraclaud quarter in the interest of public health, aided by the funds available for the new prefecture. Prostitution (like infanticide), the socialists thought, would disappear only when economic and social relations had been transformed after the revolution. In the meantime the Viraclaud quarter, including the notorious rue Froment, which "respectable" folks had avoided for half a century, disappeared.[88]

In September 1899 the Bourse du Travail thanked the municipality for improving the quality of life for workers by sponsoring a fete celebrating the close ties between the two. Whereas the *progressiste* administration had refused to contribute money toward the Seventh Corporative Congress in 1895, the municipality paid for workers to attend the Paris Exposition of 1900. Labussière routinely approved requests for workers' associations to use municipal buildings. The city contributed to workers' associations, provided assistance to the victims of tuberculosis, funded public works projects that supported unemployed workers (for example, twenty thousand francs was awarded for work on the Louyat cemetery in 1898). The council provided direct assistance to the families of porcelain workers during the 1896 Guérin strike, the shoemakers' strike the same year, and again in 1901; it also contributed one hundred thousand francs for porcelain workers in 1902, as well as aid for *maçons* and *terrassiers* in 1904. Municipal subsidies aided the *cantines scolaires* in the faubourgs and the *université populaire,* organized "to reach the people, establish meeting places in the *milieux ouvriers* where workers can come, their [work]day over, to rest, relax, and learn." Medical services available to the poor were expanded at the Bureau de bienfaisance, the hospital, and the Asile d'aliénés; a night service was also added. Expenses totaled 10 percent of the council budget. These subventions were sometimes contrasted with those of the Chénieux council, which had provided funds for the racetrack; its clients included, in the words of the shoemaker Hummel, "the marquis, counts, barons, and the *maquignons de haute volée,* who come to beg, in the name of commerce, before the council."[89]

Limoges reveled in its reputation as *la ville rouge,* taking every possible opportunity to affirm its identity and enrich its collective memory of the city's place in the socialist world. Important socialist visitors were greeted by huge throngs at the Gare des Bénédictins and taken on a tour of the city. *La visite* became a ritualized occasion of solidarity and learning. The *tour de la ville* passed the statue of Denis Dussoubs before pausing at the town hall and the Bourse de Travail. Leaders of the Bourse and the municipality showed off their city, proud

of the improvements that had been made. Only the factories were closed to inspection, protected by the gates, the concierges, and foremen of the industrialists.

Jaurès and Guesde were particularly welcome guests; the former came to Limoges in 1895, 1905, 1906, and 1913, the latter in 1886, 1894, 1900, 1902, 1903,
and 1905. Both were seasoned veterans of trains that arrived in provincial cities
and towns at odd hours. Both responded to hundreds of welcomes in France's
cities, gave innumerable speeches, and participated in countless debates. Guesde
himself spoke something like twelve hundred times between 1882 and 1890.[90]

Visits by Jaurès, Guesde, Viviani, and other socialist leaders were memorable;
they were used by socialists to generate enthusiasm and support. Similarly, May
Day became the most significant public event of the year. Bastille Day (July 14)
had lost much of its importance once the Republic's survival no longer seemed
problematic. In 1893 Mayor Chénieux had issued large, brightly colored posters
advertising booming cannon salvos, martial music, fireworks displays, and the
retraite aux flambeaux. He mounted the reviewing tribune with the bishop at his
side. When Labussière became mayor, the bishop stopped coming. In 1896 Labussière decided that the money that would have been spent on flashy celebrations
would go to the city's unemployed. His administration thereafter celebrated
Bastille Day in a muted fashion, at least partially because the military parades
associated with Bastille Day were unpopular in Limoges. The army was one
pillar of capitalism, the Church being the other. Bastille Day may have signified
the collective memory of the liberation from the nobility for *campagnards,* but
the collective memory of the urban proletariat in *la ville rouge* focused on more
recent steps in their as yet uncompleted emancipation. The first of May celebrated
class consciousness and solidarity, but it also reflected the workers' anticipated
freedom from the capitalist yoke.[91]

After the election of 1895 May Day moved from the steps of the town hall and
the working-class cafés to the streets of the city.[92] May Day affirmed the socialist
municipality and the identity of Limoges as the "red city." At the same time,
such ceremonies helped solidify the ties between socialism and the Bourse. On
the morning of May 1, 1897, 150 delegates from the unions, led by a young girl
(symbolizing the Republic) walking between two workers (symbolizing the social republic) left the Bourse de Travail and marched to the town hall, where
Labussière received a list of demands (*revendications*); both he and Treich addressed the crowd. Relatively few workers could attend this simple ceremony because they would be expected at work unless May Day fell on a Sunday or Monday. The attention given to the children of workers reflected the notion of the
"great socialist family" at home in the Bourse. The hat was passed for those
members of the "family" that were out of work, and wine and tobacco was sent
to those workers who were in the hospital. Speeches at the Bourse now often asserted the importance of combining economic and political action—for example,
in the campaign for the 8-hour day. The May Day speeches became so popular

that the events had to be moved to the municipal Cirque, when that building was completed on the place de la République, which could accommodate much larger crowds. In the afternoon the hall of the Bourse was "absolutely jammed" by more than 1,800 people as some 1,200 toys were distributed to children in a kind of socialist Christmas celebration without religion. There had been talk that Treich would confer a "socialist baptism" on several infants, as had occurred in a few socialist municipalities, but there is no evidence that this took place.[93] That night more than 4,000 people attended a concert and an annual ball that began shortly before midnight, ending at 4:45 A.M. the next morning. The May Day program varied little over the next few years, although subsequently Labussière and most of the Municipal Council went to the Bourse to receive the list of workers' demands.

The 1904 municipal elections served as a second referendum on the achievements of the reform socialists, who were now challenged by a separate list of candidates of the Guesdist *groupe ouvrier*.[94] After the turn of the century the Guesdists had called for greater financial assistance for workers. Chauly, Plaud, Teissonnière, Coussy, and Noël now declared that "those who do not want to wait until the year 3000 should vote for us," claiming that the reform socialists had reduced the number of working-class candidates on their list. Léon Betoulle, already Labussière's heir apparent, spoke for the reform socialists:

> Each day ideas of solidarity, justice, and social emancipation find more support. Each day the great socialist party, perhaps divided on the surface by entirely secondary questions but profoundly united in its ultimate goal, sees its forces grow; each day the old society crumbles a little more under the weight of its inequities. Each day brings a little more light, well-being, and happiness to those whose only lot has been, until now, suffering and misery.[95]

Betoulle and the other reform socialists emphasized the necessity of socialist unity and the accomplishments of the past nine years. They called Guesde "one of our great *patrons*" and denounced the "regime of private property."[96] Like the Guesdists, they defended the right of the individual to hold private property; like the sansculottes of the French Revolution, they opposed the ownership of too much property, or unearned property. Their war was against *les gros,* no longer the nobles but the *patronat* and the power of the bourgeois state. In the meantime workers had to free themselves economically, socially, and politically from the state and from the *patronat*. The socialist municipality provided workers with an apprenticeship that would prepare their eventual emancipation. Until the day of the liberation, the socialist municipality had to defend itself against the bourgeois state, but within the limits imposed by "national unity."

Were the Guesdists and Allemanists correct to insist that no real change could occur until the bourgeois state had fallen? Reform socialism accepted the alliance of all socialists and collaboration with radical elements of the bourgeoisie. Did reform socialism merely help strengthen the bourgeois republic by integrating workers into the political process as serious contenders for political power? To some extent this was the unintended result of such a strategy. But from the point of view of the reform socialists, municipal socialism did provide an apprenticeship for working-class political involvement and brought about concrete reforms, offering at least a little protection against, and a frame of reference opposed to, the state and capitalism. Ultimately Limoges had neither the funds nor the autonomy to push the revolution itself forward. "If we had the communal autonomy that even cities in monarchical states possessed and that the French Republic refuses us," argued Betoulle in 1903, "we could easily bring about all of the reforms that we have promised." The previous year the council had allocated 130,000 francs for unemployed workers. Betoulle had found himself defending the municipality against Chénieux and the *progressistes,* who accused the council of being "utopian" and wasting money, as well as against the Guesdist *groupe ouvrier,* who claimed it had not gone far enough. The municipality found its financial autonomy curtailed by the bourgeois constitution of the state. Yet within these limits the socialist municipality provided a setting in which workers could organize and pursue their own interests.[97] While they waited for the revolution to come, reform socialism did, in the long run, help integrate workers into the bourgeois state as contenders for national political power.[98] The revolutionary potential of socialism may have subsided, yet the socialist municipality appeared to be both an end in itself and the beginning of a revolutionary transformation of economic, social, and political power.

Led by Edouard Treich, the Bourse du Travail had maintained its close ties with the municipality, at least until Treich's departure in 1901 and, for practical purposes, until 1903. Because its leaders were socialist activists, the Bourse contributed to the politicization of class conflict in Limoges while generating momentum both for workers' organizations and for strike action. The Bourse helped make class conflict an integral part of municipal life.

During the decade that followed the inauguration of the Bourse, the number of unions more than doubled, rising from twenty-three in 1894 and thirty-nine in 1900 to fifty-three in 1905. The growth of unions in Limoges during the period was three times the national average. The number of *syndiqués* tripled, increasing from two thousand in 1897 to over six thousand in 1905, twenty-five hundred of whom were porcelain workers. Porcelain and shoemakers together accounted for 55 percent of the total number of unionized workers. At the same time, the number and percentage of unionized female workers rose with the increase of female workers in Limoges's two dominant industries.[99]

The Bourse served as the organizational nexus of working-class life in Limoges. Its purpose had been clearly stated: "We want to make the Bourse du Travail the common house of the workers, where they can go without fear of showing their joy and their pain, where they can find in shared sadness and happiness the advice and information that they need." In the perilous world of work, the Bourse would be "un asile ouvert à tous."[100] In 1898 between eight and nine hundred workers came to the Bourse each month for information about jobs in the city and its region. Henceforth workers had a place to meet; the days of renting café rooms or asking permission to use municipal buildings were over. The *syndicats* had a home.

The lights burned long into the night as the unions celebrated their anniversaries with dances, banquets, or *punches,* such as the ball of the carpenters, the fete of the *maçons,* or the dance of the porcelain workers. Other *bals populaires* on holidays brought workers of assorted trades together. How different this sociability was from the closed Cercle Turgot, or the elegant dinners at the Hôtel Continental! *Le Rappel du Centre* thus described the fete of the lithographers at the Bourse, which was attended by Labussière: "It is impossible to imagine a happier crowd, more disposed to welcome with thunderous applause the excellent artists of the theater . . . who seemed happy to be able to sing at a *fête populaire*." The Bourse's own *fanfare* came into existence. After the prefect refused to approve a lottery to raise money for the group, the municipality contributed the instruments of the defunct Société philharmonique. Music for celebrations, including those at the Hôtel de Ville, was now assured. So was food; the Bourse hired a woman who operated a café on the rue Pont St. Martial.[101] Popular culture began to follow the rhythms of political life. The Bourse fulfilled the dream of Fernand Pelloutier, the father of the Bourse du Travail, providing a center of information and leisure for workers and their families, in addition to serving as the locus for organization. It welcomed rural workers, such as the ditch diggers who came to see about starting their own union. It offered several francs to workers passing through Limoges, occasionally some clothes, and information about available jobs in Limoges or the department.[102]

The need for professional courses had been strengthened by technological advances and the increasing division of labor in the porcelain and shoemaking industries during the 1890s. "Modern industrialization," Hummel declared, "tends to compartmentalize the technical knowledge of the working class. It is therefore entirely appropriate that workers be instructed in the modifications that science is bringing to our system of production." For the moment Hummel viewed such a "field of study" as "social philanthropy" and saw it as a means of "avoiding, to a large extent, conflicts between capital and labor that are regrettable for many reasons."[103] A municipal subsidy financed trade courses. They seem to have been held irregularly at first, bringing complaints from the Ministry of Public Works. Only a course for tailors functioned smoothly during the first year. In 1897 Treich led a small delegation to Bordeaux to learn about courses organized there; subsequently courses were offered in Limoges in ceramic painting, carpentry, cabinetmaking, typography, rock cutting, and shoemaking.[104]

The Bourse's placement service ran smoothly. In its first 12 months 1,657 requests for jobs and 600 offers of employment were received, out of which 542 workers placed. During hard times requests for jobs increased, reaching 2,000 in 1897, many of which came from day laborers, and peaking at 3,742 in 1901. Domestics and servants stood the best chance of being placed. The library contained almost 600 volumes by its first summer of operation, including some professional books and volumes of commercial codes and laws donated by the Minister of Commerce. But one could also find some works by Voltaire, Molière, Rousseau, Paul de Kock, Jules Verne, several histories of France (including a copy of Louis Blanc's *History of the French Revolution* presented to the Bourse by the widow of Louis Mollat, a *quarante-huitard*), and a variety of travel books, many studies of syndicalism and cooperative societies, and a large dictionary.[105]

The first years of the Bourse were characterized by close relations with the political life of the city. The Federation, established in 1893, played a secondary role to the Bourse, at least partially because Treich headed both. In 1897 the moderate Guesdist pulled the Bourse out of the Fédération des Bourses du Travail, which was dominated by the Paris Bourse. After visiting the latter for several days, Treich returned to Limoges to say that the capital's Bourse seemed to accomplish little with respect to the emancipation of the working class, feeding off its provincial counterparts while claiming that its Limoges confrere owed it money. Thereafter, the annual fete of the Fédération des Bourses du Travail was not celebrated in Limoges, since the Bourse merged its identity with that of the city. The end result was that there seemed little that was truly revolutionary about the Limoges Bourse, whose leaders rejected a general strike as an immediate strategy while approving of it in principle.[106]

With Treich's departure in 1901, the Bourse fell, as we have seen, under the influence of the left Guesdists, and the ties with the municipality were weakened. Treich's successors as general secretary were ineffectual: Frugier, a *sabotier,* and (in 1902) Raymond, a typographer. Hummel, Noël, Teissonnière, and Parvy increased revolutionary Guesdist influence at the Bourse, particularly after 1903.[107] A new *règlement général* adopted in December 1903 reflected these changes, for it explicitly underscored the "historical fact of class struggle" and stressed the goal of "defending the interests of the working class against the imperatives, exploitation, and oppression of the employer class." The International Ceramic Federation, led locally by the Allemanist Tillet, and the Bourse's strike committee both assumed a more militant stance, pushing workers to direct action.[108] One *ordre du jour* voted upon after a lecture that year reflected the shift in tone: "The citizens gathered in the Cirque, hereby committing themselves to the struggle for the syndicalist ideal, here affirm their contempt for the capitalist society that oppresses them and assert that they can only count on themselves for their own emancipation."[108] A dramatic increase in strike activity followed in 1904, the workers winning 8 of the strikes, with 3 ending in compromise settlements. Increased organization among several specialties within the porcelain industry and the threat of further mechanization spurred the workers' resistance.[109] More female workers had joined unions, including the Chambre syndicale des ouvrières de la peinture céramique, which had 120 members in February 1904 but 400 the following year. In 1905, 1,200 female workers were unionized, representing 20 percent of all unionized workers—more than twice the national average. Thirty percent of unionized shoemakers were women, about the same percentage as in the porcelain industry. By that same year (1905) 42 percent of the members of L'Initiative were women, 12 percent more than at the turn of the century.[110] In sum, 19 percent of Limoges's workers were *syndiqués* by 1905 (6,000 out of 32,000)—a percentage considerably higher than the national average and about 5 percent higher than in 1900 (3,700 out of 25,000). These workers drew support from the non-unionized workers, most of whom were socialists.[111]

Two "waves" of strikes dominated the 1895–1905 period, sixteen in 1895–96, coinciding with the election of the new municipality and the establishment of the Bourse du Travail, and twenty-eight in 1904 and the first four months of 1905. Economic and political action merged in Limoges, for both were rooted in popular organization.[112]

One strike in particular, which occurred during the first period, merits a detailed account, for it saw skilled and unskilled workers striking together for the first time. This strike of porcelain *journaliers* suggested the possibility of future walkouts on a massive scale by workers of different skills within both the porcelain and shoe industries, as well as in other industries. This strike, then, and the possibilities it raised, weighed heavily on the *patronat*.

In April 1896 the porcelain *journaliers*, including semiskilled *caleurs, hommes du four,* and *engazetiers,* asked for a pay hike of 25 centimes per day. They withheld their demand, waiting until the municipal elections had returned the socialist majority elected the previous year. Following the election, each porcelain manufacturer received a letter reiterating their demand for high wages. On June 2, 250 *journaliers* left the Guérin factory and assembled at the Bourse. After refusing possible arbitration by the justice of the peace, the Union des fabricants posted a warning that all factories would shut down if the strikers had not returned to work by June 11. Two hundred workers walked out of the Haviland factory, on the avenue Garibaldi, in response to the company notice. Soon 8 and then 11 other factories were struck, so that only the *caleurs* remained to see that the kilns were safely extinguished. By June 10, 1,311 workers had struck, resulting in the layoff of another 400 workers.[113]

The strike immediately dislocated the city's economy. Labussière returned from Paris. Believing that the manufacturers were on the verge of granting the increase, he urged the workers to return to their jobs and await such an event. But the manufacturers refused even to discuss the demand for a raise and denounced the Bourse and the *syndicats*. Charles Haviland asserted that the workers were jeopardizing the very survival of Limoges's major industry; German and English rivals, a source of constant anxiety for the Limoges manufacturers, seemed poised to profit from the "disloyalty" of the *journaliers*. They had already copied the technology and styles of the Limoges manufacturers and were able to undersell their "more worthy" French rivals because they paid lower wages at a time when the former had to "fight for every inch" of the market.[114]

With several thousand people left without resources because of the strike, the municipality contributed seventy-five thousand francs for public works projects, but these could employ no more than several hundred workers. The Bourse distributed money, bread, and vouchers for certain stockpiled necessities. The Municipal Council of Paris sent ten thousand francs in aid, and money came from as far away as Belgium. Some strikers returned to the countryside to find farm work, and the strike went on.

On June 11, in response to the strikers' call for a general strike in the industry, the *peintres en porcelaine,* including those who worked in the remaining decoration workshops, voted to join the strike. The American firm of Bawo and Dotter demanded that their factory be placed under the protection of the American consul. Crowds of strikers thronged to the two factories that remained in operation, that of Theodore Haviland, avenue de Poitiers, and Tressemannes et Vogt, on the faubourg Montmailler. Shouts of "Vivo lô socialô" in patois echoed through the room. *Useurs de grains* and polishers joined the strike (while some warehouse workers and *emballeurs* did not). On June 16 twenty-five hundred strikers voted to stay out. The porcelain painters, in particular, vowed to resist employers' attempts to crush workers' organizations, a possibility that would set back "the forces of the working class for eight to ten years."[115]

Yet the strike soon collapsed, the reserve funds being far from sufficient to sustain the strikers. For one thing, the prefect had refused to approve the Municipal Council's use of funds for unemployed workers. Some porcelain painters and *décalqueuses* went back on June 17; the *casteurs,* too, seemed on the verge of capitulating. On June 21 the manufacturers announced that they would accept all workers back under the old working conditions. The strike ended. The defeat was costly for the unions, which had spent all of their money and now lost many members. The new *syndicat* of *journaliers* lost 450 of its 800 members.[116] Yet the failed strike demonstrated the possibility of joining skilled and unskilled workers in a massive strike action. It embittered relations between manufacturers and workers in Limoges. There were more walkouts in 1896, but there was no wave of strikes until 1904–5, when the worst fears of the manufacturers were realized.

Without detailing the fifty-three strikes that occurred during the socialist municipality's decade in Limoges, it is worth noting that there was a significant shift in the most salient strike issues. The outbreak of strikes in 1904–5, in particular, reflected an improved economic situation (salaries increased in 1902 and the cost of living grew less rapidly than did wages between 1902 and 1904, making possible union membership), continued concentration and mechanization within the porcelain and shoemaking industries, and the more aggressive leadership of labor militants.[117]

The Bourse's role in Limoges's strike activity is clear: It provided a meeting place for unions and strikers; a sense of direction and solidarity; financial support; a close link to the political struggle of the city (in which several prominent manufacturers were closely identified with the Opportunist-*progressiste* camp); support for socialist candidates; and an ideological identification of the manufacturers as the representatives of the "capitalist class." During the 1896 strike of day laborers described earlier, the manufacturers lashed out at the unions and the Bourse: "The true cause of this conflict is that we do not want to submit to the abusive and odious interference of the leaders and the unions in the smallest details of production. We revolt against their tyranny . . . the only means that we have to put an end to this ruinous disorder is to prove to the workers that the *syndicats* betrayed them in promising our defeat."[118] The *Courrier du Centre,* speaking for the manufacturers, denounced what it saw as the "disorganization of their industry piece by piece through a system of successive demands and perpetual strike threats" directed by the "professional agitators" of the Bourse, such as demands for equal wages across the industry.[119]

During the same strike Treich attacked "the egotistical and antihumanitarian ideas" of the employers, "transformed into wild beasts, counting in advance on the suffering and the anguish of our unfortunate comrades," the strikers.[120] Whereas small units of production survived in the porcelain and shoemaking industries, the major strikes were against the largest companies and the wealthiest manufacturers, including the Haviland brothers and Monteux, whose shoe company was by far the largest in Limoges (but who employed many other home workers), and who owned another factory in Paris. By 1895 one third of all shoemakers worked for him. In the mid-1890s Monteux had the reputation, at least in Limoges, of being the only somewhat paternalistic manufacturer. He had organized a *caisse de retraite* for his workers. When more than four hundred workers left his plant in 1895, he was furious, particularly when he learned that he had been dubbed the "Rességuier de Limoges," after the infamous glassworks owner of Carmaux. Monteux condemned the "tyrannical" influence of the Federation and refused to meet with any delegation not chosen from among his workers by his employees. When the strike failed, he spent the better part of a day chiding those who had left his factory. In 1904 his workers protested mechanization, the hiring of poorly paid female labor and apprentices, and the authority of foremen to enforce industrial discipline. Monteux became the target of verbal abuse and songs outside his factory.[121] During the Haviland strikes the two American brothers suffered the same kind of personal castigation, being identified with the evils of capitalism. Their defense of their assumed prerogatives as employers assumed the character of a war on the unions and the Bourse du Travail. During the 1900 printers' strike, *Le Rappel du Centre* reflected the workers' attitude toward the *patronat* (as well as the perceived alliance between capitalism and the Church): "For these modern inquisitors the worker is a human machine, a tool that one uses and then throws away when it does not bring in enough profit."[122]

Limoges's strikes were closely intertwined with local political life. Socialists, for one thing, anticipated and accepted the antagonism of labor and capital as inevitable, a view that the *progressistes* and the clerical party denounced. Strikes forced virtually the entire city to take a stand, from municipal councilmen, who allocated funds for the families of laid-off workers, to shopkeepers, who depended upon workers having income to spend and who suffered particularly heavily during the strikes of 1895–96 and 1904–5. The position of the manufacturers and of both the *progressistes* and the clerical party was clear.[123] They blamed the socialist municipality for encouraging strikes by providing material support to families of workers laid off by strikes. The *patronat* did not mince words: The Labussière administration seemed to be helping prepare the class war that lay ahead. The socialist municipality supported a mood of class contention and working-class solidarity, a position that caused bitter conflict during the municipal elections. It seemed no mere coincidence that immediately after the socialist victory in 1896 each porcelain company received a written demand for a wage hike from workers.[124] In addition to providing funds for unemployed workers, the municipality seemed willing to allow striking workers free run of the streets of the city. During the printers' strike in 1900 and a strike of shoemakers in 1904 municipal police stood by and allowed boisterous processions of workers to file by (including charivaris, in the first case), demonstrations that were clearly against the employers and their foremen. That the mayor had used his personal influence to prevent violence and to bring about negotiations and compromise on several occasions (most clearly in the 1904 shoemakers' strike) was forgotten or even resented by the manufacturers. The *progressistes* of Chénieux attacked the *régime des grèves,* underscoring the close association between strikes and politics in Limoges. Marx had made the same connection: "Every movement in which the working class comes out as a *class* against the ruling classes and tries to coerce them by pressure from without is a political movement."[125]

By 1904 Limoges's strikes had taken on something of the character of working-class crusades that challenged the manufacturers economically, socially, and politically. During the printers' strike in 1900, workers left the Bourse and marched through the streets holding flags, demonstrating nightly outside a printing company on the rue du Clocher.[126] In 1904 workers, most of them from the faubourgs, carried red and black flags with them, symbolically affirming their control of the city's thoroughfares, stopping only at the iron gates and thick wooden doors of the factories or at the houses and apartments of employers and their foremen. During the 1904 Monteux strike heated confrontations between strikers and strikebreakers occurred outside the factory located at the avenue Garibaldi and the rue de Châteauroux. Five hundred strikers blocked the factory's three gates and minor scuffles and fistfights followed. Now "L'Internationale" accompanied the "Carmagnole" linking the collective memory of past revolutionary struggles with those of the present. Street demonstrations were no longer determined according to the calendar, with the exception of May Day, as religious processions had been. In a *ville ouvrière* confident in its own identity the fact that the most important manufacturers were outsiders—Monteux lived in Paris and the Haviland brothers were both Americans, quick to dash off angry letters to their embassy—contributed to the sense of a city standing firm against capitalism. As the workers' anger against them mounted, so did the potential for violence.[127]

In April 1896 bright posters displayed during the shoemaker's strike proclaimed "No More Prison [*Bagne*]; Enough Exploitation!"[128] Wage demands appeared frequently during the economic upswing of the mid-1890s, but thereafter they occurred rarely since worker protests focused more on work conditions; strike issues became even more bitter. In 1895 seven out of nine strikes included demands for wage increases or the uniform application of rates across trades (the latter including *décalqueuses* and day laborers, as well as *sabotiers, monteurs,* and *finisseurs* in the shoe industry). Two other strikes during the ten-year period—one that same year and another in 1904—protested the assessment of the *fente* and other arbitrary fines at the Guérin factory. Only three strikes included demands for a reduction of the workday as a principal demand (that of the *sabotiers* and printers in 1895, and the *linotypistes* and *serruriers* in 1903 and 1904). The strike by Limoges's bakers in December 1903, in support of their counterparts in Paris, reflected the nationalization of working-class mobilization, as did solidarity between Monteux's workers in Limoges and those in the capital.[129]

Increasingly workers challenged the degree of control they retained over their work and work schedules. The threat of mechanization lay behind several walkouts, especially in the shoe industry (*sabotiers* in 1895, shoemakers in 1896, and *monteurs* in 1903). The strike at the Guérin factory may have ostensibly been about wages, but the implementation of machines was the real issue. In April 1895 *calibreurs* demanded a wage increase of 50 centimes from the company, which had been withholding 10 percent of their wages to pay for new machines that accomplished part of their tasks. They received the increase, but the machines stayed, the company continuing to withhold 10 percent of their wages to pay for them. A strike in July at another company—that of Barjaud de Lafon (an Opportunist)—ended in defeat. The next year *sabotiers* demanded, among other things, that their employers remove a *machine à parer;* the subsequent strike resulted in a compromise settlement. This machine, too, remained. Similarly, 48 *monteurs* and *finisseurs* failed to force the Lecointe Company to remove a machine; the company put in another machine after the workers departed. They never returned. Likewise, a strike by 110 *monteurs,* the most skilled shoemakers, at the Monteux factory in 1903 had as the ostensible cause opposition to a reduction in the piece rate, but behind this strike lay—yet again—the company's threat to bring in machines to replace the workers.[130]

The following manufacturers' strategies to reduce dependence upon higher-paid workers also generated resistance: the hiring of more apprentices; parceling out work to home workers; or taking on lower paid female workers. In 1895 *sabotiers* demanded that employers limit the number of apprentices to 6 percent of the total number of workers; and *coupeurs* forced the Vautour Company to agree not to send out work to elderly women working at home for paltry wages. Yet workers in a shop making galoshes tried unsuccessfully to force their employer to limit the number of apprentices to the same 6 percent.[131] The same year *menuisiers* lost another battle over subcontracting, long the bane of artisans and one of the most bitter complaints of workers during the Revolution of 1848.[132] Some of Lecointe's shoemakers left the same year to protest the hiring of three more female workers in an industry in which the rapid influx of females had depressed male wages. The company soon went back on an original acceptance of the workers' conditions, having used the time to install more machines.

The 1904 strike of shoe cutters revolved around the same issue. Almost 200 cutters worked for 16 manufacturers in Limoges, earning between 4.5 and 6 francs for 10 hours of work. Early that year employers began to hire many so-called apprentices. Whereas there had been only 1 or 2 apprentices for every 10 cutters, and 6 percent in at least 1 company, the ratio of apprentices to cutters had risen to almost 1 for every 2 workshops. Unlike artisanal apprentices, these young workers were not taught a true trade, or even a subtle skill, but were simply younger, poorly paid employees subject not to an artisan's gruff direction but to the written rules of the company and the sharp enforcement of the foreman. Few or no trade secrets remained. The cutters complained that these boys were asked to undertake their tasks before the rapid apprenticeship had even been completed. The manufacturers refused to acknowledge how many apprentices they employed. The Bourse du Travail estimated that there were 57 apprentices for every 100 cutters. Posters put up by the Bourse stated that this practice not only undermined the experience and, ultimately, the wages of the cutters but that the apprentices themselves would be insufficiently trained for some tasks, find future placement difficult, and "would always be subject to exploitation by the bosses." When the cutters threatened to strike all of the shoe companies, the smaller manufacturers seemed ready to limit the number of apprentices. But Monteux, by far the largest employer and the president of the employers' association, and Blanchard, owner of the second-largest company, refused. As a result, 185 of the 204 cutters walked out, causing the lay off of several hundred workers whose tasks depended on them. They held out until a compromise settlement was reached a month later. The manufacturers agreed to limit the number of apprentices to 10 percent of the number of cutters in most companies and 25 percent in the Monteux factory; the cutters, however, were not satisfied with the compromise solution, and that particular strike left bitter memories.[133]

The most explosive strike issue was that of industrial discipline, particularly the role of the foreman, who emerged as the most visible and vexing representative of the boss.[134] To many workers the foreman was an unwelcome outsider in the factory, whether or not he or she had been brought from another city. M. Vanneaud, *chef d'atelier* of the Theodore Haviland factory, was described by *Le Socialiste du Centre* as "brutally autocratic," terrorizing the "unfortunate workers placed under his orders" and trying to force them to buy corsets and belts produced at a shop operated by his wife. The manufacturers viewed industrial discipline as both a practical necessity for production and a principle to be respected, a cornerstone of class relations. Manufacturers countered the increasing influence of the Bourse, the Federation, and the *syndicats* with an emphatic insistence on the sanctity of their authority in the workplace. Whether or not they adopted the somewhat facile view—echoed by some historians—that many of the workers lacked industrial discipline because they were rural-born folk used to setting their own schedules cannot be determined.[135] But the manufacturers refused to tolerate the workers' resistance to their will.

The first strike of the period which defiantly raised the issue of industrial discipline provides an interesting example of the confrontation between two ways of life in Limoges, between the city's religious past and its secular, indeed, anticlerical evolution. Most of the 105 corset makers in Limoges were employed by the Clément Company. The *patronne* believed that workers could only obtain salvation through a combination of discipline and prayer. She distributed printed prayers to her workers and, after locking the doors of the workshop, forced them to kneel on the stone floor and pray before work, to undertake a yearly religious retreat or at least attend one mass together, and to confess their sins annually.[136]

Led by Marie Géraud (aged twenty-four), Marguerite Sadème (nineteen), and Amélie Rateau (eighteen), forty-two of the workers walked out on June 14, 1895, demanding a modest wage increase, the end of arbitrary fines, the right to come to work late (many also worked as cleaning women before beginning their regular jobs), and the end of all mandatory religious practices. The *patronne* refused and began sending out corsets to convents, where they were to be finished by nuns. Supported by the Federation and the income from several political speeches, dances, and concerts, the women held out for three weeks before half of the workers returned, their resources depleted.[137]

In September of that year four hundred of Monteux's workers struck. Monteux employed ten foremen who alone could distribute passes (*bons de sortie*) permitting a worker to leave the factory. Shoemaking had traditionally been based in small and often informally organized workshops or as home work; the Monteux factory, however, represented an astonishing concentration of work. The workers particularly detested one of the foremen, "homme à la tournure militaire et au commandement bref," who had recently replaced a more lenient colleague. He was charged with bringing a military-style discipline to the factory. But the strike failed; the workers' only gain was small indeed—the regulations now had to be posted for all to see.[138]

At the end of the same year porcelain workers made a similar move when 75 *mouleurs* and *calibreurs* employed by Lanternier went out to support their demand "to come and go as they please during the workday." The factory was near the cabarets on the rue de la Fonderie—the workers left when they had nothing to do and brought food and drink back. The company had posted a set of regulations that forbade workers from leaving without written permission from the foremen and reiterated the ban on eating or drinking in the factory. The walkout lasted but half a day.[139] A year later the *calibreurs* of the Delinières and the Barnardaud companies walked out for similar reasons. They were required to stay near their machines, whether or not the machines were actually in use. When several workers were fined 50 centimes each and walked out with a few friends, the incident touched off a major strike. As many as 125 *calibreurs* joined them when Charles Haviland threatened to lock out all of his workers if his *calibreurs* refused to replace the strikers at the other factory and if the strike did not end. The other manufacturers let go almost all of the other *calibreurs*.[140]

The issues were clear. The employers refused to accept arbitration because control of the workplace was at stake; they could never accept what they referred to as "anarchy in the factory." They blamed the municipality for giving free reign to the Bourse. The Conseil des prud'hommes had ruled in the workers' favor on another issue, namely, that the company did not have the right to withhold part of the salary of its workers to pay for the machines. The Union des fabricants stood firm, however, and the *calibreurs* returned to work on November 6, vowing to await "a favorable moment" to strike again. But they faced a grim reality, accurately yet bitterly described by the Parisian paper *Le Siècle:*

> . . . the *calibreurs* should consider one thing: It is not difficult to become a *calibreur*. He gets a ball of clay. He puts it on a wooden disk that turns. He covers it with another disk. The result is a plate. A little attention and assiduousness are the only required skills. In exchange he receives a daily salary of six francs.[141]

They could be replaced and would have to toe the line. It was a sign of the times.

Another, larger porcelain strike in 1902 also centered on the right of workers to enter and leave the factory at will. In most porcelain factories workers were allowed two breaks consisting of half an hour each during the workday for a snack (*casse-croûte*). When a law passed in 1900 limited work to ten hours in factories employing men and women, manufacturers lowered the wages of those paid by the piece. The workers had accepted this but wanted to retain the two breaks, which offered temporary relief from the heat and dust of their work. The Union des fabricants announced that any worker who did not arrive on time or who left the factory during the day would be locked out until the next bell and would thus receive no wages for that period.[142]

Two hundred decorators left one of the Haviland factories in protest. Within a few days the strike spread to twenty-one factories, involving more than fifty-eight hundred workers in many occupations and causing the layoff of another fourteen hundred workers. Mutual concessions led to a settlement, but only after six difficult weeks. The two breaks would be tolerated, but only in the factory. The doors would remain locked. Foremen would enforce these rules, making sure that no food or drink entered the factory. More than ever, the workers began to use the term *bagne,* or prison, to describe the factory. During the Dreyfus affair workers had been overheard comparing their position in the factories to that of "convicts in prison." Another strike at the Monteux factory in June 1903 was sparked because of the workers' opposition to a particularly brutal foreman.[143]

The foremen and the gates, doors, and clocks of the factories were the symbols and necessary accoutrements of industrial capitalism at the turn of the century. At the same time, though workers seemed to control the city politically, porcelain workers and shoemakers, in particular, had lost whatever control over their work they had once possessed. The factory compounds stood out as enemy strongholds in the workers' city. All these changes seemed to highlight the role of capitalism in the workers' lives. Egged on by labor organizations and encouraged by the successes of the socialist municipality, skilled and unskilled workers challenged the manufacturers and their political allies in 1905, recalling both the strike of unskilled porcelain painters in 1896 and another porcelain strike that had spread across several occupations in 1902.[144] The strikes of 1905 would be the most violent that Limoges had ever seen—or would see again.

8

Denouement:
The Strikes of 1905

The strikes of April 1905 were the last of Limoges's revolutionary *journées*. Angry workers, skilled and unskilled, carried red and black flags, singing the "Carmagnole" and the "International." Locked out by the porcelain manufacturers, they fought back. Barricades appeared in the streets. For six violent days Limoges once again captured the nation's attention.

The workers directly challenged the symbols and representatives of capitalism and the bourgeois state: the manufacturers, their foremen, and the army—the "mercenaries of capitalism"—all of whom were powerful outsiders who challenged the interests and solidarities of the workers.

Michelle Perrot has described how the worker's image of the *patron* evolved during the century: respected as a paternalistic figure (Alluaud during the Restoration, for example); mocked, castigated, and hated as personally evil or disgusting; ridiculed for being fat, gross, greedy, and lecherous; clearly identified as a symbol of capitalism.[1] The introduction of foremen in factories to enforce company rules complemented the gradual withdrawal of the employer from the workplace; the new manufacturers were rarely former skilled workers who had put together enough capital to start up on their own. The difference between Alluaud and David Haviland has already been stressed. Now the latter's two sons, Charles and Theodore, likewise Americans, symbolized the evolution of industrial capitalism in Limoges. So did Monteux, who owned the largest shoemaking factory and lived in Paris.

The workers confronted the united opposition of their employers, who were angered by the seemingly endless challenges to their authority in the factory and, above all, the many disruptive strikes that had occurred in the ten years since the newly elected socialist municipality had subsidized the establishment of the Bourse du Travail. They blamed "agitators" at the Bourse for intensifying class antagonism and felt besieged on two fronts, economic and political.

The 1905 strikes came during an economic slump that had discouraged local businessmen. The manufacturers and merchants who met at the Fédération des syndicats commerçiaux et industriels du Limousin early in April were exasperated. Porcelain manufacturers, wholesale merchants, construction entrepreneurs, grocers, barbers, and the butcher Malinvaud-Mantoue bemoaned the lack of prosperity of the last few years. Their report cited all of the following: the failure of two local banks in 1895—that same year, again; bitter disputes with the American government over import duties on porcelain; the high cost of transportation; a contraction in the market for luxury goods; stiff foreign competition; and the delays they faced in being paid by their customers. Twenty years earlier credit in Limoges seemed as sure as anywhere in France. But now one could repeatedly hear the refrain "One should invest only with *extreme* prudence." Now they faced damaging strikes. New walkouts could be disastrous.[2] The industrialists resolved not to give in to the strikers. They would teach the workers a lesson.

Foremen had become as much of a fixture in the sixteen shoe factories in Limoges as the Goodyear and Blake machines that had transformed production. On February 6 all of the workers of the Monteux Company walked out after a meeting of the Bourse, demonstrating solidarity with their Parisian counterparts in Monteux's other factory, who were demanding a raise and the rehiring of a fired comrade. The next day the Limoges shoemakers added 2 other demands, namely, that an unpopular foreman be relieved of his duties and that a worker let go several days earlier be rehired. The strike ended in defeat 3 days later. But that was time enough to bring the general secretary of the shoemakers' union in Paris to Limoges. Speaking before an audience of 600 at the Bourse, he attacked the mechanization of the industry and approved of the general strike as a weapon if demands were not met.[3] Several days later the 320 shoemakers and *sabotiers* of the Fougeras factory, on the avenue de Baudin, walked out. They wanted a raise, but above all they demanded that one of their foremen, Crouzière, be kept out of the factory. The next day they added to their list of grievances the removal of two other foremen, an office supervisor, and an end to piece rates.

The Monteux strike had particularly irritated the *patronat* because it had united skilled and unskilled workers. The Fougeras strike appeared to have been planned, in turn, as a direct challenge to the manufacturers' authority. The strikers prevented merchandise from leaving the factory. Furthermore, this strike took a frightening new direction. Workers paraded provocatively through the streets and sang the "International" while passing the hat for those out of work. Workers celebrated Carnival by displaying a hideous mask representing the hated Crouzière, described as "the perfect example of a toady foreman, thick-skinned, inflexible, authoritarian, conceited, insolent," firing anyone who challenged him. Workers defiantly gathered outside Fougeras's house, caused a commotion in the street in front of the store of one of the company's commercial suppliers, and serenaded the staff of the *Courrier du Centre* with the "International," which was not their favorite tune. Some three or four hundred workers gathered outside Crouzière's apartment, on the avenue de la Révolution, carrying an effigy of the hated foreman. Some workers scaled the walls of a garden and shouted threats. This *carnival enragé,* successor to the charivari, also served notice to another foreman who lived close by. Fougeras threatened to close his factory until September and departed, together with his foreman, for the safety of Angoulême. Before leaving he warned the prefect, Cassagneau, that "new standards of behavior seem to have been introduced among the strikers of our industry."[4]

The Fougeras workers held on, aided by contributions from other shoemakers in the city. An incident on February 17 increased their determination: A company cashier pulled a pistol on some strikers, who disarmed the man and hauled him off to the police. Fougeras, meeting with Labussière and a delegation of workers, reaffirmed his absolute right to name any foreman he wished. On March 31 strikers prevented Fougeras, several of his office employees, and two salesmen from entering the factory, sparking a scuffle in which one of the salesmen was knocked to the ground. Finally, with other strikes looming, Labussière was able to arrange a compromise: Crouzière would remain in the factory but would stay away from the workers, who would receive a small raise. The strike ended on April 6.[5]

The foremen of other companies also came under attack. Mademoiselle Joséphine Prébosc, *contremaîtresse* for the Denis and Lecointe Company, had refused to allow her workers to collect money in the workshop for the Fougeras strikers. Cries of "Joséphine, tu est malade!" echoed through the streets as the workers marched toward her apartment on the rue des Clairettes while singing revolutionary songs. Twelve *monteuses* stayed away from work for one day after she had admonished one of them for sloppy workmanship.

Protests against foremen raised a related issue: subcontracting. Madame Champard, the female foreman at the Blanchard shoemaking company, had been accused of brutality toward her workers, and especially for turning piece work done by eight workers under her direction, presumably working at home, to her own profit. In early March police dispersed a crowd protesting at the place de la République. She was fired by her employers, who could not have been happy about her lucrative side activity.[6]

A walkout at the Beaulieu factory, where about three hundred workers processed rabbit skins for use as hats, seemed to prove that the series of strikes was being orchestrated against all manufacturers in the city. A month earlier Beaulieu had agreed to pay fourteen of his workers (*sécréteurs*) fifty more centimes a day, but only on a trial basis. When he cut back these wages on March 22, seven of them left, also demanding that their foreman be fired. That evening a sizable crowd taunted those workers who stayed on. After a brief hope for compromise, Beaulieu broke off negotiations, announcing that he would replace the strikers. His employees began to block the entrance to the factory each day. On March

31—the same day that the scuffle took place outside the Fougeras factory—a female foreman confronted and "humiliated" a striker outside the gates. The following day, noting that the police appeared to tolerate the blockade, Beaulieu shut his factory and left town with his family.[7]

On March 10, 8 *moufletiers* (men who worked the kilns in which decorated plates were baked) from two factories walked out, demanding a raise. Within a few days another 150 workers joined them, putting 700 people out of work. The employers negotiated with the union, and a settlement was reached on March 20 with the help of Labussière. But 12 and then 140 warehouse workers struck the Theodore Haviland factory, soon leaving 2,400 men, women, and children without employment. These strikes, again involving workers—and, in this case, just a single specialty—encouraged the porcelain manufacturers to close ranks. They met for 3 hours on March 11 or 12, resolving to crush this strike of unskilled workers. On March 13 the Union des fabricants warned that they would close all porcelain factories if the strikers had not returned by Monday, March 20: the lockout. Haviland announced that he would not take 5 "instigators" back under any condition; his pressure succeeded and the strike ended on March 20, the same day as that of the *moufletiers*.[8]

On March 27 one of Theodore Haviland's foremen dismissed three decorators cited by another foreman, Penaud, for "inadequate work." Penaud had overseen that stage of production for twelve years. The workers detested him, claiming that he demanded sexual favors ("droit du seigneur") from his female workers. Haviland refused to fire Penaud. Workers, supported by the Fougeras strikers, tired to prevent wagons from leaving the factory by grabbing the reins of the horses. They hurled rocks at the factory and at Penaud's home. The foreman, too, left for Angoulême, which had become a place of refuge for those fleeing the Limoges strikes. Most of the other Haviland workers, skilled and unskilled, walked out in support. Haviland closed his factory on April 3.

Charles Haviland also employed an unpopular foreman, Sautour, whose brother was a leader of the small but militant Sillon group. The *mécaniciens* complained that Sautour had fired a worker whose son had been buried without benefit of a priest. Furthermore, Sautour had strictly unpopular company regulations, such as a rule governing the coming and going of workers. The *mécaniciens* demanded that he be replaced and went out on strike April 3. Sautour asked the prefect for special protection, lamenting that he was insulted and jeered everywhere he went in the city, "as is now commonplace in Limoges."[9]

On April 8 it was the typographers' turn to walk out when a 5-year union agreement with 2 companies ended. Despite the advice of Henry Clavel, assistant to Auguste Keufer of the Fédération du livre, that a strike would be ill-advised, workers demanded a reduction in the workday and 5 more centimes an hour. The walkout of 170 (out of 238) typographers threw over 700 workers into the increasingly crowded streets. Three days later negotiations between the union and employers succeeded in bringing about a compromise agreement, one that benefited only the male workers, although the workday remained fixed at 10 hours. The printing companies joined the other *patrons* in attacking the socialist municipality for a lack of "order" in the streets, claiming that the law of 1884 obliged the city to pay for minor damage that the workers inflicted on their property.[10]

Most of the public's attention, however, still rested on the porcelain strike. Would there be a general strike in Limoges's major industry? Were the manufacturers planning a lockout? It seemed that the Penaud affair could be resolved when a delegation of workers, two representatives of the Bourse, and Tillet, the general secretary of the Porcelain Federation, proposed a compromise to Theodore Haviland. Penaud would return if the company made certain that he would have no further authority over the workers. Haviland refused, defending his prerogative as the boss. He was willing to employ Penaud elsewhere for a month, but then he would return as foreman. All of the other manufacturers stood behind Haviland and Penaud. The workers' mood became more angry.[11] Demonstrations in the streets continued, one of which, on April 10, was against the army.

It was customary for sizable crowds to meet all important visitors at the Gare des Bénédictins with enthusiasm and applause. General Charles Tournier, recently given command of the 12th Military Division, headquartered in Limoges, had received another kind of reception when he disembarked on March 14. Tournier's reputation as sympathetic to clericalism had preceded him to the Limousin, and his right-wing sympathies had compromised him in the *affaire des fiches*.[12] The Municipal Council refused to greet the general. His "military exactitude, almost regal," infuriated the workers, who feared that he would use his troops against strikers. The singing and shouting of the workers drowned out the few shouts of "Long Live the Army!" from the nationalist and clerical contingent. As Tournier set off on the short ride to his new headquarters, a brawl erupted outside the Café de l'Univers between workers and nationalists. Someone spat on Chabrol, the royalist lawyer. The police seemed unable or unwilling to clear the hostile crowd from the corner of the place Tourny and the boulevard Carnot. The general was forced to take refuge in the protected courtyard of the Banque de France, which may have seemed an appropriate place for him to hide.[13]

Other boisterous and aggressive demonstrations occurred outside the military headquarters on the eighteenth and nineteenth of the month, with one gathering swelling to two thousand people. The *Courrier du Centre,* no friend of the workers, had to admit that the idea that the army was incompatible with democracy had "penetrated to the very bottom of the popular mentality." The sound of breaking glass accompanied the "International" as the nearby offices of *La Gazette du Centre* also proved an irresistible target. Antimilitary propaganda informed soldiers that they, too, were victims of militarism, subject to the same "brutalities, bad treatment, and vexations at the hands of their officers" as workers were by the owners and foremen in the factories. Toward the end of March a soldier who had insulted his sergeant, apparently while drunk, received a sentence of five years of hard labor from the Conseil de guerre. A poster distributed by *Le Socialiste du Centre* compared that decision to a case in Nancy where an officer had received a suspended sentence of thirty days in prison for having beaten a soldier with a boot. General Tournier enforced the laws of capitalism and the bourgeois state.[14]

On April 13 workers rejected the final offer of the Haviland brothers by an overwhelming majority. That evening the gates of most of the porcelain factories slammed shut. From the point of view of the workers the *pacte de famine* was on. Had not the manufacturers prepared for and eagerly awaited this day? Twenty-one factories closed, ranging in size from Batiot's small shop on the rue de Paris (which had been the first to have a strike that year) to the giant factories of the Havilands, employing over 3,600 workers between them. All told, 7,608 people were left without work; somewhere between 20,000 and 25,000 men, women, and children depended on these wages. Only 7 small factories continued to operate, employing barely one sixth of the workers in the industry.[15]

At 5:45 that same evening two thousand workers left the Bourse, preceded by fifty children and a red flag on which "Vive la grève!" had been written. This first *tour de la ville* proceeded down the avenue Garibaldi to the place Sadi Carnot, back toward the city by way of the rue de Paris, down the rue Adrien Dubouché to the place d'Aîne, and then provocatively down the rue de la Boucherie. The banners and flags were dropped off at the Bourse, to be used another day. By

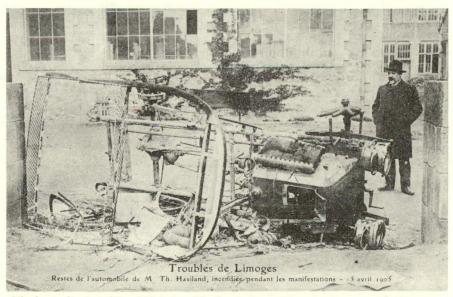

Troubles de Limoges
Restes de l'automobile de M. Th. Haviland, incendiée pendant les manifestations - 15 avril 1905

The burned automobile of Theodore Haviland, destroyed on April 15, 1905, in the courtyard of Haviland's factory

A barricade in front of the Touze factory (April 15, 1905)

7 P.M. the streets were alive. Some four thousand people packed the carrefour Tourny, again demonstrating against General Tournier and the army. A red flag waved in the crowd. Theodore Haviland wrote the American ambassador, demanding his intervention to ensure his protection. The strike had begun to take on what *Le Courrier du Centre* called a "revolutionary allure," despite the call of the unions for peaceful resistance to the lockout.[16]

On April 14, while the Municipal Council hastily adopted measures to ensure the maintenance of the *cantines scolaires,* which assisted the families of the unemployed, the workers took to the streets again. A procession dotted with red and black flags filed out of the Bourse and slowly marched up the rue du Clocher to the Guérin factory, on the rue du Petit Tour, whose owner served as president of the Union des fabricants. Several workers climbed over the wall and opened the factory gates. The municipal police arrived and urged the workers to commit no damage. They did not, moving on to Jouhanneaud and Company, where the gate again gave way to the throng, and then to chez Lanternier, rue Cruveilher, where workers were rumored to be still employed, finally arriving at the Barnardaud Company, recently established in Limoges. The workers pushed past the concierge, shouted down the angry *patron,* and convinced about twenty of his employees to leave with them. Pausing to whistle and shout before the apartment of Charles Haviland's foreman, the crowd moved on to the Haviland factory on the avenue Garibaldi. Here again the gate gave way, and some workers occupied with the maintenance of the buildings were forced to leave. Some two hundred of the marchers scattered throughout the factory buildings, searching for signs of activity.[17]

It happened that a group of about two hundred workers were nearby at the rond-point Sadi Carnot when Theodore Haviland drove past them, heading toward his factory on the avenue de Poitiers in his automobile, one of a handful in Limoges. The seething crowd ran after him, shouting, "Death to the thief. We must hang him!" Haviland drove into the factory compound. Some workers tried to force their way in by climbing over the walls or through the windows. A special police commissioner sent by the Ministry of the Interior managed to restore some semblance of order. The workers finally dispersed, returning to town in small groups at about three o'clock. Five policeman were posted at the factory.

About an hour later these guards first heard and then saw a large crowd of more than twelve hundred people carrying a red flag and two mannequins representing Penaud and Sautour. The police only had time to instruct one of Haviland's office employees to tell the American to hide his car. About half of the workers forced their way into the courtyard, some of them armed with clubs. They threw rocks at the police, turned over the automobile, and set it on fire. One worker rang the factory bell, mocking the usual procedure.

Haviland bravely emerged from his office to face insults and rocks. As soon as Labussière arrived he began to rebuke the workers for their violence, but he was drowned out by shouts of "Hang Haviland!" The police had barely saved the American flag that had been flying in the courtyard, which must have seemed like extraterritoriality to the workers. Some of the latter left the Haviland factory and proceeded, still with red flags and mannequins in hand, to the Guérin factory, and then to that of Touze, on the vieille route d'Aixe. The latter manufac-

The remnants of a barricade on the ancienne route d'Aixe, with the dead horse in the foreground (April 15, 1905)

turer and his brother-in-law were both slightly injured in a scuffle. Suddenly the cavalry charged the remaining marchers, without the obligatory *sommation*, or warnings, forcing most of the workers out of the street onto the sidewalks. Some of the demonstrators struck the horses with sticks or threw rocks at the soldiers. The commanding officer drew his saber and slashed one worker. As a second platoon arrived, some thirty or forty workers began to build a barricade, over-turning a tram and piling boxes and iron railings across the road near the Touze and Delhoume factories.

Other barricades went up. One horse was killed by a fall. After the troops and most of the workers had left, a photographer took a picture (p. 229). At dawn soldiers sent to dismantle the barricades found only a thirty-year-old porce-lain worker, normally employed by Charles Haviland, left to "guard" the barri-cades. The unpleasant task of removing the dead horse was left to municipal employees.[18]

Theodore Haviland wrote the prefect and the American ambassador describing the "state of anarchy now reigning in Limoges," the invasion of his factory, and the destruction of his automobile. "I saw," he wrote, "many *commissaires spé-ciales* but little in the way of help."[19] Mayor Labussière was in an extraordinarily difficult position. After the demonstrations on April 13 he had asked the prefect and the Minister of the Interior not to call out troops because he feared that the workers' hatred of the army would push the situation out of control. Labussière assured the minister that the street processions posed no serious threat to public order. In any case, the mayor had considerable sympathy for the workers. The porcelain manufacturers had prepared for the lockout by increasing production in the previous weeks, asking state work inspectors to look the other way as men and women worked long into the night. Several companies had kept on some workers for maintenance, which infuriated the strikers. Now, as he looked at the smoldering remains of Haviland's new automobile, Labussière told the workers that their violence had betrayed his word.[20]

When the mayor returned to his office, he learned that mounted troops had charged into a crowd at the Touze factory, the Minister of the Interior had turned his authority for policing the city over to the prefect, and that General Tournier was to oversee the military occupation of Limoges.

The night of April 15 several people broke into two gunsmiths' shops on the rue Turgot. They were believed to have carried guns to the Bourse du Travail, dropping several on the pavement of the rue Turgot. A third arms shop was later pillaged nearby. In the middle of the night a poorly made bomb exploded on the rue Cruveilher, where it was left at the door of one of Charles Haviland's office employees. The next morning the frightened population heard rumors that the churches and the *école normale* would be attacked.[21]

On Palm Sunday, April 16, gendarmes disembarked from virtually every train; Limoges was occupied by over one thousand troops. Prefect Cassagneau banned all public gatherings and demonstrations and considered shutting down the Bourse du Travail; rumor had it that hundreds of weapons were hidden there. That evening several workers defended a small boy who had been hit by a bourgeois who objected to his insulting the army. Each such small incident, blown out of proportion by rumor, increased tension in the town, particularly between the workers and soldiers.[22]

The morning of April 17 three thousand people piled into the Cirque to listen to a speech by Albert Lévy, treasurer of the C.G.T. Large crowds, defying the prefect, assembled on the Champ de Juillet, as they had in April 1848, and marched up the avenue de la Révolution to the prefecture to protest several arrests. The cortege then moved past the barracks of the 78th Infantry, with some hopeful shouts to the soldiers of "Nous sommes vos frères!" At the Church of St. Joseph several workers began climbing over the locked gates before being convinced to return to the march, which ended peacefully. Afterward several hundred workers went to the Bourse, where they picked up two red flags and one black one. Pierre Bertrand and Adrien Pressemane, a Guesdist militant, urged the prefect to rescind the ban against demonstrations and to release the prisoners. Labussière warned the prefect that he feared bloodshed. Cassagneau said that he would communicate a final decision at 6 P.M. after consulting with Etienne, the Minister of the Interior, in Paris. Once again a large crowd moved slowly from the Champ de Juillet to the place de l'Hôtel de Ville. Awaiting news in his office, Labussière received the prefect's negative response by telephone. He then took the unusual step of telephoning the minister himself, directly pleading with him

Workers entering the Cirque to listen to a speech (April 17, 1905)

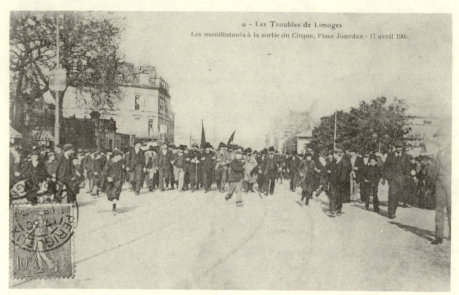

Demonstrators leaving the Cirque, place Jourdan (April 17, 1905)

to help prevent "a new Fourmies." At 6:30 P.M. the mayor sadly informed the throng that the decision was negative. Even as he called on the crowd to remain calm, shouts of "To the Prison" echoed loudly, and the procession moved up the boulevard Gambetta. Within minutes more than a thousand people threatened to storm the gates of the prison, as several municipal councilmen futilely tried to tell them that an assault on the guarded building would be useless. Pushing their way past a door weakened by the pounding of iron bars, they confronted about forty armed soldiers as mounted troops arrived. One cavalryman drew his sword and wounded a worker. The crowd scattered, as the cavalry charged into the mass of men, women, and children on the *champ de foire*. The workers again began to barricade the rue de la Mauvendière, the rue de la Reynie, and the rue de l'Amphithéâtre where it intersected with the *champ de foire,* and the entrance of the chemin de la Petit Tour. The materials used included an overturned tram, benches and iron fence railings from the Jardin d'Orsay, and wooden tables taken from storefronts. Then barricades went up on the rue Bernard-Palissy, on the faubourg Montmailler, in front of the modest Hôtel Veyras, and on the rue St. Paul. The workers were quickly chased away from the latter barricades; they responded by putting together another barricade on the faubourg des Arènes. By 9 P.M. the entire *champ de foire* had been occupied by troops, first from a small iron workshop nearby and then from the adjacent Jardin d'Orsay, whose corner was formed by the *champ de foire* and the rue de l'Amphithéâtre. Many workers, some of whom had been injured during the charge of the cavalry, had taken refuge there. An iron fence separated the Jardin d'Orsay from the street and the *champ de foire*. A staircase led from the latter up into the garden.[23]

Camille Vardelle, a nineteen-year-old porcelain worker, had been drawn to the

Demonstrators with red and black flags marching to the prefecture (April 17, 1905)

prison gate by a sense of outrage over the events of the past week. He lived on the rue de la Roche with his father, a porcelain painter, his mother, who tended a factory machine, and a young sister. Little distinguished him from the other porcelain workers, except perhaps that he had taken courses at the Ecole pratique de commerce et de l'industrie. In the words of Labussière, spoken over his grave, he was "the perfect worker, amply possessing the qualities that make a young man the pride and joy of his family." His father worked as a decorator in the industry; his son, in turn, had found work at the Pouyat factory. He contributed his salary to the family coffer. His family was "well regarded," having established a good reputation. On his father's advice he went to the morning meeting at the Cirque and then returned home to ask his father to join the demonstration. When the mounted troops arrived, he was frightened and climbed into the Jardin d'Orsay.[24]

Soldiers began to dismantle the barricades. Soon only the barricade at the base of the rue de la Mauvendière remained; rocks and bottles rained down from the Jardin d'Orsay. A thousand workers, both on the square and in the garden, shouted insults. Several municipal councilmen circulated, trying to calm the workers. The troops were becoming visibly angry. Vardelle and those around him did not hear several *sommations* announced by a trumpet. The 10th Company of the 78th Infantry ranged itself across the rue de la Mauvendière, between the remaining barricade and the *champ de foire,* facing the corner of the garden. The 11th Company was ranged to their left, on the *champ de foire.* A shot rang out, apparently fired from the corner of the garden. The bullet struck a rifle carried by one of the soldiers. Another seemed to come from the same general direction, a bit closer to the middle of the garden and a few steps from the stairway. Since the gas lamps had been smashed by the workers, and darkness was fast approaching, visibility was poor. Suddenly troops opened fire, spending fifty-two cartridges. They had not been ordered to do so. Camille Vardelle slumped to the ground, hit by a single rifle bullet. Those around him, including his father, carried him to the nearest pharmacy, but he died on the way. Four other workers were wounded. After the fusillade the news that someone had been killed caused the workers to disperse. Within a few minutes the *champ de foire* was deserted.[25]

A Parisian journalist, expecting to find "a city handed over to insurrection," found only a deathly silence and many workers in tears when he arrived.[26] Vardelle was buried on April 19. Two funeral wagons were prepared, one to carry the casket and the other covered with large wreaths and red ribbons and adorned with such signs as "A la victime du régime capitaliste," "A la victime du 17 avril," "A notre frère lâchement assassiné," and "A la victime du lockout." Ten thousand people followed the casket from the mortuary in the center of town, up the rue de Paris, with its storefronts secured, past the place Carnot, to the Louyat cemetery. Somewhere between ten and forty thousand people, according to estimates, watched the procession. It was a gray and humid day. Not a soldier was to be seen. Barely a sound could be heard, and not a single shout. Labussière, several socialist members of the departmental and arrondissement councils, the Municipal Council, and representatives of the Bourse du Travail accompanied the Vardelle family. Red flags and a few black flags could be seen in the cortege, as well as large placards bearing the names of the unions, the Parti socialiste de France, and the *université populaire*. Even as the sad procession passed the

Remains of a barricade erected on the rue Montmailler (April 17, 1905)

10. - Grèves de Limoges, 17 Avril 1905
Angle du Jardin d'Orsay où a eu lieu la fusillade
Vardelle a été tué au pied de l'arbre marqué d'une croix.

Prosper Batier, phot.-édit., Limoges. - Repr. int.

The garden of Orsay, where Camille Vardelle (insert) was shot; he fell at the foot of the tree marked by an X (April 17, 1905)

officers' club, its shutters closed, no shouts were heard. No priest accompanied the body.[27]

Four kilometers from the center of Limoges, beyond the faubourgs, the procession reached Louyat cemetery, not far from the de La Bastide château. Labussière offered a brief eulogy for the innocent victim, calling on the workers to remain calm. The repression that would follow another bloody clash would be terrible indeed. Henri Bagnol, a deputy from Paris representing the C.G.T., asked the workers to organize in order to assure a victory that would follow the power of reason, not bloodshed. Vardelle was buried. The cortege returned to town, filing in silence past the barracks of the 78th Infantry and dispersing at the Bourse. Flowers covered the tomb for months. Memorial demonstrations against the capitalist state, whose army had killed the young worker,[28] were held there for years thereafter every April 17.

The death of Camille Vardelle shocked the city, as had the death of Colonel Billet on another April evening thirty-four years earlier. The conservative press immediately treated the entire episode as the inevitable result of a socialist municipality turning the streets over to the *apaches*. They wildly exaggerated the number of soldiers injured, claiming that Vardelle had been slain while firing at soldiers in the street below. Frightened businessmen bombarded the prefect with demands for protection. A construction entrepreneur warned that his company had enough building materials to construct several hundred barricades; furthermore, he had heard that his building site would be attacked. J. Pouyat complained that his kaolin company had not been protected by troops and would be open to attack from several sides. Flammable materials could be found in the courtyard. Some six thousand guns and munitions were supposed to be hidden in the sewers between the Bourse and the railroad yards, near the river, or somewhere.[29]

The silence of mourning gave way, once again, to the sounds of anger. For the socialists French workers had suffered another Fourmies massacre. Madame Sorgue, representing the Parti socialiste de France, denounced the army in talks at the Bourse on April 21 and 22. Serious incidents between soldiers and workers continued. One lieutenant, lightly wounded on April 17, escaped a barrage of rocks after being recognized. Another soldier was knocked down in a scuffle. Primitive posters sarcastically congratulated the army on "its last great victory."[30]

Both porcelain manufacturers and their workers now seemed ready for a settlement. An arbitration panel that included both manufacturers and workers met to consider the strike. A breakthrough came when the workers' delegation agreed that the employers could name their own directors and foremen. Charles Haviland's workers accepted Sautour's return; Theodore Haviland finally agreed to sacrifice Penaud, and his employees agreed to put off a demand for a raise. Both sides were able to claim victory.[31]

Those strikes that were still under way, and subsequent walkouts, went badly for the workers. Labussière helped resolve one conflict when Charles Haviland, who had promised not to fire any workers after the strike was settled, let two *mécaniciens* go who had worked under Sautour.[32] The Beaulieu strike lost much public support, attracting only a fraction the assistance the porcelain workers had received. On May 8 strikers roughed up the young son of the concierge of the factory; public support disappeared and a week later the strike ended. It was a devastating defeat. Only about half of the workers returned to work for Beaulieu.[33] The Monteux workers went out for one day in support of their Parisian counterparts. But employers now had momentum. The lower middle class had been shocked by the violence now, too, and was tired of the constant strikes.[34] The mayor convinced thirty-five *engazetiers* to return to work after they demanded no further deductions from their wages for porcelain broken—the old issue of the *fente*. The *décalqueuses* of the Ahrenfeldt factory also lost a demand for higher wages; their employer threatened to close down the factory completely if they listened again to those who "poisoned" them with bad ideas. When they returned to work they found a warning that any worker who stepped out of line would be fired.[35] Monteux vowed not to give in to another strike that occurred at the end of May, again in support of his Parisian workers. When the strike ended in July, he took only about two thirds of his workers back, letting some three hundred go. Foremen posted the hours for entering and leaving the factory. No one could leave without permission, even if they had nothing to do. No collections could be taken up for strikers. Discipline would be enforced. Fougeras, too, defied his workers by breaking his promise and bringing Crouzière back to the factory. He broke the strike before it could start by announcing that anyone

Gendarmes and policemen guarding the Beaulieu factory after the departure of the manufacturer in May 1905

who did not return that afternoon could never come back. All returned. The prefect described the Crouzière incident as "a defeat for the workers' union." That summer a strike by joiners ended unsuccessfully. The nonunionized workers stayed on; the others left Limoges.[36]

Gradually the tension subsided in Limoges. May Day had been relatively calm: Union leaders took their list of demands to the town hall; workers heard a speech at the Bourse; and four thousand people followed the red flag to Vardelle's grave, singing the "International" and stopping to whistle and shout against the army.[37] They passed the rue de l'Amphithéâtre, now referred to as the rue de la Fusillade, where the young worker had fallen. There were about fifty sporadic incidents in the week preceding and following May Day, ranging from fights between workers and soldiers to a major disturbance at the place Sadi Carnot, where a gendarme tried to make an arrest. The police tried in vain to keep the *rond-point* clear, a focal point for gatherings by workers from the two Haviland factories. A crowd pelted cavalrymen with rocks as they rode down the rue du Collège. Touze, who had been roughed up when workers invaded his factory, reported that on May 8 several men had climbed the walls of his garden and threatened him. Drunken soldiers were seen trying to prevent workers from entering the Cirque on May 13.[38] Rumors persisted that workers were still armed and that the rich were leaving the city.[39] One producer of liqueurs received a threatening letter and two postcards from "a group of anarchists who want your skin and will have it before too long."[40]

The *progressistes* and clericals howled for Labussière's resignation. *Le Courrier du Centre* accused the mayor of having "delivered the streets of Limoges over to revolutionary marches and the worst kinds of scandals."[41] For Chénieux and his followers the force of the state was necessary because the municipal police seemed too favorably inclined toward workers. There were too few of them (fifty-three for an industrial city of eighty-five thousand); the procurer général thought that many of the policemen were unemployed workers "little disposed to aid in measures of order and repression." One had been the secretary of his union, another the concierge in a brothel, a third one of the latter's best customers. Some drank, and too many were socialists. Labussière's disgrace could lead to a *progressiste* municipality that would appoint a new police force. In the meantime most bourgeois citizens looked to the state and its troops and gendarmes for protection.[42]

The beleaguered Municipal Council declared that "a socialist municipality needs calm and order to accomplish its task and to defend, as they should, all of the legitimate demands of the working class."[43] Pierre Bertrand asserted that the true story behind the sad events of April had been the devotion of Labussière to his city. The mayor had warned of violence if the government maintained its bans on demonstrations and public gatherings and turned Limoges into an armed camp. He had done everything in his power to maintain order through persuasion, while recognizing the right of workers to protest in the streets.[44] The mayor hoped that Delaunay, a new prefect sent from Corsica, would be more reasonable than Cassagneau, who had been sent to another post. Bertrand argued that public order could not exist "in a society so profoundly divided as ours, based on bosses and wage earners, with both having interests that are absolutely and permanently opposed." The "order" that the army had brought to Limoges was nothing less than "the hypocritical expression of sheer force."[45]

Were those responsible for the violence infamous *apaches,* dangerous men on the margin of organized society, anarchists by philosophy or by deed? A few of those arrested for pillaging the gun stores were *malfamé.* One of them, Alfred Avril, was an anarchist who lived in public shelters and in houses under construction. He had taken guns from the Nicot shop to the Bourse, returned to break into Baillot's store later that evening, and had earlier been spotted among those destroying Haviland's automobile. Joseph Grosbras's parents had evicted the nineteen-year-old day laborer from their apartment after he had been convicted of an assault. Pierre Lalet, another day laborer who lived on the rue Porte-Panet, had spent three months in jail. Simon Masneuf, also a day laborer, and René Gorce, a porcelain worker on the rue du Dorat, were more respectable. The *filles* Virevialle and Biaujaud were registered prostitutes. François Texier, a metal turner from St. Germain-les-Belles, had helped Lalet plant the small explosive device outside the door of Haviland's man Chabrol. He had also suggested hiding the guns in the basement of the Bourse. Alfred Pariset, a housepainter and his friend, had lent a hand.[46]

The black flag appeared in most of the street demonstrations. Labussière himself recognized the role of the anarchists, and at one point he claimed that there were some four hundred involved. But it takes only one person to carry a black flag, and his estimate far exceeds any realistic assessment of the number of anarchists in Limoges. The central police commissioner asserted that "a small group" in the large march of April 17 carried the flag and sang "an anarchist song."[47] Were there more? Could the black flag have been taken up as a symbol of resistance to the centralized state? As a symbol of protest and an affirmation of solidarity in a working-class city confronting the *pacte de famine* of the capitalists, which was enforced by the army, both red and black flags were not incongruous. But the anarchists and the *apaches* were marginal to the entire movement. That they were responsible for catapulting the events toward violence did not mean that they shared the same goals as the workers.

The strike, however, was revolutionary in its scale, marking a confrontation with employers in both major industries—and others as well—and joining skilled and unskilled workers. The marches through the street and the *visite des usines* were a symbolic affirmation of the workers' conquest of the space of their city, acted upon the public stage of the street. But this was no movement of guns and bombs. The spontaneity of the strikes notwithstanding (within a pattern of rotating strikes from one factory to the next), the strike movement reflected the organization and political awareness of the workers, aiming to force companies to accept the removal of certain foremen. The workers' control of the streets stopped at the factory gates—thus the importance the workers attached to the symbolic conquest of the courtyards of the *bagnes* in which they labored. Those arrested in the Jardin d'Orsay or on the *champ de foire* were average workers,

The remains of a crucifix destroyed on the avenue Baudin during the Limoges strikes

mostly from the faubourgs. Henri Faucher, an eighteen-year-old *sabotier* who was also wounded, seems as typical as Vardelle. Born in nearby Condat, he lived with his parents on the rue de Nexon. His father was a fifty-year-old day laborer. The family had little money (and six children), but "were well thought of" by their neighbors.[48]

On the avenue Baudin a large crucifix fell victim to the crowd's fury. A photographer took a picture of the remains, the head of Christ almost intact on the ground, not far from the Fougeras factory and the barricades.

At some point during the events of April 17 a number of workers went to the rue de la Boucherie, threatening to knock down the only religious statue still standing on a public thoroughfare in the city, the statue of Notre-Dame-la-Pitié. The butchers, whether forewarned or simply prepared, were there to drive the workers away, or at least make them consider whether such an attack would be worth the bloodshed. We know little about that confrontation, which probably only lasted a couple of seconds, between the old and new worlds. The statue survived—and is still there—an oasis for the faithful in the socialist city.

Epilogue:
State, City, and Revolution
in Modern France

The year 1905 marked a turning point in Europe. Revolution broke out in Russia in February. Germany and France were on the verge of war during the first Moroccan crisis, and other nations fell into line behind the two enemies in a system of entangling alliances that ultimately spelled the continent's undoing. In France the separation of Church and State became official. The so-called "nationalist revival" began and socialists were now unified. In Limoges the *journées* of April led to the city's Thermidor.

Labussière resigned as mayor in December 1905 after his council refused to approve funds for the police as a form of protest against the repression during and following the strikes of April. Twenty-seven councilmen resigned shortly afterward. New elections took place in February 1906, with the violence of the preceding April the major issue. This time the throngs of workers awaiting electoral results were disappointed. The conservative republicans had retained considerable bourgeois support despite their decidedly minority position during the Labussière administration. Enough disaffected Radicals, left out in the cold by socialist unity, and a goodly number of workers abandoned the socialists to elect thirty *progressistes,* who promptly chose Chénieux as mayor. The new council would be dominated by business "well known for their devotion to the public good, and not to political life."[1] No one doubted the power of capital.

The new municipality dismissed a number of socialist employees and ended a number of subventions, such as that for free legal aid for workers.[2] Chénieux now refused the use of municipal buildings for political purposes. The council flatly rejected a request to create a "rue de la Séparation," which would have celebrated the official separation of Church and State. When the few remaining socialist councilmen objected to council actions, they were told, "You don't run things around here anymore!"[3]

The cornerstone of the *progressiste* policy was the curtailment of the Bourse du

Travail. In September 1905 the prefect reduced the Bourse's subvention from twelve thousand to fifteen-hundred francs, the goal being to prevent "political activity by those who devote themselves shamelessly to the culture of strikes and to class warfare . . . this is a state of things that we will no longer tolerate." On October 6, 1906, the council passed new regulations for the Bourse, as Chénieux had promised his constituency before the elections. Article VII banned all discussion of politics and religion, citing "les réunions bruyantes, les chants séditieux ou les manifestations quelconques, pouvant troubler l'ordre publique," while Article VIII specified that only workers of the industry or trade directly affected could be called together to discuss demands.[4]

Deprived of almost all of its subvention and facing vigorous enforcement of the new regulations, the Bourse refused municipal funds and moved out of the building on the avenue de la Gare on January 1, 1907. The Bourse's influence diminished; its general secretary admitted that the 1905 strikes had left workers uncertain and divided, afraid of the employers who had broken their strikes and their morale. For example, the shoe manufacturer Fougeras had reneged on his promise during the summer of 1905 and had brought the foreman Crouzière back into the factory. When his workers voted to walk out, he broke the strike by announcing that any worker who failed to report to work that afternoon would be considered to have quit. The tide had turned. Only financial support from the Socialist party (S.F.I.O.) and dues from members kept the Bourse going. The C.G.T. and the individual federations—particularly that of the ceramic workers—gradually assumed a larger role, while local unions lost members and momentum. The arrest and conviction of the treasurer of the Syndicat des polisseurs et useurs de grains in 1908 for pilfering funds was exploited by the conservative press, which continued to sing the virtues of the "yellow" or "mixed" unions that joined employers and workers in a few trades. At one point the Bourse seemed to do little more than serve as an intermediary between the C.G.T. and an *afficheur* who posted antimilitaristic propaganda.[5]

The weakened status and resources of the Bourse helped limit strike activity after 1905. Between January 1, 1906, and the outbreak of World War I in 1914—a period spanning more than eight years—there were thirty-three strikes in Limoges, as compared to twenty-nine in 1904–5. The vast majority of these were extremely short: At least fifteen lasted less than a week (five lasted one day or less), and in two cases the workers simply walked out and never returned. The economic crisis that struck the porcelain industry, causing layoffs and a reduction in the workday beginning in 1907, contributed to the decline of militancy. So did the absence of the socialist municipality. Désiré-Vuillemin correctly asserts that after the 1905 events workers seemed to follow the "rules of the game"; unions had to "look for action undertaken as a strategic operation, with the backing of public opinion, relying less on the doctrines of theoreticians than on the work of able tacticians."[6] It is significant that the role of the foreman almost ceased to be a strike issue; strikes over wages predominated, with negotiations and compromise the norm. With the exception of a bakers' strike in 1910, boisterous demonstrations in the streets and the specific targeting of unpopular employers and foremen disappeared.[7]

The unification of French socialists in April 1905 had been anticipated by the alliance of reform socialists and Guesdists in Limoges during the municipal elections of the previous decade. During the Millerand crisis of 1899, *Le Rappel du Centre* had expressed the hope of many: "Let us salute the coming day when the great minds of socialism—Jaurès, Guesde, Viviani, Allemane, Millerand, and the others—unified in the same love of the proletariat, will declare the dethronement of bourgeois society and will march, indissolubly united in the pursuit of universal happiness."[8] After the Russian Revolution of 1905, Limoges's socialists had joined together to protest czarist repression, putting aside their differences as they had done during the Dreyfus affair. With the declaration of unity, *Le Populaire du Centre,* the newspaper of the S.F.I.O., began publication on October 29, 1905. It followed the political direction of Jaurès, Betoulle, and Pierre Bertrand. The S.F.I.O. increased the effectiveness of socialist propaganda, making great strides in rural Haute-Vienne.

Socialist unity did not end the differences between the old reform socialists and the Guesdists and Allemanists in Limoges. The leading Guesdists did not support unity; Pressemane, for one, complained of "insufficient guarantees" for the Guesdists. The latter dominated the leadership of the departmental federation of the S.F.I.O. even though the reform socialists retained the greatest strength in the department. In 1907 the Guesdists again declared themselves opposed to Millerandism, a shadow that still hung over them.[9]

Socialists faced a more serious problem: a waning of enthusiasm and activism among workers. With the achievement of socialist unity, the activities of the political clubs tapered off. May Day demonstrations were increasingly disappointing, and after 1907 the corteges that marched to Vardelle's tomb each April grew smaller. The police commissioner described the socialist party in 1907 as being "in complete disarray."[10] In 1908 *Le Populaire du Centre* implored the workers to strive for a socialist victory in the municipal elections of that year. But the *progressistes,* who had never lost much of their middle-class constituency, won again. The Guesdist-dominated *Socialiste du Centre* called for tighter organization to ensure that the socialist party did not disintegrate in the face of diminished popular interest.[11]

Yet the potential for socialist dominance in Limoges remained. The events of 1905 had admittedly been disastrous for the socialists, but the sources of their strength survived, as the elections of 1914 would vividly demonstrate to the nation. Betoulle had been elected to the Chamber of Deputies in 1906 with only nine hundred fewer votes than Labussière had received in 1902.[12] Two issues that generated a resurgence of popular mobilization aided the socialists' return to local power: the markedly higher cost of living that began at least as early as 1907; and the debate over the law that would force Frenchmen to serve in the army for three years. At the same time, the S.F.I.O. in Limoges gradually recovered from the disorganization that followed in the wake of 1905 (for example, the loss of Labussière, who left Limoges after his resignation). Pierre Fraisseux, the Guesdist militant from Eymoutiers, later recalled Sunday trips into the villages that he and his political friends made, carrying sacks full of brochures and pamphlets.[13] In the 1908 municipal elections the socialists gained three thousand more votes than in 1906; they also gained several more seats in the cantonal elections. By 1910 the pace of political meetings had picked up before the elections of that year sent Betoulle and Pressemane to the Chamber of Deputies. The Bourse du Travail retained six thousand affiliated members. Protests against *la vie chère* brought workers together. In 1912 the socialists concentrated their efforts on winning back the Municipal Council, offering essentially the same program of decentralized municipal socialism (and still demanding control over the police).[14] Dr. Chénieux had died in March 1910; his friends on the council had named the rue de Paris after him, an irony that most of its residents, who had never voted for him, could not have missed.[15] Invoking his name, the *progressistes* conjured up memories of the 1905 strikes: "Do not forget the past: our streets invaded by hordes of rioters; our workers molested by these parasites; outbreaks of strikes, provoked and supported by sluggards—professional idlers—factories invaded; porcelain broken . . . and cars burned."[16] The socialists were swept back into power, aided by three factors: an increase of twelve-hundred workers in the city since 1908; socialist unity behind Betoulle, who became mayor; and the indecision of the Radicals. Old *limougeauds* must have started as they watched the laundresses, whose quarter had been deprived of "the poetry of yesteryear" by the new steam-cleaning plant, parading through the center of town to celebrate the return of the socialist municipality to power. In 1914 the department elected socialists for all five positions as deputy: Betoulle, Chauly, Parvy, Pressemane, and Valière, the son of a porcelain worker. The Haute-Vienne had the highest percentage of socialist votes in France.[17]

Antimilitarism contributed to the socialist resurgence in a region known for that tradition. The hostile reception given General Tournier in March 1905 reflected the intensity of popular antimilitaristic sentiments more than simply the specific circumstances of the strikes. Limoges was fertile ground for antimilitaristic propaganda even before 1900, when a soldier killed a civilian with his bayonet at the end of a drinking binge one evening and military authorities stayed away from the poor man's funeral. The memory of Vardelle's death reinforced popular animosity toward the army, particularly its officers. The use of soldiers in 1907 to repress insurgents in the Midi brought workers to the prefecture shouting "Clemenceau, assassin!" The anarchist paper *Le Combat social* faced prosecution for printing postcards, entitled "Two Ways of Obeying," showing troops killing civilians in Limoges and Narbonne.[18] *Le Populaire du Centre* and *Le Socialiste du Centre* printed many articles attacking the use of the army to defend the interests of capitalists. The socialists and the Bourse du Travail sponsored *punches* for those conscripts about to be inducted into the army.

Certainly there were signs of the "nationalist revival" in Limoges, particularly among the *progressiste* bourgeoisie and the royalist and clerical groups: patriotic gestures by the city's gymnastic clubs; the return of military marches and music to the July 14 celebrations; the Municipal Council's vote to award five hundred francs to the Société d'éducation physique et de préparation militaire; and a meeting of the Ligue patriotique des français in 1912 that attracted thirty-five hundred people. In 1907 the Action française joined two other right-wing organizations, the Action libérale and the Comité monarchiste (the names of these groups changed, but their membership remained virtually the same) to form a Fédération nationale du Centre. The twenty-one members of the Camelots du roi, mostly commercial employees and students, wore uniforms. A few shouts of "Long Live the King!" could be heard at an anti-German rally in March 1913, at which Léon Daudet warned of spies in France.[19]

Yet the evidence of antimilitaristic sympathies among Limoges's workers seems formidable. The S.F.I.O. campaigned against the law stipulating three years of military service with many protest meetings and a petition signed by 10,500 citizens in Limoges. In September 1911 the S.F.I.O. and the Bourse organized one of a series of large gatherings to protest the danger of war over the second Moroccan crisis, a situation that in the eyes of socialists seemed only to further the interests of the Schneider armaments industry. Rougerie described what such a war would entail: economic chaos; a population of widows and orphans; higher taxes; and the possible destruction of workers' organizations that had taken over forty years to build. One thousand attended a meeting to protest the court-martial of a soldier in 1912.[20] Jaurès's call for the replacement of a professional army by a national guard or militia found great echo in Limoges. In March 1913 Pressemane condemned militarism ("the wind of madness blowing in France") and confronted the issue of the socialist response to the outbreak of war. French workers would have to oppose a German advance, which would endanger the Republic, but socalists would take every possible step to stop the war, hoping that their German comrades would do the same.[21] The Municipal Council ignored the nationalist president of France, Raymond Poincaré, on his visit that same year. Some socialists may have recalled Teissonnière's prediction in 1898 that the nations of Europe would be plunged into a massive and bloody war.[22]

Limoges slipped toward war along with the rest of France and most of Europe during the hot summer of 1914. The crisis mounted following the assassination of Archduke Francis Ferdinand of Austria-Hungary in Sarajevo on June 28. As the European situation deteriorated, socialists began to anxiously consider their response. On July 28, the day Austria-Hungary declared war on Serbia, an *affiche* protesting the impending war appeared in Limoges. Two days later, the S.F.I.O. and the Bourse du Travail sponsored the largest meeting ever held in the city, which was attended by between five and seven thousand people.[23] Betoulle declared that if the workers of Germany and Austria-Hungary could not prevent their leaders from waging war, French workers would do their duty and defend the Republic against her autocratic enemies. Rougerie, representing the Bourse, admitted that there seemed to be no way of stopping the catastrophe; he almost appeared to chide the workers for having been unable to stop the bourgeoisie from beginning a war in the interests of capitalism. The assembled throng passed an *ordre du jour* asking the government to take whatever steps were necessary to maintain peace, while expressing the conviction that "the disappearance of the capitalist regime and the victory of socialism alone would permit the establishment of a definitive peace among peoples." When the prefect asked that the statement be changed to de-emphasize the desire for peace, Betoulle replied that "the best patriotism, now, consists in avoiding war." The meeting dispersed with shouts of "War Against War!"[24]

The news of the assassination of Jaurès on July 31—the same day that another demonstration, involving several thousand people, against the approaching war took place—dumbfounded the city in which the socialist leader was so popular. The Municipal Council could do little but express its shock and outrage and again call for peace. Fearing war, five hundred people lined up at the *caisse d'épargne* to withdraw their money.[25] When Germany declared war on Russia on August 1 and the French began mobilizing their forces, Betoulle ordered merchants to stop raising prices. The prefect prepared to use the army reserves and the territorials, if necessary, to repress any popular disturbances if France entered the war. He expected some ten to fifteen thousand workers to be unemployed within a few days, about a third of whom would be called into service. On August 31 Germany declared war on France.[26] Several ugly anti-German incidents occurred. In one case a large crowd gathered outside the home of an Alsatian grocer shouting "Down with the Germans! Death to the Prussians!" They left only when he could prove that he was a French Jew who had lived in the city for over thirty years.[27] A porcelain worker who shouted "Down with the War!" at the place Tourny was roughed up by onlookers.[28] By August 4 troops were boarding trains to Paris and then to the front. Unlike 1871, no one tried to stop them. Indeed, aside from a few shouts, the only incident involved a fifteen-year-old boy whom the police had to rescue from a crowd when he appeared to be making fun of a departing soldier. In fact, the boy had been amused by something the soldier had said about bringing the kaiser's head back to Limoges. The crowd sang "Allez petits soldats de la France, nos voeux vous accompagnent. Nous vous disons tous, à bientôt!"[29]

Limoges's soldiers, like all of the others, did not return before the leaves fell. Many never came back. Even two weeks into the war the prefect reported considerable discouragement in the Haute-Vienne. The "spirit" of the rural folk seemed suspect, particularly in regions that had been inundated with antimilitaristic propaganda. The crowd, waiting for news at the prefecture in Limoges, where the mood of the workers was reported to be excellent on August 18, grew ever more anxious as wounded soldiers followed bad news from Lorraine.[30]

The war went on at a murderous pace. In September 1915 the socialist Federation of Haute-Vienne, including all five deputies, called for an end to the war.[31] This was the first such public statement in Europe. When the armistice was signed more than three years later, at least 1.4 million Frenchmen had been killed (14.7 percent of those mobilized), and over 1.1 million had been seriously wounded.[32] Victorious France, like defeated Germany, seemed to have become a nation of widows and cripples. The soldiers who returned to Limoges found themselves living in a familiar city but a very different world.

Although the timing of the nineteenth-century revolutions depended upon political occurrences at the Parisian center of power, the economic and social evolution of Limoges determined events in that city.[33] The expansion of the city's commercial function and the development of the porcelain industry depended on an elite cadre of entrepreneurs who comprised the bulk of the liberal opposition to the Restoration and had unseated the Bourbons. Limoges, denied the title of a *bonne ville* during the Restoration, found its identity in the porcelain industry. The production of porcelain, in turn, concentrated porcelain workers in the city; skilled painters, turners, and moulders overcame wide differences in skill levels and remuneration to shape working-class political life in the city with the same dexterity and commitment that they shaped and embellished the plates that earned worldwide reputation. Their quest for political power was first seen in 1848 and the years of the Second Republic. Organizational changes (particularly production and decoration under the same roof) and technological advances (especially the decoration of plates by decals) transformed the industry in the 1880s and 1890s despite serious economic crises. Yet the leadership of skilled porcelain workers survived into the new era of production. Shoemaking, having long since emerged as Limoges's second industry, was transformed by factory production and even more by mechanization. After World War I it emerged as the leading industry. Shoemakers, too, became militants, even after the rapid decline in artisanal production.

Urbanization did not entail uprooting and disorganization. Rather, it brought new, organized contenders for political power to the fore: first businessmen and then workers. After the Revolution of 1830 the former feared skilled, organized workers, whose political activism during the Second Republic was precocious.

The city expanded as industrial faubourgs housed much of the working class. But here, too, where city and country met, urbanization brought not disorganization but a community of workers. The stereotypical "rural folk" of the faubourgs contributed to the political transformation of the city and its outlying regions. Limoges, comprised of two separate towns administratively before 1789, became two towns again during much of the nineteenth century. The appeal of democratic socialism and then both reform and socialism as well as Guesdism was based in the faubourgs. During the strikes of 1905 several demonstrations outside the homes of company owners and foremen in the traditional city seemed to highlight the solidarity of workers on the periphery. Beyond the statue of Denis Dussoubs workers challenged the political domination of the socially conservative bourgeoisie of the traditional city, who held power between 1830 and 1895 (and again between 1906 and 1912). The bourgeois conservatives, both the moderate republicans and Orleanists of 1871 and the *opportuno-progressistes* of the Chénieux era were the direct descendants of the *juste milieu* of the July Monarchy, no mere stereotype but a powerful social and political reality. Facing the threat from the left, they readily allied with clerical and right-wing parties in local elections.

At the same time, the persistence of a politically active nucleus of radical bourgeois throughout the nineteenth century helped perpetuate Limoges's leftist tradition. The utopian socialists of the 1840s, the *quarante-huitard* lawyers, the radical-republican era of the first decades of the Third Republic, and the reform socialists of the belle époque provided a continuity of leadership that complemented that of the skilled porcelain workers.

Small wonder that political life in Limoges during the belle époque was so charged with energy, commitment and, above all, organization. The Dreyfus affair, the Millerand ministry, the repression of striking workers by troops, and the law requiring three years of army duty intensified political life in Limoges, complementing local issues. Political clubs, meetings, and *conférences contradictoires* brought working people into political life with an understanding of the various ideological alternatives available to them. When they voted in municipal, cantonal, or departmental elections they faced clear choices. The most salient rituals and routines of municipal life were no longer religious celebrations but political occasions, following the rhythms of elections and the secular calender. The city's own collective memory of its past revolutionary experiences colored the politics of the belle époque and aided the reform socialists, who traced their ancestry back to the successes and failures of their predecessors during the Revolution of 1848 and the Commune of 1871. The electoral meetings and demonstrations were a far cry from the bread riot that had followed the Revolution of 1830; the massive strikes of 1905 were vastly different from those early walkouts by skilled porcelain workers during the 1830s; the *syndicats,* the national trade organizations, and the Bourse du Travail were a long way from the days of the first mutual aid societies. It is remarkable to consider not only the depth of these changes in economic, social, and political life but to realize that they occurred in such a relatively short time—about seventy years—which is equivalent to a normal lifespan. Daniel Lamazière, the former representative of the Haute-Vienne during the Second Republic, witnessed incredible changes in his lifetime. He was born in 1812 and lived to be almost one hundred years old. He knew Léon Betoulle, who served as mayor of Limoges from 1912 until 1956 (except for the Vichy years). Taken together, these two lives spanned the period from Napoleon's march on Moscow to the atom bomb.

Despite the generalized class consciousness and political activism of 1848–51, the wave of strikes in 1864, and the return to militancy of *l'année terrible,* the most sustained economic and political action of Limoges's workers occurred during the years of the socialist municipality. In 1905 unity seemed to have been achieved as skilled and unskilled workers, including men and women, joined together in the streets. Heres strikes truly became an extension of the political process, sustained by the atmosphere of permanent contention created by the political clubs, the *conférences contradictoires,* and the socialist municipality.

A concern for the city itself and its urban environment helped infuse municipal political life with a sense of urgency and commitment. During the 1820s and the 1860s bourgeois liberals pushed for reforms that would make Limoges a healthier and more impressive-looking place; their calls for the rights of local citizens to demand a more suitable urban environment helped account for the progress after the Revolution of 1830 and during the Empire (in the latter case benefiting from the centralized Empire's view of its role in *grands travaux*). By the 1890s socialists were calling for urban renewal and attention to the condition of life for workers. Urban projects were hotly debated in municipal elections, with the socialists promising much and the bourgeois *progressistes* relatively little; the latter concentrated attention on the central districts and on the most visible kinds of improvements. Here planning and political life closely interacted, which again helps account for the passionate nature of municipal political life in those heady days at the turn of the century. One emphasis throughout this study has been on the role of the centralized state in Limoges's political evolution. That centralization served not necessarily to *limit* municipal life, as might be expected, but also to generate such a reaction that state power itself became a lively political issue. Despite their Jacobin tradition, reform socialists were passionately engaged in a struggle for municipal liberties, much as the bourgeois liberals had been during the late Restoration and the liberal phase of the Second Empire. Issues such as control over finances and the police were an essential part of the debates that preceded municipal elections. The strong state was, furthermore, closely identified with the power of capitalists and the army that protected their interests. But despite its strength, the vision of decentralization represented wishful thinking. The state was getting stronger.

The year 1905 marked the end of an era in Limoges. The events of April 1905 were a turning point, but not because *progressistes* came to power (they held it only until 1912). Rather, combined economic and political action brought the workers of Limoges to a point of insurgency that was not far from a revolutionary situation. Thereafter the "rules of the game" predominated, even though the socialists once again held the reins of municipal power seven years later. Did the first years of this century represent a lost opportunity? Could France and Europe have been saved from the catastrophe of World War I by another revolution? But all of France was not Limoges.

Tony Judt's study of socialism in the Var, where the Guesdists successfully mobilized rural people, argues that the socialists' best chance for seizing power came relatively early in the evolution of industrial capitalism, before the combination of capitalism and the strong state had developed sufficiently so as to become virtually invulnerable.[34] Tension between the centralized state and the municipality in nineteenth-century Limoges could be easily seen, in particular in 1830 and 1870–71; the liberal bourgeoisie had wanted to shape the future of its own city, protesting a lack of municipal liberties. By the 1890s a reversal had occurred. The socialists, particularly the reform socialists, had embraced decentralization as one of their most important rallying cries (perhaps the Guesdists' identification with a centralized, Paris-centered party may have contributed to the appeal of the reform socialists). Bourgeois republicans had long since abandoned decentralization as a goal. They now looked, more than ever, to the army of the strong state to maintain social order and to fulfill their nationalistic dreams. So did the parties of the right. While the socialists demanded that the municipality control its own resources and police, bourgeois republicans applauded the army for its repression of strikers in Limoges in 1905 and in the Midi in 1907.

At the dawn of this century the French state had become so powerful that it seemed highly unlikely that the workers and their bourgeois socialist allies could assume power by means of a revolution. As Judt suggests, the tradition, organization, and experience of protest was, furthermore, rooted in artisanal and semi-skilled workers, not among the proletariat of large-scale industries like those of the St. Etienne region, the Nord, the outskirts of Paris, and a few smaller concentrations. The years 1936 and 1968 were potentially revolutionary situations. Yet those possibilities were limited, and not merely because of the superior power of the armed forces. The year 1905 only temporarily ended socialist political domination in Limoges. But the general acceptance of the "rules of the game" by workers after 1905 attested to the fact that they were integrated into the state as contenders for political power. Henceforth socialists and syndicalists used huge demonstrations and institutionalized work stoppages, orchestrated by national organizations, to obtain economic and political ends, not revolutionary goals. As Michelle Perrot put it, "A slow process of integration began that continued in the parliamentary hemicycle. The citizen replaced the comrade; and the municipal *fanfare* replaced the trumpets of the last Judgment."[35] In 1936 and 1968 the most revolutionary acts—such as the seizure of factories—were the spontaneous acts of local workers much like those in Limoges in 1905, except that they lacked the kind of coordination of national political and trade union organizations that would have been necessary to generate a successful revolutionary movement.

Workers continued to develop their consciousness as members of a class, regularly and ritually making demands of their employers and of the state, "but losing both the will and the ability to replace the political realm with something different."[36] Since World War II the French state has continued to grow stronger with the greatly increased power of the president, François Mitterand's reforms notwithstanding. Limoges is still a city of the left. But, like France, it had its last revolution in the nineteenth century.

Notes

Chapter One

1. Arthur Young, *Travels During the Years 1787, 1788 and 1789* (London, 1791), p. 14. A shorter version of the first two chapters appeared as "Restoration Town, Bourgeois City: Changing Urban Politics in Industrializing Limoges," in John M. Merriman, ed., *French Cities in the Nineteenth Century* (London, 1982).

2. Description drawn from the Archives du Ministère de la Guerre, Reconnaissances militaires, MR 1298 and 1300. A map from 1827 shows the crucifix and Beaupeyrat to the west of the city, both *en pleine campagne;* the *octroi* was beyond the crucifix.

3. Cf. Young, op. cit., p. 15: "The present Bishop has erected a large and handsome palace, and his garden is the finest to be seen at Limoges, for it commands a landscape hardly to be equaled for beauty; it would be idle to give it any other description that just enough to induce travellers to view it." Balzac offers a similar description in his novel *Le Curé du village.*

4. R. Daudet, *L'Urbanisme à Limoges au XVIIIe siècle* (Limoges, 1939), esp. pp. 26–49; Louis Guibert, "Tableau historique et topographique de Limoges," *Bulletin de la Société Archéologique et Historique du Limousin* (hereafter *BSAHL*) 59 (1909): 253.

5. Daudet, *L'Urbanisme à Limoges au XVIIIe siècle,* esp. p. 48; cf. *Almanach Limousin,* 1860, "Lettre d'un voyageur . . . sur la physionomie de Limoges en 1753": "A visit to Limoges is not particularly pleasant. The houses, built of wood, offer a sad view. There is not a single decent public place, not one remarkable building. The idea of embellishment has not yet entered the mind of the Limousin . . . Happily, the intendants have lifted this poor town out of obscurity. . . ."

6. Daudet, op. cit., esp. pp. 157–61; *Almanach Limousin* (1860), "Limoges depuis cent ans"; Monique Lachtygier, "Tableau de la vie ouvrière à Limoges de 1800 à 1848" (Mémoire pour le diplôme d'études supérieures, Université de Poitiers, 1959), pp. 20–22. See also M. J. Simmonneau, "Contribution à l'étude sociale de l'ancien régime: La Cité de Limoges à la veille de la Révolution" (Mémoire de maîtrise, Université de Limoges, n.d.). The population of the Cité was about three thousand in 1789, including the Naveix and the faubourg Boucherie. The Cité was dominated by the clergy, yet it included merchants, and artisans, and the textile manufacture of Laforest at the Porte Tourny; it did participate in the joint administration of Limoges in the eighteenth century, sending its own syndics and

deputies. The last independent meeting of the municipal council of the Cité was in December 1792, one year after the unification of the two towns.

7. MR 1300, "Mémoire sur les environs de Limoges," by A. Joinville; Lachtygier, op. cit., p. 16; *Annales de la Haute-Vienne,* January 23, 1829. The *Almanach Limousin* for 1881 cited a letter written by a German prisoner of war in 1813: "Do you want an image of Limoges? Imagine somber streets that seem to be covered by a vast umbrella. Listen to the clinking of wooden sabots. Wrap yourselves in your covers. Outside the rain falls and mud covers the ground." He added that his captors seemed to believe everything they heard.

8. 3M 3, fonds de l'évêché, letters of the Prefect of Haute-Vienne (henceforth PHV), September 22 and October 1, 1825.

9. Lachtygier, op. cit., pp. 15, 32–33; Daudet, op. cit.

10. The *Nouvelles ephémérides du ressort de la cour royale de Limoges* (Limoges, 1837), noted that between 1820 and 1835 births averaged 1,136 and deaths 1,206; the excess of deaths may have been at least partially attributable both to the presence of sizable charitable institutions with notoriously high mortality rates and to the regional prison, in which 201 of 1,266 inmates died in 1827; Lachtygier, op. cit., p. 106. Limoges's population grew as follows: 1801 (20,255); 1806 (21,025); 1821 (24,992); 1826 (25,612); and 1831 (27,070). See Charles Pouthas, *La Population française au XIXe siècle* (Paris, 1959). In 1837, 38 percent of Limoges's houses had been built within the previous twenty years. Between 1813 and 1823, 133 houses were constructed.

11. Lachtygier, p. 9, gives the population of each parish as follows:

	1821	*early in the July Monarchy*
St. Michel	10,518	13,000
St. Pierre	6,624	7,000
Cathédrale	4,102	4,000
Ste. Marie	3,748	3,000

12. A. Fray-Fournier, "Balzac à Limoges," *Bibliophile Limousin* 13 (1898): 51.

13. Ibid.

14. 1M 243, letter of Minister of Interior (hereafter Int.) July 4, 1825; Fray-Fournier, "Limoges et les bonnes villes," *BSAHL* 52 (1903): 281–352. Limoges's petition ("Will Limoges Be a Humiliating Exception?") claimed that the town had provided 10,000 troops against Caesar; its population of about 20,000 was compared to the *bonnes villes* of Bourges (16,000), Dijon (18,000), La Rochelle (17,000), Nice (18,000), and Tours (20,000). The city fathers cited the town's "miraculous progress"; Archives Municipales de Limoges (hereafter AML), "D," letters of PHV, December 6, 1816, and July 4, 1825.

15. MR 1300, Joinville, 1841; F7 9580, n.d., petition.

16. J. J. Juge, *Changements survenus à Limoges depuis cinquante ans* (Limoges, 1808 and 1817), p. 28; Henri Ducourtieux, "Les Statues dans les carrefours de Limoges," *Limoges illustré,* May 15, 1906; Lachtygier, op. cit., pp. 125–26; L. Texier-Olivier, *Statistique générale de la France: Département de la Haute-Vienne* (Limoges, 1808), p. 104. The bishop indicated in a letter of January 1, 1817 (F19 5682) that "the depravation of Limoges is considerably less than we have been told."

17. *Almanach Limousin,* 1860, "Limoges depuis cent ans"; R. Limouzin-Lamothe, *Le Diocèse de Limoges du XVIe siècle à nos jours (1510–1950)* (Strasbourg, 1953),

p. 197. The Filles-de-Notre Dame and the Sisters of Providence were among the female orders that returned. The Brothers of Christian Doctrine arrived in 1818.

18. Louis Guibert, "Les Confréries de Pénitents en France et notamment dans le diocèse de Limoges," *BSAHL* 27 (1879): 192; the *Almanach Limousin,* 1860, referring to the Récollets of St. François, so ingeniously subdivided; the Restoration Prefect de Castéja sometimes expressed his doubts about the degree of religious attachment, however, insisting, on July 12, 1816 (1M 99), that "Christian morality is singularly neglected" except by middle-class women. Most sources disagree with him.

19. The following discussion relies on Juge, op. cit., pp. 24–26; *Almanach Limousin,* 1863, "Les Ostensions"; Guibert, op. cit., pp. 5–193; idem, "Les Anciennes Confréries de la basilique de St. Martial," *BSAHL* 43 (1895); esp. pp. 286–87. See Limouzin-Lamothe, op. cit., pp. 199–200. The confraternities of St. Loup and St. Emilie also survived.

20. Guibert, "Les Confréries de Pénitents," op. cit., pp. 133–34.

21. Ibid., pp. 33, 92 (penitents were included in the degree of August 1792).

22. Ibid., pp. 173–74, 189. The prefect's estimate of 3,900 included: purple, 700; gray, 700; blue, 600; feuille-morte, 600; black, 500; and violet, 400.

23. Ibid., p. 186; 3M 3, fonds de l'évêché, PHV May 31, 1827, April 5, 1827, the latter referring to a ban on the representation of the mysteries and actions of saints in the processions; and, n.d. [1825], noting that the confraternity of St. Martial had "gravely troubled order" with their weapons.

24. MR 1300, 1842: "A group of country people arrive at the entrance to the Champ de Juillet, on the edge of three foul holes, filled with greenish, stagnant water. Each person, in turn—most with his hat in hand and head bowed—kneels down, murmurs several Our Fathers, then washes certain parts of the body—some the arm, others the hand, or even the head; they tell me that in their minds this all-powerful ritual can avoid or exorcise pain." See also Eugen Weber, *Peasants into Frenchmen: The Modernization of Rural France, 1870–1914* (Stanford, Calif., 1976), esp. pp. 23–29. Weber does not mention the fact that this rite took place on the edge of the city and not deep in "savage" countryside. See also Corbin, *Archaïsme et modernité en Limousin,* 2 vols. (Paris, 1975), pp. 619–92. Prosper de Tournefort was born in Villes-sur-Auzon in the Vaucluse in 1761; after studying law at the University of Aix, he became a priest, emigrating to Italy during the Revolution. In 1811 he was briefly imprisoned in Paris for his efforts to assist exiled cardinals. He became bishop of Limoges in 1824, replacing de Pins (1822–23), whose predecessor had been du Bourg (1802–22).

25. *Almanach Limousin,* 1860; "Les Ostensions"; 3M 2, fonds de l'évêché; 2V 3, etc. The Ostensions may have begun in 1211, and for a while they occurred several times a year. In 1827 the keys to the *chasse* containing the relics of St. Martial were kept by the mayor and the bishop, as well as by the confraternity.

26. 1M 203, *affiche,* April 30, 1821; Fıc III Haute-Vienne 10, PHV October 11, 1820.

27. *Almanach Limousin,* 1862.

28. MR 1300, report of L. J. Dulamon; see also Juge, op. cit., p. 45.

29. *Almanach Limousin,* 1862, "La Boucherie de Limoges"; AML, "F"; 123 o 7(24).

30. See Adrien Delor, *La Corporation des bouchers à Limoges* (Limoges, 1877); *Almanach Limousin,* 1862; M. le Marquis de Moussac, *Une Corporation d'autrefois encore vivante aujourd'hui* (Paris, 1892); Septime Gorceix, "La Corporation des bouchers et la confrérie de Saint Aurélien," in *Limoges à travers les siècles* (Li-

moges, 1946), pp. 35–39; see esp. Paul Verdurier, "Une survivance du moyen-age: La corporation des bouchers de Limoges," unpublished manuscript, Bibliothèque municipale de Limoges.

31. Ibid., esp. Verdurier, op. cit.
32. These nicknames were noted in the census of 1841 and in subsequent censuses, as well as in the departmental *almanachs*.
33. AML, census of 1841.
34. *Almanach Limousin,* 1862.
35. Ibid.
36. Verdurier, op. cit.; a petition of twelve butchers in 1814 (FɪC III Haute-Vienne 7) called the attention of the restored monarchy to certain officials who "ask you to give orders, apparently in the name of our paternal government, but really in the name of Robespierre and Bonaparte, whom several administrators continue to carry in their hearts and continue to criminally go after those citizens who wanted to resist their oppression."
37. 2V 3, reports on the Ostensions: *Almanach Limousin,* 1862, "Les Ostensions."
38. Verdurier, op. cit.
39. Ibid.
40. See discussion in 123 o 7(24).
41. Common complaints in 4M 43, 44, 53; reports of the commissioners of police, 1819, 1820, 1828.
42. 123 o 7(24).
43. 3M 57, "liste générale des électeurs communaux," 1834; Barthélemy Cibot *aîné dit* Sans-quartier owned such land; Cibot *aîné dit* Goudin owned land in both circumscriptions of Limoges (inter- and extra-muros) and in the commune of Ambazac, to the north, near several important markets.
44. 123 o 7(24); Verdurier, op. cit.
45. 123 o 4(7), PHV June 29, 1822, and decree of mayor, June 21, 1822 (". . . will be considered as a prostitute and submitted to such measures . . . any girl or woman designated as such by public opinion"); 4M 114, Etat nominatif des femmes publiques qui se trouvent dans la commune de Limoges au 14 novembre 1824.
46. F7 9711, PHV August 24, 1816; 133 o 4(7), PHV June 29, 1822; and mayor's decree of June 21.
47. 1M 120, mayor of Limoges, report of May 20, 1816.
48. 4M 114, PHV April 11, 1827; letter of Madame Gossély, September 9, 1830.
49. 1M 24, letter of the procureur général (henceforth PGL) and of deputy mayor, August 28, 1818, and September 29, 1818; 4M 114, "état nominatif des femmes publiques," and other reports. The *Nouvelles éphémérides* reported that in one year 178 prostitutes were admitted to the *Bons secours;* of these 135 were cured or reclaimed by their families, while 23 died.
50. AG MR 1300, "Mémoire sur les environs de Limoges," 1842; F7 9711, PHV May 6, 1819; Fray-Fournier, "Limoges et les bonnes villes," *BSAHL* 52 (1903): 351. See also Corbin, op. cit., pp. 321–35. Texier-Olivier, op. cit., remarked that the education of daughters of artisans was particularly neglected, beyond the details of keeping house and sometimes cotton spinning; the result, he believed, was "loose morals."
51. Lachtygier, op. cit., pp. 116–20.
52. Ibid., pp. 92–96; Pierre Cousteix, "La Vie ouvrière dans la Haute-Vienne sous la Restauration, *L'Information Historique* (November 1952): 181.

53. F7 9711, PHV February 4, 1818 (who indicated that all Limoges families knew how to stretch their means by baking potatoes in their bread); Lachtygier, op. cit., pp. 98–99; Corbin, op. cit., pp. 65–68.

54. Lachtygier, op. cit., p. 30.

55. See Olwen Hufton, *The Poor in Eighteenth-Century France* (Oxford, 1974).

56. Lachtygier, op. cit., p. 102; *Nouvelles éphémérides*. The Bureau de Bienfaisance helped two thousand families—one third of which resided in Limoges—in one year. See also MR 1300, which compares prices and wages in 1789, 1801, and 1831.

57. Texier-Olivier, op. cit., pp. 96, 100. He also noted that the dress of Limoges's artisans seemed halfway between that of the city and the countryside.

58. 4M 44, police reports of February 10 and June 30, 1820.

59. F7 9711, PHV June 18 and 19, 1816; Lachtygier, op. cit., p. 102.

60. 1M 133, PHV June 19, 1816.

61. 4M 53, daily reports of the municipal police, 1828; F9 1041, reporting on many deserters in the region. Nine were arrested in 1828, "a fact that should be attributed to the almost invincible disgust that the people of this department have for military service." *Nouvelles éphémérides*, p. 369. 3M 3, fonds de l'évêché, PHV December 21, 1825, complaining that despite posted laws, "mobs of beggars and vagabonds come to Limoges and form bands." He reminded the clergy that giving at the doors of churches was "the least beneficial of charities."

62. F7 9711, May 7, 1817, gendarmerie report: PHV September 3, 1824; 4M 53, police report, December 30, 1828. A judicial report in U Cour 174, for example, noted that one Joseph Loustand, a baker sentenced to five years in prison for theft, was publicly exposed at the place des Arènes, with a sign that indicated "in large and readable letters, his name, profession, home, penalty, and the reason for his condemnation"; Marie Malefont, a domestic, twenty-four years of age and born in nearby Pierre Buffière, was to be exposed for one hour after having been sentenced to one year and a twenty-five franc fine for stealing from her master's house. F7 9580, PHV December 14, 1827, June 22 and November 24, 1828.

63. The police themselves were hardly above suspicion; some of them "spent almost the whole day gambling and drinking in cafés; they know how to obtain, by vexatious means, the money necessary for such expenses" (F7 9711, July 2, 1818).

64. F7 9711, PHV May 6, 1819; *Nouvelles éphémérides*, p. 212; *Almanach Limousin*, 1875.

65. Juge, op. cit., pp. 46ff.; also noted by Joinville in MR 1300, 1842. Juge may have been contrasting them with such merchants as Bourdeau de la Judie, who made a fortune benefiting from Turgot's roads and was ennobled in 1762. See M. J. Mazabraud, "Une famille de noblesse commerçante de Limoges au XVIIIe siècle: Les Bourdeau de la Judie," Mémoire de maîtrise, Université de Poitiers, 1970.

66. F1C III Haute-Vienne 4, letter of a "friend of the king," to Int. January 18, 1816; *Nouvelles éphémérides*, pp. 224–25, written by F. Laforest, himself a textile merchant, who was undoubtedly thinking of Juge when he defended the commerce of luxury items, such as ivory, crystal, and bronze. See Michel C. Kiener and Jean-Claude Peyronnet, *Quand Turgot regnait en Limousin* (Paris, 1979), pp. 89–90.

67. 3M 57, "liste générale des électeurs communaux," 1834. Texier-Olivier had referred to "commerce intermédiare ou commerce de spéculation" (op. cit., pp. 516–17), noting that the number of "commissaires de marchandises et de roulage se sont multipliés depuis quinze ans."

68. F7 9711, PHV report of May 6, 1819; *Nouvelles éphémérides*, p. 223; Merchants like Noualhier, Pétiniaud, and Laforest seemed to have specialized in specific re-

gions like Clermont, Beaucaire, and Bordeaux. The commune of Limoges had 6,055 hectares, 2,371 of which were cultivated (39.1 percent). The remainder consisted of: meadows and pastures, 30 percent; chestnut groves, 8.6 percent; woods, 6.6 percent; buildings and roads, 6 percent; vineyards, .003 percent (16 hectares); miscellaneous (water, etc.), 3.5 percent. Limoges's hinterland offered some of the most prosperous land in the department, particularly along the Vienne. The map of the city in 1838 clearly shows the extent of gardening along the faubourgs. The commune produced 31 percent of its wheat, 30 percent of its potatoes, 75 percent of its buckwheat, and 8 percent of its oats. In addition, 5,000 annual hectoliters of small grains, vegetables, and radishes were consumed in Limoges. The woods of the commune produced about 8 percent of the wood used (including consumption in the porcelain industry). About 100 cattle or bulls, 800 cows, 400 calves, 2,500 sheep, 4,500 ewes, 500 goats, and 3,000 pigs lived in the commune in 1837, in addition to some 600 horses.

69. F7 9711, PHV May 6, 1819; Cousteix, "La Vie ouvrière dans la Haute-Vienne sous la Restauration," op. cit., pp. 178–79. Lachtygier, op. cit., pp. 38ff. The *Nouvelles éphémérides* complained about the difficulty of finding long-term credit.

70. F7 9711, PHV April 26, 1816; *Nouvelles éphémérides,* pp. 213–15, noted the lack of a "docile and laborious" work force, comparing Limoges's workers unfavorably with the inmates who worked in the regional prison, "an inexhaustible nursery of weavers who are submissive and disciplined . . ." (p. 214).

71. Juge, op. cit., p. 63; Lachtygier, op. cit., pp. 83–85; Cousteix, "La Vie ouvrière dans la Haute-Vienne sous la Restauration," op. cit., pp. 178–81. AG MR 1300 noted that over half of the 736 men and about two thirds of the women in the prison listed their occupation as weavers; almost certainly many, if not most, picked up that trade in prison. The largest spinning factory was that owned by Romanet, on the route de Paris; he employed another 150 workers in prison.

72. Camille Grellier, *L'Industrie de la porcelaine en Limousin* (Paris, 1908), offers an account of the origins of the industry; Lachtygier, op. cit., pp. 41–53; *Le Populaire du Centre,* extract, n.d., in the Archives départementales de la Haute-Vienne.

73. Grellier, op. cit.; Louis Lacrocq, "Le Flottage des bois sur la Vienne, le Taurion et leurs affluents," *BSAHL* 74 (1932); 337–67; the shore workers held a lower status and, unlike the real boatmen, were not fed nor provided with tobacco by their masters; F12 2439, letter of Tharaud (a former employee of the elder François Alluaud), February 11, 1818; 9M 29, General Director of Taxation to the PHV, February 14, 1818; the Municipal Council apparently supported Baignol's unsuccessful request for exemption.

74. Grellier, op. cit., pp. 231–36. Initial costs could be as much as sixty thousand francs.

75. Ibid., p. 236. In 1808 there had been 5 porcelain manufacturers in the region employing 324 workers (Texier-Olivier, op. cit.).

76. Grellier, op. cit., pp. 10–61; AML, census of 1841; unofficial census of 1848 (taken by the provisional government). One half of all porcelain produced in Limoges was sent to Paris for decoration; the other half, decorated or not, was sold directly from Limoges.

77. Lachtygier, op. cit., pp. 84–88.

78. Ibid., p. 104; Grellier, op. cit., pp. 231–36.

79. AG MR 1300, Joinville; Lachtygier, op. cit., pp. 24ff. Texier-Olivier believed that the Revolution had brought a flood of merchants and master artisans, in addition to peasants seeking to become artisans in the city.

80. For example, the debate between Alfred Cobban and Lenore O'Boyle, "The Middle

Class in Western Europe, 1815–48," *American Historical Review* 71, no. 3 (April 1966); 826–45; and Alfred Cobban, "The Middle Class in France, 1815–1848," *French Historical Studies* 5 (Spring 1967); 39–52. See the brilliant study of Adeline Daumard, *Les Bourgeois de Paris au XIXe siècle* (Paris, 1970). Seven nobles were among the fifty-six leading *négociants* in 1770. Michel Kiener and Jean-Claude Peyronnet have written (op. cit., p. 89) that the Limousin nobility "paraît avoir toujours répugné à quitter complètement le monde du négoce et de la marchandise avec lequel elle restait de toute manière en liaison étroite." With this in mind, the last years of the Restoration appear as a kind of aristocratic reaction.

81. 3M 57, "liste générale des électeurs communaux," 1834. The *reconnaissances militaires* undertaken in the years 1826 and 1831 divided the population of Limoges into the following categories: 900 *cultivateurs,* 300 *gens de commerce,* 4,000 artisans, 2,000 day laborers, and 2,000 domestics (1826); 400 civil and military officials, 40 *rentiers,* 60 manufacturers, 1,500 *gens de commerce,* 7,000 artisans, and 2,960 day laborers (1831).

82. Fɪc III Haute-Vienne 4, "listes des éligibles."

83. Ibid., and 3M 36, "listes des électeurs et jurés," 1829–30.

84. Fɪc III Haute-Vienne 4, "listes des éligibles"; for example, François Pouyat paid a *patente* of 45.72 francs in the commune in Isle and 187.45 francs in Limoges, out of a total tax contribution of 1,112.79 francs; even Jérome Laforest, wholesale merchant and author of the self-congratulatory section on commerce in the *Nouvelles éphémérides,* paid only 172.60 out of his 385.79 franc tax through the *patente;* one of the Ardants, a manufacturer, paid a business tax of 227.45 out of 1,917.05 francs. The growing role of commerce may itself be compared with the "Liste de cent plus forts contribuables de la commune de Limoges," July 15, 1813 (1M100)—which lists 103:

48 *agriculteurs*	10 officials	and one: baron, miller, baker, doctor, merchant,
8 *propriétaires*	2 lawyers	former soldier, engineer, transport entrepreneur,
21 *négociants*	2 innkeepers	pharmacist, manufacturer, dyer, and notary.

85. Census of 1832 (which includes only the south canton); 3M 57, "liste générale des électeurs communaux," 1834; Lachtygier, op. cit., pp. 105–6.

86. *Almanach Limousin,* 1860, "Limoges depuis cent ans."

87. 3M 57, "liste générale des électeurs communaux"; AML, census of 1841; MR 1300, "Notes militaires sur la position central de la ville de Limoges . . . par Colonel Brousseraud en 1821 et 1822."

88. This particular horse race was mentioned several times in the *Annales de la Haute-Vienne.* Texier-Olivier, op. cit., pp. 96–100. Police found it difficult to infiltrate the milieu of the laboring poor, who were set apart by language, dress, and culture.

89. Camille Jouhanneaud, "Notes pour servir à l'histoire de la musique à Limoges au XIXe siècle," *BSAHL* 55 (1905): 415ff.; 56 (1906): 68, 88ff.; *Annales de la Haute-Vienne,* June 16, 1826; F21 1226, report written for Int. November 18, 1825; Juge, op. cit.

90. Jouhanneaud, op. cit., pp. 52, 63–68, 76; F21 1226, "théâtre de Limoges," December 21, 1828. The 1828 season included "The Old Bachelor," "Robin Hood," "La Dame blanche," "Le Devin du village," and Destouches' "Le Philosophe marié."

91. Juge, op. cit., p. 92; *Annales de la Haute-Vienne,* December 29, 1826; *Almanach Limousin,* 1860, "Limoges depuis cent ans."

92. Juge, op. cit., p. 94.

93. Ibid., p. 27.
94. F7 9777, PHV May 15, 1816. The *Tableau statistique,* vol. 1, indicates that 1,400 *enfants-trouvés* were in the charitable system in 1824, 5,500 between 1824 and 1833, and 1,500 at the end of 1833. The *enfants-trouvés* were listed in the census of 1832.
95. Juge, op. cit., pp. 95–96; Prefect de Castéja also referred to the menace of luxury, of a "mob of outsiders who are in almost exclusive possession of the commerce of those items most subject to the caprices of changes in taste." (F7 9711, May 6, 1819)
96. Juge, op. cit., pp. 20–21; Texier-Olivier, op. cit., pp. 101–2, wrote that "the merchant, obsessed by his business, knows only his books and his calculations; he rarely communicates and one hardly ever sees him in the cafés or public places; he rarely goes to the theater. He avoids costly pleasures and those who seek only the charms of society complain that they cannot find them in Limoges to the same degree as in other towns of the same size."
97. 1M 225, PHV November 7, 1822.
98. 4M 102, "liste des cafés, cabinets de lecture et auberges."
99. 1M 24, mayor of Limoges, May 25, 1815; *Nouvelles éphémérides.*
100. *Annales de la Haute-Vienne,* May 16, 1828.
101. Ibid.
102. List in 1M 126.
103. *Annales de la Haute-Vienne,* February 6, 1829.
104. Ibid., see also subsequent issues.
105. Ibid., February 6, 1829.
106. *Nouvelle éphémérides,* pp. 127–28, 225. "For the successful businessman the ultimate ambition is a country house where he can spend his last years looking after a few trees and growing some flowers."
107. Juge, op. cit., p. 43, claimed that "il y a une ligne de démarcation bien prononcée entre les nobles d'extraction, les nouveaux ennoblie et les bourgeois"; The *Catalogue des Gentilshommes du Limousin par MM Louis de la Roque et Edouard de Barthélemy* (Paris, 1864), listed the families of de Roulhac, Lamy, de la Pisse, F. Martin, P. M. Chapelle, Noailhé, Bordeau, Pétiniaud, de St. Priest, de Villelume, de Montbron, de la Bastide, and Benoît de Lostende (of Isle) as having been nobles before the Revolution.
108. 8M 16.
109. A summary of the deliberations of the council can be found in AML.
110. Ibid., summaries for 1828; one member, Fray-Fournier, was replaced in 1825; he had not come to Limoges from the country, where he lived, for a year (2M 38), ordinance of March 24, 1825.
111. 2M2, fonds de l'évêché, mayor of Limoges, letter of March 21, 1828; IT 86^A, bishop of Limoges, May 6, 1828; 1M 99, PHV March 19, 1817: "The people show only a profound indifference for anything related to politics"; BB18 1157, PGL March 5, April 11, and April 23, 1828; F19 354, letter of the bishop, May 2 and 5, 1828; Int. April 26. The missionaries had, early in April, accused students of the *collège* of participating in the disturbances. Some parents blamed the sons of commercial families new to the city who were *externes* at the *collège.* Bishop Prosper blamed the march of impious godlessness and demanded that the government take strong action against "the artisans of disorder."
112. *Annales de la Haute-Vienne,* July 5, 1825; *Nouvelles éphémérides,* p. 214; Juge had associated the acquisitiveness of the new bourgeoisie with a changing attitude apparent among the workers: "On his side, the worker sang to lighten the burden of the day; he sings no longer." *Annales de la Haute-Vienne* noted that Conseil

conciliated 109 of 113 affairs considered in 1829; F7 9711, PHV July 12, 1816; and Z25, fonds Alluaud.

113. F7 9711, PHV March 3, 1817, noted also in 1M 99, PHV June 18, 1816 and May 1, 1817.

114. R 160, letter of the mayor, August 3, 1823; F7 9711, January 1, 1817, citing rumors such as a naval battle near St. Helena, Marie-Louise arriving in Lyon, and so on.

115. R 160, mayor of Limoges, January 12, 1819; and August 3, 1823; PHV May 11, 1822.

Chapter Two

1. Texier-Olivier, op. cit., p. 101. See Paul Hanson, "The Federalist Revolt of 1793: A Comparative Study of Caen and Limoges," diss., University of California, 1981. Hanson compares the federalism of Caen with the Jacobinism of Limoges, citing, among other explanatory factors, the relative underdevelopment of Limoges's economy and its greater dependence upon the state. Hanson emphasizes the "vitality of popular politics" (p. 388) and even finds "agent democracy" in Limoges, where "the commercial elite was unable to maintain control over municipal affairs (p. 387)." Lacking a homogeneous elite, rivalries between the Jacobin Club and the moderate Amis de la Paix reflected a struggle between the *moyenne* and the *haute* bourgeoisie. He notes the possible influence of the city's rich religious associational life.

2. See, for example, 4M 86, police reports, early August 1814.

3. 4M 104, Int. January 8, 1820, and PHV March 15, 1822, and July 21, 1822; F7 6741, PHV March 2 and December 31, 1819, and June 14, 1820 (asserting that "la ville de Limoges et le département de la Haute-Vienne attendent dans la paix et peut-être avec une sorte d'insouciance les événements; ils ne les provoqueront jamais"); F7 9711, July 15, 1820; 1M 125, PHV December 31, 1820; 1M 120, list of political crimes through January 28, 1816; F7 4215[13], gendarmerie report, January 4, 1820. The White Terror was quite mild in the department, as the prevotal court discussed only nine cases, meting out two life sentences for peasants arrested during grain disturbances; see F7 9711, PHV April 25, 1816, and *BSAHL* 82 (1948): *procès-verbal* 89.

4. F7 9711, PHV July 15, 1820, and F7 6755, Int. September 22, 1828, and report for that month; Sherman Kent, *The Election of 1827 in France* (Cambridge, Mass., 1975), p. 176. There is no evidence to support Kent's claim that the Limoges left was "precious close to republicanism, often with a strong Bonapartist tinge" (p. 175).

5. F7 6772, PHV July 31, 1827, noting that the public spirit in the department "s'est notablement gâté"; F7 6714, PHV November 8 and 30, 1827; F7 6777, PHV July 21, 1828; BB18 1150, PGL July 5, 1827; F1c III Haute-Vienne 4, September 20, 1827. Bankruptcies in 1826 increased by two thirds over the previous year; David H. Pinkney, *The French Revolution of 1830* (Princeton, N.J., 1972), p. 59; Kent, op. cit., pp. 1, 3, 82–84, 90–94, 117. On the economic crisis and its significance, see Paul Gonnet, "Esquisse de la crise économique en France de 1827 à 1832," *Revue d'histoire économique et sociale* 33 (1955): 249–92, and John M. Merriman, ed., *1830 in France* (New York, 1975).

6. F1c III Haute-Vienne 4, PHV November 10, 1827.

7. F1c III Haute-Vienne 4, PHV November 13, 1827.

8. Ibid., PHV September 9, 1827, estimating that out of 289 electors, 75 would vote with the ministry. Desalles Beauregard had represented the town at the coronation of Charles X in Reims and contributed to the construction of a memorial commemorating the ill-fated royalist landing at Quiberon, but he had become a liberal by 1827.

9. *BSAHL* 60, "François Alluaud," session of July 15, 1910 (443–505); F1b II Haute-Vienne 3, PHV April 30, 1815. His father had belonged to a Masonic lodge.

10. F1c III Haute-Vienne 4, PHV November 13, 1827.

11. F1c III Haute-Vienne 4, PHV October 24 and November 8, 1827.

12. F1c III Haute-Vienne 4, PHV November 18, 1827. Bourdeau received 313 votes, compared with 110 for Mousnier Buisson; the latter was elected by 87 out of 172 votes in the departmental *collège*.

13. BB18 1155, PGL February 5 and April 23; F7 677, PHV July 31, 1827; F7 6741, PHV November 30, 1827, claimed that "young men, whose social position should have rendered them more circumspect, sought to incite disorder." The *Annales de la Haute-Vienne* called the young bourgeois "our sansculottes."

14. F1c III Haute-Vienne 4, Mousnier Buisson to Royer Collard, April 18, 1828, and election results; F7 6772, PHV October 7 and November 7, 1828.

15. F7 6772, PHV July 2, 1828.

16. Ibid., PHV February 6, June 9, August 5, November 6, December 13 and 14, 1828; 6M 331, notes on inventories of the bakeries and mayor of Limoges, September 6 and November 5, 1829. The only cause for optimism was the building boom; never, Coster believed, had so many people been employed building "elegant and spacious houses." See also J. C. Parot, "1830 à Limoges" (Mémoire complémentaire pour le diplôme d'études supérieures, Université de Poitiers, 1964).

17. F7 6772, PHV November 6, 1829.

18. Ibid., PHV April 4 and October 9, 1829, and January 14, 1830; F1c III Haute-Vienne 4, PHV January 18, 1816; *Annales de la Haute-Vienne,* February 12, 1830; *Le Contribuable,* May 12, 1830. Abria was a clerk for Descoutures, a liberal notary; Peyramont was a young lawyer. Dumas had been *procureur général-syndic* of the department in 1790–91 and had founded the Société populaire in Limoges, but he fell into disfavor with the Jacobins, was charged with aiding the émigrés, namely, Pétiniaud de Beaupeyrat, and was jailed. He was released, after being in prison in Paris, when the Société populaire came to his defense (see the fifth chapter in Hanson, op cit.).

19. *Le Contribuable,* prospectus. On August 29, 1829, a letter sent from Limoges appeared in *Le Constitutionnel* indicating that commerce and industry in Limoges was suffering because of dissatisfaction with the new ministry (F7 6772, PHV September 15, 1829). Coster secretly gathered information on the porcelain industry; deputy mayor Pouyat denied that the industry was suffering, insisting that there had been no serious damage to the local economy since a bankruptcy in May 1828 (9M 29, PHV September 12, 1829, and Pouyat, September 14). Pouyat did note that some wholesale merchants had been hurt by Limoges's manufacturers increasingly selling directly to retailers.

20. *Annales de la Haute-Vienne,* April 16 and May 14, 1830, the former issue referring to "les ordures vomies par une bouche immode." F7 6772, PHV September 16, 1829, and March 1, 1830.

21. F7 6772, PHV November 29, 1829.

22. Ibid., PHV September 16, 1829, noting that "this light fermentation is only found

in *la classe des marchands en boutique,* [as] the artisans hardly get mixed up in politics."

23. Arthur Young, *Travels During the Years 1787, 1788 and 1789* (London, 1791), p. 14.

24. F19 5682, n.d. (1824); 6M 1, mayor of Limoges, July 5, 1828, sympathizing with the bishop's complaint about nude bathing: "I deplore, as you do, this usage that presents a civilized population as if they were a horde of savages"; *Annales de la Haute-Vienne,* April 13, 1827; Parot, op. cit., pp. 10–11, quoting the bishop's letter to the Minister of Foreign Affairs, February 23, 1830. In 1826 Prosper urged Charles X to take strong action against "unrestrained license, which, without any respect for the most saintly things and most sacred persons, each day spreads its corrupting poison and seeks to pervert our attachments and beliefs" (F19 5682).

25. BB18 1149, PGL June 7, 1827; *Annales de la Haute-Vienne,* February 19 and 26, 1830; F7 9711, PHV April 25, 1816; police report of April 20–21, 1828 (4M 53).

26. F7 6772, PHV January 9, 1830; *Annales de la Haute-Vienne,* January 1, 1830; 3M fonds de l'évêché, PHV December 28, 1829, and January 4, 1830.

27. F7 6772, PHV January 9, 1830; *Annales de la Haute-Vienne,* January 1, 15, and 22, 1830; *Le Contribuable,* May 12, 1830.

28. *Annales de la Haute-Vienne,* October 9, 1829. In 1824 the mayor had been accused by Descoutures—who became a leading liberal—of obtaining money for his friend, the secretary of the town hall; *Réponse de M. le Bon de la Bastide, maire de cette ville, juillet 1824* (Limoges, 1824).

29. 123 o 7(24), PHV July 21, 1830; F7 6772, PHV December 14, 1829, and July 21, 1830; *Raisons de décider,* the petition, and other relevant letters in F3 II Haute-Vienne 6; see also F2 II Haute Vienne 2 on the rue du Duc de Bordeaux, now the rue Adrien Dubouché.

30. *Le Contribuable,* May 12, 1830. See F7 6772, PHV March 1, 1830; F7 4215^14, gendarmerie report of April 8, 1830; Baron Coster worked frantically on behalf of the ministry despite intermittent illness, which necessitated several periods of recuperation (F1b II Haute-Vienne 4).

31. *Annales de la Haute-Vienne,* July 16, 1830.

32. *Le Contribuable,* July 12, 1830; Parot, op. cit., p. 12; 2M 3 fonds de l'évêché. Victor Alluaud was mentioned as Limoges's most important liberal in PHV September 16, 1829 (F7 6772); Fic III Haute-Vienne 4, PHV May 31, 1830.

33. *Le Contribuable,* July 5 and 12, 1830; Fic III Haute-Vienne 4, election. In his *profession de foi* Dumont St. Priest promised to "appeler sans cesse le regard du Roi sur l'industrie et le commerce qui vivent de l'agriculture." Dumont St. Priest received 110 of 197 votes; Bourdeau-Lajudie was elected with 102, while Mousnier Buisson received 92 votes, de Montbrun 86, and de Beaubreuil 1.

34. *Le Contribuable,* July 12 and 26, 1830; *Annales de la Haute-Vienne,* July 9 and 16, 1830.

35. BB18 1186, Coster, July 29, 1830. See Pinkney, op. cit., for the best account of the revolution in Paris.

36. BB18 1186, PHV July 29 and September 1, 1830. During the 1837 strike by turners and molders one donor to the workers' fund signed himself "un anonyme, ami des ouvriers que l'on payait en 1830 pour ne pas travailler et à qui l'on réfuse aujourd'hui le salaire nécessaire à leurs besoins, 1 franc"; another gift came from "des hommes qui n'ont jamais été de ceux qui ont payé les ouvriers pour insurger en 1830, 110 francs" (1M 130); See Paul Mantoux, "Patrons et ouvriers en juillet

1830," *Revue d'histoire moderne et contemporaine* 3 (1901): 291–96. Alluaud's appointed provisional administration held power until August 7. On August 9 *Le Contribuable* noted the rumor about de la Bastide's sentry. See also Parot, op. cit., and the *procès-verbaux* of the Municipal Council, AML.

37. *Le Contribuable,* August 9 and 16.

38. 1M 127; see James Rule and Charles Tilly, "Political Process in Revolutionary France, 1830–32," in John M. Merriman, ed., *1830 in France,* pp. 41–85.

39. Municipal Council *procès-verbaux,* AML; *Le Contribuable,* August issues, F1c III Haute-Vienne 10, PHV October 31, 1832. Philabert Chamiot-Avanturier (born 1794) was elected on the first ballot with 228 votes to Bourdeau's 117 and Bourdeau-Lajudie's 51. He paid 1,221.01 francs in taxes and had invested much of his income, which came from wholesale trade in land. Many *électeurs* paid part of their taxes in a rural commune where they owned land. Madame Léger, "Etude des listes électorales du département de la Haute-Vienne sous la monarchie de juillet (1830–48)" (Mémoire secondaire pour le diplôme d'études supérieures. Université de Bordeaux, n.d.). Subsequently the number of electors declined slightly in the arrondissement of Limoges during the July Monarchy, whereas the number in the districts of St. Yrieix and Rochechouart almost doubled. Arrondissement of Limoges, *ville:* 1832 (450); 1833 (432); 1837 (474); 1840 (508); 1843 (486); 1847 (455); and 1848 (436). Between 1845 and 1846 seventeen wholesale merchants lost their eligibility.

40. *Almanach Limousin,* 1860, "Limoges depuis cent ans," pp. 80–93.

41. *Le Nouveau Contribuable,* May 10, 1832.

42. Ibid., and other issues; 2M 38, Municipal Council.

43. *Le Nouveau Contribuable,* March 24, 1832.

44. Ibid.

45. AML, summary of meetings: 1826 (11 meetings); 1827 (7); 1828 (8); 1829 (10); 1830 (32); 1831 (30); 1832 (33); 1833 (35); 1834 (34); 1835 (28); 1836 (20); 1837 (17); 1838 (21); 1839 (15); 1840 (17); 1841 (16); 1842 (14); 1843 (17); 1844 (15); 1845 (19); 1846 (20); 1847 (20); and 1848 (50). During the first half of 1830 the porcelain manufacturers asked for a lower tax on wood brought into the city. In 1828 Limoges had 295,107 francs and six centimes in receipts, with the *octroi* contributing the major portion (252,000 francs); another 5,202f 68c from the business tax; 247f 94c in municipal fines, and 1,524f 60c from fines collected for *octroi* violations. Alluaud's speech before the municipal elections of 1832 emphasized the role of the Municipal Council in creating an improved urban environment (*Limoges illustré,* March 15, 1908), as well as the importance of electing men with business experience.

46. See 123 o 7(24), PHV November 28, 1829, and letter of Pouyat, for the mayor, December 24, 1829, PHV April 16, 1830, PHV May 9, 10, 12, 1833. Mutual accusations of bad faith and illegal slaughtering were frequent; one inspector estimated that only about half of the animals slaughtered in the city passed through the *abattoir;* some butchers of great wealth were rarely seen there. The butchers signing only with their nicknames (Tacher, Leboeuf, Curaissier, and so on) stated that "police regulations and the precautions of health should always, as much as possible, conciliate sanitary measures with the needs of commerce." The appearance of a butcher wearing a white plume on the *fête Dieu,* which drew whistles of disapproval from onlookers, may not have helped their cause (4M 54, police report, June 12–13, 1831). Several butchers were convicted of selling bad meat (4M 55, police report, November 23–24, 1833). The new slaughterhouse was built on the

ruins of the old château of Beau-séjour (*Limoges et le Limousin,* 1865). AML, series "F." Negotiations between the city and the butchers were always bitter and complicated. The butchers annually paid 58,000 francs in 1816 and 80,000 in 1834 (AML "F"). Thirty-two butchers were *censitaires* in 1834, the wealthiest Cibot *aîné dit* Sans-Quartier, the butchers claimed that their own longevity proved that there was nothing wrong with conditions on their street (AML "F," petition of the butchers' syndics, July 4, 1833). On April 4, 1831, one butcher asked the mayor to intervene to force Léonard Cibot, "whose actions paralyze and torment us," to pay his share of the tax and to stop slaughtering every day instead of three times a week" (Z 25, fonds Alluaud); see also 4M 55, police reports of May 19–20, June 3–4, 4–5, and 6–7, and August 6–7, 1833; BB18 1218, September 16, 1833.

47. F3 II Haute-Vienne 6, relevant dossier, particularly the letter of Alluaud dated October 8, 1831.

48. Alfred Leroux, "Délibérations de la Chambre consultative des arts et manufactures de Limoges," *BSAHL* 52 (1903): 200–79; for example, the response to the government circular of February 29, 1831, claiming that factories were in worse shape after the revolution.

49. Leroux, op. cit., response of May 6. The *Almanach Limousin,* 1867, noted that the Alluaud municipality covered the "sewer" of the rue Palvézy, opened the rue de l'Amphithéâtre, and worked on the rue de Paris. The Tribunal de commerce heard twenty-five hundred cases a year.

50. AML "D," Alluaud letter of February 21, 1831; F9 733, PHV October 30, 1830; Int. April 6, 1831; Dumas, September 11, 1831; 1M 209, PHV July 30, 1831; *Le Contribuable,* April 19, 1831.

51. Dumas put the strength of the Guard at 979; the "official" figures in 1831 were 6,586 eligible, of whom 1,519 were uniformed and 1,434 armed, with 2,282 fully outfitted, of whom 577 had served in the military (F9 733). *Le Contribuable,* April 26, 1831; F9 733, PHV August 13, and mayor of Limoges, September 20, 1833, indicate that the proposed reorganization by quarter never occurred, as does subsequent correspondence in 1840 and 1847 (R 161).

52. F7 4215[14], gendarmerie report, October 7 and December 6, 1831; F9 733, PHV May 4, 1833. "Groups" formed to receive news of the Lyon insurrection; the National Guard received live ammunition.

53. Municipal Council *procès-verbaux,* AML, *Le Contribuable,* August, 1830, passim.

54. F7 4215[14], Commander of 11th Gendarmerie Division, September 10; 1M 127, PHV September 1 and 6, 1830; and BB18 1187, September 1. The bakers received damages from the Municipal Council. Several groups of workers had asked that the price of bread be lowered.

55. BB18 1187, PHV September 1.

56. U Cour 174 and 190; BB18 1187, PGL September 3; those born outside Limoges included two workers from St. Léonard, and one each from Condat, Beaume, Neuvic, the Dordogne, and the Cantal. The porcelain worker was an *engazetier.*

57. AML, "D," letters from workers dated September 1, 3, and 9.

58. *Le Constitutionnel* for December 20 reported two bankruptcies in Limoges.

59. Leroux, op. cit., p. 198.

60. Grellier, op. cit., pp. 237–40; the municipality considered establishing a *société anonyme,* which would serve as a *banque de secours.* A loan of 200,000 francs was authorized by the government on January 5, 1831. Loans from the government and private citizens helped finance the purchase of 3,370 hectoliters of grain costing over 63,000 francs.

61. 1M 127, PHV September 23; Minister of Finance, October 1. Tax receipts dropped rapidly, and on September 5 the PHV requested that troops remain in the city. See also 4M 105, Alluaud, September 23; PHV September 23; director of tax office, September 15; and 1M 100, PHV March 26, 1831.

62. *Le Contribuable*, August 23, 1830.

63. *Le Contribuable*, August 30, 1830.

64. 1M 127, October 2, 1830; the Minister of Interior blamed the Société des amis du peuple.

65. *Le Contribuable*, October 25, 1830; Parot, op. cit., p. 17.

66. *Le Contribuable*, June 7, 1831.

67. June 21 and November 29; Fıc III Haute-Vienne, PHV October 18, 1833; Dumont St. Priest, whom the PHV called "le flambeau du barreau de la cour royale," was born on March 24, 1786; by 1834 he had become only number 137 among the leading taxpayers (315,99 francs). Several nights of disturbances followed his decoration with the Légion d'honneur, with cries of "A bas le juste milieu!" (*Le Contribuable*, June 7, 1831, and 1M 128, PHV June 2, 1831).

68. *Le Contribuable*, June 7 and 21, 1831.

69. *Le Contribuable*, October 18, 1830; Limouzin-Lamothe, op. cit., p. 202; 1M 127, Int. September 21, 1830; 4M 105, Prosper de Tournefort, December 7, 1820. The new members on the council included François Pouyat père, A. Laporte, P. Lezeau, and G. Pouyat, all of whom began serving on September 10; *Analyse des actes et délibérations de l'administration municipale de Limoges*, vol. 2 (Limoges, 1896).

70. 4M 105, PHV September 9 and 29, 1830, Int. February 23, 1831, mayor of Limoges, September 11 and December 10, 1830 (mentioning rumors of secret Carlist meetings near the Poitou); *Le Contribuable*, May 21 and September 20, 1831; 6M 4, mayor, September 20, 1830, and February 24, 1831; F7 4215^{14}, PHV February 22 and 23, 1831; gendarmerie report, March 6, 1831; and police report, June 1, 1832; 2V 9, Minister of Public Instruction, October 21, 1831; F19 481$^{1-3}$, PHV September 29, 1830, Int. February 23 and March 24, 1831; bishop, September 10, 1830, and January 24, 1831; F19 481^{A}, bishop, January 24, 1831, and PHV February 11, 1831; 1M 128, PG February 23, 1831; F7 5733, Commander of 5th Military Division, March 1, 1831, MG, February 23, 1831, and PHV October 25, 1831. Prosper died at 2 P.M. on March 7, 1844, at the age of eighty-three, and was entombed in the Cathedral of St. Etienne.

71. *Le Contribuable* September 20, 1831, and police reports for that month; see also F7 4215^{14}, police report of June 1, 1832.

72. *Le Nouveau Contribuable*, April 19 and 25, 1832, and June 27, 1832, which applauded the temporary lowering of the tax on liquor.

73. *Le Nouveau Contribuable*, July 4, 1832.

74. *Le Nouveau Contribuable*, March 17, 1832, and subsequent issues. The bank favored manufacturers with many workers and had less to offer those needing long-term credit.

75. AML, "D," address of August 6, 1830; *Le Contribuable*, March 21 and June 14, 1831; *Le Nouveau Contribuable*, June 31, 1832; BB18 1326, Int. March 14, 1832 (noting that Dumont St. Priest had asked for one thousand francs for the use of secret police in Limoges); 1M 128, PHV March 16, 1831, and April 23, 1833, mayor of Limoges, October 6, 1832; 4M 54, police report of March 14-15, 1831.

76. 4M 54, police reports of March 15-17, April 18-19, 24-25, and others; 4M 55, October 12-14, and November 9-10, 1833; 1M 128, PGL August 27, 1832; F9 733, PHV May 4, 1833; 1M 100, PHV March 26, 1831; Fıc III Haute-Vienne 10, PHV

October 31, 1832. The only evidence of Napoleonic attachment was one cry of "Long Live Napoléon II" in June 1832, after the controversial arrest of a *plafonnier* for shouting "Long Live Charles X!"

77. F7 4215[14], gendarmerie report, December 6, 1831, noting Saint-Simonian disciples among the "classes aisées"; 4M 54; police reports of May 24–25 and July 29–30, 1831.

78. *Le Contribuable,* November 8, 1831.

79. *Le Contribuable,* August 30 and November 15, 1831; June 20 and October 31, 1832.

80. 4M 55, police reports of February 2–3; 1M 128, police report of May 12, 1833; letter of Rivet, May 20; and PHV May 15 and June 1, 1833; Fic III Haute-Vienne 10, PHV October 31, 1832.

81. F7 6784, PHV July 25 and 27, 1833, mayor of Limoges, July 31, and gendarmerie reports of July 27 and 29; BB18 1217, PGL, July 27 and 28, 1830; F9 733, report of mayor, July 21, 1833, and F7 4215[15], gendarmerie report for 1833. On August 3 the prefect wrote that on the occasion of the anniversary of the revolution, "public enthusiasm was shown for the Revolution of 1830, but not for the person of the king as one would have expected" (F7 6784). Mourgnes was born in 1772 in Montpellier; a former military diplomat and general secretary in the Ministry of the Interior (where he undoubtedly acquired his reputation), he also served as the prefect of the Haute-Marne and the Dordogne (2M 12).

82. See BB18 1217, PGL August 8, 18, and 22, 1833. The two porcelain workers were sent before the Cour d'assises, while the other appeared before the Police Correctional Court. Bac received a twenty-four-hour jail sentence.

83. BB18 1218, PGL September 16 and October 15, 1833, Int. November 4; 4M 55; police reports of September 23–25 and October 12–14, 1833; 1M 128, Int. December 30, 1831. In the first week of September the spinners of Pétiniaud and Jabet, working near Limoges, threatened to strike unless their wages were increased. Dumont St. Priest and the Conseil des prud'hommes intervened to prevent the strike, but the factory soon closed (*Nouvelles éphémérides,* op. cit.). Neither workers nor employers met openly to avoid the appearance of a "coalition." See also J. P. Aguet, *Les Grèves sous la monarchie de juillet* (Geneva, 1954), pp. 101–2; Grellier, *op. cit.,* p. 240; France, Direction du Travail, *Les Associations professionelles ouvrières,* vol. 3 (Paris, 1903), pp. 523–24. About the same time the *relieurs* formed a "coalition," agreeing to do no work for the Maison centrale, whose director had arranged to establish a workshop there, where inmates were paid extremely low wages (4M 55, police report, June 24–25, 1833).

84. Fic III Haute-Vienne 4, PHV October 18, 1833, April 2 and 3, 1834; AML "D," Alluaud, July 27, 1833, banning charivaris. During the next few years the preoccupation with business was such that it was virtually impossible to find anyone who would serve as mayor. One candidate after another begged off; Juge St. Martin did so in 1832, citing "the need to consecrate all of my time to the business of my family" (2M 59).

85. 1M 209, PHV July 25, 1832; *Le Contribuable,* September 20, 1830. See also Z 25, fonds Alluaud, note. The *reconnaissance militaire* of 1842 (MR 1300) mentioned that "since 1830, public officials and the ambitious, that is, the majority of those one calls *the* Haute-Vienne, have withdrawn from the penitents." One can grasp something of this sense of progress and pride in Pierre Grellier, *Tableau descriptif de la ville de Limoges* (Limoges, 1838).

86. *Le Contribuable,* May 23, 1831. The newspaper was called *Nouveau* as of No-

vember 29, 1831. Late in 1832 it had 180 subscribers in the department, compared to 99 of the legitimist *Amis des Lois* and 88 of the *Annales de la Haute-Vienne,* which survived as the organ of the prefecture and a journal of *petites annonces.* *Le Nouveau Contribuable* published its last issue on February 16, 1833, and was followed briefly by *Le Patriote.* Of the Parisian papers, the legitimist *Gazette de France* had the most subscribers in the department (25), followed by the *Constitutionnel* (24), the *Journal des Débats* (24), and *Le National* (12).

87. FIC III Haute-Vienne 4, PHV January 11 and October 18, 1833. Chamiot-Avanturier defeated Bourdeau in the election.

88. *Le Nouveau Contribuable,* April 11, 1832.

89. 4M 55, police reports of June 17 and 18, 1833.

90. John M. Merriman, "Social Conflict in France and the Limoges Revolution of April 27, 1848," *Societas* 4, no. 1 (Winter 1974): 21–38.

91. BB20 361, PGL April 30, 1848.

92. 1M 130, PHV April 17, 21, 28 and May 3 (and subsequent issues), 1837.

93. 1M 130, PHV July 12, 14, August 4, 1837, Int. August 28.

94. *Précis sur la situation véritable des ouvriers et artistes en porcelaine* (Limoges, 1837), 1M 130.

95. M 777 (old *côte*), "Tableau général des sociétés de secours mutuels."

96. BB18 1451, PGL March 23, 1847; Archives départementales de la Creuse, 4M 72.

97. F9 733, mayor, August 18, 1831.

98. Ibid., petition.

99. BB18 1385, PGL July 20 and 27, 1840.

100. See John M. Merriman, *Agony of the Republic: The Repression of the Left in Revolutionary France, 1848–51* (New Haven, Conn., 1978), pp. 7–10.

101. Ibid., pp. 10–13; BB30 361 passim.

102. See Merriman, op. cit., pp. 138–54.

103. Ibid., p. 148.

104. Ibid., pp. 153–54.

Chapter Three

1. M. A. de Louguemar, *Limoges et le congrès scientifique en 1859* (Poitiers, 1859), esp. pp. 21–26 and 66–76. De Louguemar, who noted the "sunny" (?), climate of Limoges, was fascinated both by the speed with which porcelain was shaped and by the enormous heat of the oven that cooked the product in some thirty-six hours: "Cette dernière partie de l'opération est confiée à des chauffeurs dont la vie est sans cesse menacée par les fluxions de poitrine amenées par la brusque et continuelle alternative d'une chaleur intense et de courants d'air auxquels ils sont presque toujours exposés." The scientists were entertained by one Madame Fanny Desnoix-Desvergnes, "la muse du congrès," who recited her "gracious and touching compositions," which included her poem "Mon chat," and sang to honor the victorious in the Crimean War.

2. *Limoges et le Limousin: Guide pour l'étranger* (Limoges, 1865), pp. 142–43; Grellier, op. cit., pp. 248, 255.

3. See Michelle Perrot, "The Three Ages of Industrial Discipline in France," in Merriman, ed., *Consciousness and Class Experience,* pp. 149–68; *Limoges et le Limousin.*

4. Grellier, op. cit., pp. 242–62; Corbin, op. cit., pp. 316–17.

5. Grellier, op. cit. In 1837, of the 250 to 300 workers occupied in the decoration of Limoges porcelain, 80 were *peintres* and *doreurs* and 150 were *brunisseuses*. Auguste Renoir, born in Limoges in 1841, worked as a decorator in Sèvres before moving on to other work.

6. *Almanach Limousin,* 1862 and 1865; Grellier, op. cit., pp. 257–58. In 1861 twenty-nine kilns were fueled by wood and twenty-two by coal; five years later twenty-one were fueled by wood and forty-two by coal (*Almanach Limousin,* 1868). Gas lighting had been introduced about 1845.

7. Grellier, op. cit.; Corbin, op. cit., p. 45; C 968, for 1848; 4M 57, police report of March 31, 1857; BB30 378, PGL October 5, 1861. The *Almanach Limousin,* 1868, counted a total of 3,625 workers in the industry, a significant increase from the 2,162 given by the *Statistique de la France: Industrie,* vol. 4 (Paris, 1852).

8. C 968; Corbin, op. cit., pp. 33 and 35; *Almanach Limousin,* 1868.

9. C 968; Corbin, op. cit., p. 46. *Almanach Limousin,* 1867.

10. *Almanach Limousin,* 1868.

Occupations in Limoges, 1856	
industry	38.1
artisanal	19.5
military	10.8
agriculture	10.5
liberal professions, administration, clergy	5.7
commerce	5.4
rentiers	5.4
others	4.6

Source: Corbin, op. cit., p. 19.

11. *Almanach Limousin,* 1864.

12. AML, census of 1848.

13. Census of 1876.

14. 6M 12, census of 1876; *Almanach Limousin,* 1861ff. With the exception of 1853, more people died in Limoges than were born in the city each year from 1851 through 1859. Between 1849 and 1858 (inclusive) there were 14,330 births (11,185 "legitimate") and 15,776 deaths. Limoges prospered in a moribund region, and her growth came at the expense of the rest of the department.

15. AML, census of 1848. This census, unfortunately, is incomplete; it lists only males because it was prepared with the National Guard in mind.

16. Ibid.

17. Ibid; census of 1876.

18. Jean-Paul Brunet, *Saint Denis: La Ville rouge, 1890–1939* (Paris, 1980), p. 15; cf. Corbin, op. cit., p. 767: "Ce sont les ouvriers des faubourgs qui forment de très loin la majorité au sein de la Société populaire." The census of 1841 listed 112 porcelain workers on the faubourg Montmailler and another 119 day laborers (21.2 percent and 22.6 percent, respectively) of the 526 residents with an occupation listed).

19. Corbin, op. cit., p. 83.

20. *Limoges et le Limousin.* One of the employers who testified after the "Commune" of Limoges asserted that the migrants were apt to be those who owned their own houses (C 3023). Encouraged by a committee of patronage and the Municipal

Council, an investment group, the Société immobilière, drew up plans for a quarter in the faubourgs. The new neighborhood was to encompass about 120,000 square meters, about four times the size of the place Dauphine, at the intersection of the route de Paris and the avenue du Crucifix. Schools and gardens were promised, as well as a "promenade précieuse." Investors were assured of up to 90 percent on their return, and four banks sold shares at 500 francs each (*Almanach Limousin*, 1866).

21. Louis Guibert, "La Foire de St. Loup," *Almanach Limousin*, 1861. Only the magician Gervais seemed to be absent from the 1864 fair; his usual stall was left vacant in the hope that he would return.

22. Ibid.

23. *Almanach Limousin*, 1862.

24. *Almanach Limousin*, 1861. The *Almanach* of 1865 noted the "obnoxious behavior" of the revelers on the *train de plaisir* to Bordeaux the previous year.

25. *Almanach Limousin*, 1861.

26. *Almanach Limousin* 1861, and 1863; *Le Grelot,* June 15, 1862. The *Almanach* of 1863 claimed that the entrepreneurs had depended too much on music to attract the public.

27. *Almanach Limousin*, 1862.

28. Louis Guibert, "Les Confréries de pénitents en France et notamment dans le diocèse de Limoges," *BSAHL* 27 (1879): 5–193.

29. Ibid.

30. *Almanach Limousin*, 1863; 2V 3, fonds de l'évêché.

31. Several confraternities still survive in Limoges.

32. *Almanach Limousin*, 1862.

33. *Almanach Limousin*, 1860, 1862, 1863, 1865; *Le Grelot,* March 22, 1863; Fɪc III Haute-Vienne 11, PHV October 14, 1862, and March 22, 1863; *Limoges illustré,* May 15, 1906. Contemporaries noted that the poor no longer grovelled for coins tossed to them at funerals.

34. *Limoges et le Limousin.*

35. *Almanach Limousin*, 1862. In 1872 Limoges had only 152 non-Catholics, many of them refugees from Alsace-Lorraine. The opening of a Protestant church in Limoges in 1853 had attracted 130 Protestants from the region and a few curious onlookers (Fɪ9 5815, PHV January 1, 1853). See Corbin, op. cit., pp. 619–92, and particularly Marguerite Le Saux, "Approche d'une étude de la déchristianisation: L'Evolution réligieuse du monde rural dans trois cantons de la Haute-Vienne (Ambazac, Le Dorat, Limoges) du milieu du XIXe siècle à la première guerre mondiale," Mémoire de maîtrise, Université de Poitiers, 1971. In 1844 only 12 percent of baptisms took place more than three days after a child's birth; by 1871, 40 percent were so delayed. Le Saux stresses that the religion of the Limousin was a natural religion, emphasizing ignorance and fear while honoring the dead and the cult of saints.

36. *Almanach Limousin*, 1865; *Le Grelot,* March 22, 1863.

37. *Almanach Limousin*, 1860.

38. *Le Grelot,* December 14, 1862.

39. *Almanach Limousin*, 1862.

40. Ibid.

41. Ibid.

42. Ibid.

43. Ibid. Albert de Laborderie, "L'Eglise Saint Aurélien," *BSAHL* 81 (1945): 239,

asserted that the butchers "had a peasant soul, the same spirit . . . encountered at the cattle markets for more than a thousand years."

44. 1M 142, police report, August 7, 1855.

45. AML "D," report of the colonel commanding the 4th Regiment, April 12, 1838.

46. *Almanach Limousin,* 1864; census of 1876. Other residents on the street were Jean Fournier, born in Laurière, who undoubtedly met his wife, a Cibot, at the cattle market there; Antoine Soula, born in Oradour-sur-Vayres, whose wife was a Cibot; Jean Thomas, born in St. Brice, whose wife was also a Cibot; and Jean Magnaud, from the Corrèze, likewise married to a Cibot, with six children. Of the nonbutchers on the street, one was a Cibot without a listed profession who owned the building at number 42, a butcher's shop operated by Cibot *dit* le Chantre; Barthélemy Thomas, a grocer from Limoges with a wife and five children; Langlade, a barber from St. Léonard, living with his wife, one child, and two servants; Champaud, a joiner, born in Eymoutiers (also a cattle market town), living with his wife, a seamstress; and Juge, a grocer, married to a Cibot who had been born in Eymoutiers. Paul Verdurier, "Une corporation au XXe siècle: Les Bouchers de Limoges," *La Revue des Idées* 2, no. 18 (June 15, 1905): 461, citing Adrien Delor, claimed that the population of the quarter was as high as 800 in 1877, but that is not borne out by any census. The number of butchers residing in Limoges were as follows: 1816 (57); 1830 (58); 1843 (64); 1848 (64); 1860 (60, including 4 outsiders); and 1862 (72, including 3 outsiders and 6 persons living in other quarters of the city).

47. Prostitution in Limoges was regulated by a municipal decree of 1849, supplementing those of the early 1820s: the *femmes de joie* were to be properly registered and inspected four times a month. They were forbidden from circulating after sunset, forming groups, approaching the barracks, or leaving their residences for more than twenty-four hours without authorization. At the theater they were to sit in specially isolated loges to prevent them from beckoning to potential clients in the audience (which might have been the last thing in the world some of their occasional clients would have wanted). Limoges's prostitutes were still overwhelmingly from the immediate region, many of whom had been unable to piece together a living doing textile work, such as in the so-called "renaissance" textiles, where young women earned little more than fifty centimes a day in the commune of Panazol (4M 87, CC March 23, 1857). See 4M 114, "statistiques"; decree of July 25, 1849; mayor of Condat, April 21, 1856; commander of the 21st Military Division, December 29, 1858; police commissioner, January 17, 1859; report of May 27, 1879, "ville de Limoges"; mayor of Condat, April 21, 1856. Count E. de Coëtlogon, *De l'assistance charitable à tous les points de vue et de l'extinction de la mendicité vagabonde* (Limoges, 1858), offered the figure of fifteen thousand "registered" poor, which was probably accurate since the author was the prefect. Prostitutes sometimes stole to augment their income, as in the case of one man who lost his wallet to a prostitute at the place d'Orsay who had "lavished him with caresses" (4M 88, police report of January 2–3, 1856).

48. H.D. [Hippolyte Ducourtieux] "Limoges depuis cent ans: L'Abbessaille et le Naveix à vol d'oiseau," *Almanach Limousin,* 1863. The name Abbessaille originated with certain feudal rights once enjoyed by the abbey there. Naveix came from Naves-port-au-bois. Among the wood merchants there was one who sold "moonwood"—wood taken from neighbors when there was no moon. On the ponticauds, see also Georges-Emmanuel Clancier, *La Vie quotidienne en Limousin au XIXe siècle* (Paris, 1976), pp. 325–47.

49. *Almanach Limousin,* 1862.

50. David H. Pinkney, *Napoleon III and the Rebuilding of Paris* (Princeton, N.J., 1958); Charlene-Marie Leonard, *Lyon Transformed: The Public Works of the Second Empire* (Berkeley, Calif., 1961).

51. Pierre Lavedan, *Histoire de l'urbanisme,* vol. 3 (Paris, 1952); Leonardo Benevolo, *The Origins of Modern Town Planning* (Cambridge, Mass., 1971).

52. *Almanach Limousin,* 1862ff.; see also F2 II Haute-Vienne 2; the city took out loans in 1862 and 1864, but only in 1861 was the Municipal Council decidedly in the red by 43,557 francs.

53. *Limoges et le Limousin,* pp. 223–24.

54. "Les Questions de travaux publiques." The *Almanach* of 1873 looked back upon a period of progress, "new quarters, magisterial roads correctly laid out, new or restored monuments, promenades turned over to the public."

55. Ibid. Other important projects included the widening of the place de la Mairie, the completion of the asylum at Naugeat, work on the cathedral tower, some repairs to the several churches and the *lycée,* and the planting of trees on the place Royale. The *Almanach Limousin,* 1862, noted the destruction of several old houses, one at the entrance of the rue Rafilhoux ("la maison du bon coin") and another on the rue des Murailles.

56. *Almanach Limousin,* 1865; Fɪc III Haute-Vienne 11, PHV August 16, 1864; ɪM 100, CP September 14, 1864. One enterprising man, a certain Duqueyroux-Lagrange, began a tiny museum commemorating the fire and published an account of the conflagration in the form of a brochure entitled "Relation authentique du grande incendie de Limoges" (1865).

57. *Almanach Limousin,* 1865, 1866, 1868; Louis Guibert, *Mélanges 1879–1886* (Limoges, n.d.). Only three out of thirty-five large public fountains were left in the city (Barres, Aigoulène, and Boucherie); some had gone the way of that on the place Dauphine, which was eliminated to expedite the flow of traffic at what had become probably the busiest intersection in Limoges. There were nine reservoirs. It seems strange that in such a rainy region the amount of water available per capita was relatively low (ten liters per person by one estimate, twenty-eight by another, compared to about sixty-nine in Paris). Much of the water lay under the houses, occasionally causing buildings to collapse. It also nurtured innumerable rats (*Almanach Limousin,* 1861). On the failure of the public works of the period, see Corbin, op. cit., p. 83.

58. Corbin treats this vast subject thoroughly in a chapter entitled "La Faiblesse du niveau culturel," (op. cit., pp. 321–417). See also Fɪ7 6846, for example, the report of June 21, 1864, and inspectors' reports in Fɪ7 6848; *Almanach Limousin,* 1859. AML, Régistre pour l'inscription des livrets ouvriers, 1856–57 (nos. 5884 to 8140). In the census of 1872, 24,883 of the city's 55,134 inhabitants (including children of all ages) could neither read nor write (*Almanach Limousin,* 1873). See also "La Bibliothèque bleue de Limoges," *Bibliophile limousin,* 19, 2ᵉ sér., 1 (Jan. 1904): 139–50; and Fɪ8 2309, statistics on printing, February 1, 1851. The imperial *lycée* graduated between 105 and 171 students each year between 1853 and 1863; the bishop held regular inspections to make sure that sufficient attention was given to religious instruction.

59. Corbin, loc. cit.; Fɪ7 9373, report of September 30, 1856, indicating that only 15,105 out of 25,162 boys and only 6,006 out of 23,747 girls of school age were in school. The Haute-Vienne also led France in infanticides.

60. *Almanach Limousin,* 1860, 1861ff.; F21 1226, PHV April 15, 1848, and Int. September 30, 1851; PHV March 11, 1862.
61. *Almanach Limousin,* 1865, 1866.
62. *Almanach Limousin,* 1863, 1864, and 1865; A. Audiganne, *Les Populations ouvrières et les industries de la France* (Paris, 1860), pp. 365–66. 1M 142, Tableau indicatif des sociétés savantes existant dans le département de la Haute-Vienne (1855). Corot spent some time in St. Junien (a "site Corot" now marks the spot where the artist placed his easel above the picturesque glove-making town). See Marilyn Brown, "The Image of the Bohémien from Diaz to Manet and Van Gogh," diss., Yale University, 1978, pp. 414–15. Brown claims "the fact that the artist chose a provincial town for the rare public exhibition of one of his figure paintings again indicates the private nature of these images, which he never showed in the artistic mainstream of Paris."
63. Fic III Haute-Vienne 11, PHV October 1 and 12, 1860.
64. *Almanach Limousin,* 1868, 1870, and 1882. Dubouché was born in 1818, the son of a cloth merchant. His marriage in 1846 to the daughter of a wealthy manufacturer of eau-de-vie gave him the possibility of following his own interests. He served on the Municipal Council and died in 1881.

Chapter Four

1. F12 5406^A, renseignements statistiques sur les sociétés de secours mutuels; *Almanach Limousin,* 1862.
2. 1M 145, CP May 30, 1856, and mayor, May 4, 1868.
3. A.P.O. III, p. 527; BB30 390, report of PGL second trimester 1867.
4. BB30 378, PGL January 12, 1855; Fic III Haute-Vienne 10, PHV February 16, 1853.
5. BB18 1540, PGL October 20, 1856, and February 24, 1855. 10M 96, including: an 1853 attempt by *ouvriers en cercles* to force a raise; a walkout by fourteen porcelain workers when Tarnaud let an *enfourneur* go; workers planning a protest meeting on the anniversary of the Second Republic before being dispersed; a brief strike of railroad workers in 1856; and a brief walkout by day laborers working for the porcelain factory of Gibus, Redon, and Margaine in 1862.
6. BB30 415, PGL November 28, 1855.
7. See William H. Sewell, Jr., *Work and Revolution in France* (Cambridge, Mass.: and New York, 1981).
8. See Christopher Johnson, "Patterns of Proletarianization" in Merriman, ed., *Consciousness and Class Experience,* pp. 65–84; Joan W. Scott, *The Glassworkers of Carmaux* (Cambridge, Mass., 1974); Ronald Aminzade, *Class, Politics, and Early Industrial Capitalism* (Albany, N.Y., 1981).
9. Michael P. Hanagan, *The Logic of Solidarity* (Urbana, Ill., 1980).
10. The phrase occurs in the ninth chapter of Sewell, op. cit.
11. Charles Tilly and Lynn Lees, "The People of June, 1848," in Price, ed., *Revolution and Reaction,* pp. 170–209.
12. See E. P. Thompson, *The Making of the English Working Class* (New York, 1963); see also Aminzade, op. cit.
13. Albert Soboul, *The Sans-culottes* (New York, 1969); Agulhon, *La République au village,* op. cit.; Margadant, op. cit.; Merriman, *The Agony of the Republic.*

14. Sewell, op. cit.; Moss, op. cit.

15. Scott, op. cit.; Hanagan, op. cit.; Louise A. Tilly and Joan W. Scott, *Women, Work and Family* (New York, 1978).

16. Susanna Barrows, *Distorting Mirrors* (New Haven, Conn., 1981); see also 4M 87 and 4M 154, including PHV decree, December 3, 1857.

17. Theodore Zeldin, *The Political System of Napoleon III* (New York, 1958).

18. BB30 378, PGL July 9, 1858; he thought that the problem with the upper class was that it had not had to suffer "our political trials, but they have had in their education the new ideas that commercial and industrial freedoms have further destroyed" (BB 30 378, April 8, 1866).

19. Fᴵᴄ III Haute-Vienne 8, PHV April 9 and July 1, 1854; July 1, 1855, and January 5, 1866; 1M 142, police report, July 4, 1853. The newspaper *Le XX décembre* (January 4, 1853) subscribed to a view of the recent history of France to which the republican opposition would have agreed completely: The Restoration had "only the support of the traditional aristocracy," while the July Monarchy had "somewhat enlarged its base of support by depending on the bourgeoisie."

20. AML "D"; R 196, commander of 21st Military Division, March 6, 1853; Int. March 6, 1852. The Guard was officially reorganized at the end of 1852; the *état nominatif* listed 1,075 members, including bourgeois and master artisans. The uniform was made obligatory. Most officers were *fabricants* or *négociants*.

21. 1M 141, PHV June 1853. Even the St. Vincent de Paul Society, which sometimes served as a legitimist front in other cities, was inactive in Limoges (Fᴵᴄ III Haute-Vienne 11, PHV September 10, 1861). See 1M 129 on legitimists during the July Monarchy.

22. Fᴵᴄ III Haute-Vienne 11, PHV February 13, 1855; Fᴵᴄ III Haute-Vienne 10, PHV December 12, 1852, and March 1, 1853. Bac came to defend *octroi* employees caught helping merchants avoid paying the tax on liquor. One policeman emphasized the fact that rich people looked only for order (4M 87, March 25, 1857).

23. 1M 141, September 16, 1853. On electoral abstentions, see Corbin, op. cit., pp. 859–65.

24. See Tilly, "Food Supply and Public Order in Modern Europe," in *The Formation of National States in Western Europe,* pp. 380–455.

25. 1M 142, police report, March 27–28, 1853, and January 1 and 18–19, 1854.

26. 4M 87, police report, September 30, 1854; 4M 88, police report, January 23–24, 1854; 1M 141, police report, September 16, 1853; 1M 142, PHV September 28, 1854, and November 30, 1855; BB30 378, PGL June 11 and July 10, 1853.

27. 1M 141.

28. Ibid. A priest related a conversation with a porcelain worker who insisted that there were still "too many traitors and enemies of the little people." The priest chided the worker, saying that it was idleness and the bad habits of the workers that were to blame for their miserable condition; he accused the man of echoing the radical catechism he picked up in his workshop. He then asked the man if he were republican, and the latter asked defiantly, "Since when do you have the right to interrogate people about their opinions?" and walked away (Abbé P. Labrune, *Mystères des campagnes* [Limoges, 1858]), p. 301.

29. BB30 415, PGL January 3, 1856; BB30 447, PGL February 25 and May 13, 1858. The latter list recommended that nineteen men be interned, one expelled, one sent to an island prison, and noted that another forty people should be arrested in Limoges at the first sign of trouble.

30. Corbin, op. cit., pp. 833–925, esp. pp. 844–50 and 866–84.

31. Corbin, op. cit., p. 870; BB30 378, PGL January 28, 1857. In the plebiscite of 1852, 32.9 percent of the ballots cast in Limoges were negative.

32. BB30 378 PGL January 28, 1857; July 9, 1858; January 1 and April 14, 1861; and May 3, 1862. Bac received 41.9 percent in the northern canton and 33.5 percent in the southern canton; he lost to Péconnet, 2,395 votes to 2,334 (BB18 1694, PHV June 19, 1864). The police noted examples of what the procureur général meant: a nineteen-year-old day laborer sentenced to six months in prison for having said in a café that "the workers are out of work and it's the emperor's fault," followed by a hint that the next time a would-be assassin would not fail, as Orsini had (1M 141, May 30, 1858). Numerous other examples could be noted.

33. BB30 278, PGL January 1 and July 20, 1863, and report for October 1864; Corbin, op. cit., p. 882. Bac was defeated in 1863, winning support only in the towns of the Haute-Vienne.

34. *Le Libéral,* February 25, 1869; F12 5406[A]. Honorary members usually contributed twenty-five francs a year. La Scieuse, founded in 1851, joined ten *encasteurs* whose slogan was "no more poverty for the sick worker, nor for he whom age has condemned to rest." In 1853 the carpenters celebrated the feast of their patron saint in the church of St. Pierre, carrying an image of the saint through the streets (*Le XX décembre,* March 23, 1853).

35. *Almanach Limousin,* 1864.

36. Bernard Moss, *The Origins of the French Labor Movement* (Berkeley, Calif., 1976).

37. F12 4638.

38. See 8M 29, PHV December 30, 1865; A.P.O. III, pp. 532–38; Cousteix, op. cit., pp. 130–34; F1c III Haute-Vienne 10, police report, July 26, 1852; Corbin, op. cit., pp. 537–38. A cooperative bakery had three hundred members in 1868, each of whom paid a fee of fifty francs and earned 5 percent interest, thereby benefiting from slightly cheaper bread. A cooperative grocery failed the same year.

39. A.P.O. III, op. cit., p. 542.

40. BB18 1694, PGL May 17, 1864; Cousteix, op. cit., pp. 125–28; and Corbin, op. cit., pp. 542–47.

41. BB18 1694; PGL reports, May 17 through June 16, 1864; 10M 130, letter of workers to PHV and police reports, May 21ff.; F12 4651, PHV May 29, 1864; A.P.O. III, pp. 539–41.

42. BB18 1694, PGL reports, May 17 through June 16, 1864. The weavers, washerwomen, and shoemakers appear to have been the only workers who gained from the strike, although there is some indication from a strike at the Gibus factory in January 1871 that those workers won a concession.

43. Corbin, op. cit., p. 543; BB18 1694, PGL June 16, 1864; the Minister of the Interior referred to the events as a "general strike" in his letter of June 15 (10M 130). Several of the militants had worked for Bac's election.

44. 10M 130, police report, June 3 and n.d., [1864]; BB 18 1694, PGL June 6 and 10 and July 2, 1864; F12 4651, PHV June 5, 9, 28, and July 2 and 5, 1864. Alluaud turned away those workers who returned before all of the workers had capitulated; the prefect seemed relieved that the workers returned "without any conditions," with the manufacturers returning the *fente.*

45. F12 4651, PHV May 29 and 30; 10M 130, PHV June 16 and Int. May 30, 1864; BB18 1694, PGL May 19 and June 16, 1864. The PGL noted the calmness of the workers: "The *patrons* have not ceased to be the object of deference and they are greeted . . . with the same *politesse.*"

46. Corbin, op. cit., p. 546; F12 4651, PHV May 29, June 5 and 28, 1864; 10M 130, Int. May 27 and June 7; BB18 1694, PGL May 19, 1864.

47. Corbin, op. cit., pp. 543–44.

48. 1M 100, PHV September 14, November 29, and December 29, 1864; BB18 1694, PGL May 19, 1864, noted that the *carrossiers* believed that the "emperor does not want us to work more than ten hours a day." Nincieux, a radical porcelain worker who had served on the strike committee, was proposed as a member in the republican-dominated Masonic lodge.

49. BB30 378, PGL October 9, 1865; BB30 390, report of PGL first trimester 1867 and 1868; *Almanach Limousin,* 1867.

50. BB30 389, PGL October 13, 1868; BB18 1794[1], procureur général's report, November [*sic* for December] 16, 1868, PGL March 22, 1869; BB30 378, PGL October 4, 1867; *Almanach Limousin,* 1870.

51. *Le Libéral,* February 27, 1869; on March 24 it asserted: "Certes, la ville de Limoges était vraiment digne d'éloges en disant à ses travailleurs: Lisons pour devenir meilleur."

52. *Le Libéral,* February 16, March 5 and 12, and August 15, 1869; Fic III Haute-Vienne 8, PHV July 3 and 12, 1867; BB30 390, PGL report of first trimester 1868 and January 6, 1870. *Le Libéral* criticized Péconnet for putting fancy gates on a garden and ignoring the water problems of the city. As for the PGL, he believed that centralization could be a useful tool for keeping radicals in check if local authorities were armed "with real powers to act" (BB390, PGL January 6, 1870).

53. *Le Libéral,* August 13 and 15, 1869.

54. Denis Poulot, *Le sublime, ou le travailleur comme il est en 1870, et ce qu'il peut être,* with an introduction by Alain Cottereau (1870; rpt. Paris, 1980).

55. Fic III Haute Vienne 11, PGL March 25, 1870.

56. BB30 389, PGL January 13, 1869.

57. Ibid.

58. Maurice Moissonnier, "Les Communes provinciales: Propositions pour une étude," *Mouvement social* 79 (April–June 1972): 124. See also Jeanne Gaillard, *Communes de province, commune de Paris 1870–1871* (Paris, 1971); Louis M. Greenberg, *Sisters of Liberty: Marseille, Lyon, Paris and the Reaction to a Centralized State, 1868–1871* (Cambridge, Mass., 1971).

59. BB30 390, PGL July 5, 1870. Fic III Haute-Vienne 8. PHV January 1870. C 2883, testimony of manufacturers; 10M 152, *rapport sommaire.* See Alain Dalotel, Alain Faure, and Jean-Claude Freiermuth, *Aux origines de la Commune: Le Mouvement des réunions publiques à Paris, 1868–1870* (Paris, 1980); see also Poulot, *Le Sublime.* In February sixty-five *lycée* students barricaded themselves in their quarters, singing the "Marseillaise" and shouting "Long Live the Republic! Long Live [Henri] Rochefort!"

60. 10M 152, particularly the "Relevé des réunions des chambres syndicales." The first meeting was held on January 23, the last on July 17, 1870. They occurred as follows: January (3), February (6), March (11), April (5), May (1), June 1, and July (3). The meetings took place in the salle Renon (rue Banc-Léger), the salle Dérignac, and the *bains chinois,* as well as in the salle Palvézy. The breakdown by trade was as follows: *porcelainiers* (4); *tailleurs de pierre* and *maçons* (3); *menuisiers* (3); *employés de commerce* (3); *tisseurs, filateurs,* and *teinturiers* (2); *carrossiers* and *forgerons* (2); *cordonniers* (2); *peintres sur porcelain, relieurs, corroyeurs,* and *sabotiers* (1); *peintres et moufletiers, useurs de grains, garçons de magasin, ouvriers*

boulangers, and *charpentiers* (1 each). Two meetings brought together workers of various trades.

61. 10M 152, August 18, 1873, *rapport sommaire;* C2883, Commission of Inquiry, which began its study July 11, 1871; see E. Dolléans, *Histoire du mouvement ouvrier,* vol. 1 (Paris, 1936), p. 335; the Bâle congress was held from June 6 to 12, 1868; The two Parisians probably were sent by the Société civile du crédit mutuel et de solidarité des ouvriers de la céramique de Paris.

62. Fɪc III Haute-Vienne 11, March 25, 1870, and PHV April 21, 1870.

63. 10M 153, Int. to PHV, April 2, 1870; statutes; 10M 152, PHV April 19, 1870. The Chambre syndicale would intervene in disputes between *patrons* and workers, inform *pères de famille* regarding possible replacement of children in apprentice-ships, consider creating a professional library, and pay striking workers an indem-nity of fifty centimes per day.

64. 10M 152, Int. to PHV, April 19, 1870.

65. Fɪc III Haute-Vienne 11, PHV, July 1 and 13, 1870; C 2883, extracts of police reports, July 13–19, 1870. On August 1 Bergeron called upon them "à se rendre indépendant par le produit de leur travail, c'est à dire en entrainant les entre-preneurs à les payer plus cher." Workers promised to give between ten and fifty centimes a day of their salary to support the *tailleurs de pierre and maçons* out on strike, and to help find them jobs. The *chambres syndicales* also discussed possible candidates for the Municipal Council.

66. BB30 390, PGL July 5, 1870. *Almanach Limousin,* 1869; Corbin, op. cit., pp. 902–3: in Limoges, 75.5 percent of eligible voters participated in the plebiscite; 49 percent voted in the negative and 25.3 percent in the affirmative.

67. BB30 390, PGL July 26, 1870. C 2883, extract of the Commissaire central de police (henceforth CC) July 27.

68. 10M 152; Fɪc III Haute-Vienne 11, PHV Sept. 1, 1870; *Analyse,* IV, Feb. 13, 1871. Three of eight *accusés* were convicted. The council voted 4,662.12 francs to Geanty, the *armurier* whose store was pillaged.

69. 4M 66, CC reports, September 13, October 10, 22, 1870. *Almanach Limousin,* 1871; *Analyse,* IV; *Défense républicaine,* November 29, 1870. On July 29 a mob had gone to the police office on the rue Fitz-James to find that Prussian spies turned out to be Alsatians.

70. *Analyse,* IV; *Almanach Limousin,* 1871; *Défense nationale.* The council approved the forced loan by a vote of 13 to 9, and several councilmen resigned in protest. The Société populaire had demanded that the tax be two million francs. Haviland preferred the creation of a municipal bank that would print bills of five, ten, and twenty francs, to be backed by a voluntary loan. The commission of ten included six councilmen as well as Victor Alluaud and Haviland. F12 4547 provides the following information on the number of workers and manufacturers still occupied:

Industry	July 23, 1870	Jan. 1, 1871
porcelain (factories)	3,839 (33)	2,108 (16)
decoration (ateliers)	1,218 (46)	297 (23)
relieurs (patrons)	37 (11)	9 (5)
shoemaking *(patrons)*	828 (68)	293 (32)
sabotiers (patrons)	221 (28)	35 (14)

71. *Almanach Limousin,* 1872, "La Dette Beaupeyrat."

72. *La Discussion,* October 19, 26, and 28, 1870.

73. Ibid. The commission proposed that the loan, which would be reimbursed at 5 percent interest, would be levied on all those who paid more than 200 francs annually in *impôt foncier* and *portes-fenêtres,* or the *cote mobilier* above 88.50 francs. A prefectorial decree of December 1 voided the Municipal Council decision.

74. Peter H. Amann, *Revolution and Mass Democracy: The Paris Club Movement in 1848* (Princeton, N.J., 1975).

75. *La Confiance,* December 30, 1970; January 1, 1871; *Analyse,* IV. This paper, published from October 16, 1870, through January 16–17, 1871, supported the "independents" in Limoges, "cité catholique par excellence."

76. Corbin, op. cit., p. 913, notes that the Société included 35 members of the liberal professions, 23 *négociants, marchands,* and bankers, 29 artisans, 2 *propriétaires,* 6 industrialists, 2 *ouvriers,* 4 soldiers, 1 *employé de commerce,* 1 *cadre supérieur de l'administration*—totaling 103 members whose profession could be identified.

77. See pp. 107 and 115. A similar society in St. Junien adhered to the statutes of the Society for Republican Defense; *Défense nationale,* October 3.

78. 4M 66, CC September 12.

79. *Défense nationale,* September 18.

80. *Défense nationale,* September 16 and December 11, 1870; January 8, 1871. The Société populaire demanded the immediate expulsion of the clergy.

81. *Défense nationale,* October 17, November 1, December 7, and following issues. The paper appeared daily—in principle—after November 13.

82. *Défense nationale,* November 13.

83. 4M 66, CC September 22.

84. *Défense républicaine,* December 21, 22, and 31. The Société populaire complained that "certain reactionaries" opposed the second demonstration. On December 7 the Society for Republican Defense demanded that the government pay more attention to the victims of the coup d'état of December 2, 1851.

85. *Défense républicaine,* December 23, 24, and 25, January 8, 1871. The *Défense nationale* and the *Défense républicaine* merged, becoming the *Défense nationale,* which was published by the Société de défense républicaine du Centre; on April 1 the *Défense républicaine* appeared again. The soldier killed was Langle fils.

86. Only 3,381 out of 11,421 voted in the election. 10M 152; *Almanach Limousin,* 1871, *La Discussion,* December 28, 1871.

87. 10M 152, PHV Aug. 18, 1871; *Défense nationale,* January 14 and 16; the workers complained that they were being forced to enter and leave the factory at fixed hours announced by the factory bell, which they called "a type of servitude."

88. C 2883.

89. *Analyse,* IV; *Défense nationale,* January 21; C 2883. The *chambre syndicale* of shoemakers asked the Municipal Council for exclusive rights to the concessions of contracts for military boots; in the future the *syndicats* would be recognized as bidders for contracts.

90. See Corbin, op. cit., pp. 918–20; Fic III Haute-Vienne 11, January 3, 1866; there was irritation in Limoges over the fact that the law of August 7, 1851, dictated that urban hospices had to accept the rural sick (BB30 390, PGL July 5, 1870). Reports of urban marauders noted in *Défense nationale,* October 4 and 13, November 22, and following issues. The article of October 4 spoke of "vagabonds" devastating harvests: "Les paysans les dénomment villaux, en d'autres termes, ouvriers de la ville." The 71st *mobiles* suffered casualties on the order of 53 killed, 87 dead as a result of illness, 55 wounded, 71 taken prisoner, and 150 missing.

91. See Chapter Two. *La Discussion,* February 5 and 6; the paper aimed at rural

voters, describing the Orleanist Benoît de Buis surrounded by trusting peasants who lived near his estate.

92. F12 4547, report of the Chamber of Commerce on the industrial situation in Haute-Vienne, March 21, 1871, by Victor Alluaud. This contrasted sharply with the "good conditions" reported on January 29, 1870, and the "good year" of 1869.

93. *Analyse,* IV. *Défense nationale,* January 23 and following issues. Prefect Massicault left early in April to become prefect of the Hautes-Pyrénées; he was replaced by Delpon. The National Guard may have begun to meet independently; the Société populaire met only a few times at the end of February. Early in March two thousand workers were still in the municipal workshops (*Défense nationale,* March 17).

94. For more details, see Stewart Edwards, *The Paris Commune, 1871* (New York, 1971); *Défense républicaine,* April 2; *Analyse,* IV. The council met on the 19th, unaware of the events in Paris.

95. *Analyse,* IV; 10M 152, *rapport sommaire; Défense nationale,* March 3 and following issues; *Almanach Limousin,* 1872. Ransom tried to resign several times, expressing the hope that another administration would have the confidence of the capitalists. At the same time (March 17), the newspaper announced that it would soon readopt its old title of *Défense républicaine* to underline the necessity of mobilizing support for the Republic.

96. *Analyse,* IV; *Défense nationale,* March 23, 24, and following; *Almanach Limousin,* 1872.

97. *Analyse,* IV; *Défense nationale,* April 1. The council had already spent almost 750,000 francs on the workshops (10M 152, PHV August 18, 1873).

98. *Défense nationale,* April 1.

99. *Défense républicaine,* April 2. Rumors that Limoges workers were moving into the countryside spread throughout rural Haute-Vienne. In Eymoutiers the National Guard responded to a rumor that *insurgés* were heading their way. Yet in that small market town a balloon ascent was greeted with shouts of "Long Live Paris! Long Live the Republic!"

100. BB30 386, PGL April 3.

101. *Analyse,* IV; C 2885, CC March 23, April 4; C 2883, the testimony of Louvet; *Almanach Limousin,* 1872. On March 26 the Municipal Council announced that guns would be distributed on the twenty-sixth, with the youngest to be armed first. The review was postponed because the mayor said that he knew that seven red flags were to be used during the review of April 2 (testimony of Douai).

102. C 2883, testimony, Captain Calmel and others. The concierge at the town hall said that he had distributed *billets* for lodging to troops until he learned that they were for troops that had gone to the station. The one indication of the attitudes of the soldiers during the disturbances on the fourth comes from Gaillard, op. cit., p. 65.

103. C 2883, testimony of Tarrade. Dubois seems to have been interrogated, perhaps fleeing during the process.

104. C 2883, testimony of Alphonse Alexandre (a tailor), the prefect, and others. One witness related the story of a guardsman who asked a lieutenant colonel of the Guard for permission to leave a post to which he had been assigned. The guardsman said that his orders had come from "the Commune," to which the lieutenant colonel replied, "If the Commune had put him there, the Commune would have to relieve him."

105. C 2883, testimony of Paul Etienne Durand, former captain in the National Guard; testimony of Jouhaud, *horloger,* rue du Consulat; testimony of Villegoureix,

bijoutier, place St. Michel. Aubalie Laplaud, place St. Michel, noted that the men were *en blouse.*

106. *Défense républicaine,* April 6, 8, and following issues; C 2883, testimony of officer Chalvin; BB30 486, PGL April 6.

107. Corbin, op. cit., p. 932; Moissonnier, op. cit., p. 132; Greenberg, op. cit.

108. C 2883, *rapport sommaire;* Gaillard, op. cit., p. 60; Moissonnier, op. cit., p. 130-31. See Aminzade, op. cit., pp. 262–67.

109. 10M 152; C 2885, *Almanach Limousin,* 1871. Sixty-two men were tried: Dubois and Rebeyrolle were sentenced to death in absentia; 25 men were condemned to penalties of varying length, including 1 to life imprisonment; there were also 27 *non-lieu* and eight acquittals. The Conseil de guerre dealt harshly with a former convict named Bléamont, *journalier,* who admitted firing a shot, but only after the death of Billet ("le Colonel a ordonné la charge sur le peuple"); he admitted helping build a barricade and received 20 years in prison. Fessal, a National Guard corporal, received a sentence of life imprisonment; Bondy, *porcelainier,* got 10 years; Join fils, *sans profession,* got 5 years; and Soudenas, *cordonnier,* got 3 years. Virtually all were workers. The list of those still under surveillance in the department in August 1871 was dominated by 130 workers, including 17 shoemakers and 13 day laborers, plus 15 *cultivateurs.* See also *Défense républicaine,* April 10–11 and following issues; May 5. Ths newspaper claimed that the newly elected council had a republican majority of twenty to fourteen. The editors were called before the Conseil de guerre because of a May 7 editorial stating that the streets of Lyon "n'ont pas encore été souillées par la troupe," referring to the government of the "fusillade blanche," attacking "les décorés, les canroberts, et autres traîneurs de sabre de même farine." Its last issue appeared on May 27.

110. C 2883; the commission began its work on July 11, with Ardant presiding in Limoges. Its stated goal was to obtain precise information on contracts "with the savage undertakings of Paris." The report of the commander of the 21st Military Division (C 2885, July 22, 1871) tried to link the International, whose members alone he guessed numbered about thirty-five hundred in Limoges, to the secret society Marianne, which he claimed had influence in Limoges. Chamiot, the procureur général, offered a more dispassionate analysis, finding no emissaries from Paris, but he did mention that the Société populaire sent two representatives to Paris, which is confirmed by their account in *Le Populaire du Centre* of 1907; however, they failed in their attempt to see anyone from the central committee. (BB30 486, March 29, 1871). The *Enquête parlementaire sur l'insurrection du 18 mars* (Paris, 1872), vol. 1, pp. 299–309, summarized as follows the biased testimony of C 2883: "Depuis bien des années, la ville de Limoges a eu le triste honneur de rivaliser avec Lyon, St. Etienne, et Marseille pour l'exaltation de ses sentiments révolutionnaires . . ." (p. 300).

111. 10M 152, esp. CC June 21, 1873, and C 2883; C 3023, report of the Commission of Inquiry; 10M 153, CC reports of June 24, 1872, and January 29, 1874.

112. *La Nation française,* April 13, 1871.

113. *La Nation française,* July 14.

114. IT 86ᴬ.

115. IT 86ᴬ, letter of the bishop, January 1, 1872; the prefect forced the Municipal Council to give 5,200 francs to the *fabriques.*

116. *Almanach Limousin,* 1872.

117. 4M 66, CC reports of August 6–7, 1871, and September 10, 1872; 1M 149, police report of March 4, 1873.

Chapter Five

1. Roland Duchalard, *Visages d'antan* (Limoges, 1977), pp. 11–13.
2. Censuses of 1872 and 1891, reported in *Almanach Limousin,* 1874, 1893, and 1901. See Chapter Six. In 1883, 31.48 percent of the population of the department was considered illiterate.
3. 123 o 6(14); *Analyse,* IV; *Almanach Limousin,* 1874; *Limoges illustré,* February 1, 1900 (on the occasion of the banquet commemorating the centenary of the *octroi*). In 1904 there were seventy-nine employees of the Limoges *octroi*. The latter was extended for the last time on February 7, 1938, disappearing with World War II.
4. *Limoges illustré,* December 1, 1902.
5. *Almanach Limousin,* 1894.
6. *Limoges illustré,* April 10, 1898, and February 1, 1900; *Almanach Limousin,* 1894, 1898, 1900. The newer quarters, too, celebrated fetes, such as those of the route d'Ambazac and the rond-point Sadi Carnot.
7. *Almanach Limousin,* 1900; *Limoges illustré,* October 15, 1902. The building L'Etoile had 16 units, each consisting of from one to three rooms, with electricity and running water, renting for between 140 and 255 francs per year.
8. *Almanach Limousin,* 1897. These houses thus also held somewhat fewer households and fewer people than the houses of the center city, not only because of their smaller size but as a result of the arrival of young single men and women looking for work.
9. 123 o 9(45). The faubourg Montmailler was aligned between 1889 and 1893 (authorized by the council on May 12), a measure first considered in 1879. Stormy negotiations with *propriétaires* followed. The owners of numbers 8 and 10 received 9,500 and 11,300 francs, respectively, for their houses; the municipality had already paid 9,000 francs for number 20 in 1893. Those who rented, however, got only 1 franc, since they were not covered by the law of 1841 or a decree issued in 1870, which permitted the expropriation of houses in the public interest. One *lingère* who had lived in the quarter for 26 years and whose husband was without work protested that 1 franc was hardly compensation for having to move. The renters at numbers 5 and 7 got to stay, although the facades of the houses were chopped back. See also the *Almanach Limousin* for 1901.
10. *Almanach Limousin,* 1897 and 1902. Between 1891 and 1896 the Creuse, Corrèze, Charente, Dordogne, Vienne, and Indre all lost between 3,000 and 13,000 inhabitants to migration. The Haute-Vienne grew by 2,816 people, but only because of Limoges's addition of 5,006 inhabitants. Five years later Limoges's population increase of 6,418 inhabitants accounted for all of the department's growth of 6,029; the rest of the department decreased in population. In 1906 all of the capitals of the above departments had lost population except for Châteauroux and Limoges.
11. *Almanach Limousin,* 1901 (Isle); 1904 (Condat); 1906 (Le Palais). In the late 1870s a military officer noted that most of the communes surrounding Limoges had more men than women because many females found work as domestics in the city. In Bosmie 117 of the 149 *propriétaires* in 1824 owned less than 6 hectares, and 71 of these owned less than 1.
12. *Almanach Limousin,* 1909 (St. Just); 1907 (Feytiat); 1902 (Panazol) as well as 1901, 1904, 1906, 1908, and 1909; MR 2269 and 2284.
13. Roger Shattuck, *The Banquet Years: The Origins of the Avant-Garde in France,*

1885 to World War I (New York, 1968), pp. 18, 23. See *Limoges illustré,* February 1, 1903, on Limoges's sad temperament; October 21, 1900, on the tavern of the Hôtel Central. Camille Jouhanneaud noted the *froide* nature of Limoges and its inhabitants in the *Almanach Limousin* for 1900.

14. *Almanach Limousin,* 1884; 4M 138, dossiers on associations; *Limoges illustré,* November 15, 1902; Clancier, op. cit., p. 264. Three hundred gymnastic societies met in Limoges in 1891 (*Almanach Limousin,* 1892). Other circles catered to specialized interests, such as the Cercle central du Limousin (1900), which sought "to procure for its members satisfactions from the world of science, the arts, and literature"; the Cercle Gay Lussac, which organized two scientific expositions and published a journal for a short period; and the Société botanique (4M 124).

15. *Almanach Limousin,* 1884 and 1897; *Le Rappel,* June 6 and December 26, 1897; and *Limoges illustré,* May 15, 1901, and October 15, 1903. Each wagon held 50 people, with receipts averaging about 1,300 francs per day. A Société anonyme des tramways was begun in February 1884, selling 2,000 shares at 500 francs each, with a guarantee of 3 percent interest (*Le Petit Centre,* February 12, 1884).

16. Shattuck, op. cit.

17. *Almanach Limousin,* 1903, 4M 55, esp. CC March 27, 1886.

18. *Limoges illustré,* July 1 and November 15, 1900, noted "the absolute indifference that the majority of the population professes for the pleasures that are taken in café concerts in other cities"; Clancier, op. cit., p. 266. See also 4M 155 for earlier café concerts; the hair fair was noted by Cousteix, "Le Mouvement ouvrier limousin," p. 61. See *Limoges illustré,* May 15, 1904, on the fete of the barbichet.

19. 4M 125, PHV November 21, 1899.

20. Shattuck, esp. pp. 3–42.

21. *Almanach Limousin,* 1901; *Limoges illustré,* February 1, 1903.

22. Paul Ducourtieux, "Les Statues de la Vierge aux carrefours du vieux Limoges," *Limoges illustré,* May 15, 1906. See F19 5817, CP n.d. (1880). On the new churches, see 1T 86D, report of *fabriqué,* and 1T 86H. In December 1872 the municipal council had agreed to give 7,700 francs to the existing parishes. Ste. Valérie was authorized in 1875 to serve the Pont Neuf quarter, and St. Paul–St. Louis, inaugurated in 1889, was constructed near the railroad station. St. Joseph's had 6,800 parishioners, at least nominally, and Sacré-Coeur had only slightly less.

23. Weber, op. cit., pp. 23–29, 357–74; Le Saux, op. cit., pp. 27ff. See also Corbin, op. cit., pp. 619–93.

24. Le Saux, p. 29.

25. Limouzin-Lamothe, op. cit., p. 242; Robert, op. cit., p. 125.

26. Le Saux, op. cit., p. 37.

27. Ibid., pp. 37–42. Pierre Henri Lamajou, named bishop of Limoges in 1881, fared no better—for other reasons. After seeing the condition of the cathedral shortly after his arrival, he spent much of his time trying to get transferred from the city. He turned down an appointment to Gap, which did not seem like much of an improvement. Finally rewarded for his patience with Amiens, a real plum, the poor man died a week after leaving his palace in the Vienne (see F19 2529, esp. the letter of Député Lecomte of the Mayenne).

28. Le Saux, op. cit., p. 39.

29. Louis Pérouas, "Limoges, une capitale régionale de la Libre-pensée à l'orée du XXᵉ siècle," *Annales du Midi* 91, no. 142 (April-June 1979): 165–85. Pérouas also notes the role of Jean Thabard, a socialist porcelain painter. *La Libre-Pensée de Limoges* appeared briefly after 1882; *Le Libre-Penseur du Centre* began in Novem-

ber 1905. The weak influence of the Church in Limoges probably contributed to the rather limited activities of the Libre-Pensée group. Within the group there was a split between those members of the radical tradition and those suspicious of collaboration with the bourgeoisie. Royalist businessmen included the printers Chapoulaud and Barbou des Courrières, textile manufacturers Jabet and Romanet de Caillaud, and merchants Pétiniaud and Lajudie.

30. *Almanach Limousin,* 1882; *Limoges illustré,* June 15, 1902. A bequest helped pay for it.

31. Clancier, op. cit., p. 247.

32. Ernest Vincent, "Les Crieurs publics en Limousin," *BSAHL* 82 (1947): 249–68; *Limoges illustré,* December 1, 1909.

33. Weber, op. cit., esp. pp. 377–496.

34. *Limoges illustré,* June 1, 1902 and August 1, 1909.

35. *Limoges illustré,* March 1 and 15 and April 15, 1902; *Le Rappel du Centre,* June 27, 1896.

36. M. le Marquis de Moussac, *Une corporation d'autrefois encore vivante aujourd'hui* (Paris, 1892), p. 81.

37. Ibid., p. 56; Adrien Delor, *La Corporation des bouchers à Limoges* (Limoges, 1877), pp. 12, 40–47.

38. Moussac, p. 81; Delor, op. cit., p. 30.

39. Archives municipales de Limoges, censuses of 1876 and 1906; *Almanach Limousin,* each year following a census. See also Delor, op. cit., p. 35, and Paul Verdurier, "Une survivance du moyen âge: La corporation des bouchers de Limoges," unpublished manuscript, Bibliothèque municipale de la ville de Limoges, who referred to "[une] certaine débilité de race." The number of heads of household did decline: 58 (1830); 60 (1860); 50 (1893); and 44 (1906).

40. Census of 1906. Verdurier, op. cit., gave both figures.

41. *Almanach Limousin,* 1894. Petit, op. cit., pp. 110–22; Verdurier, op. cit.; Delor, op. cit., p. 46, estimated the population of the quarter at 800. Verdurier stated that in 1887 twelve master butchers could not read. The corporation elected four syndics; members had to pay a hundred-franc fine if they broke the butchers' rules covering the fairs and markets of the region and were still required to attend the funerals of other members. The Cercle St. Aurélien "regularized" its status in 1887 (following the passage of the law on associations of March 21, 1884). The Syndicat professionel de la boucherie was formed in 1891 with the goal of "establishing relations and links of fraternity among its members." According to Petit, a few of the butchers refused to pay their fees to the corporation, indicating that the old solidarity might have been ebbing. He also claimed that twenty of the patriarchs had between two hundred and three hundred thousand francs in assets, with several having more than half a million francs, which is very unlikely. The first *syndicat* of the *confrérie* of St. Aurélien was also president of the circle and of the Chambre syndicale; the second syndic was also vice president of both. The syndicate and the corporation were one of the same.

42. 123 o 9(28), plan, 1875, PHV decree of December 26, 1876; butchers petition for paving, October 3, 1870; letter of Cibot *dit* le Pape, January 22, 1877; Verdurier, "Une corporation"; Septime Gorceix, "Une vieille corporation se prolonge jusqu'à nos jours," *Le Populaire du Centre,* February 26, 1958, claimed that the butchers protested when the Municipal Council sent a commission to investigate the possibility of establishing latrines on the street.

43. Moussac, op. cit., pp. 56–64.

44. *Almanach Limousin,* 1881; *La Corporation de MM. les Bouchers de Limoges et l'arrêté du 7 mai 1880. Par un ouvrier* [J. B. Laroudie], n.d.
45. Ibid.
46. Ibid.
47. *Almanach Limousin,* 1898; 2 V 3, CC June 6 and PHV June 3 and 15, 1897.
48. *Journal des Débats,* February 16, 1943; Delor, op. cit., p. 46; Joseph Petit, *Une ancienne corporation et ses survivances: La corporation de messieurs les bouchers de Limoges* (Paris, 1906), p. 155; Gorceix, op. cit. The 1914 *Almanach Limousin* listed the following among the city's 143 butchers: 10 Cibot, 10 Plainemaison, 9 Malinvaud, 9 Parot, 5 Pouret, and 4 Juge. The butchers were the subject of articles in *Action Française,* November 23, 1909, and August 3, 1940.
49. 10M 103, CC December 11, 1896, and Commissaire spécial (henceforth CS), December 11, 1896.
50. The butchers blamed the instigation of the strike on the L'Union. Throughout the strike the butchers' workers were careful to avoid violating the "freedom of work," although there was one *procès verbal* for *entravement;* one butcher, François Cibot *dit* Menot, was charged with attacking a striker but got off easy when it could not be proved that the visible battle scars he carried had come from that particular encounter. The butcher made some sort of concession, but it is not clear on what issue. (CC December 12–19, 22, 24, 28, 1896, and official strike summary). The new cooperative apparently opened a stall at the *marché* Dupuytren at the market. The sixteen butchers who were struck included Malinvaud *dit* l'Ange, Malinvaud Baptiste, Jean Parot *dit* Aîné, Pouret *dit* Jambon, Parot *dit* Nez plat jeune, Malinvaud Rubanex, Edouard Parot, Léon Parot, Lucas Parot, Juge *dit* Jeune, Cibot *dit Parpaillot,* and two butchers not part of the families.
51. Maurice Agulhon, *Marianne au combat* (Paris, 1979).
52. F21 4413, mayor July 31, 1884.
53. *Limoges illustré,* November 1, 1902; F21 4413, letter of Labussière, July 7, 1888; letter of Minister of Public Instruction, May 17, 1890; 1M 229, PHV April 2, 1892. A fountain had been demolished there in 1854. The Municipal Council first discussed placing the statue on the promenade d'Orsay.
54. F21 4413, Minister of Public Instruction, May 17, 1890.
55. 1M 229, PHV April 2, 1892; *Le Courrier du Centre,* April 26, 1892. On February 15, 1882, the Municipal Council had voted to change the name of the square to place Denis Dussoubs.
56. 1M 229, PHV July 16, 1897, and CC July 27, 1897. There was also a bronze representation of *La Céramique* at the place d'Orsay.
57. 1M 229, PHV September 20 and 26, 1899; CC September 20, 1899.
58. Ibid., and *Le Rappel du Centre.*
59. Ibid.
60. Shattuck, op. cit., pp. 4–5, 24.
61. *Le Rappel du Centre,* March 11 and 25, April 15, and May 2, 1900.
62. *Limoges illustré,* August 15, 1903.

Chapter Six

1. 3M 355, "Aux électeurs de la septième circonscription." Malinvaud had been a delegate to the congress held in Paris in 1876 and served as president of the association of sabot makers. Cousteix calls him a mutalist: "He expressed a

working-class humanism . . . discovered in the study of moral truths that an educated worker discovers by the daily routine of work" ("Le Mouvement ouvrier limousin de 1870 à 1939," op. cit., pp. 37–38).

2. *Le Républicain de la Haute-Vienne,* May 23, 1878.
3. *La Haute-Vienne,* February 12, 1876. The *Journal de la Haute-Vienne*'s depiction of the generic worker probably did not help the royalists' image: "A thug, cap tilted to one side, exposing a love-lock [*accroche-coeur*], pipe riveted in his mouth, hands in pockets, strolls about philosophically, saying, 'The laboring classes, that's me!'" (March 25, 1875); the paper first appeared in October 1874.
4. *L'Union conservatrice* took up the struggle in September 1877 but lasted only until the end of the year.
5. *Journal de la Haute-Vienne,* August 4 and October 16, 1875; the "comités d'hommes de la classe dirigeante" were to organize the *cercles catholiques.*
6. Henri Baju, *Rapport sur les associations ouvrières catholiques et sur le cercle de la jeunesse de Limoges* (Limoges, 1877), p. 3; 1M 160, "Etat des cercles catholiques" lists slightly higher figures; between sixty and seventy members for all three in 1878. One third of the members of the Cercle St. Joseph were "associate" or honorary members. In 1876 the latter organization had more honorary members (eighty-five) than regulars (sixty-four).
7. 1M 160, n.d.; members of the former club included nineteen porcelain painters, four other porcelain workers, two *mécaniciens,* two barbers, two sabot makers, and two other painters; *Journal de la Haute-Vienne,* August 4 and October 16, 1875.
8. 1M 160, CC December 6, 1882; there were also several associations of ecclesiastics, such as that for the Propagation of the Faith. See Louis Pérouas, "Limoges, une capitale régionale de la Libre-Pensée à l'orée du XXᵉ siècle," op. cit. The working-class militant Emile Noël also belonged to the Libre-Pensée, along with other workers.
9. 1M 188, CC July 4, 1878. The crowd was estimated at about seven hundred people.
10. The *Almanach Limousin,* 1873, noted the council's sentiments with considerable disgust, yet the 1872 council did vote to establish seven more primary schools (four for girls), turning them over to the congregations.
11. F17 9277, reports of inspectors: November 11, 1876; May 9, 1879; and July 1881.
12. *Almanach Limousin,* 1880–84; F19 6059; *Le Républicain de la Haute-Vienne,* January 3, 1878. See the *Analyse* for the decisions of the Municipal Council in the 1870s. At the beginning of the laicization campaign the municipality had more than once justified its decisions by the fact that the nuns did not have a *brevet complet,* as was required beginning in 1875; now they were quite willing to ask the prefect to assign lay teachers carrying only a *brevet simple.* One of the justifications for shutting down convents was that they engaged in commerce and did not pay taxes. In 1880 a locksmith had to be called to open the door of the small Jesuit house on the rue des Clairettes (*Almanach Limousin,* 1881).
13. Ducray, op. cit., p. 172.
14. Ibid., pp. 133–35; 10M 39, PHV n.d., notes three *syndicats* that were not reconstituted after the Commune; 10M 153. L'Initiative had 600 members; the other associations of porcelain workers during the mid-1870s included La Loyale (*useurs de grains, polisseurs,* and *garçons de magasin*), with 100 members; L'Econome, with 500; and another of the *moufletiers,* with 150. The prefect called attention to the "constant solidarity" between L'Initiative and the shoemakers' association, which had been established in February 1870.

15. 10M 152, statutes of the porcelain painters. See Bourdelle, p. 41. The *compagnon-nage* had been relatively unimportant in Limoges. The *compagnons du devoir* of Maître Jacques and Père Soubise had members in several trades, dominated by the blacksmiths. Two *auberges* served them: Madame Chenaud, at the Hôtel Saint Maurice on the rue des Petites Maisons, for the blacksmiths, forgerons and bakers; and Madame Girodelle, boulevard de la Cité, for the carpenters. The blacksmiths paid two francs a month (one and a half francs for their mutual aid fund and fifty centimes for the cost of their correspondence and assistance for compagnons arriving in Limoges); see Alfred Leroux, note in *BSAHL* 54 (1904), *procès-verbal:* 691.

16. 10M 130, PHV n.d., and August 26, September 11 and 24, 1873; CC September 24, 1873; author unknown, August 28, 1873; 10M 153, CC July 28, 1872, noting that "tout le monde se traite de citoyen"; Bourdelle, op. cit., p. 52; Grellier, op. cit., p. 267. The Touze Company employed 120 people; the *tourneurs* earned between 6 and 7.5 francs a day and asked for a raise of between 10 and 15 percent.

17. 10M 130, PHV September 24 and n.d. 1873; Ducray, op. cit., p. 172.

18. 10M 153, CC June 24, 1872, and January 29, 1874; CP November 8, 1874. When the police tried to show collusion between L'Initiative and other associations, they compiled a list of militants that included: François Celeries, who frequented civil burials and public meetings; F. Nadalon, an "able and intelligent propagandist"; L. Pourch, a freethinker "capable of leading an insurrection"; and Alexandre Lavergne, who lived at 70, rue de Paris and also showed up at civil burials.

19. 10M 153, PHV May 9, 1889.

20. Ducray, op. cit., pp. 147–53.

21. J. M. A. Parantaud, *Une coopérative de consommation: L'Union de Limoges* (Limoges, 1944), pp. 44–54; "Société coopérative L'Union" (n.p., n.d.); 1M 165, PHV December 16, 1894; BB18 1992, PGL January 10, 1895; "Son caractère politique est suffisamment indiqué part le fait que l'anarchiste Tennerie est l'agent comptable et que l'anarchiste Barbet fait partie du conseil d'administration." "Le Progrès" had included 260 Haviland workers (10M 175). L'Union sold 4,000 shares at 25 francs each, paying 4 percent interest.

22. Parantaud, op. cit., pp. 54–58, who argued that the cooperative was in the tradition of 1848, "le conviction que l'homme peur agir sur les choses" (p. 142). L'Union was still going strong in the 1930s, having added eighteen showers, a library, and the sponsorship of a *colonie des vacances*. Its growth may be seen as follows:

year	members	annual business
1881	45	875f
1885	417	20,000
1891	3,528	1,247,000
1900	8,758	3,875,000
1913	10,303	
1919	14,701	
1939	26,463	

23. BB18 1892; January 10, 1895; Jean Rougerie, for one.

24. Ibid., and Int. to MJ, January 1, 1895; 1M 165, CS December 16, 1894. Labussière continually claimed that the true enemy of small commerce were the *grands magasins*.

25. For example, 3M 437, Commissaire de police (henceforth CP), first arrondisse-

ment, May 8, 1896; *Le Socialiste de la Haute-Vienne,* December 20, 1903; Parantaud, op. cit., p. 142.

26. Archives of the Prefecture of Police, BA 182, report of October 1879. The carpenters also asked for weekly pay, a ten-hour summer workday, and exemption from having to pay for their own tools and 2 percent of their wages for insurance. See also F12 4664, PHV July 18, 1882, and May 25, 1883; 10M 130, CC September 6 and 15, 1882; Ducray, op. cit., pp. 132–36; 10M 153; 10M 171; 10M 175. In the strike by the *useurs de grains,* a strike committee called for solidarity against the manufacturers, who refused to negotiate and replaced the strikers with other workers. The strikers had wanted a raise from 1.70 francs to 2 francs a day. An insignificant strike of porcelain workers at the Vultury and Aragon Company in 1881 was settled by compromise (F12 4664 and *Almanach Limousin,* 1883).

As of January 1, 1884, the number of *syndicats* and members were as follows: porcelain workers (120); *sabotiers* (100); carpenters (25); *useurs de grains* (25); cabinetmakers (8); stonecutters and masons (20); *gazetiers* (10); day laborers in porcelain (51); building painters (12); polishers (25); porcelain painters (245); typographers (70); waiters (28); shoemakers (32); and sabot makers (25). There were also *syndicats patronales* of bakers (47); *entrepreneurs en bâtiment* (56); printers, typographers, and lithographers (18); and porcelain manufacturers (29). The one "mixed" *syndicat* was that of the musicians.

27. 10M 130, CC November 27 and December 13, 1882, and January 3, 1883; PHV January 4 and 29 and May 25, 1883; F12, 4664, PHV May 25, 1883; Archives of the Prefecture of Police, BA 182, reports of December 19, 1882, and January 5, 12, and 13, 1883. The Municipal Council vigorously debated its right to aid the strikers, drawing an angry attack from the *Journal des débats* for asking the Senate and the Chamber of Deputies to help the workers. One report in BA 182 indicated that Chabert had been sent by the national committee of the Union Fédérative, charged with "orchestrating the strike and exhorting the workers to resist their employers." Another police report suggests that the merchants of the city, hurt by the strike, pressed the manufacturers to compromise.

28. 10M 130, esp. CC February 6, 1883, claiming that the strikers had been "excited" by Boudaud and Roulhac, two Allemanist municipal councilmen: "Imbus des doctrines collectivistes, leur résistance avait en réalité pour but de créer une agitation politique destinée à favoriser le développement du parti ouvrier." One strike meeting heard Boudaud describe the employers as "thieves and liars"; the police claimed that the manufacturers held out because "they do not want socialism implanted in the working class here, which, until now, has been uninterested in politics" (BA 182, January 17, 1883). Malinvaud, who gave a talk to raise money for the strikers, told the workers, "I was uninterested in politics and the working-class movement, but I perceived that a peril threatens everyone and the Republic. Support the strike without failure, for if the employers win, you are lost." Chabert's visit is described in 4M 102, PHV August 12, 1879, and 10M 192, PHV October 10, 1879. The subject of his talk, "The Necessity of Organizing the Proletariat: A Comparative Study of the French Revolution and Our Era," was advertised by "The Committee of Initiative" as an appeal to "the devotion of the democracy of workers in Limoges." See also 10M 130, PHV January 10 and 14 and February 1, 1883, and *Le Petit Centre,* November 29, 1882.

29. 10M 130, PHV January 4 and 29, February 6 and 10, and May 15, 1883; the president of the Conseil des prud'hommes heard both sides make their cases. Grellier, op. cit. pp. 270–71. The organization of the *useurs de grains* disbanded

after the strike. *Le Figaro,* reporting from Limoges on January 31, noted that the employers, "qui n'avait jamais vu que peu de grèves dans la contrée . . . ont saisi cette occasion de former un comité défensif de leurs intérêts."

30. Ducray, op. cit., pp. 123–25; the manufacturers met once a year, paying twenty-five francs per kiln to belong.

31. 10M 155, January 23, 1883, and statutes, Archives of the Prefecture of Police, BA 182, esp. the report of January 17, 1883; Bourdelle, op. cit., p. 45. The Federation stated its goal "to support and fortify the government of the Republic . . . the interests of all workers being identical, it is incumbent on them to seek the means to defend themselves." Its leaders included Camille Machette, a *plâtrier,* originally from the Isère, "of good reputation." Chieppe, a porcelain painter left with three children when his wife died, was a good worker, but the police thought he neglected his family somewhat for other pleasures, one of which was socialism. Another leaders was Martial Ruby, a tailor, "who owns nothing and whose only resource is his labor; nonetheless, his household has the appearance of being well kept up, and they live quietly enough" (10M 156, signalements).

32. The blacksmiths won a raise of about 25 percent after three days (F12 4664, PHV January 29 and February 1, 1886); thirty shoemakers stopped working for one manufacturer in 1883 after they were refused a raise, and they did not return (10M 130, Gendarmerie report of July 23 and 10M 111, CC July 23, 1883). In 1889 *ouvriers sabotiers* struck Fougeras frères (10M 111); and in August 1891, one hundred *monteurs* left the Monteux factory, demanding a raise of 25 percent, but they returned eight days later in defeat (BB18 1857, PGL August 8, 1891). The police commissioner claimed that the latter strike was intended to give Boulanger, whom a number of the workers supported, some publicity in the wake of his recent decline in popularity (10M 111, CC August 22, 1891). The *finisseurs* refused to follow the *monteurs,* which ended the strike. The typographers' one-day strike was against Charles Lavauzelle, who, after lunching with his workers, agreed not to cut wages by 20 percent (10M 126, CC March 17–18, 1892; F12 4669; F12 4664, PHV September 8–14, 1896).

Michelle Perrot points to "the growing role of organizations in strikes, which, little by little, substitute their wisdom" for the leadership of impassioned leaders during the period 1871 to 1890 (Perrot, *Les Ouvriers en grève,* vol. 2, p. 723). Cool rationality did not always lie behind strikes, and spontaneity still was important, as were "political circumstances" that could explain periods of militancy and quiescence. In March 1889 Boulanger supporters appeared to have urged about 150 unemployed workers to present demands to the prefect and mayor (F12 4665, PGL February 15, 1890).

33. See Shorter and Tilly, op. cit., esp. pp. 76–77.

34. *Almanach Limousin,* 1892.

35. Grellier, op. cit., pp. 269–79, 287–90, and 304–22; Bourdelle, op. cit., p. 7; 5M 51, authorizations for constructions of new kilns. In 1882 there was but 1 kiln more than 100 cubic meters in size; in 1907 forty-five were larger than 100 cubic meters, with several 140 to 150 cubic meters in size (p. 287). The year 1907 marked the apogee of the industry, with 40 factories and some 14,000 workers—5 factories and 1,000 more workers than in 1905.

36. Grellier, op. cit., pp. 345–54. David Haviland died in 1879.

37. Ibid., pp. 270–73. American officials accused French manufacturers of making false declarations of the value of porcelain to be imported. The former thus attempted to impose uniform duties on porcelain, as if all companies exported first-quality porcelain, which hurt the smaller companies in Limoges. In 1900 there were only

217 *journées* fueled by wood and 2,791 fueled by coal. About .39 kilograms of coal were used for each kilo of wood. The first attempt to use gas occurred in 1845.

38. Ibid., pp. 329–45; *Almanach Limousin, 1876*. Chromolithography was first used in Paris in 1818. Eight manufacturers produced their own *feuilles de décalque*. In 1907 there were *crématoires* in Limoges. Decoration by impression was accomplished with copper or zinc. A few *chambrelains* still decorated certain items at home.

39. *Almanach Limousin, 1876*. By hand a turner could produce 100 plates a day; with the machine a turner and two assistants could turn out between 450 and 600 a day. See Grellier, op. cit., pp. 274–75, 287, 311, and 341; the number of *modeleurs* increased with a decline in the need for workers with other skills. Apprenticeships, which averaged between two and three years for a porcelain painter, took one year for a *décalqueuse*. Corbin, op. cit., p. 44, claimed that labor amounted for 41 percent of the porcelain manufacturers' total costs, 25 percent of which went for skilled labor.

40. Bourdelle, op. cit., pp. 7–10.

41. Boutaud, op. cit., pp. 27–30. The *Rapports sur les lois réglementant le travail* 23 (1903), noted that in the Haute-Vienne many family workshops were not observing the law, implying that shoe manufacturers were parceling out work to home workers. Based upon Amdur's sample, op. cit., pp. 46–47, the number of artisanal shoemakers fell from 79 percent in 1891 to 8 percent in 1921. In the porcelain industry foremen earned between 8 and 10 francs a day, 166 to 233 percent more than day laborers; *ouvriers,* in the middle, earned 4.75 francs in 1895, 58 percent more than day laborers. Piece rates continued for some skilled workers until 1905. Salaries did not reach the level of 1882 until 1900.

42. Perrot, "The Three Ages of Industrial Discipline in France."

43. BB18 1892, report of the Commission supérieure du travail dans l'industrie, session of June 12, 1895, in the wake of the death of a *poudreuse* from saturnine poisoning in one of the Haviland factories. See F12 4945, *établissements insalubres;* Dr. E. Raymondaud, *Hygiène et maladies des porcelainiers* (Paris, 1891); Dr. H. Boulland, *Etat sanitaire de Limoges en 1890* (Limoges, 1890); *Almanach Limousin,* 1893; and Boutaud, op. cit., pp. 36–38.

44. See Perrot, "The Three Ages of Industrial Discipline in France," and Ducray, op. cit., pp. 86–98, 200–204.

45. Boutaud, op. cit., pp. 13–14, 18. See F12 4654, "Rapport sur le travail des enfants dans les manufactures" (1879); and 10M 13. Alcoholism was a great problem (Ducray, op. cit., p. 199).

46. Ducray, op. cit., pp. 70–72; and 6M 513.

Purchasing Power (in Francs) of Day Laborers
in the Porcelain Industry

year	salary	cost of living	purchasing power
1882	100	100	100
1886	88	103	85
1895	91	96	94
1902	100	106	94
1904	116	113	102

Source: Boutaud, "Les Ouvriers porcelainiers de Limoges de 1884 à 1905" (Mémoire de maîtrise, Université de Poitiers, 1970), pp. 32–33.

47. Ducray, op. cit., p. 198; *Almanach Limousin, 1900.*

48. Dr. Pierre Charbonnier, "Limoges qui se transforme," *Limoges illustré*, May 15, 1908, quoting Dr. Jacques Bertillon in the *Journal*, March 31, 1908. In 1901 "le foyer Limousin" offered housing for workers for 390 francs rent per year toward eventual purchase, but only the quite well-off workers, Boutaud argues (p. 40), could afford such a move because of taxes. Limoges's *cité ouvrière* amounted to a single house, put up at the base of the faubourg Montjovis by the Etoile association in 1909.

49. Clancier, *La Vie quotidienne*, p. 253.

50. Ducray, op. cit., pp. 191–97.

51. Census of 1906, Boutaud, op. cit., pp. 3a–4 and 9–10; Ducray, op. cit., pp. 191–97. Amdur, op. cit., says that in 1891 60 percent of the porcelain workers in Limoges had been born there, compared to 40 percent of the shoemakers. References to the workers' patois include *Le Rappel*, July 14, 1895, and May 29, 1898; a soldier was insulted in patois without knowing it (4M 85, CC June 11, 1899).

52. Boutaud, op. cit., pp. 4–9, who says that 74.5 percent of the female porcelain workers had been born in Limoges.

53. Amdur, op. cit., p. 60, argues that rural birth would not have weakened artisans' claims to leadership among shoemakers, but it undercut their claim to lead the workers' movement, at least with the expansion of the shoe industry after World War I. Of the Monteux workers in 1906, 359 had been born in Limoges and 245 had been born elsewhere (1906 census). She contends that shoemakers had anarchist tendencies because their rural origins weakened participation in the dominant socialist movement. It is also possible that a move to the city enhanced militancy because unions provide a means of integration into a community; Shorter and Tilly, op. cit., pp. 271–73, write that "motors of militancy are set in motion not by the marginal, the integrated and the recently arrived, but by workers who belong to firmly established networks of long standing at the core of urban industrial society." In the long run, however, it must be admitted that the city aids mobilization by providing its own dominant tradition and serving as the cement that joins workers together.

54. Boutaud, op. cit., pp. 4–9; Ducray, op. cit., pp. 196–97; *Limoges illustré*, March 15, 1902, spoke of someone "moitié campagnard, moitié citadin." Boutaud shows, among other things, that 55 percent of the porcelain painters were sons of porcelain workers or shoemakers; they sometimes married *institutrices. Ouvriers en porcelain,* among whom the author probably included turners and moulders, had even more modest origins: 40 percent were sons of workers, 25 percent were sons of farmers, and 25 percent were sons of day laborers. Only 10 percent were born into "somewhat well-off [*un peu aisées*] families." Of *ouvrières* in Boutaud's sample (four hundred), 7 percent were daughters of farmers, 20 percent were daughters of porcelain workers, and 45 percent were daughters of day laborers. One third of the day laborers were sons of day laborers, and only 10 percent were sons of artisans or shopkeepers.

55. Jean Lenoble et al., *La Gauche au pouvoir depuis un siècle en Limousin* (Limoges, 1978), p. 22. On the Comité républicain national ouvrier de la Haute-Vienne see 1M 176, PHV July 20 and August 12, 1889, and Ferrand's letters to PHV March 12 and July 9, 1889, requesting an audience for "personal business"—he wanted a job. Planteau drew considerable anger from many workers for supporting Boulanger. The Municipal Council voted a credit of eight thousand francs to celebrate the centenary of the French Revolution (1M 2220, PHV May 7, 1889).

56. 3M 367 (1881); *La France Centrale,* December 11 and 26, 1880, and July 1, 6, and 11, 1881; and 3M 393 (1885), 394 (1886), and 398 and 404 (1888). The Municipal Council protested the General Council's decision, which may have been motivated by a fear of Boulanger, but the Radical majority on the council left little doubt that the sectioning would hurt them (*Almanach Limousin,* 1893). Before the 1878 elections a meeting of over twelve hundred people resulted in the drawing up of a list of radical candidates. Malinvaud's "Adresse des ouvriers de Limoges au Président de la République" in February 1879 (B.N. LB⁵⁷ 7028) reveals the moderate tone of workers' demands, emphasizing an amnesty for Communards, anticlericalism, republicanism, education, protection for workers against economic crisis, "le travail et les salaires de plus en rapport avec les besoins et le bien-être du travailleur," all of which was to lead to a gradual "grand effacement des distinctions et catégories sociales."

57. 3M 355–56 and 367. The Radicals included *quarante-huitards* Daniel Lamazière and Mollat, as well as Tarrade and Ransom, who had been part of the republican opposition at the end of the Empire.

58. 4M 125. The Cercle démocratique seems to have been a formalized continuation of the pre-electoral meetings of 1878, organized by the Radicals. The Cercle des droits de l'homme et du citoyen began with ninety-seven members, principally workers; its symbol was a bust of Marianne wearing a Phrygian cap (4M 125).

59. Jean Maitron, ed., *Dictionnaire biographique du mouvement ouvrier français* (Paris, 1974), vol. 3. Labussière defeated Chénieux, garnering 12,390 votes to his 8,123 in the 1898 legislative elections.

60. 3M 424–25. The 1892 election again demonstrated the solidarity of the second section behind the left; eleven of the twelve candidates elected on the first ballot were republican-socialists, led by Labussière, and eight were in the second section. A coherent republican-socialist program appealed to workers; as an *affiche* in the fifth section put it, "Without even leaving the limits of the municipality, many good things can be effected immediately." The Opportunists swept the first and third sections. Five workers were elected: Chalard, Pfrimmer, Balleroy, Hummel, and Barbois. François Chénieux, first elected to the Municipal Council in 1891, was born in 1845 in St. Pont-le-Betoux, in the Yonne. After serving as a surgeon's aide in the Franco-Prussian War, he became a doctor in 1873 and in 1893 was named director of the small medical faculté in Limoges. See *Le Petit Centre,* May 3, July 18 and 22; August 16–17, 1892.

61. *Le Rappel du Centre,* March 4, 1900; 4M 125.

62. 4 M 125–26. Following defeat in 1896, the number of members dropped to 160, each of whom paid 12 francs a year to belong.

63. 4M 125, CS November 21, 1889; *Le Rappel du Centre,* October 16, 1898, and March 4, 1900.

64. 4M 127, CC August 16, 1898; 1M 164, CC March 17, 1891; Maitron, *Dictionnaire biographique,* vol. 3. Boudaud fell into disfavor with the workers for helping elect the Boulangist Le Veillé in 1889 against Périn, yet he was reelected to the council in 1900.

65. 1M 179, CC April 28, 1890, PHV May 3, 1890, and April 5 and May 2, 1891; CC May 1, 1891; 1M 164, CC March 17, 1891, listed sixteen militants, including Hummel and Neveu: four porcelain painters, four shoemakers, two porcelain workers, and one porcelain polisher, one cabinetmakers, one *mouleur,* one wine merchant, one grocer, and an *octroi* employee.

66. 1M 164, Int. March 22, 1894; 4M 127, CC August 16, 1898; 3M 437; L'Emancipa-

tion, with its statutes stating that only workers could belong, probably included both Allemanists and Guesdists.

67. 1M 164. In 1898 the club established electoral committees in each section (CC July 26, 1898). Boudaud admitted that the Allemanists should have followed the lead of the Guesdists; when Guesde came to Limoges in 1894, the Avant-garde group held a *punch* for him, while Dr. Chénieux refused to allow him to speak in a municipal building. See also CC July 3, 1896; of the forty-seven workers in attendance at a meeting in 1895, thirty were sabot makers (CS July 2, 1895).

68. BB18 1972, PGL May 13, 1894; 1M 164 CS May 13, 1894. Malinvaud's letter is noted in a report in BA 199, "Pamphile à X." The letter, dated January 1, 1879, insisted that it be hand delivered.

69. 1M 179.

70. See Chapter Seven, pp. 195–201.

71. 4M 315; 4M 127, CC August 16, 1898. Threatening letters were sent to porcelain manufacturers by anarchists in 1891; copies of *La Révolte,* sent from Paris, turned up at the railroad station. Jean Lenoble et al., op. cit., p. 29, estimate that there were less than one hundred anarchists in the entire department.

72. Pierre Cousteix, "Influence des doctrines anarchistes en Haute-Vienne sous la IIIe République," *L'Actualité de l'histoire* 13 (November 1955): 26–27.

73. 4M 315, CC March 19, 1893, April 10, 1894, and December 12, 1897; 1M 165, CS April 21, 1895, and BB18 2000, PGL April 23, 1895.

74. 3M 398 (1888), *affiche* of the Allemanist candidates.

75. 3M 398. On the first ballot the independent radicals (Opportunists) received 6,522 votes and the Radicals received 5,126. Hummel, Neveu, and the other workers running for the council attacked Prefect Sée's campaign against the *syndicats.*

76. 3M 398 and 402.

77. Ibid.

78. 1M 165, CC September 28 and PHV October 4, 1890; 3M 418, 425–26.

79. *Le Petit Centre,* May 3, 14, and 30, June 30, July 18 and 22, August 16–17 and 21, and October 24 and 29, 1891. The newspaper waged a campaign against the socialists, accusing them of wanting to take the peasantry's land, importing a doctrine from Germany, and labeling those who headed small businesses "bourgeois."

80. 3M 418, 424–25. In this election the first and second sections were represented by nine seats, the third and fifth by five seats each, and the fourth by eight seats.

81. Maitron, *Dictionnaire biographique,* vol. 3; 10M 156, *signalement.* Treich, born in 1860, stressed the importance of combining economic and political action (see *Le Rappel,* May 23, 1897); he was an unsuccessful candidate in the 1898 legislative elections.

82. 10M 156, *signalements;* PHV November 28, 1893; statutes, which excluded consumer cooperatives. The Federation, representing thirty-four trades and occupations, opposed the immediate declaration of a general strike while accepting it in principle (10M 99, PHV January 26, 1895; 10M 156, CC July 8 and December 10, 1893).

83. 10M 156, PHV November 28 and December 10, 1893. Treich to mayor, March 16, 1893, and CS April 19, 1894; 10M 153, CC September 23, 1894. Labussière served as honorary president of the Federation's annual fete in 1894. For the strikes, see 10M 111, CC August 12, 1893, CC January 19, 1894, PHV January 18, 1894; *Le Courrier du Centre,* January 22, 1894; BB18 1970, PGL May 2, 1894; F12 4672, PHV April 19, 1893, summary reports in F12 4675, January 18 and PHV March 7, 1894; 10M 126, CC March 18–24, and April 24, 1893.

84. 10M 183, PHV July 24 and September 24, 1895, CS September 12 and CC September 29, 1895. Labussière presided over a banquet for the delegates. After Labussière defeated Chénieux by 2,684 votes to the latter's 2,629, 16 *progressistes* resigned, provoking the election. The new municipality had offered a *punch* for the congress of metallurgists that took place earlier in September (10M 182, CC September 21, 1895); see also BB18 2013 and 3M 435. There was no election in the second section, which had no Opportunist councilmen. One of the council's first acts was to send 500 francs support to the strikers in Carmaux.

85. F7 13622, PHV September 8, 1896, and December 28, 1905; extract of Municipal Council meeting, March 11, 1896.

86. F7 13622, statutes.

87. Ibid., CS January 27 and August 1, 1896.

88. Ibid.

89. 123 o 7(23), Municipal Council meeting, December 11, 1895; Bourdelle, op. cit., p. 78, quoting *La Fédération,* January 1, 1896.

Chapter Seven

1. 3M 442, CC May 1, 1896; 3M 437, CC May 1 and 2, 1896; F7 13622, CS May 1, 1896. The building was the former factory of Dalpeyrat and Depelley.

2. 3M 442, CC February 7, 1896; 1M 161, CC March 9, 13, and 17, 1896, on the clerical gatherings; 3M 437, *affiche* of progressistes in the second arrondissement; CC April 10, 14, 17, 28, and 30, 1896.

3. 3M 442, *affiche;* 3M 437, CP third arrondissement, May 2, 1896; CP first arrondissement, April 30, 1896; CC April 30.

4. 3M 437, CP first arrondissement, April 29, 1896.

5. 3M 437, CP second arrondissement, May 1, 1896, CC April 23, 1896, reporting on a meeting of sixty people, presided over by Tabaton-Tuilière, and letter of Millet, of the Avant-garde, appearing in *Le Courrier du Centre,* April 14, 1896; 1M 164, CS July 2, 1896, noting the insistence of Allemanists that workers be represented by workers.

6. 3M 437, CC April 23, May 1 and 8, 1896; 3M 437, CS May 1 and CP first arrondissement, April 30, 1896: "on ne remarquait que des ouvriers."

7. 3M 437, CP first arrondissement, May 1, CP second arrondissement, May 1, 1896, and following.

8. He also discussed his split with Treich. The latter saw strikes as a "means of defense and of social emancipation and not as an arm of war." Universal suffrage offered, Treich thought, "the suffering class the possibility of ultimately controlling the means of production" (see 3M 437, CS May 5 and 8, CC May 1, 1896).

9. 3M 437, CP first arrondissement, May 1, and CP third arrondissement, May 2, 1896. On the revolutionary heritage, see, for example, *Le Rappel du Centre,* July 17, 1898, for an article on the Revolutions of 1789, 1848, and 1871; December 22, 1895, for an article on Pierre Leroux; and June 21, 1896, for a summary of the importance of Albert, the worker in the provisional government of 1848.

10. 3M 437, CP first arrondissement, May 1, and CP third arrondissement, May 2, 1896.

11. 3M 437, CP first arrondissement, April 29, 1896; *Le Rappel du Centre* attacked Chénieux and his friends for their luxurious lifestyle, implying that they drank too much, while people in the faubourgs did not have enough to eat (February 23 and May 7 and 10, 1896).

12. 3M 437, CP first arrondissement, April 29, 1896. Raymond himself was attacked by the Allemanists for being bourgeois (CC April 10, 1896).

13. 3M 442, general commanding the 12th Military Division, May 9; 3M 437, CC May 10 and 11, and PHV May 2, 1896. Troops were readied at the Hôtel de Ville and put on alert in the barracks; at least eighty gendarmes and police were posted at several locations. 3M 438, results, and CC May 11, 1896; 3M 437, CC May 10 and general commanding the 12th Military Division, May 9, 1896; *Le Rappel du Centre,* May 24, 1896.

14. *Almanach Limousin,* 1898, referring to the meeting of May 29, 1896.

15. BB18 1972, PGL May 13, 1894; 1M 165, CS May 13, 1894. Whereas in the 1885 election only 2,326 out of 17,277 eligible voters participated, in 1896 3,547 out of 5,144 voters turned out in the second section and 1,636 out of 2,239 turned out in the fifth section (3M 400).

16. 1M 165, CS July 7, 1895, and *Le Petit Centre,* July 8. When Chauvière, a deputy representing the Seine, arrived in September to speak before seven hundred people, the police noted that it was the ninth such *conférence contradictoire* that year. *Le Rappel du Centre* (March 21, 1897) reported on a meeting in which the councilmen from the fifth section recounted their first year in office to two hundred people, who approved their work by acclamation; see also *Le Rappel du Centre* for May 2, 1897.

17. 1M 165, CS April 21 and May 4, 1895; *Le Rappel du Centre,* May 1, 1895. See 4M 102, "Registre des déclarations de réunions ou conférences publiques," March 1881 to March 1907 (which seems incomplete).

18. See Dalotel et al., op. cit.

19. *L'Univers,* July 10, 1895.

20. 1M 160, CS December 7, 1899; *Le Rappel du Centre,* November 8, 1900. Noël and Pressemane debated Marc Sangnier in 1903 (1M 159, CC June 27, 1903).

21. Abbé Jean Desgranges, *L'Organisation des conférences* (Limoges, 1928), p. 22.

22. Ibid., pp. 22–23. Desgranges estimated that some six or seven thousand of Limoges's twenty-five thousand workers heard him speak.

23. Ibid., pp. 86–116 (quotation from p. 109). Among the priest's suggestions was to put the guest speaker in an apartment and to "feed him according to his tastes or diet, having him drink a little of the good wine of France, not to excess, however" (p. 75).

24. Madame Louis Gerardin, "La Presse catholique à Limoges—fin du XIXe—début du XXe," *Association française pour l'avancement des sciences* (Limoges, 1974), citing *La Croix,* May 26, 1895.

25. 1M 176, PHV July 20 and August 12, 1889, and Ferrand's letters to PHV, March 12 and July 9, 1889, requesting to see him—he wanted a job. CS April 17, 1897; 4M 128, CS November 21, 1899; BB18 1816, PGL May 2, 1890; F7 12462, CS September 15, 1899. *Le Tout Limoges* was published from December 4, 1892, through January 29, 1893.

26. 1M 156, PHV August 7 and November 13, 1898.

27. F7 12462, CS September 15, 1899; BB18 2118B, PGL September 19, 1899; 1M 156, CC September 4, 6, and 8, 1899.

28. BB18 2118B, PGL September 19–20 and December 15, 25, and 26, 1899. Another activist, Chaisematin, left town because he feared arrest.

29. 1M 138, CC January 7 and February 19, 1899; F7 12457, CS August 25, 1900. They agreed to meet occasionally and wrote the Ligue de la partie française for advice (which was to keep meeting).

30. 1M 191, CC November 18, 1898; 1M 161, CC August 14 and September 1, 1898, and March 2, 1899; 1M 138, CC January 1 and February 2, 1899, May 18 and June 18, 1900; 4M 84, CC June 3, 1899; 1M 191, CC September 1, October 11, November 16 and 18, 1898, March 2 and August 11, 1899, and PHV September 3 and 10, 1899. The League of the Rights of Man was also active.

31. 1M 161, CC September 1, October 21 and 30, and November 7 and 22, 1898, CS November 21, 1898; 1M 166, CS July 15 and October 19, 1900. Rumors of a coup d'état by rightists reached Limoges. In June 1903 some members of a fishing party returning to the city were arrested for shouting "Down with Dumont!" (4M 84, CC June 3 and 18, 1903). The Allemanists accused the Guesdists of excluding them from a *punch populaire* of "republican protest" in October 1898.

32. 1M 161, CS January 12, 1901; 1M 138, CC October 26 and 27, 1902; CS January 28, 1902; CC February 13 and 16, 1902; F7 2457, CC February 16, 1902, and police report for November 4, 1901.

33. See, for example, 1M 160, CS June 30, 1899, and February 15, 1903; 1M 128, CC March 16, 1902; 1M 156, CS January 17 and March 22, 1903. When nationalist and clerical speakers came, socialists sometimes packed the hall, drowning out the anti-republican *ordre du jour* (for example, 1M 138, CC October 26; F7 12457, CC February 16, 1902).

34. 1M 161, CC October 27, 1902; 1M 138, CC February 13 and 16, 1902; 1M 156, CC June 23 and October 24, 1902; CS January 17, March 9 and 23, 1903. The police commissioner listed Clappier and Fayout (both lawyers), two wine merchants (including Gardelle), two café owners, one of the Malinvaud butchers, five soldiers, and two *quincaillers* as noteworthy rightists. A Spanish priest, Isasi, was expelled from France in 1902 for his political activities as Ardant's right-hand man (F19 5912, PHV January 16 and May 23, 1902).

35. F19 2529, PHV October 28 and November 11, 1889; Madame Louis Gerardin, "L'Action social catholique en Haute-Vienne: Deux abbés 'démocrates,'" mémoire de maîtrise, Université de Limoges, 1975. The author also discusses Abbé Goguyer, the *chanoine* of the Church of St. Joseph, who entered the priesthood after his wife's death. See F19 5912, PHV (Monteil), April 9, 1901, calling Marévéry one of the most active of the enemies of the Republic.

36. See Abbé Jean Desgranges, *Les Vraies Idées du Sillon* (Limoges, 1905); pp. 81–83.

37. Ibid.

38. 1M 160, CS April 23, 1900; Gerardin, "L'Action sociale catholique." Desgranges admitted that no more than ten or twelve workers attended his meetings, and that most of the audience sometimes consisted of priests from the region. In July 1904 a confrontation took place at the place Dussoubs between members of Sillon's "moral elite" and workers singing the "International" (1M 159, CC July 11, 1904).

39. 1M 160, CS February 19, May 20, and April 23, 1900; 1M 159, CC June 26 and 28, 1903, and July 10, 1904.

40. 1M 160, CS June 27, 1899.

41. Madame Louis Gerardin, "L'Action social catholique"; 1M 160, CC November 3 and 9, 1899; CS June 27, 1899; 1M 161, CC March 9, 1896. At one social Catholic talk police noted that the audience included butchers, habitués of the Catholic clubs, and several merchants (4M 456, CC April 4, 1900).

42. See Maitron, *Dictionnaire biographique,* vol. 3, for a biographical summary of Faure.

43. 4M 315, CC January 19, March 21–27, and CP third arrondissement, March 28, 1897. According to Pierre Cousteix, "Influence des doctrines anarchistes," p. 27,

Beaure had to pawn his watch so Broussouloux could move on. Broussouloux, *dit* Pintelon, *dit* Rouard, *dit* Viochot, *dit* Louis l'Algérien, was born in Algiers in 1863 and lived in Paris (Maitron, *Dictionnaire biographique,* vol. 3).

44. 4M 315, CS January 15 and 19, 1899; 1M 191, CC October 30, 1898; F7 13622, PHV September 8, 1896; 1M 165, CS April 21, 1895, and March 28, 1897. One minor incident was reported (4M 84, *procès-verbal,* November 2, 1898) when forty people, angry because Faure had not appeared, as scheduled, went to the offices of *Le Petit Centre* and *Le Courrier du Centre,* shouting, "Vive la Sociale!" Julie Louise Paujaud, *dite* Séraphine, was born in 1859.

45. *Le Mouvement socialiste en France (1893–1905): Les Guesdists,* p. 510.

46. Ibid., pp. 316–17, 510; 3M 475; Lenoble, et al., op. cit., pp. 51–52.

47. 1M 164, CC January 1 and 27, February 3, 17 and 29, March 2 and 15, 1896; *Le Rappel du Centre,* September 19 and 22, 1897; F7 13622, CS December 30, 1897, noting that the schism between Guesdists and reform socialists was well under way. Coussy was a member of the Conseil des prud'hommes.

48. Bobe, op. cit., pp. 38–40, 3M 456, CC May 1, 1900. See *La Bataille sociale* and *L'Avenir.* The former began publication March 12, 1898; Treich wrote an editorial for each issue, which began with articles on the *affaire de Limoges.* In 1900 the newspaper became the property of the Associations ouvrières de Limoges et du Centre and ceased publication in June 1901.

49. Bobe, op. cit., pp. 38–39.

50. Docteur Fraisseux, *Au long de ma route* (Limoges, 1946), pp. 27, 41, and 52.

51. Based upon Maitron, *Dictionnaire biographique,* vol. 3. See also 1M 164 for a list of members of the Parti ouvrier limousin. Of the thirty-seven people noted, sixteen were porcelain painters.

52. Maitron, *Dictionnaire biographique,* vol. 3. Hummel, who died in 1899, could not read or write until his militant years (*Le Rappel du Centre,* November 26, 1899); Bobe, op. cit., p. 27.

53. Bobe, op. cit., p. 44.

54. *Le Rappel du Centre,* October 3, 1897.

55. Joan W. Scott, "Mayors Versus Police Chiefs: Socialist Municipalities Confront the French State," in Merriman, ed., *French Cities in the Nineteenth Century,* p. 232.

56. 4M 84, CC June 3, 1899; 1M 164, CS August 5, 1899, December 1900, and January 8, October 19 and 30, 1900, CC August 1 and 5, 1899.

57. F7 12305, CS January 21, 1900; 1M 164, CS January 21 and 29, February 5, 1900, CC March 1–5; *Le Rappel du Centre,* December 24, 1899; *La Bataille sociale,* March 4, 1900; F7 13622, PHV December 28, 1905. Even during this crisis, *Le Rappel du Centre* paid tribute to Guesde in its "Men of Revolution" series (February 4, 1900). Treich was having well-publicized marital problems with Madeline Darthout, to whom he had been married since 1882.

58. 3M 456, CP second arrondissement, May 5, CP fourth arrondisement, May 12; CS March 23 through May 17, 1900; 1M 164, CS February 17 and 26, 1900; *Le Rappel du Centre,* September 16, 1900. Labussière, later accused by his Guesdist enemies of lacking character, fought a duel with the editor of *La Gazette* in 1900.

59. 3M 456, CC April 3, 1900.

60. *Le Rappel du Centre,* September 16, 1900; 3M 456, CC April 22 and May 6, 1900; *affiches,* such as "Appel aux travailleurs."

61. 3M 461, CC May 20, 1900; 3M 456, *affiches* and CS May 9, CC May 12 and following 1900; 3M 457, results; see *Le Rappel du Centre* for the period preceding and following the election, including an electoral appeal in patois. One ballot was

marked "A bat [*sic*] Nicolas, Vive sa femme!" Labussière referred to the second section as "the Belleville of Limoges," CP second arrondissement, May 5 (3M 456). The section had picked up two extra seats since 1892 because of its growth.

62. F7 13622, PHV December 28, 1905; 1M 164, CC June 6 and 27, July 27, August 13, and December 3, 1900, CS July 20–30, 1900; *Le Rappel du Centre*, December 23, 1900; *Almanach Limousin*, 1902. The declaration was signed by Boudaud, Tabaton-Tuilière, Chauly, Dutreix, Coussy, Chambaret, Noël, Plaud, and Millet, who accepted the resolutions of the congress of Paris, 1899.

63. 1M 164, CC March 1 and 18 and December 3, 1900, February 8 and 18, 1901; CS June 25 and 26, PHV November 23, 1900. The Cercle d'unité celebrated the anniversary of the Commune, but the Cercle démocratique did not.

64. 1M 164, CS April 19, 1903; *L'Avenir* was published from December 2, 1900, until April 5, 1903. See Bobe, op. cit., p. 14.

65. Bobe, op. cit., p. 41; *Le Socialiste de la Haute-Vienne*, January 22, 1903, and January 10, April 17, and November 6, 1904; *Le Réveil du Centre*, June 6, 1904; Chauly and Baudaud voted against support for the Université populaire, arguing that it was unnecessary to have one in each quarter (*Almanach Limousin*, 1905). They feared it might detract from their own educational efforts. The Federation dissolved itself in June 1904 (10M 156).

66. *Le Rappel, du Centre*, August 25, 1895, and November 20 and 27, 1898.

67. *Le Rappel du Centre*, October 13, 1895, and August 15 and November 27, 1898; *Almanach Limousin*, 1894 and 1898, summary of Municipal Council sessions of July 27 and August 5, 1896. The council vote was twenty-four to eleven, with the *progressistes* all voting against the measure. During the debate in 1893, Hummel told the *progressistes*, "What you consider an honorary post the worker considers a post of combat."

68. *Le Rappel du Centre*, April 24, 1898; 1M 179, CC April 30 and June 5, 1897; *Almanach Limousin*, 1899, leading Chénieux to say to the socialists, "You threaten us constantly with violent revolution. I forbid you the right to speak of May 1 as an international holiday." In 1891 the socialists had accused the prefect of trying to prevent schools from being used for electoral meetings; during the 1896 election campaign the prefect instructed police to attend and report on such gatherings (for example, F7 13622, police spy, February 20, 1897).

69. *Le Rappel du Centre*, December 25, 1898; also November 27 and December 4, 1898; *La Bataille sociale*, May 6, 1900.

70. *Le Rappel du Centre*, December 3, 1899 and June 4, 1900; *Almanach Limousin*, 1898, 1901, and 1902; 1M 164, CC December 1, 1898.

71. *La Semaine religieuse*, 1882 (pp. 917–21). On October 25, 1899, the council voted eighteen to six to congratulate the government on its measures against "the clerical-reactionary coalition," *Almanach Limousin*, 1901.

72. F19 5817, police report, n.d. [July 1880] and 6M 4 fonds, bishop May 15, July 31, and August 15, 1880; *La Bataille sociale*, May 6, 1900.

73. Abbe Marévéry was fined five francs for an infraction of the decree (BB18 2022, PGL June 22, 1896).

74. *Almanach Limousin*, 1893, summary of council meeting of June 17, 1891.

75. 2V 3, CC May 15, 1890, PHV April 5, 1890, decree affirmed May 13; CC June 6, 1897; *Almanach Limousin*, 1896, F19 6059, including *L'Univers*, November 20 and 24, 1894; *La Croix*, November 11, 1894.

76. 2V 3, CC June 6, 1897, PHV June 3 and 15, 1897 *Almanach Limousin*, 1897 and 1898; that year a *comité des processions* protested the suspension of such ceremonies

by walking together in small groups after a meeting in the city's churches (BB18 2052, PGL June 8, 1897; F19 6059, PHV June 15, 1897). It is interesting to note that *Le Rappel du Centre* for June 17, 1894, also gave the date as "29 prairial an 2."

77. *La Bataille sociale,* November 26, 1898; *Le Rappel du Centre,* December 15, 1895, June 4, 1900; *Almanach Limousin,* 1887, 1891, 1903, 1904, and 1905; Camille Jouhanneaud, "Les Changements des noms des rues à Limoges," *Almanach Limousin,* 1899.

78. *Almanach Limousin,* 1899.

79. *Almanach Limousin,* 1902 and 1904. Socialist pressure for more lay *crèches* was marred by one incident. Mademoiselle Hebrard, a former nun, was the victim of an unsavory campaign by the Guesdists in 1901 and 1902; they claimed she had been sleeping with two reform socialist friends (1M 198, CC October 1, 1901, and February 12, 1902).

80. 1M 198, CC August 2–11, 1900 and following; CS August 10; *Almanach Limousin,* 1903; *Le Courrier du Centre,* October 19, 1902; *La Gazette,* January 26, 1902; *Le Bonhomme Limousin,* March 14, 1901. Madame Noualhier eventually was successful in one of two lawsuits against her detractors.

81. *Almanach Limousin,* 1902 (Municipal Council meeting of January 23, 1901); *Limoges illustré,* March 1, 1901.

82. 1M 188, extract of Municipal Council meeting, April 22, 1901; *Almanach Limousin,* 1893 and 1901. Monteil broke with custom and visited a Municipal Council meeting (*Le Rappel du Centre,* December 2, 1900); because of his anticlerical campaign, Monteil was the only prefect of the Haute-Vienne who enjoyed relatively good relations with the socialists.

83. 6M 4 fonds, July 4, 1854.

84. F19 5818, anonymous, April 9, 1881; BB18 1193, PGL April 18, 1892; 1M 177, PHV September 27, 1895. A number of incidents occurred as a result of the Church's opposition to Sunday work; in 1899 several students broke the windows of shops that remained open (BB18 2125, PGL June 5, 1899).

85. *Almanach Limousin,* 1904; *Limoges illustré,* June 15, 1904. The Libre-Pensée organized a large anticlerical meeting in August featuring Labussière and Pressemane (*Le Socialiste de la Haute-Vienne,* August 7, 1904).

86. *Le Rappel du Centre,* June 23 and December 15, 1895.

87. *Almanach Limousin,* 1897, noting that the quarter included seventy-eight children at the time of Dr. Boulland's report. The mortality rate for Viraclaud was forty-five per every thousand individuals and thirty-six for the rest of Limoges. See also *Almanach Limousin,* 1900.

88. *Almanach Limousin,* 1889, 1890, 1897, 1900, and 1904; Louis Guibert, *Limoges qui s'en va* (Limoges, 1897). The expropriation took three months, and some of the quarter was not demolished until 1908. By the spring of 1898, 1.2 million francs had been spent on such projects as the Aigueperse sewer, electric lights, and the modification of "eccentric quarters" (*Le Rappel du Centre,* May 5, 1898).

89. *Le Rappel du Centre,* September 10, 1895, April 24 and September 4, 1898, and September 2, 1899; yearly summaries of Municipal Council meetings in the *Almanach Limousin,* 1901, 1903, 1904; F7 13622, PHV December 28, 1905. The subvention proposed for the 1895 congress had been voted down fifteen votes to twelve (*Almanach Limousin,* 1897). The socialist council voted assistance for the municipal theater because workers seemed to attend in fairly large numbers (*Almanach Limousin,* 1898). Labussière claimed that Chénieux had falsified the

commune's financial situation to paint a rosy picture of the *progressiste* regime, while his earlier administration had never had to borrow money. Chénieux did leave a surplus of over 135,000 francs.

90. Willard, op. cit., p. 32.

91. Pierre Vallin, "Fête, mémoire et politique: Les 14 juillet en Limousin (1880–1914)," *Revue française de science politique* 32, no. 6 (December, 1982): 958–60; 1M 213, mayor July 5, 1889; *affiches,* and subsequent reports. July 14 was celebrated at the Bourse du Travail with a *bal populaire,* as well as by festivities in individual quarters (*Le Rappel du Centre,* July 15, 1900).

92. 1M 179, CC May 1, 1899, and April 28, 1900; *affiches.* Dr. Chénieux had previously announced that he would not take responsibility for the "absolutely revolutionary scenes that occur" on May Day (*Almanach Limousin,* 1896); see also 1M 179, CC May 2, 1894, and PHV May 2, 1891.

93. 1M 179, CC April 21, 28, and 30, and May 2 and June 5, 1897; CS May 1, 1897; PHV May 2, 1897; *Le Rappel du Centre,* May 9, 1897. See also Scott, op. cit., pp. 240–43.

94. *Le Réveil du Centre,* April 30, 1904; 3M 491, PHV April 26, 1904; 3M 475, CC April 28, 1904.

95. *Almanach Limousin,* 1904, summary of Municipal Council meeting, December 29, 1902. The *groupe ouvrier* began calling for more assistance for workers in 1900 (*Almanach Limousin,* 1902).

96. 3M 475, *affiches* and PHV April 26, 1904; 3M 480, results; *Le Réveil du Centre,* April 30, 1904. Betoulle, the illegitimate son of a seamstress, was born in the Sablard quarter. He left school to take a job as a clerk with the Theodore Haviland Company. After the election the prefect noted Labussiere's good relations with the administration, adding that he was "très écouté par la population ouvrière. Il jouit à Limoges d'une grande popularité." (3M 491 PHV May 15, 1905).

97. *Almanach Limousin,* 1905, quoting Betoulle at the meeting of December 29, 1903. *La Bataille sociale,* May 29, 1898. See Scott, op. cit., p. 245.

98. Here my interpretation differs from that of Scott, op. cit., p. 245.

99. Bourdelle, op. cit., pp. 95, 103–4. Bobe, op. cit., p. 64; Boutaud, op. cit., p. 65; F7 13622. At the end of 1905, 19 percent of the workforce was unionized (Bourdelle, op. cit., p. 95). Sixty percent of the porcelain workers were unionized in 1902 and 77 percent by 1914 (Amdur, op. cit., p. 104). Ducray, op. cit., pp. 141–45, describes the "mixed" unions, such as the "corporation Saint-Antoine de Padoue," established in 1891 by Madame Guérin, with one hundred women as members. Such "unions" struggled.

100. Bourdelle, op. cit., p. 90, quoting *La Fédération,* January 1, 1898.

101. F7 13622, CS August 9, September 10, October 25 and 27, and November 24, 1897; *Le Rappel du Centre,* March 21 and December 19, 1897; *Limoges illustré,* May 15, 1901; Bourdelle, op. cit., p. 93, quoting the Bourse's report for 1901: "Même dans les centres imbus du plus grand esprit réactionnaire, nos musiciens n'ont pas craint à l'ombre du drapeau rouge de faire entendre à tous les échos notre belle internationale."

102. F7 12734, CP May 29, 1901. See Jacques Julliard, *Fernand Pelloutier et les origines du syndicalisme d'action directe* (Paris, 1971). Pelloutier, however, would not have approved of the reformist and politicized nature of the Limoges Bourse.

103. 123 o 7(23), Municipal Council meeting, October 26, 1894, and December 11, 1895; *Almanach Limousin,* 1896; Bourdelle, op. cit., pp. 79–81, 88–89.

104. 123 o 7(23), Municipal Council meetings of September 17 and October 25, 1897, CC August 28, 1898; F7 13622, CS September 9, 1896, and May 22 and June 23, 1897.

105. *Le Rappel du Centre,* October 4, 1896, March 3, August 2, and October 3, 1897; F7 13622, "Opérations du Bureau de placement gratuit de la Bourse du Travail de Limoges." Bourdelle, op. cit., pp. 84–88, who gives the following numbers for requests and placements effected: 1896 (803/177); 1899 (1,285/545); 1900 (1,400/610); 1901 (3,742/2,143); 1904 (1,741/1,216); 1905 (1,265/1,002).

106. F7 3622, CC September 10, 1897, and CS October 25, 1897. In 1895 Treich argued that "the strike is a murderous weapon, the use of which is as harmful for the employers as for the workers" (10M 111, CC May 7, 1895). In September 1896 the special commissioner described the Limoges Bourse as "a powerful means of electoral action" (F7 13622, CS September 8, 1896). See Peter Schöttler, "Politique sociale ou lutte des classes: Notes sur le syndicalisme 'apolitique' des Bourses du Travail," *Mouvement social* 116 (July–September, 1981): 3–20.

107. F7 13622, PHV December 28, 1905.

108. Ibid., règlements.

109. Bourdelle, op. cit., p. 92.

110. Ibid., pp. 98–102.

111. Ibid.

112. On strike waves see Shorter and Tilly, op. cit. For strikes in Limoges, see Bourdelle, op. cit., esp. pp. 106–27.

113. BB18 2025, PGL June 2–August 8, 1896; F12 4682, summary. At first Treich did not support the strike; when he asked if the workers did not have confidence in him, they allegedly replied "Pas trop!" But Treich had infuriated the employers in a letter to them, in the fall of 1895, demanding that they raise the wages of their lowest-paid workers.

114. *Le Courrier du Centre,* June 3–20, esp. June 9, 1896; F12 4682, letters of PHV June 10 and following. The manufacturers particularly resented Treich's claim to speak for the workers.

115. *Le Courrier du Centre,* June 12 and 18, 1896, and following; F12 4682 PHV June 10 and following. The strike is thoroughly documented. The *garçons de magasin* and the *emballeurs* voted against the strike, while the *useurs de grains* and polishers supported it. The *Almanach Limousin* for 1897 noted the patois shouts.

116. F12 4682, PHV June 17–28, 1896; Ducray, op. cit., pp. 175–79; Grellier, op. cit., pp. 280–82; *Le Rappel du Centre,* June 14, 21, and 28, 1896.

117. Bourdelle, op. cit., p. 145, and appendix number 4.

118. F12 4682, extract from *Le Temps,* June 18, 1896.

119. *Le Courrier du Centre,* June 10, 1896. The manufacturers were angered at receiving notices such as the one from Hummel, sent during the strike of *finisseurs* in June 1895. "Vous devez vous adresser, non aux ouvriers, mais à la Fédération, légalement instituée et chargée de défendre des intérêts ouvriers" (10M 111, CC June 1, 1895).

120. *Le Courrier du Centre,* June 8, 1896.

121. 10M 111, summary; PHV September 6, 1895, CC September 7, 1896; 10M 112, summary; Minister of the Interior, December 27, 1904, CC December 7, 9, and 23, 1904; F12 4678, PHV September 4–7, 1895. Among the alleged insults were the following: "Salaud, cochon, sale juif."

122. *Le Rappel du Centre,* June 17, 1900, on the Dumont strike see 10M 126. Theodore

Haviland was awarded the Légion d'honneur at the end of 1903 (*Limoges illustré,* January 15, 1904). The workers castigated the latter for letting one worker go who had four children, the oldest of whom was seven years old.

123. See the brief discussion on the *progressistes* in Jean-Marie Mayeur, *Les Débuts de la IIIe République, 1871–1898* (Paris, 1973), pp. 211–17.

124. *Le Courrier du Centre,* June 4, 1896.

125. Cited with emphasis in original, by Shorter and Tilly, op. cit., p. 349.

126. The workers sang, a song that included the following refrain: "Ah! Mon ami / Quel sale outil / Le vilain, nom / Que celui de Dumont / Non d'un pétard / Quel sale cafard / Qui fait crever / de faim des ouvriers." See 10M 126, CC June 13–15; CS May 23 and following; BB18 2153, PGL May 30 and June 12 and 13, 1900; F12 4682, PGL May 30, 1900.

127. 10M 112, CC December 7 and following.

128. 10M 111, summary of Lecointe strike.

129. BB18 2244, PGL December 25 and 28, 1903; Bourdelle, op. cit., pp. 103–13.

130. BB18 2244, PGL June 23, 1903; F12 4678, summary, 10M 111, summary; BB18 1997, PGL April 27 and August 21, 1895; 10M 130, CC July 5, 10, and following.

131. 10M 111, summary and CC June 3–7 and November 10, 19, and 20, 1895; BB18 1997, summary.

132. 10M 11, summary and PHV April 4, 1896; *Le Rappel du Centre,* August 11, 1895.

133. *Le Réveil du Centre,* September 29, 1904; BB18 2274, PGL November 18 and 28 and December 3–15, 1904; 10M 112, gendarmerie report, December 9, 1904, and summary. The cutters earned four and a half to six francs a day, while *monteurs* earned four to four and a half francs. The former denied that they were trying to maintain their particular privileged situation as the highest-paid shoemakers, insisting that they asked nothing more than security for the future. The strike generated considerable bitterness, particularly after one manufacturer reneged on a promise. The PGL wrote that a poorly organized show of force by troops or gendarmes could only lead to "great trouble and grave disorders" (BB18 2274, PGL December 9, 1904).

134. Perrot, "The Three Ages of Industrial Discipline"; Ducray, op. cit., p. 127: "Ils paraissent surtout avoir une sainte horreur de tout ce qui a l'air de les enrégimenter; ils haïssent la dépendance, et se montreraient très défiants à l'égard de tout ce que les patrons pourraient tenter."

135. *Le Socialiste du Centre,* October 23, 1904; Pierre Cousteix, "Le Mouvement ouvrier limousin," p. 27; Bobe, op. cit., p. 35, speaks of the impact of "un milieu sociologique ouvrier et paysan disposé à recevoir les idées collectivistes."

136. BB18 1997, PGL June 22, 1895; *Le Petit Centre,* July 6, 1895; F12 4678, summary and CC July 10, 1895.

137. BB18 1997, PHV October 4, 1895.

138. F12 4678, summary and PHV September 4, 6, and 7, 1895.

139. F12 4678; 10M 130, CC December 5, 1895, and January 1, 1896.

140. F12 4682, summary and PHV October 19, 27, and 31, and November 1, 1896; BB18 2025, PGL October 21, 30, and 31, and November 2 and 11, 1896.

141. *Le Siècle,* November 13, 1896, extract in F12 4682.

142. 10M 131, summary and CC April 11 and 30 and May 16, 1902; Boutaud, op. cit., p. 17; BB18 2216, PGL May 30, April 3, 4, 5, 7, and 22, and May 16, 1902. A law passed in 1900 limited the workday to ten hours for factories employing men and women, which may have caused employers to put pressure on workers' wage demands. The Municipal Council voted one hundred thousand francs to assist unem-

ployed workers, and contributions and benefits raised another twelve thousand francs.

143. 1M 191, CC November 18, 1898; BB18 2244, PGL June 23 and 25, 1903; 10M 111, CC June 17, 1903.

144. BB18 2216, PGL March 30, April 3, 4, and following; 10M 131, summary. See notes 113–16 in this section.

Chapter Eight

1. Michelle Perrot, "Le Regard de l'autre: les patrons français vus par les ouvriers (1880–1914)," in Maurice Levy-Leboyer, ed., *Le Patronat de la seconde industrialisation* (Paris, 1979).

2. 10M 132, report of April 5, 1905.

3. 10M 112, PHV February 18, 1905, CC February 7; Geneviève Désiré-Vuillemin, "Les Grèves dans la région de Limoges de 1905 à 1914," *Annales du Midi* 85 (January–March 1973): 53–56. The *piqueuses* earned between 1.5 and 2.5 francs a day; *coupeurs* between 4.5 and 6; machinists between 4 and 5; and day laborers between 3 and 4. The first strike of the year was that of 50 porcelain workers employed by Batiot, who demanded and won a raise; the strike lasted from January 30 to February 3.

4. 10M 112, summary report; CC February 17 and 22, March 3 and 15, and April 1, 1905. The *Courrier du Centre* published a letter from one "Fargéas" asking the workers to return; the letter was probably sent by Malinvaud, who sold raw materials to the Fougeras factory, which explains why the workers demonstrated in front of that shop; see Désiré-Vuillemin op. cit., pp. 54–57. The description of Crouzière comes from Gabriel Beaubois, "Le Mouvement ouvrier à Limoges," *Mouvement socialiste,* 2nd series, vol. 7, nos. 155–56 (May 15 and June 1, 1905): 83.

5. 10M 112, summary report and CC April 1, 1905; the women's salaries were raised by 20 to 25 centimes a day, to between 2.5 and 2.75 francs, the men's salaries by 50 centimes to 6 and 6.5 francs; *sabotiers* got a raise from 3.5 to 4.5 francs.

6. 10M 112, CC, Feb. 28; 10M 122, CC March 3, 28; one meeting at the Bourse drew 2,000 workers.

7. BB18 2294, PGL April 1, 1905; Désiré-Vuillemin, op. cit., pp. 57–59.

8. 10M 131, summary report and CC March 14; BB18 2294, PGL March 11, 16, 18, and 20, 1905. The *moufletiers* earned 4.20 to 5.4 francs per day; 8 out of 10 struck, asking 1.20 more francs a day.

9. BB18 2294, PGL April 4, 5, and 6, 1905; Désiré-Vuillemin, "Une grève révolutionnaire: Les porcelainiers de Limoges en avril 1905," *Annales du Midi* 83 (January–March 1971): 54–57. See A. Corbin, *Les Filles de noce* (Paris, 1982), p. 354, noting the article "Le Droit de jambage à Limoges," *Le Libértaire,* April 23, 1905.

10. BB18 2294, PGL April 10 and 11, 1905, and 10M 127, CC April 4, and 5, 1905.

11. Désiré-Vuillemin, "Une grève révolutionnaire, pp. 58–60; 10M 132, CC April 14, 1905.

12. See Désiré-Vuillemin, "Une grève révolutionnaire," pp. 51–54, who suggests the importance of Tournier's anti-Masonic sentiments; BB18 2298, PGL March 15, 1905.

13. Désiré-Vuillemin, "Une grève révolutionnaire"; BB18 2298, PGL March 18–20, 1905.

14. *La Gazette de France, Le Courrier du Centre,* and *Le Réveil du Centre,* all

March 15, 1905. BB18 2290. The *affiche* was signed "Le Groupe socialiste révolutionnaire de Limoges—Parti socialiste de France."

15. 10M 132, CC April 14, 1905; the vote was 260 to 67 against accepting the manufacturer's offer.

16. *Le Réveil du Centre,* April 15; BB18 2294, PGL April 15, 1905. The recently established Bernardaud company, successor to R. Delinières, wrote to complain that five hundred workers had entered his factory after forcing open the door at 4:30 P.M., invading the workshops. Bernardaud himself was in New York (10M 132, company letter, April 14, 1905).

17. BB18 2294, PGL April 16, 1905; *Le Réveil du Centre,* April 16, 1905.

18. 10M 132, CC April 16, and 17, 1905, CP report, n.d.; *Le Réveil du Centre,* April 17, 1905.

19. 10M 132, his letter of April 15, 1905.

20. *Le Réveil, du Centre,* April 16 and 17, 1905.

21. *Le Réveil du Centre,* April 17, 1905; BB18 2294, PGL April 16, 1905; letter of director, April 16, 1905.

22. *Le Réveil du Centre,* April 18, 1905; apartments searched were at 20, rue Porte-Panet, 4, rue Dorat, and 25, boulevard St. Maurice. *Le Réveil du Centre* claimed that six thousand troops had arrived.

23. 10M 132, CC April 17, 1905; *Le Réveil du Centre,* April 19, 1905; Désiré-Vuillemin, "Une grève révolutionnaire," pp. 64–67.

24. 10M 132, CC April 18, 1905. Vardelle's grandfather owned two houses worth between ten and twelve thousand francs. An autopsy, witnessed by the family doctor, showed that Vardelle died from a single rifle shot that penetrated his thigh, rupturing an artery.

25. 10M 132, report of commander of 78th Infantry, April 18, 1905. CP April 17, 1905, CC (Dhermal) April 17, 1905; *Le Réveil du Centre,* April 19, 1905. Betoulle, Fèbre, and Borde were among the municipal councilmen circulating, attempting to prevent a clash. Several other people were wounded: A fifteen-year-old apprentice *sabotier,* living with his mother and her husband at 43, rue de Paris; Fernand Favarès, twenty-six, a commercial employee living at 8, rue du Consulat; Henri Faucher, eighteen, a *sabotier,* residing at route de Nexon (hit in the head by a bullet); 10M 132, CC April 18, 1905.

26. *Journal,* April 20, 1905.

27. 10M 132, unsigned letter, n.d., PHV April 22, 1905; *Journal,* April 20, 1905.

28. 10M 132, PHV April 22, 1905.

29. 10M 132, letters of Rouveroux frères, Pénicaud et Cie, and J. Pouyat, all April 18, 1905.

30. BB18 2294, PGL April 19, 21, and 23, and May 10, 1905. Twelve out of eighteen that were still in custody had been freed by the time of the amnesty. There had been a total of thirty-one arrests, eighteen for unlawful gathering, seven for "outrages," and six for the pillage of arms. Major disturbances occurred in St. Junien. (10M 132, PGL April 20, 1905).

31. 10M 132, PHV April 22, 1905. BB18 2294, April 22 and 23, 1905. Désiré-Vuillemin, "Une grève révolutionnaire," p. 70. The procureur général stated that two legal *sommations* had occurred, and that the tenth company had "returned" fire when two shots came from the Jardin d'Orsay (BB18 2294, PGL April 29, 1905). The arbitration committee included the justice of the peace, the president of the Tribunal de Commerce, three manufacturers, the general secretary of the Fédération de la céramique, and three porcelain workers.

32. BB18 2294¹, PGL April 28 and 29 to May 28, 1905.

33. BB18 2294, PGL May 9, and 17, 1905; Désiré-Vuillemin, "Les Grèves dans la région de Limoges," p. 61.

34. 10M 112, summary report. Exactly 189 shoemakers won a small raise from Lecointe et Denis on May 1, after a three-day strike.

35. 10M 131, CC May 16, 1905; summary report, Ahrenfeldt strike. The *décalqueuses* earned between 1.75 and 2.5 francs a day.

36. 10M 112, PHV October 3, 1905; BB18 2294, PGL July 7 and 8, 1905; 10M 122, summary report, Monteux strike; BB18 2294¹, PGL reports, May 25 to July 25, 1905.

37. 1M 180, CC May 1, PHV May 1 and CS May 1, 1905.

38. BB18 2294, PGL May 9, 13, and 15, 1905; 10M 132, gendarmerie report, May 10 and letter of Touze, May 10, 1905. CP May 10, 1905. All but two of the men arrested during the Beaulieu confrontation were convicted, the latter two let go only because they were fifteen. Two of those arrested at the rond-point Carnot incident were workers living on the rue de Paris, and another was from the adjacent rue Aigueperse. The location of the covered market nearby also brought people to that square. The procureur général contended that leniency shown those arrested during such incidents served to perpetuate them.

39. See Désiré-Vuillemin, "Une grève révolutionnaire," pp. 71–73.

40. 10M 132, letter of April 18, printed in its entirety by Désiré-Vuillemin, "Une grève révolutionnaire," p. 80. The man, O. Lafon, was called "more voracious than the lions of the forests of North America" and "le plus crapule de patron de Limoges."

41. Ibid.

42. BB18 2294, PGL May 2 and 11, 1905.

43. *Arrêté* of May 15, 1905; interview with Pierre Bertrand, extract from the *Petite République,* May 13, 1905, in BB18 1294. On May 12 the council announced it would not resign.

44. *Le Réveil du Centre,* May 2 and 31, 1905. The Chamber of Deputies voted to provide money for the "victims" of the strike, which angered the workers.

45. Ibid.

46. BB18 2294, *acte d'accusation,* Sept. 16, 1905, also found in F7 13622. There was a government *enquête,* headed by Constantin, who interviewed the president of the Chamber of Commerce, a number of manufacturers, and Rougerie, the general secretary of the Bourse du Travail. All those arrested were freed by the end of the year as part of an amnesty agreement.

47. 10M 132, CC April 17, 1905; see correspondence in BB18 2294.

48. Most were in their twenties; only four of the twenty-one were over thirty years of age. Five lived on the ancienne route d'Aixe, on which the Touze factory stood. One lived on the faubourg Pont Neuf, on the other side of the Vienne, and another on the rue du Rajat in Abbessaille. (10M 132, CC April 18, 1905). Two lived on the rue de Paris: Sylvain Pouhol, twenty-five, who lived at number 20, and Henri Bontemps, seventeen, who lived at number 43. Simon Mazelot lived on the rue du Collège. Other streets included the chemin des Rouchoux and the faubourg d'Angoulême.

Epilogue

1. BB18 2994, PGL December 30, 1905; the vote was fourteen to thirteen. *Almanach Limousin,* 1907. See *Le Populaire du Centre,* January 28 and 30 and February 6,

1906. Four hundred businessmen had met before the election with an eye to "preventing the kind of disorders that victimized our town." Tony Judt, *Socialism in Provence, 1871–1914* (New York, 1979), p. 80, notes that Radicals after 1905 were treated as enemies, or "no more than occasional allies," by the socialists. *Le Populaire du Centre*'s first issue noted that *Le Réveil du Centre* did not "accept the reality of class struggle." One café owner wrote a letter urging shopkeepers not to vote for the *progressistes* (*Le Populaire du Centre*, February 6, 1906).

2. The *groupe socialiste* protested the dismissal of socialist employees, "une politique d'iniquité et de violence sans précédent" (*Le Populaire du Centre*, August 7, 1906). The new council refused all subventions for workers to attend trade union or professional congresses and picked only nonsocialists for the task of taking the 1906 census (*Le Populaire du Centre*, November 1 and February 26, 1906).

3. *Almanach Limousin*, 1908.

4. Ibid.; F7 13622, PHV September 16, 1905, regulations of November 7, 1906, and PHV October 26, 1907. A group of young militants formed a new organization called "Jeunesse syndicaliste" or "le Bataillon sacré" and began a cooperative restaurant, La Coopé, located at L'Union, rue de la Fonderie, which served four hundred people on the first day.

5. BB18 2294, PGL July 7 and 8, 1905; F7 13622, PHV December 17, 1908; 10M 151. The Bourse moved first to the rue de la Fonderie and then to the rue Manigne in 1911. The Bourse had 6,604 affiliated members in 1910 and 6,606 in 1912 (10M 151). Several "yellow" unions signed petitions against strikes in 1908 (*Le Populaire du Centre*, August 15).

6. Désiré-Vuillemin, "Les Grèves dans la région de Limoges de 1905 à 1914," pp. 52, 66, and 81 ("one no longer fought in the street; one negotiated with authorities"). Analysis based on BB18 2333, 10M 134, 10M 136, BB18 2356[1], F7 12768, F7 12791, BB18 2402[1], B18 2431, and 10M 112. The only strikes of any length were (1) an unsuccessful 1907 walkout, lasting two months, by eighteen *gazetiers* who demanded that their company no longer withhold 20 percent of their wages to pay for work expenses and damages; (2) an unsuccessful 1908 strike, lasting twelve days, by gas workers seeking a small wage increase and some indemnity during illness; (3) a successful 1909 strike by typographers and linographers for a raise and a nine-hour day, and (4) an attempt by *ouvriers boulangers* in 1911 to force their employers to end night baking, which failed after three months.

7. There were two exceptions. In 1913 seven workers demanded the dismissal of a foreman at the Lanternier porcelain factory, claiming that he continually threatened to fire them and intervened in their discussions with the company. In 1912 shoe cutters at the Hétier Company also demanded that a foreman be fired; they complained of his "pride and the manner in which he gives instructions to workers who are much older and more experienced than he." (*Le Populaire du Centre*, September 14 and October 12, 1913; 10M 122, CC March 12, 1912).

8. *Le Rappel du Centre*, November 5, 1899.

9. Bobe, op. cit., pp. 23 and 43. For details of the split between Betoulle, Parvy, and Goujaud see 1M 166, CC March 17.

10. 1M 166, CC October 9, 1907; in April 1909 the Limousin section of the S.F.I.O. had only 360 francs left after spending 16,000 in three years (4M 85, CC April 9, 1909).

11. 3M 493; the *progressistes* won thirty of the thirty-six seats; *Le Populaire du Centre*, April 20–21, 1909; *Le Socialiste du Centre*, January 26, 1908, called for controlled, centralized discussions of political issues.

12. Lenoble et al., op. cit., p. 56. Betoulle received 8,500 votes to Lamy de la Chappelle's 7,535. Neither the anarchist group nor the right improved its positions significantly during the years that followed 1905. The socialist emphasis on antimilitarism and resistance to the centralized state undoubtedly weakened the appeal of anarchism. Three successive anarchist papers, *L'Ordre, Le Combat sociale,* and *L'Insurgé,* were essentially local editions of Parisian papers, ceasing publication in 1911. Although police usually estimated the number of anarchists in Limoges at between 30 and 100 (including some revolutionary syndicalists), only 4 people showed up for a 1909 meeting presided over by a fifteen-year-old.

   The right increasingly split between the social Catholics, led by Desgranges (although he split from Le Sillon in 1909), and the traditional monarchists. Desgranges's acceptance of the Republic infuriated the royalist clique; when a *fanfare* played the "Marseillaise" on the occasion of several speeches sponsored by the Oeuvres terriennes in 1907, consisting of social Catholics, "the music was not sweet to the ears of the clerical party," as the prefect put it. The royalists found that the *progressistes* easily outbid them for the support of the nationalistic bourgeois conservatives, who became as anti-German as they were. In 1907 the Action française joined two other right-wing organizations, the Action libérale and the Comité monarchiste to form a Fédération nationale du Centre. A retired general, du Bessol, presided, assisted by St. Marc Girardin, a descendant of the Orleanist deputy.

13. Fraisseux, op. cit., p. 59; 10M 192, CP November 26, 1908. For meetings protesting *la vie chère* see 4M 85, CC November 4, 1911.

14. Lenoble, et al., op. cit., p. 66; 3M 493. On public meetings see 4M 85, reports of February 8 and following.

15. Chénieux was succeeded by Dantony. Emile Labussière continued to serve on the departmental General Council until 1906; he accepted a position as *trésorier-payeur* on the island of La Réunion, and then in Indochina (1900). He died in Perpignan on February 21, 1924, after having been named to the same position there.

16. 3M 493.

17. 3M 512, esp. CP first arrondissement, May 3, 1912. See Jean-Jacques Becker, *1914: Comment les français sont entrés dans la guerre* (Paris, 1977), p. 327. See also Cousteix, "Le Mouvement ouvrier," p. 49.

18. BB18 2372, PGL October 5, 1908, indicating that the trial was dismissed without a verdict: 1M 183, CC March 15–19, 1900; BB18 2158, PGL April 7, 1900; 1M 192, PHV and CS June 22, 1907, describing a *manifestation* of five thousand people protesting repression in the Midi.

19. 1M 156, PHV March 3, 1913; 4M 85, CC March 10, 1912; *Almanach Limousin,* 1913.

20. *Le Populaire du Centre,* September 26, 1911; 4M 85, CC September 20 and November 24, 1911.

21. 4M 85, CC March 15, 1913.

22. *Almanach Limousin,* 1914; see *L'Humanité,* October 17, 1913, on Poincaré's visit. Bourdelle, op. cit., p. 69, notes Teissonnière's prediction.

23. Becker, *op. cit.,* pp. 156 and 158; *Le Courrier du Centre,* July 31, and *Le Populaire du Centre,* July 30–31.

24. *Le Populaire du Centre,* July 30–31; see Becker, op. cit., pp. 158 and 170, who notes that the "International" had been heard in Limoges (p. 178). Limoges's *syndicalistes* apparently associated themselves with a large demonstration planned for July 31 in Paris (p. 208).

25. *Le Populaire du Centre,* July 30–31, 1914; *Le Réveil du Centre,* August 2, 1914.
26. F7 12939, PHV August 2, 1914; *Le Réveil du Centre,* August 3, 1914.
27. 4M 84, CC August 5, 1914.
28. Becker, op. cit., p. 353, n. 184.
29. 4M 84, CC August 5, 1914; *Le Réveil du Centre,* August 4, 1914.
30. F7 12939, August 18, 25, 27, and 29, 1914. The prefect was worried about wild rumors and considered various ways of keeping people from talking to the wounded in hospitals and preventing officers lodged in private homes from talking about events at the front.
31. F7 13622, PHV September 25, 1915. Those signing included two deputy mayors.
32. Colin Dyer, *Population and Society in Twentieth-Century France* (New York, 1978), p. 40.
33. Here I would disagree with Amdur, op. cit., who portrays local political issues as being unimportant, little more than a reflection of national issues.
34. Judt, op. cit., pp. 306–8.
35. Michelle Perrot, "Les Socialistes français et les problèmes du pouvoir," in Michelle Perrot and Annie Kriegel, *Le Socialisme français et le pouvoir* (Paris, 1966), p. 38.
36. Judt, op. cit., p. 292.

Bibliography

Primary Sources

NATIONAL ARCHIVES (PARIS)

Series BB18: Ministry of Justice

BB18				
1140	1376	1794^1	2118^b	2309
1149	1885	1795	2125	2309^4
1150	1449	1816	2153	2324^2
1155	1451	1857	2158	2333
1157	1468	1970	2179	2349^1
1186	1470	1972	2182	2356^1
1187	1470^c	1983	2216	2372
1193	1474^a	1992	2244	2377
1217	1474^b	1997	2274	2402^1
1218	1481	2013	2284^1	2431
1240	1540	2022	2290	2440^1
1318	1694	2025	2294	2443^5
1326	1788	2052	2294^1	

Series BB30: Ministry of Justice

BB30				
333	378	390	415	*424
361	386	296	418	447
372	389	405	422	486

Series C: National Assembly

C	968
	1335
	1577
	2883
	2885
	3023

Series F: General Administration

F1b II Haute-Vienne 2	F1c III Haute-Vienne 10
F1b II Haute-Vienne 4	F1c III Haute-Vienne 11
F1c III Haute-Vienne 3	F2 II Haute-Vienne 2
F1c III Haute-Vienne 4	F3 II Haute-Vienne 1
F1c III Haute-Vienne 7	F3 II Haute-Vienne 5
F1c III Haute-Vienne 8	F3 II Haute-Vienne 6
F1c III Haute-Vienne 9	

Series F7: Police

F7	3884	6741	9711	12543	12791
	4215^7	6742	12365	12545	12822
	4215^{13}	6755	12457	12704	12912
	4215^{14}	6772	12461	12723	12939
	4215^{15}	6784	12462	12768	13344
	5733	6993	12503	12773	13622
	6706	9580	12515		

Series F9: Military

F9	338
	732
	733
	1041
	1071

Series F11: *Subsistances*

F11 736

Series F12: Commerce and Industry

F12	2439	4652	4666	4675	4714
	4547	4654	4668	4678	4945
	4638	4664	4669	4682	5406^A
	4651	4665	4672	4706	

Series F17: Education

F17	6848
	9277
	9281
	9373
	9374

Series F18: Press

F18	208
	263
	511^A
	511^B
	2309

Series F19: Religion and Clergy

F19	354	5606	5817	5912	6784
	481^A	5682	5818	6059	9373
	2529	5733			

Series F20: Statistics

F20 147

Series F21: Beaux Arts
    F21   430
            588
            1220
            1226
            4413

ARCHIVES OF THE MINISTRY OF WAR (VINCENNES)

Series E5: Correspondence of the Ministry of War, July Monarchy
    E5   1–2

Series F1: Correspondence of the Ministry of War, Second Republic
    F1   1–50

Series MR: *Reconnaissances militaires*
    MR   1298
             1300
             1303
             2262
             2269
             2284

MUNICIPAL ARCHIVES OF LIMOGES

Series "M," "D," "F," and "I": Miscellaneous reports

Registre pour l'inscription des livrets, 1856–57

Registre de la correspondance concernant la police et renseignements divers, 21 mars 1831 à 2 février 1855

Censuses of 1841, 1848 (incomplete and unofficial), 1876, 1896, and 1906

Archives of the Prefecture of Police, Paris
    BA   182
           189

ARCHIVES DEPARTEMENTALES DE LA HAUTE-VIENNE (LIMOGES)

Series 1M: General Administration, Prefectorial Reports

1M	24	119	129	142	156
	33	120	130	143	158
	39	124	133	144	159
	99	125	134	145	160
	100	126	135	147	161
	117	127	138	148	162
	118	128	141	149	163

164	179	188	199	220
165	180	191	203	229
166	183	192	209	243
176	186	198	213	244
177				

Series 2M: Administrative Personnel

2M	12
	38
	57
	59

Series 3M: Plebiscites, Elections, Electoral Lists

3M	36	378	398	435	487
	57	380	400	456	491
	355	384	404	457	492
	356	392	416	461	493
	366	393	418	475	494
	367	394	420	476	512
	371	396	424	480	513

Series 4M: Police

4M	7	64	102	128	168
	43	66	104	130	315
	44	72	114	136	316
	45	84	115	138	321
	53	85	122	154	416
	54	86	124	155	418
	55	87	125	160	435
	56	88	126	161	456
	57	101	127	162	

Series 5M: Public Health and Hygiene

5M	50
	51

Series 6M: Population, Economy, Statistics

6M	1
	12
	331
	332
	512
	513

Series 8M: Commerce and Tourism

8M	11
	16
	24
	27
	29
	30
	31

Series 9M: Industries, Handicrafts
  9M 29
      30
      44

Series 10M: Work
  10M 13   105   131   153   172
       21   111   132   155   175
       39   112   134   156   183
       71   113   135   157   186
       96   122   140   161   192
       98   126   151   170   193
       99   127   152   171
      103   130

Series O: Communal Administration and Bookkeeping
    123 O 4(7)
    123 O 6(14)
    123 O 7(23)
    123 O 7(24)
    123 O 9(28)
    123 O 9(38)
    123 O 9(45)

Series R: Military Affairs
  R   12   163   169   184   196
      160   168   181   192   197
      161

Subseries T: Churches
  1T 86^A
  1T 86^D
  1T 86^H

Series U: Justice
  U Cour 174
          190
          191
          432
          435
          438
          440
          441
          447

Series V: Religion
  2V 3
  2V 9

Series Z: Private Papers
  Z 25 *fonds* Alluaud

Archives of the Bishop
  2M 2

2M 3
3M 1
3M 2
3M 3
6M 1
6M 4
8M 6

NEWSPAPERS

L'*Ami des lois*
Les Annales de la Haute-Vienne
L'*Avenir*
L'*Avenir national*
La Bataille sociale
Le Carillon républicain
Le Combat social
Le Conciliateur
La Confiance
Le Contribuable
Le Courrier du Centre—le 20 décembre
Le Courrier du Centre
Le Cri social
La Croix
La Défense nationale
La Défense républicaine
Le Diable à quatre
La Discussion
L'*Echo du Palais*
La France centrale
La Gazette du Centre
Gazette du Haut- et Bas-Limousin
Le Grelot
Le Gros Bourdon
La Haute-Vienne
Journal de la Haute-Vienne

Le Journal de Limoges
Le Libéral du Centre
Limoges
Limoges illustré
La Nation française
Le Nouveau Contribuable
L'*Ordre*
Le Persévérant
Le Petit Centre
Le Peuple
Le Populaire du Centre
La Province
Le Radical du Centre
Le Rappel du Centre
Le Républicain de la Haute-Vienne
Le Républicain du Centre
Le Réveil du Centre
Le Réveil républicain de Limoges
La Semaine religieuse
Le Socialiste de la Haute-Vienne
Le Socialiste du Centre
Le Tout Limoges
Le Travailleur
L'*Union conservatrice*
Le XX décembre

Secondary Sources

Almanach Limousin, 1859–1914.

Amdur, Kathryn. "Unity and Schism in French Labor Politics: Limoges and Saint-Etienne, 1914–1922." Diss., Stanford University, 1978.

Analyse des actes et délibérations de l'administration municipale de Limoges. 4 vols., 1896–1903.

Audiganne, A. *Les Populations ouvrières et les industries de la France.* Paris, 1860.

Baju, Henri. *Rapport sur les associations ouvrières catholiques et sur le cercle de la jeunesse de Limoges.* Limoges, 1877.

Beaubois, Gabriel. "Le Mouvement ouvrier à Limoges." *Mouvement socialiste,* 2nd series, vol. 7, nos. 155–56 (May 15 and June 1, 1905): 73–86, 155–78.

Becker, Jean-Jacques. *1914: Comment les français sont entrés dans la guerre.* Paris, 1977.

Bobe, Bernard. "Contribution à l'histoire de l'idée socialiste durant la seconde internationale: Essai sur le département de la Haute-Vienne." Mémoire présenté et soutenu pour le diplôme d'études supérieures des sciences politiques, Université de Paris, 1969.

Boisserie, Gaston. *Les Coopératives ouvrières de production dans l'industrie de la porcelaine à Limoges de 1848 à nos jours.* Paris, 1912.

Bouillon, Jacques. "Les Élections législatives du 13 mai 1849 en Limousin." *Bulletin de la Société Archéologique et Historique du Limousin* [*BSAHL*], 84 (1954): 467–96.

Boulland, Dr. H. *Etat sanitaire de Limoges en 1890.* Limoges, 1890.

———. "La Topographie de Limoges dans ses rapports avec l'hygiène." *Almanach Limousin,* 1893, pp. 117–34.

Bourdelle, Francine. "Evolution du syndicalisme ouvrier à Limoges, 1870–1905." Mémoire de maîtrise, Université de Limoges, 1973.

Boutaud, Roger. "Les Ouvriers porcelainiers de Limoges de 1884 à 1905." Mémoire de maîtrise, Université de Poitiers, 1970.

Chambre de Commerce de Limoges, 1858–1958.

Charbonnier, Dr. Pierre. "Limoges qui se transforme." *Limoges illustré,* May 15, 1906.

Chazalas, Victor. "Une épisode de la lutte des classes à Limoges, 1848." *Revue d'histoire de la révolution de 1848* 7 (November–December, 1910): 161–80, 240–56, 326–49, 389–412; 8 (January–February, 1911): 41–66.

Clancier, Georges-Emmanuel. *Le Pain noir.* Paris, 1959.

———. *La Vie quotidienne en Limousin au XIXe siècle.* Paris, 1976.

Clément-Simon, G. "La 'bibliothèque bleue' de Limoges." *Bibliophile limousin* 19 (2nd series), no. 1 (January 1904): 139–50.

Cöetlogon, Comte E. de. *De l'assistance charitable à tous les points de vue, et de l'extinction de la mendicité vagabonde.* Limoges, 1858.

Coissac, G. Michel. *Mon Limousin.* Paris, 1913.

Compte final d'administration rendu par le maire de Limoges. Etat de situation de 1830. Limoges, 1831.

La Confrérie et la corporation de Saint-Aurélien à travers les siècles. Limoges, 1930.

Corbin, Alain. *Archaïsme et modernité en Limousin au XIXe siècle, 1845–1880.* 2 vols. Paris, 1975.

La Corporation de MM. les bouchers de Limoges et l'arrêté du 7 mai 1880. Par un ouvrier [J. B. Laroudie]. Limoges, 1880.

Cousteix, Pierre. "L'Action ouvrière en Haute-Vienne sous la IIe République." *BSAHL* 84 (1954): 497–511.

———. "L'Influence des doctrines anarchistes en Haute-Vienne sous la IIIe République." *L'Actualité de l'histoire* 13 (November 1955): 26–34.

———. "Le Mouvement ouvrier limousin de 1870 à 1939." *L'Actualité le l'histoire* 20–21 (December 1957): 27–96.

———. "L'Opposition ouvrière au Second Empire en Haute-Vienne." *BSAHL* 86 (1955): 119–34.

———. "La Vie quotidienne à Limoges sous le Second Empire." *L'Information Historique* 13 no. 4 (July–October 1951): 135–38.

————. "La Vie ouvrière dans la Haute-Vienne sous la Restauration." *L'Information Historique* 14, no. 5 (November 1952): 178–81.

Daudet, R. *L'Urbanisme à Limoges au XVIIIᵉ siècle.* Limoges, 1939.

Delor, Adrien. *La Corporation des bouchers à Limoges.* Limoges, 1877.

Desgranges, Abbé Jean. *L'Organisation des conférences.* Limoges, 1928.

————. *Les Vraies Idées du Sillon.* Limoges, 1905.

Désiré-Vuillemin, Geneviève. "Une grève révolutionnaire: Les Porcelainiers de Limoges en avril 1905." *Annales du Midi* 83 (January–March 1971): 25–86.

————. "Les Grèves dans la région de Limoges in 1905 à 1914." *Annales du Midi* 85 (January–March 1973): 51–84.

Duchalard, Roland. *Visages d'antan.* Limoges, 1977.

Ducourtieux, Hippolyte. "Les Cris de Limoges: Esquisse de moeurs." *Almanach Limousin,* 1859.

————. "Limoges depuis cent ans: *Alamanch Limousin,* 1860–64.

Ducourtieux, Paul. "Les Statues de la Vierge aux carrefours du vieux Limoges." *Limoges illustré,* May 15, 1906.

————. *Histoire de Limoges.* Limoges, 1925.

————. *Limoges et ses environs.* Limoges, 1905.

————. *Le Vieux Limoges.* Limoges, 1923.

Ducray, Gaston. *Le Travail porcelainier en Limousin: Etude économique et sociale.* Angers, 1904.

Enquête parlementaire sur l'insurrection du 18 mars. Vol. 1. Paris, 1872.

Faure, J. M. L. *Histoire de l'octroi de Limoges de 1370 à 1900.* Limoges, 1902.

Fraisseux, Docteur. *Au long de ma route.* Limoges, 1946.

France, Direction du Travail. *Les Associations professionnelles ouvrières.* Vol. 3. Paris, 1903.

Fray-Fournier, A. "Balzac à Limoges." *Bibliophile Limousin* 13 (1898): 49–65.

————. "Les Fêtes nationales et civiques dans la Haute-Vienne pendant la Révolution." *Limoges illustré,* November 15, 1901; December 1, 1901; January 1, 1902; February 1, 1902; February 15, 1902; and March 1, 1902.

————. "Limoges et les bonnes villes." *BSAHL* 52 (1903): 281–352.

Fusade, E. "Les Habitations ouvrières." *Limoges illustré,* October 15, 1902.

Gerardin, Madame Louis. "L'Action sociale catholique en Haute-Vienne: Deux abbés 'démocrates.'" Mémoire de maîtrise, Université de Limoges, 1975.

————. "La Presse catholique à Limoges—fin du XIXᵉ siècle—début du XXᵉ." *Association française pour l'avancement des sciences.* Limoges, 1974.

Gorceix, Septime. "La Corporation des bouchers et la confrérie de Saint Aurélien." *Limoges à travers les siècles.* Limoges, 1946, pp. 35–39.

————. "Une vieille corporation se prolonge jusqu'à nos jours." *Le Populaire du Centre,* February 26, 1958.

Grellier, Camille. *L'Industrie de la porcelaine en Limousin.* Paris, 1908.

Guibert, Louis. "Les Confréries de Pénitents en France et notamment dans le diocèse de Limoges." *BSAHL* 27 (1879): 5–193.

————. "Etude sur la foire de St. Loup." *Almanach Limousin,* 1861.

————. "La Dette Beaupeyrat." *Almanach Limousin,* 1872.

————. *Limoges qui s'en va.* Limoges, 1897.

————. *Mélanges, 1879–1886.* Limoges, n.d.

————. "Les Ostensions," *Almanach Limousin,* 1862, pp. 63–71; 1863, pp. 74–87.

————. *Le Quartier Viraclaud.* Limoges, 1897.

————. "Tableau historique et topographique de Limoges." *BSAHL* 59 (1909): 205–336.

Hanson, Paul. "The Federalist Revolt of 1793: A Comparative Study of Caen and Limoges." Diss., University of California at Berkeley, 1981.

Jouhanneaud, Camille. "Les Changements des noms des rues à Limoges." *Almanach Limousin,* 1890.

————. "Limoges, fin de siècle." *Almanach Limousin,* 1901, pp. 112–21.

————. "Notes pour servir à l'histoire de la musique à Limoges au XIXᵉ siècle." *BSAHL* 55 (1905): 392–419; 56 (1906): 48–108.

————. "Les Transformations de Limoges." *Almanach Limousin,* 1900, pp. 99–105.

Juge, J. J. *Changements survenus dans les moeurs des habitans de Limoges depuis une cinquantaine d'années.* 2nd ed. Limoges, 1817.

Kiener, Michel C., and Jean-Claude Peyronnet. *Quand Turgot régnait en Limousin.* Paris, 1979.

Labordie, Albert de. "L'Eglise Saint Aurélien." *BSAHL* 81 (1945): 227–43.

Labrune, Abbé P. *Mystères des campagnes.* Limoges, 1858.

Lachtygier, Monique. "Tableau de la vie ouvrière à Limoges de 1830 à 1848." Mémoire pour le diplôme d'études supérieures, Université de Poitiers, n.d.

Lacrocq, Louis. "La Flottage des bois sur la Vienne, le Taurion et leurs affluents." *BSAHL* 74 (1932): 337–67.

Léger, Madame Jean. "Etude des listes électorales du département de la Haute-Vienne sous la monarchie de Juillet (1830–48). "Mémoire sécondaire—diplôme d'études supérieures, Université de Bordeaux, n.d.

Lenoble, Jean. "L'Evolution politique du socialisme en Haute-Vienne sous le IIIᵉ République." Thèse, Université de Paris, 1950.

————, Maurice Robert, Serge Dunis, and J. P. Gendillou. *La Gauche au pouvoir depuis un siècle en Limousin.* Limoges, 1978.

Leroux, Alfred. "Délibérations de la Chambre consultative des arts et manufactures de Limoges," *BSAHL* 52 (1903): 197–279.

————. *Histoire de la porcelaine de Limoges.* Limoges, 1904.

Le Saux, Marguerite. "Approche d'une étude de la déchristianisation: L'Evolution religieuse du monde rural dans trois cantons de la Haute-Vienne (Ambazac, Le Dorat, Limoges) du milieu du XIXᵉ à la première guerre mondiale." Mémoire de maîtrise, Université de Poitiers, 1971.

Limoges et le Limousin: Guide pour l'étranger. Limoges, 1865.

Limouzin-Lamothe, R. *Le Diocèse de Limoges du XVIᵉ à nos jours (1510–1950).* Strasbourg, 1953.

Louguemar, M. A. de. *Limoges et le congrès scientifique en 1859.* Poitiers, 1859.

Maitron, Jean, ed. *Dictionnaire biographique du mouvement ouvrier français.* 6 vols. Paris, 1964– .

Malinvaud, G. "Adresse des ouvriers de Limoges au Président de la République." Limoges, 1879.

Mazabraud, M. J. "Une famille de noblesse commerçante de Limoges au XVIIIᵉ siècle: Les Bourdeau de la Judie." Mémoire de maîtrise, Université de Poitiers, 1970.

Merriman, John M. *The Agony of the Republic: The Repression of the Left in Revolutionary France, 1848–51.* New Haven, Conn., 1978.

————. "Incident at the Statue of the Virgin Mary: The Conflict of Old and New in Nineteenth-Century Limoges." In Merriman, ed., *Consciousness and Class Experience in Nineteenth-Century Europe.* New York, 1979.

————. "Radicalisation and Repression: A Study of the Demobilisation of the *'Démoc-Socs'* during the Second French Republic." In R. D. Price, ed., *Revolution and Reaction: 1848 and the Second French Republic.* London, 1975.

————. "Restoration Town, Bourgeois City: Changing Urban Politics in Industrializing Limoges." In Merriman, ed., *French Cities in the Nineteenth Century.* London, 1982.

————. "Social Conflict in France and the Limoges Revolution of April 27, 1848." *Societas—A Review of Social History* 4 (Winter 1974): 21–38.

Moussac, Marquis de. *Une corporation d'autrefois encore vivante aujourd'hui.* Paris, 1892.

Nouvelles Ephémérides du ressort de la cour royale de Limoges. Limoges, 1837.

Observations des bouchers de la ville de Limoges. Limoges, 1832.

Parantaud, J. M. A. *Une coopérative de consommation: L'Union de Limoges.* Limoges, 1944.

Parot, J. C. "1830 à Limoges." Mémoire complémentaire supérieur, Université de Poitiers, 1964.

Pérouas, Louis. "Limoges, une capitale régionale de la Libre-Pensée à l'orée du XXᵉ siècle." *Annales du Midi* 91, no. 142 (April–June 1979): 165–85.

Parrelon, P. *Théodore Bac: Notice biographique.* Paris, 1867.

Perpillou, A. *Le Limousin: Etude de géographie physique régionale.* Chartres, 1940.

Perrier, Antoine. "Limoges, étude d'économie urbaine." *Annales de géographie,* 33 (1924): 352–64.

————. "La Société populaire de Limoges en 1848." *Actes du quatre-vingt-sixième congrès des sociétés savantes.* Paris, 1966.

Petit, Joseph. *Une ancienne corporation et ses survivances: La corporation de messieurs les bouchers de Limoges.* Paris, 1906.

Pittle, A. *Une esquisse du mouvement ouvrier à Limoges depuis le XIXᵉ siècle.* Angoulême, 1929.

Précis sur la situation véritable des ouvriers et artistes en porcelaine sans travail de la ville de Limoges, pour servir à faire apprécier à leur juste valeur des dires de certains ennemis des ouvriers. Limoges, 1837.

Rapports sur les lois réglementant le travail 23 (1903).

Raymondaud, Dr. E. *Hygiène et maladies des porcelainiers.* Paris, 1891.

Réponse de M. Descourtures à M. le Bᵒⁿ de la Bastide, maire de cette ville, juillet 1824. Limoges, 1824.

Robert, M. *La Société limousin, 1870–1914.* Limoges, 1971.

Roque, Louis de la, and Edouard de Barthélemy. *Catalogue des gentileshommes du limousin,* Paris, 1864.

Royère, Pierre. *La Confrérie de Saint Aurélien et la corporation des bouchers de Limoges.* Paris, 1970.

Simmonneau, M. J. "Contribution à l'étude sociale de l'ancienne régime: La Cité de Limoges à la veille de la révolution." Mémoire, pour le diplôme d'études supérieures, Université de Bordeaux, n.d.

Société coopérative L'Union. n.p., n.d.

Statistique de la France. Industrie. Vol. 4. Paris, 1851.

Texier-Olivier, L. *Statistique générale de la France: Département de la Haute-Vienne.* Limoges, 1808.

Vallin, Pierre. "Fête, mémoire et politique: Les 14 juillet en Limousin (1880–1914)." *Revue française de science politique* 32, no. 6 (December 1982): 949–72.

Verdurier, Paul. "Une corporation au XXe siècle: Les Bouchers de Limoges." *Revue des Idées* 2, no. 18 (June 15, 1905): 438–63.

———. "Une survivance du moyen age: La corporation des bouchers de Limoges," unpublished manuscript, Bibliothèque municipale de la ville de Limoges.

Verynaud, Georges. *Histoire de Limoges*. Limoges, 1973.

Vincent, Ernest. "Les Ateliers nationaux à Limoges en 1848." *BSAHL* 83 (1951): 336–44.

———. "Les Crieurs publics en Limousin." *BSAHL* 82 (1947): 249–68.

Willard, Claude. *Le Mouvement socialiste en France (1893–1905): Les Guesdistes*. Paris, 1965.

Young, Arthur. *Travels During the Years 1787, 1788, and 1789*. London, 1791.

RELATED STUDIES

Aguet, J. P. *Les Grèves sous la monarchie de juillet*. Geneva, 1954.

Agulhon, Maurice. *Marianne au combat*. Paris, 1979.

———. *La République au village*. Paris, 1970.

———. *Une ville ouvrière au temps du socialisme utopique; Toulon de 1815 à 1851*. Paris, 1970.

Amann, Peter. *Revolution and Mass Democracy: The Paris Club Movement in 1848*. Princeton, N.J., 1975.

Aminzade, Ronald. *Class, Politics, and Early Industrial Capitalism: A Study of Mid-Nineteenth-Century Toulouse*. Albany, N.Y., 1981.

Barrows, Susanna. *Distorting Mirrors: Visions of the Crowd in Late Nineteenth-Century France*. New Haven, Conn., 1982.

Bastié, Jean. *La Croissance de la banlieue parisienne*. Paris, 1964.

Benevolo, Leonardo. *The Origins of Modern Town Planning*. Cambridge, Mass. 1971.

Bezucha, Robert J. *The Lyon Uprising of 1834*. Cambridge, Mass., 1974.

Briggs, Asa. *Victorian Cities*. Harmondsworth, Eng., 1968.

Brunet, Jean-Paul. *Saint-Denis: La Ville rouge, 1890–1939*. Paris, 1980.

Castells, Manuel. "Structures sociales et processus d'urbanisation: Analyse comparative intersociétale." *Annales: Economies, sociétés, civilisations* 25 (1970): 1155–99.

Chevalier, Louis. *Laboring and Dangerous Classes in Paris During the First Half of the Nineteenth Century*. Princeton, N.J., 1981.

Cobb, Richard. *Paris and Its Provinces*. London, 1975.

———. *The Police and the People*. Oxford, Eng., 1970.

———. *Promenades*. Oxford, Eng., 1980.

———. *A Second Identity*. London, 1969.

———. *A Sense of Place*. London, 1975.

———. *Tour de France*. London, 1976.

Crew, David. *Town in the Ruhr*. New York, 1979.

Dalotel, Alain, Alain Faure, and Jean-Claude Freiermuth. *Aux origines de la Commune: Le Mouvement des réunions publiques à Paris, 1868–1870*. Paris, 1980.

Daumard, Adeline. *Les Bourgeois de Paris au XIXe siècle*. Paris, 1970.

Deyon, Pierre. *Amiens, capitale provinciale*. Paris, 1967.

Duby, Georges, ed. *Histoire de la France urbaine*. Vol. 3: *La Ville classique*. Paris, 1981; vol. 4: *La Ville de l'âge industriel*. Paris, 1983.

Duveau, Georges. *1848: The Making of a Revolution*. New York, 1967.

———. *La Vie ouvrière en France sous le Second Empire*. Paris, 1946.

Dyos, H. J. *Victorian Suburb: A Study of the Growth of Camberwell*. Leicester, Eng., 1961.

———, ed. *The Study of Urban History*. London, 1968.

Edwards, Stewart. *The Paris Commune, 1871*. New York, 1971.

Elwitt, Sanford. *The Making of the Third Republic: Class and Politics in France, 1868–1884*. Baton Rouge, La., 1975.

Faure, Alain. *Carême prenant: Du carnival à Paris au XIXᵉ siècle*. Paris, 1978.

Foster, John. *Class Struggle and the Industrial Revolution*. London, 1974.

Friedmann, Georges, ed. *Villes et campagnes: Civilisation urbaine et civilisation rurale en France*. Paris, 1953.

Gaillard, Jeanne. *Communes de province, commune de Paris 1870–1871*. Paris, 1971.

———. *Paris: La Ville, 1852–1870*. Paris, 1977.

Garden, Maurice. *Lyon et les lyonnais au XVIIIᵉ siècle*. Paris, 1971.

Gelu, Victor. *Marseille au XIXᵉ siècle*. Paris, 1971.

Girault, Jacques. *La Commune et Bordeaux, 1870–1871*. Paris, 1971.

Gourevitch, Peter A. *Paris and the Provinces*. Berkeley, Calif., 1980.

Greenberg, Louis. *Sisters of Liberty: Marseille, Lyon, Paris and the Reaction to a Centralized State, 1868–1871*. Cambridge, Mass., 1971.

Guillaume, Pierre. *La Population de Bordeaux au XIXᵉ siècle*. Paris, 1972.

Guin, Yannick. *Le Mouvement ouvrier nantais*. Paris, 1976.

Hanagan, Michael P. *The Logic of Solidarity: Artisans and Industrial Workers, 1871–1914*. Urbana, Ill., 1980.

Haug, C. James. *Leisure and Urbanism in Nineteenth-Century Nice*. Lawrence, Kan., 1982.

Hobsbawm, E. J. *The Age of Capital, 1848–1875*. New York, 1975.

———. *The Age of Revolution: Europe, 1789–1848*. London, 1962.

Hufton, Olwen. *Bayeux in the Late Eighteenth Century*. Oxford, Eng., 1967.

Johnson, Christopher H. *Utopian Communism in France: Cabet and the Icarians, 1839–1851*. Ithaca, N.Y., 1974.

Johnson, Robert Eugene. *Peasant and Proletarian: The Working Class of Moscow in the Late Nineteenth Century*. New Brunswick, N.J., 1969.

Jones, Gareth Stedman. *Outcast London: A Study in the Relationship Between Classes in Victorian Society*. Harmondsworth, Eng., 1976.

Judt, Tony. *Socialism in Provence, 1871–1914*. New York, 1979.

Kemp, Tom. *Economic Forces in French History*. London, 1971.

Lequin, Yves. *Les Ouvriers de la région lyonnaise (1848–1914)*. 2 vols. Lyon, n.d.

Magraw, Roger. *France 1815–1914: The Bourgeois Century*. Oxford, Eng., 1983.

Margadent, Ted W. *French Peasants in Revolt: The Insurrection of 1851*. Princeton, N.J., 1979.

Mayer, Arno J. *The Persistence of the Old Regime*. New York, 1981.

Meacham, Standish. *A Life Apart: The English Working Class, 1890–1914*. Cambridge, Mass., 1977.

Merriman, John M., ed. *Consciousness and Class Experience in Nineteenth-Century Europe*. New York, 1979.

———. *1830 in France*. New York, 1975.

———. *French Cities in the Nineteenth Century*. London, 1982.

Moch, Leslie P. *Paths to the City: Regional Migration in Nineteenth-Century France*. Beverly Hills, Calif., 1983.

Moss, Bernard H. *The Origins of the French Labor Movement.* Berkeley, Calif., 1976.

Mumford, Lewis. *The City in History.* New York, 1961.

Murard, Lion, and Patrick Zylberman. *L'Haleine des faubourgs.* Fontenay-sous-Bois, 1978.

——, eds. *Le Petit Travailleur infatigable ou le prolétaire régénéré.* Fontenay-sous-Bois, 1976.

Ozouf, Mona. "Le Cortège et la ville: Les Itinéraires parisiens des fêtes révolutionnaires." *Annales: Economies, Sociétés, Civilisations* 26 (September–October, 1971): 889–916.

——. *La Fête révolutionnaire, 1789–1799.* Paris, 1976.

Perrot, Jean-Claude. *Genèse d'une ville moderne: Caen au XVIII*ᵉ *siècle.* 2 vols. Paris, 1975.

Perrot, Michelle. *Les Ouvriers en grève.* 2 vols. Paris, 1974.

——. "Le Regard de l'autre: Les Patrons français vus par les ouvriers (1880–1914)." In Maurice Levy-Leboyer, ed., *Le Patronat de la seconde industrialisation.* Paris, 1979.

Pierrard, Pierre. *La Vie ouvrière à Lille sous le Second Empire.* Brionne, 1965.

Pinkney, David H. *Napoleon III and the Rebuilding of Paris.* Princeton, N.J., 1958.

——. *The French Revolution of 1830.* Princeton, N.J., 1972.

Poulot, Denis. *Le sublime, ou le travailleur comme il est en 1870, et ce qu'il peut être.* Introduction by Alain Cottereau. 1870; rpt. Paris, 1980.

Pouthas, Charles. *La Population française pendant la première moitié du XIX*ᵉ *siècle.* Paris, 1956.

Price, Roger. *The French Second Republic: A Social History.* Ithaca, N.Y., 1972.

——, ed. *Revolution and Reaction.* New York, 1978.

Roche, Daniel. "Urban History in France: Achievements, Tendencies and Objectives." *Urban History Yearbook,* 1980.

Rudé, George. *The Crowd in the French Revolution.* London, 1967.

Schöttler, Peter. "Politique sociale ou lutte des classes: Notes sur le syndicalisme 'apolitique' des Bourses du Travail." *Mouvement social* 116 (July–September, 1981): 3–20.

Scott, Joan W. *The Glassworkers of Carmaux.* Cambridge, Mass., 1974.

——. "Mayors Versus Police Chiefs: Socialist Municipalities Confront the French State." In John M. Merriman, ed., *French Cities in the Nineteenth Century.* London, 1982.

——, and Louise A. Tilly. *Women, Work and Family.* New York, 1978.

Sewell, William H., Jr. "La Classe ouvrière de Marseille sous la Seconde République: Structure sociale et comportement politique." *Mouvement social* 76 (July 1971): 27–63.

——. *Work and Revolution in France: The Language of Labor from the Old Regime to 1848.* New York, 1980.

Shattuck, Roger. *The Banquet Years.* New York, 1968.

Shorter, Edward, and Charles Tilly. *Strikes in France, 1830–1968.* New York, 1974.

Sutcliffe, Anthony. *The Autumn of Central Paris.* London, 1970.

——, ed., *The Rise of Modern Urban Planning, 1800–1914.* New York, 1980.

Thernstrom, Stephan, and Richard Sennett. *Nineteenth-Century Cities.* New Haven, Conn., 1969.

Tilly, Charles. "The Changing Place of Collective Violence." In Melvin Richter, ed., *Essays in Theory and History.* Cambridge, Mass., 1970.

——. *The Contentious French.* Cambridge, Mass., in press.

————. "Food Supply and Public Order in Modern Europe." In Charles Tilly, ed., *The Formation of National States in Western Europe*. Princeton, N.J., 1975.

————. *From Mobilization to Revolution*. Reading, Mass., 1978.

————. *The Vendée*. Cambridge, Mass., 1976.

————, Louise Tilly, and Richard Tilly. *The Rebellious Century*. Cambridge, Mass., 1975.

Tilly, Charles, and Lynn Lees. "The People of June, 1848." In Roger Price, ed., *Revolution and Reaction: 1848 and the Second French Republic*. London, 1975.

Trempé, Rolande. *Les Mineurs de Carmaux, 1848–1914*. 2 vols. Paris, 1971.

Walker, Mack. *German Home Towns*. Ithaca, N.Y., 1971.

Wallace, Anthony F. C. *Rockdale: The Growth of an American Village in the Early Industrial Revolution*. New York, 1972.

Weber, Eugen. *Peasants into Frenchman: The Modernization of Rural France, 1870–1914*. Stanford, Calif., 1976.

Zeldin, Theodore. *The Political System of Napoleon III*. New York, 1971.

Index